HISTORICAL LAW-TRACTS

NATURAL LAW AND
ENLIGHTENMENT CLASSICS

Knud Haakonssen
General Editor

Henry Home, Lord Kames

NATURAL LAW AND
ENLIGHTENMENT CLASSICS

Historical Law-Tracts

The Fourth Edition
with Additions and Corrections

Henry Home, Lord Kames

Edited and with an Introduction by
James A. Harris

Major Works of Henry Home, Lord Kames

LIBERTY FUND

This book is published by Liberty Fund, Inc., a foundation established
to encourage study of the ideal of a society of free and responsible individuals.

𒂼𒄄

The cuneiform inscription that serves as our logo and as a design element in
Liberty Fund books is the earliest-known written appearance of the word
"freedom" (*amagi*), or "liberty." It is taken from a clay document written
about 2300 B.C. in the Sumerian city-state of Lagash.

Frontispiece and cover (detail): Portrait of Henry Home, Lord Kames, by David Martin.
Reproduced with permission of the National Galleries of Scotland.

19 20 21 22 23 C 5 4 3 2 1
19 20 21 22 23 P 5 4 3 2 1

Library of Congress Cataloging-in-Publication Data
Names: Kames, Henry Home, Lord, 1696–1782, author. | Harris, James A.
(James Anthony), writer of introduction.
Title: Historical law-tracts / by Henry Home, Lord Kames ; edited and with
an introduction by James A. Harris
Description: Fourth Edition with Additions and Corrections | Carmel, Indiana :
Liberty Fund Inc., 2019. | Series: Natural law and enlightenment classics |
Includes index.
Identifiers: LCCN 2018058310 | ISBN 9780865976177 (hardback) |
ISBN 9780865976184 (paperback) | ISBN 9781614879282 (pdf)
Subjects: LCSH: Law—England—History. | Law—Scotland—History. |
BISAC: PHILOSOPHY / History & Surveys / Modern.
Classification: LCC KD612 .K36 2019 | DDC 349.41—dc23
LC record available at https://lccn.loc.gov/2018058310

LIBERTY FUND, INC.
11301 North Meridian Street
Carmel, Indiana 46032-4564

CONTENTS

INTRODUCTION

When he published *Historical Law-Tracts* in 1758, Henry Home was 62.[1] He had been elevated to the Court of Session, and had assumed the title Lord Kames, six years previously, in February 1752. Since its creation in 1532 the Court of Session had been the supreme civil court in Scotland. As Kames explains in the tract "Of Courts," it "hath an original jurisdiction in matters of property, and in every thing that comes under the notion of pecuniary interest" (226).[2] Elevation to the Court was the culmination of a legal career that had begun when Kames was called to the bar in 1723.

1. The best biography remains Ian Simpson Ross, *Lord Kames and the Scotland of His Day* (Oxford: Clarendon Press, 1972). The most comprehensive study of Kames's thought is now Andreas Rahmatian, *Lord Kames: Legal and Social Theorist* (Edinburgh: Edinburgh University Press, 2015). But see also: William C. Lehmann, *Henry Home, Lord Kames, and the Scottish Enlightenment* (The Hague: Martinus Nijhoff, 1971); David Lieberman, "The Legal Needs of a Commercial Society: The Jurisprudence of Lord Kames," in Istvan Hont and Michael Ignatieff (eds.), *Wealth and Virtue: The Shaping of the Political Economy of the Scottish Enlightenment* (Cambridge: Cambridge University Press, 1983), pp. 203–34; David Lieberman, *The Province of Legislation Determined: Legal Theory in Eighteenth-Century Britain* (Cambridge: Cambridge University Press, 1989), pp. 144–75; Michael Lobban, *A History of the Philosophy of Law in the Common Law World 1600–1900* (Dordrecht: Springer, 2007), pp. 114–21; David M. Walker, *The Scottish Jurists* (Edinburgh: W. Green, 1985), pp. 220–47. For an account of the development of Scots law up to 1832, see John Cairns, "Historical Introduction," in Kenneth Read and Reinhard Zimmermann (eds.), *A History of Private Law in Scotland* (Oxford: Oxford University Press, 2000), vol. i, pp. 14–184. Cairns's chapter sketches the context for many of the issues explored by Kames in *Historical Law-Tracts*. See also John Cairns, "Attitudes to Codification and the Scottish Science of Legislation, 1600–1832," *Tulane European and Civil Law Forum* 22 (2007): 1–78.

2. Kames predicts, though, that in time it will be accepted "[t]hat it is the province of this court, to redress all wrongs for which no other remedy is provided" (pp. 228–29). For the place of the Court of Session in eighteenth-century Scottish political culture, see N. T. Phillipson, *The Scottish Whigs and the Reform of the Court of Session 1785–1830* (Edinburgh: Stair Society, 1990), pp. 1–41.

One thing that had helped to advance that career was the remarkable energy Kames devoted to a series of books intended to give order to two centuries of the Court's decisions. The first of these was *Remarkable Decisions of the Court of Session, from 1716 to 1728* (1728), intended as a supplement to Stair's *Institutions of the Law of Scotland* (1681), and preoccupied, like the *Institutions,* with uncovering the fundamental principles of law in Scotland. Stair's question had been "Whether law may or should be handled as a rational discipline, having principles from whence its conclusions may be deduced?"[3] Kames had no doubt that the answer was that it may and should—in other words, that those lawyers were mistaken who, as Stair had put it, "esteem[ed] law, especially the positive and proper laws of any nation, incapable of such a deduction, as being dependent upon the will and pleasure of lawgivers."[4] Kames went on to produce a huge two-volume work entitled *The Decisions of the Court of Session from Its Institution to the Present Time, Abridged and Digested under Proper Heads, in Form of a Dictionary* (1741). This was a further attempt to show that the opinions of the judges on the Court were "founded . . . for the most part, upon solid principles"—to show, in other words, that it was not a fatal flaw in Scottish law that it had so little foundation in statute.[5] Late in life Kames told Boswell that he didn't like to remember how much time this dictionary took to complete. However, he had the energy to press on to a consideration of Scottish statute law, *Statute Law of Scotland Abridged, with Historical Notes* (1757). In the years before *Historical Law-Tracts* he also wrote two more miscellaneous books: *Essays upon Several Subjects in Law* (1732) and *Essays on Several Subjects concerning British Antiquities* (1747).

Kames was a man of extraordinary energy and intellectual range. He was interested in philosophy as well as law, because he wanted to expose law's philosophical foundations, but also because he found metaphysical and moral questions fascinating in their own right. He had the confidence to engage in correspondence with Samuel Clarke about *a priori* arguments for

3. James, Viscount of Stair, *The Institutions of the Law of Scotland,* ed. David M. Walker (Edinburgh and Glasgow: The University Presses of Edinburgh and Glasgow, 1981), p. 89.

4. Stair, *Institutions,* ed. Walker, p. 89.

5. Kames, *The Decisions of the Court of Session,* 2nd ed., vol. i, p. vii.

the existence of God and with Joseph Butler about various issues raised in his *Sermons Preached at the Rolls Chapel.* Kames was part of the active intellectual community based in the Scottish Borders in the 1730s, a community that included the young David Hume, for a time so close a friend that the pair are said by some to have laid plans to start a new Edinburgh-based journal.[6] Kames's conversations with Hume, and his inability to accept the younger man's scepticism, gave rise to his first non-legal work, *Essays on the Principles of Morality and Natural Religion* (1751). In this book Kames gave systematic expression to a belief that underlies all of his writing on law: that there is such a thing as natural law, prior to and independent of all positive law, and revealed to us, not by reason or by divine will, but rather by human sentiment. The true ground of our knowledge of the primary laws of nature, Kames argued, was human nature. The laws of nature could be defined as "*Rules of our conduct founded on natural principles approved by the moral sense, and enforced by natural rewards and punishments.*"[7] One of these natural principles was a "principle of justice," consisting of two branches, "one to abstain from harming others, and one to perform our positive engagements."[8] Another was benevolence. Kames gave particular emphasis to the naturalness of principles of justice conceived of as grounded in an innate sense of duty distinct from the sense of benevolence, and in this he meant himself to be understood as correcting Francis Hutcheson. But of course the language of a moral sense was Hutcheson's language, and it is probably right to see Kames's moral philosophy as, at bottom, Hutchesonian in inspiration.[9] What differentiated Kames from Hutcheson, and from Hume for that matter, was his interest in how universal principles of human nature found different particular expressions in different times and places.

This was an interest Kames shared with Montesquieu, and it is usual to group Kames with those Scots whose intellectual life was fundamentally

---

6. See, e.g., Ross, *Lord Kames and the Scotland of His Day,* pp. 81–82.

7. Kames, *Essays on the Principles of Morality and Natural Religion,* ed. Mary Catherine Moran (Indianapolis: Liberty Fund, 2005), p. 56.

8. Kames, *Essays on the Principles of Morality and Natural Religion,* ed. Moran, p. 56.

9. See David Fate Norton, *David Hume: Common-Sense Moralist, Sceptical Metaphysician* (Princeton: Princeton University Press, 1982), pp. 174–89.

altered by the publication of Montesquieu's *De l'Esprit des Lois* in the late autumn of 1748. In his *Life of Adam Smith* (1794), Dugald Stewart described Kames in the *Historical Law-Tracts* as having "given some excellent specimens" of Montesquieu's consideration of laws "as originating chiefly from the circumstances of society." He provided further instances of the attempt "to account, from the changes in the condition of mankind, which take place in the different stages of their progress, for the corresponding alterations which their institutions undergo."[10] John Craig, in his 1806 "Life of John Millar," likewise claimed that in his history of property law, Kames had followed Montesquieu's way of deploying a comparative study of law in relation to human nature in order to "deduce the causes of those differences in laws, customs, and institutions, which, previously, had been remarked merely as isolated and uninstructive facts."[11] Kames, though, had already made a historical turn in his thinking about law in *Essays upon Several Subjects in Law* and *Essays on Several Subjects Concerning British Antiquities,* both published before *De l'Esprit des Lois.* Furthermore, he could be seen as rather self-consciously refusing to acknowledge any significance for Montesquieu in the writing of *Historical Law-Tracts.* By 1758 the intellectual life of Scotland was more or less saturated by Montesquieu.[12] When John Dalrymple published *An Essay towards a General History of Feudal Property* in 1757, he made no bones about the influence upon

10. Dugald Stewart, "An Account of the Life and Writings of Adam Smith, LL.D.," in Adam Smith, *Essays on Philosophical Subjects,* ed. W. P. D. W. Wightman, J. C. Bryce, and I. S. Ross (Oxford: Clarendon Press, 1980), pp. 294–95.

11. [John Craig], "Account of the Life and Writings of John Millar, Esq.," in John Millar, *The Origin of the Distinction of Ranks,* ed. Aaron Garrett (Indianapolis: Liberty Fund, 2006), p. 20.

12. An edition of *De l'Esprit des Loix* had been published in Edinburgh in 1750, along with a special translation of the two chapters which bore most closely on the question of the constitution of England and the character and manners that it was likely to produce. In 1756 Nugent's translation was published in a new edition in Aberdeen. Editions of the *Considérations sur les Causes de la Grandeur des Romains et de leur Décadence* were published in Edinburgh in 1751 and in Glasgow in 1752. A fourth version of the Glasgow edition came out in 1758. A translation of *Lettres Persanes* appeared in Glasgow in 1751. For a general account of Montesquieu's influence in eighteenth-century Scotland, see James Moore, "Montesquieu and the Scottish Enlightenment," in Rebecca E. Kingston (ed.), *Montesquieu and His Legacy* (Albany: State University of New York Press, 2009), pp. 179–95.

his book of "the greatest genius of our age." Montesquieu was quoted on the title page, and if Kames "directed" Dalrymple's thoughts in the *Essay,* as Dalrymple wrote in the dedication to him, those thoughts were later revised by Montesquieu himself. In the Preface, Montesquieu is said to have been one of the first to have "suggested . . . that it was possible to unite philosophy and history with jurisprudence, and to write even upon a subject of law like to a scholar and a gentleman."[13] Books 30 and 31 of *De l'Esprit des Lois* are then cited repeatedly in Dalrymple's "History of the Introduction of the Feudal System into Great Britain." In *Historical Law-Tracts,* by contrast, there is not a single mention of Montesquieu or of *De l'Esprit des Lois.* In the Preface, the authority cited "in order to recommend the history of law" is, of all people, Bolingbroke—an author, as Kames himself says, "in whose voluminous writings not many things deserve to be copied" (viii).

Kames certainly read Montesquieu and admired him greatly. In his magnum opus *Sketches of the History of Man,* published in 1774, Kames describes the author of *De l'Esprit des Lois* as "the greatest genius of the present age."[14] The remark is made in the context of a discussion of manners and their causes. This is significant because on this topic Kames disagrees with Montesquieu profoundly, and at great length. Like Hume, Kames found the case made for the influence of climate made in Book 14 of *De l'Esprit des Lois* quite unpersuasive. Montesquieu may have been, as Kames says elsewhere in the *Sketches,* "a judicious writer, to whom every one listens with delight,"[15] but this did not mean that everyone, least of all Kames himself, agreed with everything that Montesquieu said. The majority of the references made to Montesquieu in *Sketches of the History of Man* are critical in tone. So the greatness of Montesquieu's genius was not, for Kames, a matter of his always having been right.

In one important respect, even so, the agenda of *Historical Law-Tracts* is notably similar to that of Montesquieu. In its treatment of criminal law,

---

13. John Dalrymple, *An Essay towards a General History of Feudal Property in Great Britain,* 2nd ed. (London: 1758), p. ix.

14. Kames, *Sketches of the History of Man,* ed. James A. Harris (Indianapolis: Liberty Fund, 2007), p. 163 fn.

15. Kames, *Sketches of the History of Man,* ed. Harris, p. 511.

De l'Esprit des Lois, before it is anything else, is a plea for moderation and the relaxation of senselessly severe regimes of punishment. The rigor of punishments is argued to vary in direct proportion to the liberty allowed by a state's form of government. "Severity in penalties suits despotic government, whose principle is terror," Montesquieu observes, "better than monarchies and republics, which have honor and virtue for their spring."[16] Even in a despotism, however, it is possible for penalties to be too severe, as is shown by the case of Japan, where punishments are so excessive that, as Montesquieu puts it, "one is often obliged to prefer impunity."[17] In a despotism there is only one judge, the despot himself. It is a mark of the freedom of a republic, in Rome and, Montesquieu adds, "in many other cities," that citizens are permitted to accuse one another, for it is in the spirit of a republic, "where each citizen should have boundless zeal for public good, where it is assumed that each citizen has all the rights of the homeland in his hands."[18] Between these two extremes lies what is appropriate in a monarchy, where citizens cannot be supposed to have that kind of zeal for the public good and where it is a danger that prosecutions might be attempted merely in order to please the prince. "At present we have an admirable law," Montesquieu writes; "it wants the prince, who is established in order to see the execution of laws, to appoint an officer in each tribunal who will pursue all crimes in his name."[19] In the tract "Criminal Law" Kames makes the same case for the need for a public prosecutor "[i]n modern governments" (60). This is a necessary restraint on the passion of private resentment, which is the origin of all criminal law, but which is admitted as the guiding principle of punishment only among savages. The public prosecutor, who should have no personal stake in any legal process, can be supposed to have only the public good in view in his determinations of appropriate punishment. It may well have been the case for the distinction of punishment from revenge that prompted Bentham to declare that

16. Charles de Secondat, Baron de Montesquieu, *The Spirit of the Laws,* ed. and trans. Anne M. Cohler, Basia C. Miller, and Harold S. Stone (Cambridge: Cambridge University Press, 1989), p. 82 (VI.9).

17. Montesquieu, *The Spirit of the Laws,* p. 88 (VI.13).

18. Montesquieu, *The Spirit of the Laws,* p. 81 (VI.8).

19. Montesquieu, *The Spirit of the Laws,* p. 81 (VI.8).

"A very ingenious and instructive view of the progress of nations, from the least perfect states of political union to that highly perfect state of it in which we live, may be found in Lord Kaims's *Historical Law Tracts*."[20] The point here, though, is not that Montesquieu should be supposed to have been an influence on Kames. Rather, both were part of a larger, pan-European, movement for the reform and modernization of criminal law.[21]

In *Historical Law-Tracts* Kames gives full expression to a long-standing antipathy to the feudal system. In the aftermath of the Jacobite rebellion of 1745 one key feudal form, the "regality," or hereditary jurisdiction, was completely and finally abolished. In Tract VI Kames described the process whereby the regalities had in fact already, and naturally, ceded power as regards both civil and criminal matters to centralized and professional courts. This meant that, in truth, the Hereditable Jurisdictions Act of 1746 was "no harsh measure" (222). It is worth remembering that in a letter to Montesquieu of April 1749, Hume pointed to this act as proof of the truth of Montesquieu's "novel and striking" remark that "In order to favour liberty, the English have removed all the intermediate powers that formed their monarchy. They are quite right to preserve that liberty; if they were to lose it, they would be one of the most enslaved peoples on earth."[22] "The consequences that you predict would certainly take place," Hume wrote, "if there were a revolution in our government"—if, in other words, Britain's monarchy were to take a despotic turn.[23] Adam Ferguson shared Hume's concern about the dangers inherent in the stripping away in Britain of the intermediate powers that, on Montesquieu's analysis of monarchy, provided the surest protection of the individual from the power of the crown.[24] So did Dalrymple. Kames did not. He can have had no sympathy for the implicit case made by Montesquieu in Books 29, 31, and 32 of *De l'Esprit des Lois* for the need, even in a modern monarchy, for the preser-

---

20. Jeremy Bentham, *A Comment on the Commentaries and A Fragment on Government*, ed. J. H. Burns and H. L. A. Hart (Oxford: Clarendon Press, 1977), p. 430.

21. Lieberman, "Legal Needs of a Commercial Society," p. 215.

22. Montesquieu, *The Spirit of the Laws*, pp. 18–19 (II.4).

23. J. Y. T. Greig (ed.), *The Letters of David Hume*, 2 vols. (Oxford: Clarendon Press, 1932), vol. i, p. 134.

24. See Iain McDaniel, *Adam Ferguson in the Scottish Enlightenment: The Roman Past and Europe's Future* (Cambridge, Mass.: Harvard University Press, 2013).

vation of a traditional, which is to say feudal, balance of power between the king and the other powers of the state. Kames might have agreed, instead, with Smith's assertions in his lectures on jurisprudence that, under feudalism, "the nobility are the greatest opposers and oppressors of liberty that we can imagine," and that "[t]hey hurt the liberty of the people even more than an absolute monarch."[25]

Wherever he saw the continuing presence of the spirit of feudalism in Scottish law, Kames saw something to be reformed. The feudal system, he writes in the tract on property, "was a violent and unnatural system, which could not be long supported in contradiction to love of independence and property, the most steady and industrious of all human appetites" (141). But the spirit of feudalism had penetrated deep into Scottish property law, in ways that were often only apparent to the judge whose business it was to decide hard cases concerning land and the various kinds of rights pertaining to it. Through the process of the normalization of the ownership and inheritance of land, the substance of feudal law might have been reduced to nothing. Yet the forms remained in place. For example, a purchaser of land, as Kames puts it in the tract on "Securities upon land for payment of debt," "contrary to the nature of the transaction, was metamorphosed into a vassal," and so was subjected to a variety of duties and fees (170). "When the substantial part of the Feudal law has thus vanished," Kames observes, "it is dismal to lie still under the oppression of its forms, which occasion great trouble and expence in the transmission of land-property" (171). In several tracts Kames mounted a sustained attack on ways in which the continuing influence of feudal forms upon the law of inheritance in Scotland made it difficult, sometimes to the point of impossibility, for creditors to extract repayment of loans from the heirs of debtors. The spirit of feudalism was incompatible with an owner of land using that land as a means of raising loans, and thus the preservation of feudal legal forms was incompatible with one of the driving forces of a commercial society. It made borrowing more risky than it needed to be, and more expensive. There was reason to hope, now that the benefits of easy borrowing and low

25. Adam Smith, *Lectures on Jurisprudence,* ed. R. L. Meek, D. D. Raphael, and P. G. Stein (Oxford: Clarendon Press, 1978), p. 264.

interest rates were obvious, that the dead hand of feudal forms would be felt less and less in legal disputes between debtors and creditors, and in the decisions of the Court of Session in particular. And yet, astonishingly, the great landowners had managed to arrest this natural process, with the passing in 1685 of a statute enshrining in law the right of entail.

Montesquieu's view was that entails and other forms of "substitution" were appropriate to a monarchy but not to a republic. They were a means of keeping property in families, and were thus a means of reinforcing the "dignity" of noble and his fief, on which, in turn, the dignity of the monarch depended. In a republic, by contrast, all possible measures should be taken to restore fortunes to equality by the division of inheritances. Substitutions, he noted, "hamper commerce."[26] This was also Kames's principal objection to entails. The very idea of an owner of land determining the line of succession for generations to come had its origin in the rights of a feudal superior. It had no basis, Kames insisted, in common law. It was a perversion of the perfectly natural sentiment of ownership, in the form of an attempt to maintain ownership forever, even after the death of the immediate heir. "No moderate man can desire more than to have the free disposal of his goods during his life," Kames argued, "and to name the persons who shall enjoy them after his death" (154–55). No one in ancient Greece or Rome had imagined the rights of property to extend any further. It is interesting to contrast Kames's unequivocal opposition to entails with the position developed by Dalrymple in his pamphlet *Considerations upon the Policy of Entails* (1764). Having argued against statutory abolition of entails in his earlier book on feudal property, Dalrymple now made a positive case for their preservation, and did so in language that was redolent of Montesquieu's description of moderate monarchy. "[T]hat state of despotism is, of all others, the most irretrievable," he intoned, "where the antient families of a country, being divested of their estates, there is no rank in the State, except that of Prince and Tenant; terms which will soon be converted, if not in name, yet in effect, into those of Master and Slave."[27] It is tempting to suggest that, in the disagreement between Kames and

---

26. Montesquieu, *The Spirit of the Laws,* pp. 54–55 (V.8–9).

27. John Dalrymple, *Considerations upon the Policy of Entails in Great Britain* (Edinburgh: 1764), p. 62.

Dalrymple about entails, we see a disagreement as to whether, in Montesquieu's terms, Britain was fundamentally a republic or a monarchy. In truth, though, and needless to say, Kames was no republican. His criticism of feudal legal forms was grounded, rather, in a sober pragmatism about what Scotland needed to do to have a chance of improving itself and competing with England on more or less equal commercial terms.

"I am afraid of Kames' *Law Tracts*," Hume wrote to Adam Smith in April 1759. "A man might as well think of making a fine sauce by a mixture of wormwood and aloes, as an agreeable composition by joining metaphysics and Scottish law."[28] Despite the book's merits, Hume continued, few people would take the trouble to read it. Hume seems to have been wrong about that. *Historical Law-Tracts* went through four editions (new and corrected editions were issued in 1761, in 1776, and, posthumously, in 1792), and the tracts on criminal law and property were translated into French in 1766.[29] William Robertson reviewed it in glowing terms in *The Critical Review*. Kames, according to Robertson, showed that it was possible to write on law in a more rational and instructive manner than had usually been managed hitherto. "[T]hough researches of this kind be, necessarily, intricate and profound," Robertson added, "our author writes with remarkable perspicuity, and in a vigorous and manly stile. A subject seemingly dry and abstruse becomes, in his hands, not only instructive but amusing."[30] *Historical Law-Tracts* was well received also by *The Monthly Review*, where, like Robertson, the reviewer gave particular attention to the tract on the history of the criminal law, "a subject of general import, and of the highest concern to every member of a free state; as the preservation of Liberty depends chiefly on the perfection of the laws in criminal cases." Despite the amount of technical discussion of Scottish law, the reviewer judges that

28. Greig (ed.), *The Letters of David Hume*, vol. i, p. 304.

29. *Essais Historiques sur les Loix, Traduits de l'Anglois, par Mr. Bouchand* (Paris: 1766). "L'immortel Montesquieu nous a donné l'esprit des Loix," the translator writes in the Introduction. "Voici un Auteur Ecossois, dont nous ignorons le nom, qui a tenté d'en equisser l'histoire. Son objet est de remonter à l'origine des Loix, sur les points de Jurisprudence les plus importans, & de tracer les changemens progressifs de ces Loix, dans les différens âges du monde & les différentes nations" (pp. v–vi).

30. William Robertson, review of *Historical Law-Tracts*, *The Critical Review* 7 (April 1759): 356–67, p. 358.

in the book taken as a whole "the Author discovers a thorough knowledge of human nature, and a very intimate and extensive acquaintance with History and Jurisprudence."[31] Bentham's approval of Kames's jurisprudence has been noted above. On the basis of his achievement in the *Law-Tracts,* Kames was invited to become a member of a "Society of Citizens" to be based in Berne with the aim of improving moral science and the science of legislation.[32] *Historical Law-Tracts* was also read with interest in revolutionary America.[33] John Adams endorsed Kames's critique of feudalism, and Thomas Jefferson ranked Kames with Blackstone as a legal authority. In the lectures he gave in the College of Philadelphia in the 1790s, James Wilson recommended his own program for the study of law in the following terms:

> It comes to you supported with all the countenance of and authority of Bacon, Bolingbroke, Kaims—two of them [i.e., Bacon and Kames] consummate in the practice, as well as in the knowledge of the law—all of them eminent judges of men, of business, and of literature; and all distinguished by the accomplishment of an active, as well as those of a contemplative life.[34]

There is recognition here of Kames's achievement in turning himself into a notably well-rounded man of law, expert not only in the law itself but also in much else pertinent to understanding law's function in a free society.

---

31. [Anon.], review of *Historical Law-Tracts, The Monthly Review* 21 (July 1759): 302–11, pp. 304, 303. *The Monthly Review,* however, lamented that, while Kames had adopted an "enlarged and liberal method of prosecuting legal investigations," "his doctrines are generally fallacious; and while he gives too great a scope to conjecture and to fancy, he is destitute of erudition, and discovers a propensity to adopt as his own the inventions of other men" ([Anon.], review of *A Collection of Curious Discourses Written by Eminent Antiquaries, The Monthly Review* 47 (July 1772): 361–65, p. 362). I am grateful to Silvia Sebastiani for drawing these reviews to my attention.

32. See Ross, *Lord Kames and the Scotland of His Day,* pp. 216–17.

33. For a general account of Kames's influence in America, see Rahmatian, *Lord Kames,* pp. 316–33.

34. Quoted in Rahmatian, *Lord Kames,* p. 329.

EDITORIAL PRINCIPLES

Text

This edition of *Historical Law-Tracts* is based on the edition published ten years after Kames's death:

> *Historical Law-Tracts.* The Fourth Edition. With Additions and Corrections. Edinburgh: Printed for T. Cadell, in the Strand, London; and Bell & Bradfute, and W. Creech, Edinburgh. 1792.

This edition incorporates Kames's final alterations. It also incorporates the page numbers of the 1792 addition, inserted within angle brackets in the main body of the text.

Earlier editions are as follows:

> *Historical Law-Tracts.* 2 vols. Edinburgh: Printed for A. Millar, at Buchanan's Head in the Strand; and A. Kincaid, and J. Bell, Edinburgh. 1758.
>
> *Historical Law-Tracts.* The Second Edition. Edinburgh: Printed by A. Kincaid, His Majesty's Printer, for A. Millar in the Strand, London; and A. Kinkaid and J. Bell, Edinburgh. 1761.
>
> *Historical Law-Tracts.* The Third Edition. With Additions and Corrections. Edinburgh: Printed for T. Cadell, in the Strand, London; and J. Bell and W. Creech, Edinburgh. 1776.

Major differences between the 1792 and earlier editions are indicated in footnotes to the text. The 1758 and 1761 editions are mostly identical, as are the 1776 and 1792 editions.

None of these four editions has the author's name on its title page. The table of contents was added in 1776. In 1758 and 1761, the title of every tract apart from Tract XIV begins with "History of . . . ." Thus in these two editions, Tract I is "History of Criminal Law," Tract II is "History of Promises and Covenants," and so on.

Annotation

Full references to all works cited by Kames are provided in the bibliography. Most of Kames's footnote references (shorter ones indicated by symbols: *, †, ‡, etc.; longer ones indicated by Arabic numerals within parentheses) are easy enough to make sense of. Where this is not the case, sufficient information (inserted within double square brackets) has been added to enable the reader to identify the passage that Kames refers to. A small number of footnotes (indicated by Arabic numerals) have been added to explain legal and historical matters likely not to be readily comprehensible to the nonspecialist.

Kames frequently cites Scottish and English, and British, statute law. He also regularly cites decisions of the Court of Session, and a variety of bodies of ancient British and continental European law. These citations can be pursued using the following reference works:

Statute Law of Scotland

For the period beginning with the accession of James I in 1406 Kames would have used:

Glendook, Sir Thomas Murray of. *Laws and Acts of Parliament made by King James the First, [. . .], King Charles the Second who now presently reigns, Kings and Queens of Scotland.* Edinburgh, 1681.

The standard reference work is now:

The Acts of the Parliament of Scotland, A.D. *MCXXIV–MDCCVII.* Ed. Cosmo Innes and Thomas Thomson. 12 vols. London, 1814–52.

A complete list of acts of the Scottish Parliament to 1707, including a chronological table of statutes from 1424 to 1707, is provided by the database Records of the Parliaments of Scotland to 1707: http://www.rps.ac.uk

Statute Law of England and Great Britain

Kames would have used one or other of the successive editions of *Statutes at Large,* a list of statutes ratified by the English Parliament beginning with Magna Carta. E.g.,

> *The Statutes at Large, from Magna Charta, to the Thirtieth Year of George the Second, Inclusive.* Ed. John Cay. 6 vols. London, 1758.

Ancient British and European Law

Kames's source for his citations from the laws of the Angli and Thuringi, Bavarians, Burgundians, Longobards, Ripuarians, Saxons, and Visigoths, and from the Salic Law, was almost certainly:

> *Codex Legum Antiquarum.* Frankfurt, 1613.

The definitive modern editions of these laws are to be found in the volumes of the *Monumenta Germaniae Historica* (Hanover, Berlin, Munich: 1819–).

Kames's sources for his citations from ancient British law were:

> Lambard, William. *Archaionomia, sive, De Priscis Anglorum Legibus Libri.* London, 1568. [Cited by Kames as "Lambard's Collection."]
> Wilkins, David. *Leges Anglo-Saxonicae Ecclesiasticae et Civiles.* London, 1721.

Identifying the particular laws which Kames refers to in these collections is relatively straightforward, and there seemed no need to supplement footnotes containing such references.

Decisions of the Court of Session

Decisions of the Court of Session are most easily consulted via the website of the British and Irish Legal Information Institute: http://www.bailii.org /scot/cases/ScotCS/

Legal Terminology

A comprehensive glossary of Latin, Scots, and other legal terms is provided below, pp. 301–31.

ACKNOWLEDGMENTS

I have needed much expert help as I have worked on this edition, and have received it from Adam Beresford, Sarah Broadie, Michael Lobban, Tom Pye, Silvia Sebastiani, Adam Tomkins, and, especially, John Cairns. I am very grateful indeed to Karen Baston for the glossary of legal terminology, and to Norman Reid, along with David McOmish and Peter Maxwell-Stuart, for translations from Latin. Knud Haakonssen has been, as ever, a peerless source of wisdom and advice.

HISTORICAL LAW-TRACTS

Historical Law-Tracts

The Fourth Edition.
With Additions and Corrections.

EDINBURGH:

Printed for T. Cadell, in the Strand, London;
and Bell & Bradfute, and W. Creech, Edinburgh.

MDCCXCII.

PREFACE

The history of man is a delightful subject. A rational enquirer is no less entertained than instructed, in tracing the progress of manners, of laws, of arts, from their birth to their present maturity. Events and subordinate incidents are, in each of these, linked together, and connected in a regular chain of causes and effects. Law in particular, becomes then only a rational study, when it is traced historically, from its first rudiments among savages, through successive changes, to its highest improvements in a civilized society. And yet the study is seldom conducted in that manner. Law, like geography, is taught as if it were a collection of facts merely: the memory is employed to the full, rarely the judgment. This method, were it not rendered familiar by custom, would appear strange and unaccountable. <iv> With respect to the political constitution of Britain, how imperfect must the knowledge be of that man who confines his reading to the present times? If he follow the same method in studying its laws, have we reason to hope that his knowledge of them will be more perfect?

Such neglect of the history of law, is the more strange, that in place of a dry, intricate, and crabbed science, law treated historically becomes an entertaining study; entertaining not only to those whose profession it is, but to every person who hath any thirst for knowledge. With the generality of men, it is true, the history of law makes not so great a figure, as the history of wars and conquests. Singular events, which by the prevalence of chance or fortune excite wonder, are much relished by the vulgar. But readers of solid judgment find more entertainment, in studying the constitution of a state, its government, its laws, the manners of its <v> people; where reason is exercised in discovering causes and tracing effects through a long train of dependencies.

The history of law, in common with other histories, enjoys the privilege of gratifying curiosity. It enjoys beside several peculiar privileges. The feu-

3

dal customs ought to be the study of every man who proposes to reap instruction from the history of modern European nations: because among these nations, public transactions, no less than private property, were some centuries ago regulated by the feudal system. Sovereigns formerly were many of them connected by the relation of superior and vassal. The King of England, for example, held of the French King many fair provinces. The King of Scotland, in the same manner, held many lands of the English King. The controversies among these princes were generally feudal; and without a thorough knowledge of the feudal system, one must be ever at a loss <vi> in forming any accurate notion of such controversies, or in applying to them the standard of right and wrong.

The feudal system is connected with the municipal law of this island, still more than with the law of nations. It formerly made the chief part of our municipal law, and in Scotland to this day makes some part. In England, indeed, it is reduced to a shadow. Yet, without excepting even England, much of our present practice is evidently derived from it. This consideration must recommend the feudal system, to every man of taste who is desirous to acquire the true spirit of law.

But the history of law is not confined to the feudal system. It comprehends particulars without end, of which one additional instance shall at present suffice. A statute, or any regulation, if we confine ourselves to the words, is seldom so perspicuous as to prevent errors, perhaps gross <vii> ones. In order to form a just notion of any statute, and to discover its spirit and intendment; we ought to be well informed how the law stood at the time, what defect was meant to be supplied, or what improvement made. These particulars require historical knowledge; and therefore, with respect to statute-law at least, such knowledge appears indispensable.

In the foregoing respects, I have often amused myself with a fanciful resemblance of law to the river Nile. When we enter upon the municipal law of any country in its present state, we resemble a traveller, who, crossing the Delta, loses his way among the numberless branches of the Egyptian river. But when we begin at the source and follow the current of law, it is in that course no less easy than agreeable; and all its relations and dependencies are traced with no greater difficulty, than are the many streams into which that magni-<viii>ficent river is divided before it is lost in the sea.

An author, in whose voluminous writings not many things deserve to be copied, has however handled the present subject with such superiority of thought and expression, that in order to recommend the history of law, I will cite the passage at large.

I might instance (says he) in other professions the obligation men lie under of applying themselves to certain parts of history, and I can hardly forbear doing it in that of the law, in its nature the noblest and most beneficial to mankind, in its abuse and debasement the most sordid and the most pernicious. A lawyer now is nothing more, I speak of ninety-nine in a hundred at least, to use some of Tully's words, *nisi leguleius quidem cautus, et acutus praeco actionum, cantor formularum, auceps syllabarum.*[1] But there have been lawyers that were orators, philosophers, historians: there <ix> have been Bacons and Clarendons. There will be none such any more, till in some better age, true ambition or the love of fame prevails over avarice; and till men find leisure and encouragement to prepare themselves for the exercise of this profession, by climbing up to the *vantage ground,* so my Lord Bacon calls it, of science, instead of groveling all their lives below, in a mean, but gainful, application to all the little arts of chicane.[2] Till this happen, the profession of the law will scarce deserve to be ranked among the learned professions: and whenever it happens, one of the vantage grounds to which men must climb, is metaphysical, and the other, historical knowledge. They must pry into the secret recesses of the human heart, and become well acquainted with the whole moral world, that they may discover the abstract reason of all laws: and they must trace the laws of particular state, especially of their own, <x> from the first rough sketches to the more perfect draughts; from the first causes or occasions that produced them, through all the effects, good and bad, that they produced.*

---

* Bolingbroke of the Study of History, p. 353, quarto edit. [[Bolingbroke, *Works,* vol. ii, p. 353.]]

1. "than a circumspect and sharp kind of pettifogger, a crier of legal actions, a chanter of legal formulas, a trapper of syllables." Cicero, *De Oratore,* Bk 1, § 55. Trans. Sutton.

2. The reference is to Bacon's essay "Of Truth": "no pleasure is comparable to the standing upon the vantage ground of Truth . . . and to see the errors, and wanderings, and mists, and tempests, in the vale below" (*Essays or Councils, Civil and Moral,* p. 4).

The following discourses are selected from a greater number, as a specimen of that manner of treating law which is here so warmly recommended. The author flatters himself, that they may tend to excite an historical spirit, if he may use the expression, in those who apply themselves to law, whether for profit or amusement; and for that end solely has he surrendered them to the public.

An additional motive concurred to the selection here made. The discourses relate, each of them, to subjects common to the law of England and of Scotland; and, in tracing the history of both, tend to intro-<xi>duce both into the reader's acquaintance. I have often reflected upon it as an unhappy circumstance, that different parts of the same kingdom should be governed by different laws. This imperfection could not be remedied in the union betwixt England and Scotland; for what nation will tamely surrender its laws more than its liberties? But if the thing was unavoidable, its bad consequences were not altogether so. These might have been prevented, and may yet be prevented, by establishing public professors of both laws, and giving suitable encouragement for carrying on together the study of both. To unite both in some such plan of education, will be less difficult than at first view may be apprehended; for the whole island originally was governed by the same law; and even at present, the difference consists more in terms of art than in substance. Difficulties at the same time may be overbalanced by advantages: the proposed plan has great advantages, not only by re-<xii>moving or lessening the foresaid inconvenience, but by introducing the best method of studying law; for I know none more rational, than a careful and judicious comparison of the laws of different countries. Materials for such comparison are richly furnished by the laws of England and of Scotland. They have such resemblance, as to bear a comparison almost in every branch; and they so far differ, as to illustrate each other by their opposition. Our law will admit of many improvements from that of England; and if the author be not in a mistake through partiality to his native country, we are rich enough to repay with interest, all we have occasion to borrow. A regular institute of the common law of this island, deducing historically the changes which that law hath undergone in the two nations, would be a valuable present to the public; because it would make the study of both laws a task easy and agreeable. Such institute, it is true, is an undertaking too great for any <xiii> one hand. But if men of knowledge and genius would undertake particular branches, a general system might in time be completed from their works. This subject, which has frequently occupied the author's thoughts, must touch every Briton who wishes a complete union; and a North-Briton in a peculiar manner. Let us reflect but a moment upon the condition of property in Scotland, subjected in the last resort to judges, who have little inclination, because they have scarce any means to acquire knowledge in our law.[3] With respect to these judges, Providence it is true, all along favourable, hath of late years been singularly kind to us. But in a matter so precarious, we ought to dread a reverse of fortune, which would be severely felt. Our whole activity is demanded, to prevent if possible the impending evil. There are men of genius in this country, and good writers. Were our law treated as a rational science, it would find its way into England, and be studied there <xiv> for curiosity as well as for profit. The author, excited by this thought, has ventured to make an essay; which, for the good of his country more than for his own reputation, he wishes to succeed. If his Essay be relished, he must hope, that writers of greater abilities will be moved to undertake other branches successively, till the work be brought to perfection. <1>

3. After the 1707 Union of Parliaments, the House of Lords in Westminster acted as the final court of appeal for all civil and criminal cases in both Scotland and England. See p. 182 below.

Criminal Law

Of the human system no part, external or internal, is more remarkable than a class of principles, intended obviously to promote society, by restraining men from harming each other. These principles, as the source of the criminal law, must be attentively examined: and to form a just notion of them, we need but reflect on what we feel when we commit a crime, or witness it.[1] Upon certain actions, hurtful to others, the stamp of *impropriety* and *wrong* is impressed in legible characters, visible to all, not excepting even the delinquent. Passing from the action to its author, we perceive that he is *guilty;* and we also perceive, that he ought to be punished for his guilt. He himself, having the same perception, is filled with remorse; and, which <2> is extremely remarkable, his remorse is accompanied with an anxious dread that the punishment will be inflicted, unless it be prevented by his making reparation or atonement. Thus in the breast of a man a tribunal is erected for conscience: sentence passeth against him for every delinquency; and he is delivered over to the hand of Providence, to be punished in proportion to his guilt. The wisdom of this contrivance is conspicuous. A sense of wrong is of itself not sufficient to restrain the excesses of passion: but the dread of punishment, which is felt even where there is no visible hand to punish, is a natural restraint so efficacious, that none more perfect can be imagined.* This dread, when the result of atrocious or unnatural crimes, is itself a tremendous punishment, far exceeding all that have been invented

---

* Essays on the Principles of Morality and Natural Religion, part 1. ess. 2. chap. 3.

1. 1758, 1761 add: "The first reflection will unfold Divine justice carried into execution with the most penetrating wisdom."

8

by men. Happy it is for society, that instances are rare, of crimes so gross as to produce this natural dread in its higher degrees: it is, however, still more rare, to find any person so singularly virtuous, as never to have been conscious of it in any degree. When we peruse the history of mankind, even in their most savage state, we discover it to be universal. One instance I must mention, because it relates to the Hottentots, of all men <3> the most brutish. They adore a certain insect as their deity; the arrival of which in a kraal, is supposed to bring grace and prosperity to the inhabitants; and it is an article in their creed, that all the offences of which they had been guilty to that moment, are buried in oblivion, and all their iniquities pardoned.* The dread that accompanies guilt, till punishment be inflicted or forgiven, must undoubtedly be universal, when it makes a figure even among the Hottentots.

For every wrong, reason and experience make us apprehend the resentment of the person injured: but the horror of mind that accompanies every gross crime, produceth in the criminal an impression that all nature is in arms against him. Conscious of meriting the highest punishment, he dreads it from the hand of God, and from the hand of man:

> And Cain said unto the Lord, My punishment is greater than I can bear. Behold, thou hast driven me out this day from the face of the earth: and from thy face shall I be hid, and I shall be a fugitive and a vagabond in the earth, and it shall come to pass, that every one that findeth me shall slay me.†

Hence the efficacy of human <4> punishments in particular, to which man is adapted with wonderful foresight, through the consciousness of their being justly inflicted, not only by the person injured, but by the magistrate or by any one. Abstracting from this consciousness, the most frequent instances of chastising criminals would readily be misapprehended for so many acts of violence and oppression, the effects of malice even in judges; and much more so in the party offended, where the punishment is inflicted by him.

---

* Kolben's Present State of the Cape of Good Hope, vol. i. p. 99.
† Genesis, iv. 13. 14.

The purposes of Nature are never left imperfect. Corresponding to the dread of punishment, is, first, the indignation we have at gross crimes, even when we suffer not by them; and next, resentment in the person injured, even for the slightest crimes: by these, ample provision is made for inflicting the punishment that is dreaded. No passion is more keen or fierce than resentment; which, when confined within due bounds, is authorised by conscience. The delinquent is sensible, that he may be justly punished; and if any person, preferably to others, be entitled to inflict the punishment, it must be the person injured.[2]

Revenge, therefore, when provoked by injury or voluntary wrong, is a privilege that belongs to every person by the law of Nature; for we have no criterion of right or wrong more illustrious than the approbation or dis-approbation of <5> conscience. And thus, the first law of Nature regarding society, that of abstaining from injuring others, is enforced by the most efficacious sanctions.

An author of the first rank for genius, as well as blood, expresses himself with great propriety on this subject:

> There is another passion very different from that of fear, and which, in a certain degree, is equally preservative to us, and conducing to our safety. As that is serviceable in prompting us to shun danger, so is this in for-tifying us against it, and enabling us to repel injury, and resist violence when offered. 'Tis by this passion that one creature offering violence to another, is deterred from the execution, whilst he observes how the at-tempt affects his fellow, and knows by the very signs which accompany this rising motion, that if the injury be carried further, it will not pass easily, or with impunity. 'Tis this passion withal, which, after violence and hostility executed, rouses a creature in opposition, and assists him in returning like hostility and harm on the invader. For thus as rage and despair increase, a creature grows still more terrible; and, being urged to the greatest extremity, finds a degree of strength and boldness unexper-

2. 1758, 1761: the paragraph continues with a quotation from Pope's translation of Homer: "'—But at the Tyrant's name,/ My rage rekindles, and my Soul's on flame;/ 'Tis *just* Resentment, and becomes the Brave;/ Disgrac'd, dishonour'd, like the vilest Slave.'/ ILIAD ix. 759."

ienced till then, and which had never risen except through the height of provocation.* <6>

But a cursory view of this passion is not sufficient. It will be seen by and by, that the criminal law in all nations is entirely founded upon it; and for that reason it ought to be examined with the utmost accuracy. Resentment is raised in different degrees, according to the sense one hath of the injury. An injury done to a man himself, provokes resentment in its highest degree. An injury of the same kind done to a friend or relation, raises resentment in a lower degree; and the passion becomes gradually fainter, in proportion to the slightness of the connection. This difference is not the result of any peculiarity in the nature of the passion: it is occasioned by what is inherent in all sensible beings, that every one has the strongest sense of what touches itself. Thus a man hath a more lively sense of a kindness done to himself, than to his friend; and the passion of gratitude is in proportion. In the same manner, an injury done to myself, to my child, to my friend, makes a greater figure in my mind, than when done to others in whom I am less interested.

Every heinous transgression of the law of Nature raiseth indignation in all, and a keen desire to have the criminal brought to condign punishment. Slighter transgressions are less regarded. A slight injury done to a stranger, with whom we have no connection, raiseth our indignation, it is true, but so faintly as not to prompt any <7> revenge. The passion in this case, being quiescent, vanisheth in a moment. But a man's resentment for an injury done to himself, or to one with whom he is connected, is an active passion, which is gratified by punishing the delinquent, in a measure corresponding to the injury. And many circumstances must concur before the passion be completely gratified. It is not completely gratified with the suffering of the criminal: The person injured must inflict the punishment, or at least direct it; and the criminal must be made sensible, not only that he is punished for his crime, but that the punishment proceeds from the person injured. When all these circumstances concur, and not otherwise, the passion is completely gratified; and commonly vanisheth as if it had never been. Ra-

---

* Characteristics, vol. 2. p. 141. [[In fact the quotation is from pp. 144–45. Kames omits four sentences between ". . . violence when offered" and "'Tis by this passion . . .".]]

cine understood the nature of this passion, and paints it with great accuracy in the following scene.

CLEONE.
Vous vous perdez, Madame. Et vous devez songer—

HERMIONE.
Que je me perde, ou non, je songe à me venger.
Je ne sai même encor, quoi qu'il m'ait pu promettre,
Sur d'autres que sur moi, si je dois m'en remettre.
Pyrrhus n'est pas coupable à ses yeux comme aux miens,
Et je tiendrois mes coups bien plus sûrs que les siens. <8>
Quel plaisir, de venger moi-même mon injure;
De retirer mon bras teint du sang du parjure;
Et pour rendre sa peine et mes plaisirs plus grands,
De cacher ma rivale à ses regards mourans!
Ah! si du-moins Oreste, en punissant son crime,
Lui laissoit le regret de mourir ma victime!
Va le trouver. Dis-lui qu'il aprenne à l'ingrat,
Qu'on l'immole à ma haine, et non pas à l'état.
Chére Cléone, cours. Ma vengeance est perdue,
S'il ignore, en mourant, que c'est moi qui le tue.
ANDROMAQUE, act. 4. sc. 4.[3]

---

3. *Cleone:* You're courting self-destruction. Think again.
   Hermione: If nothing else, I'll savour retribution.
   I'm worried by my trust in what *he* says—
   I'm not convinced by my "doting Orestes."
   To his eyes Pyrrhus seems less steeped in guilt:
   I'd stab with more conviction—to the hilt.
   Far better were my own right hand to pull
   The knife out, quivering, and beautiful,
   As he pays back for what he's done to me;
   And then I wouldn't even let her *see*
   Her dying consort: I'd shield him from her eyes
   As fickle, faithless Pyrrhus slowly dies!
   I'd be consoled, though, should my second-hand
   Assassin tell him it's at *my* command
   He's murdered. Go and find him. Tell him hate
   Dictates this sacrifice, and not the State:
   I'll not have "duty," justifying "Greece,"

Injury, or voluntary wrong, is commonly the cause of resentment; we are taught, however, by experience, that sudden pain is sufficient sometimes to raise this passion, even where injury is not intended. If a man wound me by accident in a tender part, the sudden anguish, giving no time for reflection, provokes resentment, which is as suddenly exerted upon the involuntary cause. Treading upon a gouty toe, or breaking a favourite vase, may upon a warm temper produce this effect. The mind engrossed by bodily pain, or any pain which raises bad humour, demands an object for its resentment; and what object so ready as the person who was the occasion of the pain? that it was undesigned is never thought of. In the same manner even a stock or a stone becomes sometimes the object of resentment. Striking my foot by accident against a stone, a smart pain en-<9>sues: Resentment, suddenly enflamed, prompts me to bray the stone to pieces. The passion is still more irregular in a losing gamester, when he vents it on the cards and dice. All that can be said as an apology for such absurd fits of passion, is, that they are but momentary, and vanish upon the first reflection. And yet such indulgence was by the Athenians given to this irrational emotion, that if a man was killed by the fall of a stone, or other accident, the instrument of death was destroyed.* (1) Resentment raised <10> by

---

Get in the way of loathing's masterpiece.
Oh, run, Cleone: I'll be satisfied
If, when he dies, he knows his jilted bride
Took her revenge.—Trans. Dunn.

* Meursius de leg. Atticis, l. 1. cap. 17.

(1) The *Actio Noxalis* among the Romans, founded also upon the privilege of resentment, appears not altogether void of reason. Animals, it was thought, were not to be exempted from punishment more than men; and when a domestic animal did mischief contrary to its nature, the law required, that it should be given up to the person who was hurt, in order to be punished. To make this law effectual, the *Actio Noxalis* was given, which followed the animal, though even in the hands of a purchaser *bona fide.*— § 5. *Inst. de Noxal. Action* [[i.e., *Justinian's Institutes* 4.8.5]].—So far it was well judged, that property should yield to the more essential right of self-preservation, and to the privilege of punishing injuries. It is probable, that originally there was a necessity to deliver the animal to punishment, without admitting any alternative. But afterward, when passions were more under subjection, and the connection of property became more vigorous, which last will be the subject of a following discourse, an alternative was indulged to the defendant to repair the damage, if he chose to be at that expence, rather than surrender his animal.—*l.* 1. *pr. D. Si quadrupes pauperiem fecisse dicatur* [[i.e., *Digest*

voluntary wrong, which is a rational and useful passion, is in a very different condition. It subsists till the sense of the injury be done away, by punishment, atonement, or length of time.

But all the irregularities of this passion are not yet exhausted. It is still more savage and irrational, when, without distinguishing the innocent from the guilty, it is exerted against the relations of the criminal, and even against the brute creatures that belong to him. Such barbarity <11> will scarce find credit with those who have no knowledge of man but what is discovered by experience in a civilized society; and yet, in the history and laws of ancient nations, we find this savage practice, not only indulged without redress, but, what is still more astonishing, we find it authorised by positive laws. Thus, by an Athenian law, a man committing sacrilege, or betraying his country, was banished, with all his children;* and when a tyrant was killed, his children were also put to death.† By the law of Macedon (2), the punishment of treason was extended against the relations of the criminal.‡ By a Scythian law, when a criminal was punished with death,

---

9.1.1]].—Among modern nations, in Scotland at least, this action went into disuse with the privilege of private punishment. As at present it belongs to the magistrate only to inflict punishment, the mischief done by irrational animals is not regarded, but for preventing the like mischief in time coming. The satisfaction of private revenge is quite disregarded.

Ulpian seems not to have understood the nature or foundation of the *Actio noxalis,* in teaching the following doctrine, That the proprietor is primarily liable to repair the mischief done by his animal, and that the alternative of delivering up the animal, was afterward indulged by the law of the Twelve Tables.—*l. 6. § 1. De re judicata.*—The law of Nature subjects no man to repair the mischief done by his horse or his ox, if not antecedently known to be vicious. All that can be incumbent upon him, by any rational principle, is, to deliver up the animal to be punished; and hence it is evident, that the privilege indulged by law, was not that of giving up the animal, but that of retaining it upon repairing the damage.

(2) Hanno, one of the most considerable citizens of Carthage, formed a design to make himself tyrant of his country, by poisoning the whole senate at a banquet. The plot being discovered, he was put to death by torture, and his children, with all his relations, were at the same time cut off without mercy, though they had no share in his guilt.—*Justin* [[i.e., Marcus Junianus Justinus]], *l. 21. cap. 4.*

* Meursius, l. 2. cap. 2.
† Meursius, l. 2. cap. 15.
‡ Quintus Curtius, l. 6. cap. 11.

all his sons were put to death with him: His daughters only were saved from destruction.* In the laws of the Bavarians,† the use of women was forbidden to clergymen, "lest (as in the text) the people be destroyed for the crime of their pastor": A very gross notion of divine punishment. And yet the Gre-<12>cians entertained the same notion; as appears from the Iliad, in the beginning:

> Latona's son a dire contagion spread,
> And heap'd the camp with mountains of the dead,
> The King of men his rev'rend priest defy'd,
> And for the King's offence the people died.[4]

Lucan, for a crime committed by the King, thought it not unjust to destroy all Egypt.‡ But it may appear still more surprising, that this savage and absurd practice continued very long in some parts of the Roman empire, though governed by laws remarkable for their equity. Of this the following statute of the Emperors Arcadius and Honorius‖ is clear evidence.

> Sancimus ibi esse poenam ubi et noxia est. Propinquos, notos, familiares, procul a calumnia submovemus, quos reos sceleris societas non facit. Nec enim adfinitas vel amicitia nefarium crimen admittunt. Peccata igitur suos teneant auctores: Nec ulterius progrediatur metus quam reperiatur delictum. *Hoc singulis quibusque judicibus intimetur.*[5]

At the same time, these very Emperors, however mild and rational with regard to others, talk a very different language upon a crime which affected

---

* Herodotus, l. 4.
† Tit. I. § 13.
‡ L. 9. l. 145.
‖ L. 22. C. De poenis.
4. Homer, *Iliad*, trans. Pope. Bk. 1, ll. 10–14.
5. "We order that punishment shall be inflicted only upon those who are liable to it, and We exclude all relatives, acquaintances, and companions from the imputation of calumny, as association with criminals does not necessarily render them guilty, and neither affinity nor friendship presumes implication in crime. Therefore, let each one be responsible for the offences which he himself commits, and let the fear of punishment go no further than the detection of guilt. This law shall be communicated to all judges." *Codex* 9.47.22.

themselves: After observing, that will and purpose alone, without any ouvert act, is treason, subjecting the guilty person to a capital punishment and forfeiture of <13> goods, they go on in the following words.

> Filii vero ejus, quibus vitam Imperatoria specialiter lenitate concedimus, (paterno enim deberent perire supplicio, in quibus paterni, hoc est hereditarii, criminis exempla metuuntur), a materna, vel avita, omnium etiam proximorum hereditate ac successione habeantur alieni: Testamentis extraneorum nihil capiant: Sint perpetuo egentes, et pauperes, infamia eos paterna semper comitetur, ad nullos prorsus honores, ad nulla sacramenta perveniant: Sint postremo tales, ut his, perpetua egestate fordentibus, sit et mors solatium, et vita supplicium.*[6]

Every one knows, that murder committed by a member of any tribe or clan, was resented, not only against the criminal and his relations, but against the whole tribe or clan: A species of resentment so common as to be distinguished by a peculiar name, that of *deadly feud*. So late as the days of King Edmond, a law was made in England, forbidding deadly feud, except betwixt the relations of the deceased and the murderer himself; and declaring, that these relations shall forfeit all their goods, if they prosecute with deadly feud the relations of the murderer. In Japan, to this day, it is the practice to involve children and relations in the punishment of capital crimes.[†] <14>

A tendency to excess, so destructive in the passion of resentment, is often in other passions the occasion of good. Joy, when excessive, as well as gratitude, are not confined to their proper objects, but expand themselves upon

---

* L. 5. § 1. C. Ad leg. Jul. Majest.

† See Kemfer's History of Japan.

6. "The sons of a person convicted of such an offense, to whom by special Imperial indulgence We grant the privilege of life (for they should be put to death by the same punishment as their father, as in their cases his example, that is the inclination to commit a crime, is inherited), shall be excluded from the estates and successions of their mothers and grandmothers, and all their remaining nearest relatives. Nor shall they be able to receive anything under the wills of strangers, but shall always remain in want, and poor; and the infamy of their fathers will always attach to them, nor shall they afterwards be eligible to any office, or be qualified to perform public duties; in short, such men shall remain in such a condition of perpetual indigence that death will be a consolation to them, and life a punishment": *Codex* 9.8.5.1.

whatever is connected with these objects. In general, all our active passions, in their nascent state and when moderate, are accompanied with a sense of fitness and rectitude; but when excessive, they enflame the mind, and violently hurry it to action, without due distinction of objects.

And this leads to a reflection upon the irregular tendency of resentment here displayed. If it be the nature of all active passions, when immoderate, to expand themselves beyond their proper objects, which is remarkable in friendship, love, gratitude, and all the social passions, it ought not to be surprising, that resentment, hatred, envy, and other dissocial passions, should not be more regular. Among savages, this tendency may perhaps have a bad effect, by adding force to the malevolent passions: But in a civilized state, where dissocial passions are softened, if not subdued, this tendency is, upon the whole, extremely beneficial.

It is observed above, that revenge is a privilege bestowed by the law of Nature on those who suffer by a voluntary injury; and the correspondence hath also been observed betwixt this privilege and the sense of merited punishment, which <15> makes the criminal submit to the punishment he deserves. Thus by the law of Nature, the person injured acquires a right over the delinquent, to chastise and punish him in proportion to the injury; and the delinquent, sensible of the right, knows he ought to submit to it. Hence punishment is commonly said to be a sort of debt, which the criminal is bound to pay to the person he hath injured (3); and this way of speaking may safely be indulged as an analogical illustration, provided no consequence be drawn that the analogy will not justify. This caution is not unnecessary; for many writers, influenced by the foregoing semblance, reason about punishment unwarily, as if it were a debt in the strictest sense. By means of the same resemblance, a notion prevailed in the darker ages of the world, of a substitute in punishment, who undertakes the debt and suffers the punishment that another merits. Traces of this opinion are found in the religious ceremonies of the ancient Egyptians and other ancient nations. Among them the conceptions of a Deity were gross, and of morality no less so. We must not therefore be surprised at their notion of a trans-

(3) Upon this resemblance, the expression in the Roman language, *solvere* or *pendere poenas,* is founded.

ference of punishment, as of debt, from one person to another. They were imposed upon by the slight analogy above-mentioned; which reasoning taught <16> them not to correct, because reasoning at that time was in its infancy.[7] The prevalence of this notion in the religious ceremonies of the ancient Egyptians, is vouched by Herodotus.* A bull is chosen pure white, for a sacrifice to their god Apis. The victim is brought to the altar, a fire kindled, wine poured out, and prayers pronounced. The bull is killed; and his head is thrown into the river, with the following execration: "May all the evils impending over those who perform this sacrifice, or over the Egyptians in general, be averted on this head." Even in later times, when a Roman army was in hazard of a defeat, it was not uncommon for the general to devote himself to death, in order to obtain the victory.[†] Is not this practice founded upon the same notion? Let Lucan answer the question.

> O utinam, coelique Deis, Erebique liberet
> Hoc caput in cunctas damnatum exponere poenas!
> Devotum hostiles Decium pressere catervae:
> Me geminae figant acies, me barbara telis
> Rheni turba petat: cunctis ego pervius hastis
> Excipiam medius totius vulnera belli.
> Hic redimat sanguis populos: hac caede luatur
> Quicquid Romani meruerunt pendere mores.
>
> L. 2. l. 306.[8] <17>

And the following passage of Horace, seems to be founded on the same notion.

---

* Book 2.

† Tit. Liv. l. 8. § 9.; and again, l. 10. § 28. 29.

7. 1758, 1761: "because reasoning at that time was in its infancy" = "because reasoning at that time was not so far advanced as to overbalance the weight of natural prejudices."

8. "But would it were possible for me, condemned by the powers of heaven and hell, to be the scapegoat for another nation! As hordes of foemen bore down Decius when he had offered his life, so may both armies pierce this body, may the savages from the Rhine aim their weapons at me; may I be transfixed by every spear, and may I stand between and intercept every blow dealt in this war! Let my blood redeem the nations, and my death pay the whole penalty incurred by the corruption of Rome." Trans. Duff.

At tu, nauta, vagae ne parce malignus arenae
    Offibus et capiti inhumato
Particulam dare. Sic, quodcunque minabitur Eurus
    Fluctibus Hesperiis, Venusinae
    Plectantur sylvae, te sospite.

CARM. l. 1. ode 28.[9]

That one should undertake a debt for another, is a matter of consent, not repugnant to the rules of justice. But with respect to the administration of justice among men, no maxim has a more solid foundation or is more universal, than that punishment cannot be transferred from the guilty to the innocent. Punishment, considered as a gratification of the party offended, is purely personal; and, being inseparately connected with guilt, cannot admit of substitution. A man may consent, it is true, to suffer that pain which his friend the offender merits as a punishment; but the injured person is not satisfied with such transmutation of suffering: his resentment is not gratified but by retaliating upon the very person who did the injury. Yet, even in a matter obvious to reason, so liable are men to error when led astray by any bias, that to the foregoing notion concerning punishment, we may impute the most barbarous practice ever prevailed among savages, that of substituting human crea-<18>tures in punishment, and compelling them to undergo the most grievous torments, even death itself. I speak of human sacrifices, which are deservedly a lasting reproach upon mankind, being of all human institutions the most irrational, and the most subversive of humanity. To sacrifice a prisoner of war to an incensed deity, barbarous and inhuman as it is, may admit some excuse. But that a man should sacrifice his children as an atonement for his crimes, cannot be thought of without horror (4). Yet this savage impiety can rest upon no other foun-

9. "But you, seafarer, do not be so mean as to grudge a grain of wind-blown sand to my unburied skull and bones. Then, whatever threats are hurled by the East Wind at the waves of Westland, may the woods of Venusia bear the brunt while you are safe." Trans. Rudd.

(4) When Agathocles King of Syracuse, after a compleat victory laid siege to Carthage, the Carthaginians, believing that their calamities were brought upon them by the anger of the gods, became extremely superstitious. It had been the custom to sacrifice

dation than the slight resemblance that punishment hath to a debt; which is a strong evidence of the influence of imagination upon our conduct. The vitious hath ever been solicitous to transfer upon others the punishment they themselves deserve; for nothing is so dear to a man as himself.

> Wherewith shall I come before the Lord, and bow myself before the high God? <19> shall I come before him with burnt offerings, with calves of a year old? Will the Lord be pleased with thousands of rams, or with ten thousand rivers of oil? shall I give my first-born for my transgression, the fruit of my body for the sin of my soul?

But this is not an atonement in the sight of the Almighty.

> He hath shewed thee, O man, what is good; and what doth the Lord require of thee, but to do justly, and to love mercy, and to walk humbly with thy God?*

I beg indulgence for a reflection that arises naturally from this branch of the subject; that the permitting vicarious punishment is subversive of humanity, and no less so of moral duty. Encourage a man to believe that without repentance or reformation of manners he can atone for his sins, and he will indulge in them for ever.[10] Happy it is for mankind, that by the improvement of our rational faculties, the open profession of compounding for sin is banished from all civilized societies: And yet from the selfishness of human nature this doctrine continues privately to influence our conduct more than is willingly acknowledged, or even suspected. Many men give punctual attendance at public worship, to compound for hidden vices; many are openly charitable, to compound for private oppression; and many are willing to do God good service in <20> supporting his established

---

to their god Saturn, the sons of the most eminent persons; but the later practice was, to purchase and breed up children for that purpose. That they might therefore without delay reform what was amiss, they offered, as a public sacrifice, two hundred of the sons of the nobility.   *Diodorus Siculus, book* 20. *ch.* 1.

   * Micah vi.

   10. 1758, 1761: "Encourage a man to believe that without repentance . . . he will indulge in them for ever" = "Men we see have been misled so far, as fondly to flatter themselves, that without repentance or reformation of manners, they could atone for their sins; and by this pernicious notion have been encouraged to indulge in them without end."

church, to compound for aiming at power by a factious disturbance of the state. Such pernicious notions, proceeding from a wrong bias in our nature, cannot be eradicated after they have once got possession; nor be prevented, but by early culture, and by frequently inculcating the most important of all truths, That the Almighty admits of no composition for sin; and that his pardon is not to be obtained, without sincere repentance, and thorough reformation of manners.

Having discoursed in general of the nature of punishment, and of some irregular notions that have been entertained about it, I am now ready to attend its progress through the different stages of the social life. Society, originally, did not make a strict union among individuals. Mutual defence against a more powerful neighbour, being in early times the chief or sole motive for joining in society, individuals never thought of surrendering to the public, any of their natural rights that could be retained consistently with mutual defence. In particular, the privileges of maintaining their own property and of avenging their own wrongs, were reserved to individuals full and entire. In the dawn of society accordingly, we find no traces of a judge, properly so called, who hath power to interpose in differences, and to force persons at variance to submit to his opinion. If a dispute about property, or about <21> any civil right, could not be adjusted by the parties themselves, there was no other method, but to take the opinion of some indifferent person.[11] This method of determining civil differences was imperfect; for what if the parties did not agree upon an arbiter? Or what if one of them proved refractory, after the chosen arbiter had given his opinion? To remedy these inconveniencies, it was found expedient to establish judges, who at first differed in one circumstance only from arbiters, that they could not be declined. They had no magisterial authority, not even that of compelling parties to appear before them. This is evident from the Roman law, which subsisted many centuries before the notion obtained of a power in a judge to force a party into court. To bring a disputable matter to an issue, no other means occurred, but the making it lawful for the complainer to drag his party before the judge *obtorto collo,* as expressed by the

11. 1758, 1761: "some indifferent person" = "some indifferent person, whose opinion should be the rule."

writers on that law: And the same regulation appears in the laws of the Visigoths.* But jurisdiction, at first merely voluntary, came gradually to be improved to its present state of being compulsory, involving so much of the magisterial authority as is necessary for explicating jurisdiction, viz. power of calling a party into court, and power of making a sentence effectual. And in this <22> manner, civil jurisdiction in progress of time was brought to perfection.

Criminal jurisdiction is in all countries of a much later date. Revenge, the darling privilege of undisciplined nature,[12] is never tamely given up; for the reason chiefly, that it is not gratified unless the punishment be inflicted by the person injured. The privilege of resenting injuries, was therefore that private right which was the latest of being surrendered, or rather wrested from individuals in society. This revolution was of great importance with respect to government, which can never fully attain its end, where punishment in any measure is trusted in private hands. A revolution so contradictory to the strongest propensity of human nature, could not by any power, nor by any artifice, be instantaneous. It must have been gradual; and, in fact, the progressive steps tending to its completion, were slow, and, taken singly, almost imperceptible; as will appear from the following history. And to be convinced of the difficulty of wresting this privilege from individuals, we need but reflect upon the practice of duelling, so customary in times past; which the strictest attention in the magistrate, joined with the severest punishment, have not altogether been able to repress.

No production of art or nature is more imperfect than is government in its infancy, com-<23>prehending no sort of jurisdiction, civil or criminal. What can more tend to break the peace of society, and to promote universal discord, than that every man should be the judge in his own cause, and inflict punishment according to his own judgment? But instead of wondering at the original weakness of government, our wonder would be better directed upon its present state of perfection, and upon the means by which it hath arrived to that state, in opposition to the strongest and most active principles of human nature. This subject makes a great figure in the history

---

* L. 6. tit. 4. § 4.
12. 1758, 1761: "undisciplined nature" = "human nature."

of man; and that it partly comes under the present undertaking, I esteem a lucky circumstance.

A partiality rooted in the nature of man, makes private revenge a most dangerous privilege. The man who is injured, having a strong sense of the wrong done him, never dreams of putting bounds to his resentment. The offender, on the other hand, under-rating the injury, judges a slight atonement sufficient. Further, the man who suffers is apt to judge rashly, and to blame persons without cause. To restrain the unjust effects of natural partiality, was not an easy task; and probably was not soon attempted. But early measures were taken to prevent the bad effects of rash judgment, by which the innocent were often oppressed. We have one early instance among the Jews: Their <24> cities of refuge were appointed as an interim sanctuary to the man slayer, till the elders of the city had an opportunity to judge whether the deed was voluntary or casual. If casual, the man was protected from the resentment of the party offended, called in the text *the avenger of blood:* but he was to remain in that city until the death of the high priest, to give time for resentment to subside. If the man taking benefit of the sanctuary was found guilty, he was delivered to the avenger of blood that he might die.* In the laws of the Athenians, and also of the barbarous nations who dismembered the Roman empire, we find regulations that correspond to this among the Jews; and which, in a different form, prevented erroneous judgment still more effectually than was done by the cities of refuge. If a crime was manifest, the party injured might avenge himself without any ceremony. Therefore it was lawful for a man to kill his wife and the adulterer found together.† It was lawful for a man to kill his daughter taken in the act of fornication. The same was lawful to the brothers and uncles after the father's death.‡ And it was lawful to kill a thief apprehended under night with stolen goods.‖ <25> But if the crime was not manifest, a previous trial was required, in order to determine whether the suspected person was guilty or innocent. Thus a married woman suspected of adul-

---

* Numbers xxxv. Deut. xix.
† Meursius de leg. Atticis, l. 1. c. 4.; Laws of the Visigoths, l. 3. tit. 4. § 4.; Laws of the Bavar. tit. 7. § 1.
‡ Laws of the Visig. l. 3. tit. 4. § 5.
‖ Laws of the Bavar. tit. 8. § 5.

tery, must be accused before the judge; and, if found guilty, she and the adulterer are delivered over to the husband to be punished at his will.* If a free woman live in adultery with a married man, she is delivered by the judges to the man's wife to be punished at her will.† He that steals a child, shall be delivered to the child's relations to be put to death, or sold, at their pleasure.‡ A slave who commits fornication with a free woman, must be delivered to her parents to be put to death.‖

In tracing the history of law through dark ages, unprovided with records, or so slenderly provided as not to afford any regular historical chain, we must endeavour to supply the broken links, by hints from poets and historians, by collateral facts, and by cautious conjectures drawn from the nature of the government, of the people, and of the times. If we use all the light that is afforded, and if the conjectural facts correspond with the few facts that are distinctly vouched, and join all in one regular chain, more <26> cannot be expected from human endeavours. Evidence must afford conviction, if it be the best of the kind. This apology is necessary with regard to the subject under consideration. In tracing the history of the criminal law, we must not hope that all its steps and changes can be drawn from the archives of any one nation. In fact, many steps were taken and many changes made, before archives were kept, and even before writing was a common art. We must be satisfied with collecting the facts and circumstances as they may be gathered from the laws of different countries: and if these put together make a regular chain of causes and effects, we may rationally conclude, that the progress has been the same among all nations, in the capital circumstances at least; for accidents, or the singular nature of a people, or of a government, will always produce some peculiarities.

Emboldened by this apology, I proceed chearfully in the task I have undertaken. The necessity of applying to a judge, where any doubt arose about the author of the crime, was probably, in all countries, the first instance of the legislature's interposing in punishment. It was a novelty; but it was such as could not readily alarm individuals, being calculated not to restrain the

* Laws of the Visig. l. 3. tit. 4. § 3.
† Ibid. l. 3. tit. 4. § 9.
‡ Ibid. l. 7. tit. 3. § 3.
‖ Laws of the Bavar. tit. 7. § 9.

privilege of revenge, but only to direct revenge to its proper object. The application to a judge was made necessary among the Jews, by <27> the privilege conferred upon the cities of refuge; and, among other nations, by a positive law without any circuit. That this was the law of the Visigoths and Bavarians, hath already been said; and that it was also the law of Abyssinia and Athens, will appear below. The step next in order, was an improvement upon this regulation. The necessity of applying to a judge, removed all ambiguity about the criminal, but it did not remove an evil repugnant to humanity and justice, that of putting the offender under the power of the party injured, to be punished at his pleasure. With relation to this point, I discover a wise regulation in Abyssinia. In that empire, the degree or extent of punishment, is not left to the discretion of the person injured. The governor of the province names a judge, who determines what punishment the crime deserves. If death, the criminal is delivered to the accuser, who has thereby an opportunity to gratify his resentment to the full.* This regulation must be approved, because it restrains in a considerable degree excess in revenge. But a great latitude still remaining in the manner of executing the punishment, this also was rectified by a law among the Athenians. A person suspected of murder was first carried before the judge; and, if found guilty, was delivered to the relations of the deceased, to be put to death if they thought pro-<28>per. But it was unlawful for them to put him to any torture, or to force money from him.† Whether the regulations now mentioned, were peculiar to Athens and Abyssinia, I cannot say; for I have not discovered any traces of them in the customs of other nations. They were remedies so proper for the disease, that one should imagine they must have obtained every where some time or other. Perhaps they have been prevented, and rendered unnecessary, by a custom I am now to enter upon, which made a great figure in Europe for many ages, that of pecuniary compositions for crimes.

Of these pecuniary compositions, I discover traces among many nations. It is natural to offer satisfaction to the party injured; and no satisfaction is for either party more commodious, than a sum of money. Avarice, it is true,

* Father Lobo's voyage to Abyssinia, ch. 3.
† Meursius de leg. Atticis, l. 1. cap. 20.

is not so fierce a passion as resentment; but it is more stable, and by its perseverance often prevails over the keenest passions. With regard to man-slaughter in particular, which doth not always distress the nearest relations, it may appear prudent to relinquish the momentary pleasure of gratifying a passion for a permanent good. At the same time, the notion that punishment is a kind of debt, did certainly facilitate the introduction of this custom; and there was opportunity for its becoming universal, during the <29> period that the right of punishment was in private hands. We find traces of this custom among the ancient Greeks. The husband had a choice to put the adulterer to death, or to exact a sum from him.* And Homer plainly alludes to this law, in his story of Mars and Venus entangled by the husband Vulcan in a net, and exposed to public view:

> Loud laugh the rest, ev'n Neptune laughs aloud,
> Yet sues importunate to loose the god:
> And free, he cries, oh Vulcan! free from shame
> Thy captives, I ensure the penal claim.
> Will Neptune (Vulcan then) the faithless trust?
> He suffers who gives surety for th' unjust:
> But say, if that leud scandal of the sky
> To liberty restor'd, perfidious, fly,
> Say, wilt thou bear the mulct? He instant cries,
> The mulct I bear, if Mars pefidious flies.
>
> ODYSS. viii. l. 381.

The Greeks also admitted a composition for murder; as appears from the following passage:

> Stern and unpitying! if a brother bleed,
> On just atonement, we remit the deed;
> A sire the slaughter of his son forgives,
> The price of blood discharg'd, the murd'rer lives;
> The haughtiest hearts at length their rage resign,
> And gifts can conquer ev'ry soul but thine.
> The gods that unrelenting breast have steel'd,
> And curs'd thee with a mind that cannot yield.
>
> ILIAD, ix. l. 743. <30>

---

* Meursius de leg. Atticis, l. 1. cap. 4.

Again,

> There in the forum, swarm a num'rous train;
> The subject of debate, a town's-man slain:
> One pleads the fine discharg'd, which one deny'd,
> And bade the public and the laws decide.
>
> ILIAD xviii. l. 577.

One of the laws of the Twelve Tables was "Si membrum rupit, ni cum eo pacit, talio esto."* And Tacitus is very express upon this custom among the Germans:† "Suscipere tam inimicitias seu patris seu propinqui quam amicitias necesse est: nec implacabiles durant; luitur enim etiam homicidium certo armentorum ac pecorum numero, recipitque satisfactionem universa domus." We find traces of the same thing in Abyssinia,‡ among the negroes on the coast of Guinea,‖ and among the blacks of Madagascar.§ The laws of the barbarous nations cited above, insist longer upon these compositions than upon any other subject; and that the practice was established among our Saxon ancestors, under the name of *Vergelt,* is known to all the world.

This practice at first, as may reasonably be conjectured, rested entirely upon private consent. <31> It was so in Greece, if we can trust Eustathius in his notes on the foregoing passage in the Iliad first quoted.[13] He reports, that the murderer was obliged to go into banishment one year, unless he could purchase liberty to remain at home, by paying a certain fine to the relations of the deceased. While compositions for crimes rested upon this foundation, there was nothing new or singular in them. The person injured might punish or forgive at his pleasure; and might remit the punishment upon terms or conditions. But the practice, if not remarkable in its nascent

---

* Aulus Gellius, l. 20. cap. 1. [["If one has broken another's limb, there shall be retaliation, unless a compromise be made." Trans. Rolfe.]]

† De moribus Germanorum. [[[XXI]. "It is incumbent to take up a father's feuds or a kinsman's not less than his friendships; but such feuds do not continue unappeasable: even homicide is atoned for by a fixed number of cattle and sheep, and the whole family thereby receives satisfaction." Trans. Peterson.]]

‡ Lobo, chap. 7.

‖ [[Bosman,]] Description of the coast of Guinea, letters 10. and 11.

§ Drury, p. 240.

13. Eustathius of Thessalonica (d. ca. 1194) wrote a commentary on the *Iliad.* Kames probably draws on Pope's notes to his translation: see *Iliad,* trans. Pope, vol. iii, p. 80.

state, made a great figure in its progress. It was not only countenanced, but greatly encouraged, among all nations, as the likeliest means to restrain the impetuosity of revenge: till becoming frequent and customary, it was made law; and what at first was voluntary, became in process of time necessary. But this change was slow and gradual. The first step probably was to interpose in behalf of the delinquent, if he offered a reasonable satisfaction in cattle or money, and to afford him protection if the satisfaction was refused by the person injured. The next step was to make it unlawful to prosecute resentment, without first demanding satisfaction from the delinquent. And in the laws of King Ina* we read, that he who takes revenge without first demanding satisfaction, must restore <32> what he has taken, and further be liable in a compensation. The third step completed the system, which was to compel the delinquent to pay, and the person injured to accept, a proper satisfaction. By the laws of the Longobards,† if the person injured refused to accept a composition, he was sent to the king to be imprisoned, in order to restrain him from revenge. And if the criminal refused to pay a composition, he also was sent to the king to be imprisoned, in order to restrain him from doing more mischief. After composition is made for manslaughter, the person injured must give his oath not further to prosecute his feud;‡ and if he notwithstanding follow out his revenge, he is subjected to a double composition.‖

Altars, among most nations, were places of sanctuary. The person who fled to an altar, was held to be under the immediate protection of the deity, and therefore inviolable. This practice prevailed among the Jews, as appears by the frequent mention of laying hold on the horns of the altar. Among the Grecians,§

> Phemius alone the hand of vengeance spar'd,
> Phemius the sweet, the heav'n-instructed bard. <33>
> Beside the gate the rev'rend minstrel stands;

---

* Lambard's Collection, law 9.
† Laws of the Longobards, l. 1. tit. 37. § 1.
‡ Ibid. l. 1. tit. 9. § 34.
‖ Ibid. l. 1. tit. 9. § 8.
§ Meursius de leg. Atticis, l. 2. cap. 32.

The lyre, now silent, trembling in his hands;
Dubious to supplicate the chief, or fly
To Jove's inviolable altar nigh.

ODYSSEY xxii. l. 367.

Aedibus in mediis, nudoque sub aetheris axe,
Ingens ara fuit; juxtaque veterrima laurus,
Incumbens arae, atque umbra complexa Penates.
Hic Hecuba, et natae nequicquam altaria circum
Praecipites atra ceu tempestate columbae
Condensae, et Divum amplexae simulacra tenebant.
Ipsum autem sumptis Priamum juvenilibus armis
Ut vidit: Quae mens tam dira, miserrima conjux,
Impulit his cingi telis? aut quo ruis? inquit.
Non tali auxilio, nec defensoribus istis
Tempus eget: Non, si ipse meus nunc afforet Hector.
Huc tandem concede: Haec ara tuebitur omnes,
Aut moriere simul. Sic ore effata, recepit
Ad sese, et sacra longaevum in sede locavit.

AENEID, l. 2. l. 512.[14]

Altars prevailed also among Christians.[15] Thus by the law of the Visigoths,*
if a murderer fly to the altar, the priest shall deliver him to the relations of
the deceased, upon giving oath that, in prosecuting their revenge, they will
not put him to death. Had the prosecutor, at this period, been bound to
accept of a composition, the privilege of sanctuary would have been un-

---

* L. 6. tit. 5. § 16.

14. "In the middle of the palace and beneath the open arch of heaven was a huge
altar, and hard by an ancient laurel, leaning against the altar and clasping the household
gods in its shade. Here, round the shrines, vainly crouched Hecuba and her daughters,
huddled together like doves swept before a black storm, and clasping the images of the
Gods. But when she saw even Priam harnessed in the armour of his youth, 'My poor
husband,' she cries, 'what dreadful thought has driven you to don those weapons? Where
are you rushing to? The hour calls not for such aid or such defenders, not though my
own Hector were here himself! Come hither, pray; this altar will guard us all, or you will
die with us!' Thus she spoke, then drew the aged man to her and placed him on the holy
seat." Trans. Fairclough.

15. 1758, 1761: "Altars prevailed also among Christians" = "The same notion prevailed
among Christians, and altars served the purpose of the cities of refuge among the Jews."

necessary. <34> By this time, however, the practice of compounding for crimes had gained such authority, that it was thought hard, even for a murderer to lose his life by the obstinacy of the dead man's relations. But this practice gaining still more authority, it was enacted in England,* That if any guilty of a capital crime fly to the church, his life shall be safe, but he must pay a composition. Thus it appears, that the privilege of sanctuary, though the child of superstition, was extremely useful while the power of punishment was a private right: But now that this right is transferred to the public, and that there is no longer any hazard of excess in punishment, a sanctuary for crimes, which hath no other effect but to restrain the free course of the criminal law and to give unjust hopes of impunity, ought not to be tolerated in any society.

When compositions first came in use, it is probable that they were authorised in slight delinquencies only. We read in the laws of the Visigoths,† That if a free man strike another free man on the head, he shall pay for discolouring the skin, five shillings; for breaking the skin, ten shillings; for a cut which reaches the bone, twenty shillings; and for a broken bone, one hundred shillings: But that greater crimes shall be more severely punished; maiming, dismember-<35>ing, or depriving one of his natural liberty by imprisonment or fetters, to be punished by the *lex talionis*.‡ But compositions growing more and more reputable, were extended to the grossest delinquencies. The laws of the Burgundians, of the Salians, of the Almanni, of the Bavarians, of the Ripuarii, of the Saxons, of the Angli and Thuringi, of the Frisians, of the Longobards, and of the Anglo-Saxons, are full of these compositions, extending from the most trifling injury, to the most atrocious crimes, not excepting high treason by imagining and compassing the death of the king. In perusing the tables of these compositions, which enter into a minute detail of the most trivial offences, a question naturally occurs, why all this scrupulous nicety of adjusting sums to delinquencies? Such a thing is not heard of in later times. The following answer will give satisfaction, That resentment, allowed scope among barbarians,

---

* Laws of King Ina, collected by Lambard, law 5.
† L. 6. tit. 4. § 1.
‡ Laws of the Visigoths, l. 6. tit. 4 § 3.

was apt to take flame by the slightest spark (5). <36> Therefore, to provide for its gratification, it became necessary to enact compositions for every trifling wrong, such as at present would be the subject of mirth rather than of serious punishment. For example, where the cloaths of a woman bathing in a river, are taken away to expose her nakedness;* and where dirty water is thrown upon a woman as a mark of contumely.† But as the criminal law is now modelled, private resentment being in a good measure sunk in public punishment, nothing is reckoned criminal, but what encroaches on the safety or peace of society; and such a punishment is chosen, as may have the effect of repressing the crime in time coming, without much regarding the gratification of the party offended.

As these compositions were favoured by the resemblance that private punishment has to a debt, they were apt, in a gross way of thinking, to be considered as reparation to the party injured for his loss or damage. Therefore, in adjusting these compositions, no steady or regular distinction is made betwixt voluntary and involuntary acts.[16] He who wounded or killed a man by chance, was liable to a composition;‡ and even where a man was killed in self-defence, a <37> full composition was due.‖ A distinction was made by a law among the Longobards, enacting, That involuntary wrongs should bear a less composition than voluntary.[17]§ And the same rule did no doubt obtain among other nations, when they came to think more accu-

---

(5) In the year 1327, most of the great houses in Ireland were banded one against another, the Giraldines, Butlers, and Breminghams, on the one side, and the Bourkes and Poers on the other. The ground of the quarrel was no other, but that the Lord Arnold Poer had called the Earl of Kildare, *Rimer.* This quarrel was prosecuted with such malice and violence, that the counties of Waterford and Kilkenny were destroyed with fire and sword. *Affairs of Ireland by Sir John Davies.* [[For the episode Kames describes, see pp. 147–48.]]

* Laws of the Longobards, l. 1. tit. 12. § 6.

† Ibid. § 8.

‡ Laws of the Angli and Thuringi, § 10.; Laws of Henry 1. of England [[see Wilkins, *Leges Anglo-Saxonicae*]], law 70.

‖ Laws of the Longobards, l. 1. tit. 9. § 19.

§ Law 1. tit. 2 § 11.

16. 1758, 1761: "acts" = "wrongs."

17. 1758, 1761: "A distinction . . . than voluntary" = "Voluntary and involuntary crimes were generally put upon the same footing. But this was altered by a law among the Longobards, enacting, That the latter should bear a less composition than the former."

rately about the nature of punishment (6). But such was the prevalency of resentment, that though at first no alleviation or excuse was sustained to mitigate the composition, aggravating circumstances were often laid hold of to enflame it. Thus he who took the opportunity of fire or shipwreck to steal goods, was obliged to restore fourfold.* These compositions were also proportioned to the dignity of the persons injured; <38> and from this source is derived our knowledge of the different ranks and titles of honour among the barbarous nations above mentioned. And it is a strong indication of their approach to humanity and politeness, that their compositions for injuries done to women are generally double.

As to the persons entitled to the composition, it must be obvious, in the first place, that he only had right to the composition who was injured: But if a man was killed, every one of his relations was entitled to a share, because they were all sufferers by his death. Thus, in the Salic laws,† where a man is killed, the half of the composition belongs to his children; the other half to his other relations, upon the side of the father and mother. If there be no relations on the father's side, the part that would belong to them accrues to the fisk. The like if there be no relations on the mother's side. The Longobards had a singular way of thinking in this matter. Female relations got no part of the composition; and the reason given is, That they cannot assist in prosecuting revenge, *Non possunt ipsam faydam levare.*‡ But women are capable of receiving satisfaction or atonement for a crime committed

---

(6) What is said above about the nature of resentment, that when suddenly raised it makes no distinction betwixt a voluntary and involuntary wrong, may help to explain this matter. It is certain, that such grossness of conception was not peculiar to the barbarous nations. The polite Grecians appear to be as little sensible of the distinction as the others. Aristotle talks familiarly of an involuntary crime [[It is not obvious what in Aristotle Kames is alluding to here, but it is probably a passage in *Nicomachean Ethics* V.ii (1131a) where Aristotle discusses "rectificatory" justice, and divides the kinds of actions that fall under the scope of such justice into the voluntary and involuntary.]]: And that this was not merely a way of speaking, appears from the story of Oedipus, whose crimes, if they can be called so, were, strictly speaking, involuntary. And by an express law among the Athenians, involuntary slaughter was punished with banishment, without liberty of returning till the relations of the deceased were satisfied. *Meursius de leg. Atticis, l.* 1 *cap.* 16.

* Laws of the Visigoths, l. 7. tit. 2. § 18.

† Tit. 65.

‡ L. 1. tit. 9. § 18.

against their relation, and <39> therefore are entitled in justice to some share of the composition (7).

Before entering upon a new branch, I must lay hold of the present opportunity, to bestow a reflection on this singular practice of compounding for crimes. However strange it may appear to us, it was certainly a happy invention. By the temptation of money, men were gradually accustomed to stifle their resentment. This was a fine preparation for transferring the power of punishment to the magistrate, which would have been impracticable without some such intermediate step: for while individuals retain their privilege of avenging injuries, the passion of resentment, fortified by universal practice, is too violent to be subdued by the force of any government.

We are now arrived at the last and most shining period of our history; which is, to unfold the means by which criminal jurisdiction, or the right of punishment, was transferred from private hands to the magistrate. There perhaps never was in government a revolution of greater importance. While criminal jurisdiction is engrossed by every individual for his own behoof, there must be an overbalance of power in the people, inconsistent with any stable administra-<40>tion of public affairs. The daily practice of blood, makes a nation fierce and wild, not to be awed by the power of any government. A government, at the same time, destitute of the power of the sword, except in crimes against the public which are rare, must be so weak, as scarce to be a match for the tamest people: for it cannot escape observation, that nothing tends more to support the authority of the magistrate, than his power of criminal jurisdiction; because every exercise of that power, being public, strikes every eye. In a country already civilized, the power of making laws may be considered as a greater trust: But in order to establish the authority of government, and to create awe and submission in the people, the power of making laws is a mere shadow, without the power of the sword.

In the original formation of societies, to which mutual defence against some more powerful enemy was the chief or sole motive, the idea of a common interest otherwise than for defence, of a public, of a community, was scarce understood. War, indeed, requiring the strictest union among

(7) See in the Appendix, No 1. the form of an amicable composition for murder, termed in our law, *Letter of Slains*. [[Note, and Appendix, added 1776.]]

individuals, introduced the notion of a number of men becoming an army, governed, like a single person, by one mind and one council. But in peaceable times, every man relied upon his own prowess, or that of his clan, without having any notion of a common interest, of which no signs appeared. There was, indeed, <41> from the beginning, some sort of government;[18] but it was so limited, that the magistrate did not pretend to interpose in private differences, whether civil or criminal. In the infancy of society, the idea of a public is so faint and obscure, that public crimes, where no individual is hurt, pass unregarded. But when government hath advanced to some degree of maturity, the public interest is then recognised, and the nature of a crime against the public understood. This notion must gain strength, and become universal in the course of a regular administration, spreading itself upon all affairs which have any connection with the common interest. It naturally comes to be considered, that by all atrocious crimes the public is injured, and by open rapine and violence the peace of the society broke. This introduced a new regulation, that in compounding for gross crimes, a fine, or *fredum,* should be paid to the fisk, over and above what the person injured was entitled to claim.

It cannot be doubted, that the compositions for crimes established by law, paved the way to these improved notions of government. Compositions were first solicited, and afterward enforced by the legislative authority. It was now no longer a novelty for the chief magistrate to interpose in private quarrels. Resentment was now no longer permitted to rage, but was <42> brought under some discipline: And this reformation, however burdensome to an individual during a fit of passion, was agreeable to all in their ordinary state of mind. The magistrate, having thus acquired such influence even in private punishment, proceeded naturally to assume the privilege of avenging wrongs done to the public merely, where no individual is hurt. And in this manner was the power of punishing crimes against the state, established in the chief magistrate.

To public crimes in the strictest sense where no individual is hurt, was at first this new-assumed privilege confined. In the laws of the Bavarians,*

* Tit. 6. § 1.
18. 1758, 1761: "There was indeed . . . sort of government" = "There behoved indeed, from the beginning, to be some sort of government."

we find that the goods of those who contract marriage within the prohibited degrees, are confiscated. In the laws of King Ina,* he who fights in the King's house forfeits all his substance, and his life is to be in the king's power. The judge who knowingly doth injustice, shall lose his liberty, unless the king admit him to redeem the same.†

It being once established, that there is a public, that this public is a politic body, which, like a real person, may sue and defend, and in particular is entitled to resent injuries; it was an easy step, as hinted above, to interest the <43> public even in private crimes, by imagining every atrocious crime to be a public as well as a private injury; and in particular, that by every open act of violence, the peace of the public or country is broke. In the oldest compositions for crimes that are recorded, there is not a word of the public; the whole is given to the private party. In the Salic laws, there is a very long list of crimes, and of their conversion in money, without any fine to the public. But in the tables of compositions for crimes among the Burgundians, Allamanni, and Longobards, supposed to be more recent, there is constantly superadded a fine, or *fredum,* to the king. And in the laws of King Canute,‡ "If murder be committed in a church, a full compensation shall be paid to JESUS CHRIST, another full compensation to the king, and a third to the relations of the deceased." The two first compositions, are evidently founded upon the foregoing supposition, that the peace of the church, and the king's peace, are broke by the murder.

After establishing compositions for crimes, which proved a very lucky exertion of legal authority, the public had not hitherto claimed any privilege but what belonged to every private person, viz. that of prosecuting its own resentment. But this practice of converting punish-<44>ment into money, a wise institution indeed to prevent a greater evil, was yet, in itself, too absurd to be for ever supported against enlightened reason. Certain crimes came to be reckoned too flagrant and atrocious to admit a pecuniary conversion; and, perhaps, the lowness of the conversion contributed to this thought; for compositions established in days of poverty, bore no proportion to crimes after nations became rich and powerful. That this was the case of

* Lambard's Collection, law 6.
† Laws of William the Conqueror, Wilkins's edition, law 41.
‡ Lambard's Collection, law 2.

the old Roman compositions, every one knows who has dipped into their
history. This evil required a remedy, and it was not difficult to find one. It
had long been established, that the person injured had no claim but for the
composition, however disproportioned to the crime. Here then was a fair
opportunity for the king, or chief magistrate, to interpose, and to decree an
adequate punishment. The first instances of this kind had probably the consent of the person injured; and it is not difficult to persuade any man of
spirit, that it is more for his honour, to see his enemy condignly punished,
than to put up with a trifling compensation in money. However this be, the
new method of punishing atrocious crimes gained credit, became customary,
and passed into a law. If a punishment was inflicted adequate to the crime,
there could be no claim for a composition, which would be the same as paying
a debt twice. And <45> thus, though indirectly, an end was put to the right
of private punishment in all matters of importance.

Theft is a crime that greatly affected the public after the security of property came to be a capital object; and therefore theft afforded probably the
first instances of this new kind of punishment. It was enacted in England,
That a thief, after repeated acts, shall have his hand or foot cut off.* Among
the Longobards, the third act of theft was punished with death.† By the
Salic laws, theft was punished with death, if proved by seven or five credible
witnesses.‡ And that the first instances of this new punishment had the
consent of the person injured, is made probable from the same Salic laws,
in which murder was punished with death, and no composition admitted
without consent of the friends of the deceased.‖

A power to punish all atrocious crimes, though of a private nature, was
a valuable acquisition to the public. This acquisition was supported by the
common sense of mankind, which, as observed in the beginning of this
discourse, entitles even those to inflict punishment who are not injured by
the crime; and if such privilege belong to private persons, there could be
no doubt that <46> the magistrate was peculiarly privileged. Here, by the
way, may be remarked, a striking instance of the aptitude of man for society.

* Laws of King Ina, Lambard's Collection, law 18.
† L. 1. tit. 25. § 67.
‡ Tit. 70. § 7.
‖ Tit. 70. § 5.

By engrossing the right of punishing, government acquired great vigour. But did nature dictate that none have right to punish but those who are injured, government must for ever have remained in its infantine state: for, upon that supposition, I can discover no means sufficient to contradict human nature so far, as to confine to the magistrate the power of dispensing punishments.

The criminal jurisdiction of the magistrate being thus far advanced, was carried its full length without meeting any longer with the slightest obstruction. Compositions for crimes were prohibited, or wore out of practice; and the people were taught a salutary doctrine, That it is inconsistent with good government to suffer individuals to exert their resentment, otherwise than by applying to the criminal judge; who, after trying the crime, directs an adequate punishment to be inflicted by an officer appointed for that purpose; admitting no other gratification to the person injured, but to see the sentence put in execution, if he be pleased to indulge his resentment so far.

But as this signal revolution in the criminal law, must have been galling to individuals, un-<47>accustomed to restrain their passions (8), all <48>

---

(8) For some time after this revolution was completed, we find, among most European nations, certain crimes prevailing, one after another, in a regular succession. Two centuries ago, assassination was the crime in fashion. It wore out by degrees, and made way for a more covered, but more detestable method of destruction, and that is poison. This horrid crime was extremely common, in France and Italy chiefly, almost within a century. It vanished imperceptibly, and was succeeded by a less dishonourable method of exercising revenge, viz. duelling. This curious succession is too regular to have been the child of accident. It must have had a regular cause; and this cause, I imagine, may be gathered from the history now given of the criminal law. We may readily believe, that the right of punishment, wrested from individuals and transferred to the magistrate, was at first submitted to with the utmost reluctance. Resentment is a passion too fierce to be subdued till man be first humanized and softened in a long course of discipline, under the awe and dread of a government firmly established. For many centuries after the power of the sword was assumed by the magistrate, individuals, prone to avenge their own wrongs, were incessantly breaking out into open violence, murder not excepted. But the authority of law, gathering strength daily, became too mighty for revenge executed in this bold manner; and open violence, through the terror of punishment, being repressed, assassination was committed privately, in place of murder committed openly. But as assassination is seldom practicable without accomplices or emissaries of abandoned morals, experience showed that this crime is never long concealed; and the fear of detection prevailed at last over the spirit of revenge, gratified in this hazardous manner. More secret

measures were taken to make the yoke easy, by directing such a punishment as tended the most to gratify the person injured. Whether this was done in a political view, or through the still subsisting influence of the right of private <49> revenge, is not material. But the fact is curious, and merits attention; because it unfolds the reason of that variation of punishment for the same crime, which is remarkable in different ages. With respect to theft, the punishment among the Bavarians was increased to a ninefold restitution, calculated entirely to satisfy the person injured, before they thought of a corporal punishment.* The next step was demembration, by cutting off the hand or foot; but this only after repeated acts.† Among the Longobards, it required a third act of theft before a capital punishment could be inflicted.‡ And at last theft was to be punished with death in all cases, if clearly proved.‖ By this time, it would appear, the interest of the public, with respect to punishment, had prevailed over private interest; or at least had become so weighty as to direct a punishment that should answer the purpose of terror, as well as of private resentment. There is a curious fact relating to the punishment of theft, which must not be overlooked. By

---

methods of gratification were now studied. Assassination repressed made way for poisoning, the most dangerous pest that ever invaded society, if, as believed, poison can be conveyed in a letter, or by other latent means that cannot be traced. Here legal authority was at a stand; for how can a criminal be reached who is unknown? But nature happily interposed, and afforded a remedy when law could not. The gratification which poisoning affords, must be extremely slight, when the offender is not made sensible from what quarter the punishment comes, nor for what cause it is inflicted. Repeated experience showed the emptiness of this method of avenging injuries; a method which plunges a man in guilt, without procuring him any gratification. This horrid practice, accordingly, had not a long course. Conscience and humanity exerted their lawful authority, and put an end to it. Such, in many instances, is the course of Providence. It exerts benevolent wisdom in such a manner as to bring good out of evil. The crime of poisoning is scarce within the reach of the magistrate: But a remedy is provided in the very nature of its cause; for, as observed, revenge is never gratified unless it be made known to the offender that he is punished by the person injured. To finish my reflections upon this subject, duelling, which came in the last place, was supported by a notion of honour; and the still subsisting propensity to revenge blinded men so much, as to make them see but obscurely, that the practice is inconsistent with conscience and humanity.

  * Tit. 8. § 1.
  † Laws of King Ina, Lambard, l. 18.
  ‡ L. 1. tit. 25. § 67.
  ‖ Salic Laws, tit. 70. § 7.

the laws of the Twelve Tables, borrowed from Greece, theft was punished with death in a slave, and with slavery in a free man. But this law was afterwards mitigated, by converting the punishment into a pecuniary composition; subjecting the *furtum manifestum* to a <50> fourfold restitution, and the *furtum nec manifestum,* to the restitution of double. The punishment of theft, established by the law of the Twelve Tables, might suit some of the civilized states in Greece, which had acquired the notion of a public, and of the interest which a public has to punish crimes *in terrorem.* But the law was unsuitable to the notions of a rude people, such as the Romans were in those days, who of punishment understood no other end but the gratification of private resentment. Nor do I find in any period of the Roman history, that theft was considered as a crime against the public, to admit of a punishment *in terrorem.* Toward such improvement there never was a step taken but one, which was not only late, but extremely slight, viz. that a thief might be condemned to an arbitrary punishment, if the party injured insisted for it.*

I make another remark, that so long as the gratification of the prosecutor was the chief aim in punishing theft, the value of the stolen goods was constantly considered as a preferable claim;[†] for unless the prosecutor obtain restitution of his goods, or their value, there can be no sufficient gratification. But after the interest of the public came chiefly to be considered in punishing theft, the prosecutor's claim of resti-<51>tution was little regarded; of which our act 26. parl. 1661, is clear evidence; witness also the law of Saxony, by which if a thief suffer death, his heir is not bound to restore the stolen goods.[‡]

For the same reason, a false witness is now punished capitally in Scotland, though not so of old. By the Roman law,[||] and also by our common law,[§] the punishment of falsehood is not capital; which is also clear from act 80. parl. 1540, and act 22. parl. 1551. Yet our supreme criminal court has, for more than a century, assumed the power of punishing this crime

---

* L. ult. De furtis. [[I.e., *Digest* 47.2.93.]]
† Judicia civitatis Lundoniae, Wilkins, p. 65.
‡ Carpzovius, part 4. const. 32. def. 23.
|| L. 1. § ult. De leg. Cornel. de fals. [[I.e., *Digest* 48.10.33.]]
§ Reg. Maj. l. 4. cap. 13; Stat. Alex. II. cap. 19.

capitally, as well as that of bearing false witness, though warranted by no statute. The notions of a public, and of a public interest, are brought to perfection; and the interest of the public to be severe upon a crime so prejudicial to society, hath in these instances prevailed over even the strict rules of the criminal law (9). <52>

Upon this head an observation occurs, which will be found to hold universally. It regards a material point, that of adjusting punishments to crimes, when criminal jurisdiction is totally engrossed by the public. After this revolution in government, punishments at first are found extremely moderate; not only for the reason above given that they are directed chiefly to gratify the persons injured, but for a separate reason. Though the power of the sword adds great authority to a government, yet this effect is far from being instantaneous; and till authority be fully established, great severities are beyond the strength of a legislature. But when public authority is firmly rooted in the minds of the people, punishments more rigorous may be ventured upon, which are rendered necessary by the yet undisciplined temper of the people. At last, when a people have become altogether tame and submissive under a long and steady administration, punishments, being less and less necessary, are commonly mild, and ought always to be so (10). <53>

(9) Durum est, torquere leges ad hoc ut torqueant homines. Non placet igitur extendi leges poenales, multo minus capitales, ad delicta nova. Quod si crimen vetus fuerit, et legibus notum, sed prosecutio ejus incidat in casum novum a legibus non provisum; omnino recedatur a placitis juris, potius quam delicta maneant impunita. *Bacon de augmentis scientiarum, l. 8. cap. 3. aphor.* 13. [["It is a hard Case to torture Lawes, that they may torture Men. *We would not therefore* that Laws Penal, much lesse Capital, should be extended to new Offences: *yet if it be an old Crime, and known to the Lawes, but the Prosequution thereof falls upon a new Case, not fore-seen by the Lawes; we must by all means depart from the* Placits of Law, *rather than that offences passe unpunisht.*" Trans. Watts.]] By the law of Egypt, perjury was capital: for it was said to involve the two greatest crimes, viz. impiety to the gods, and violation of faith and truth to man. *Diodorus Siculus, book* 1. *ch.* 6. This, and many other laws of the ancient Egyptians show, that public police was carried to a considerable degree of perfection in that celebrated country.

(10) We discover a similar progress in the Civil Law of this country. Some ages ago, before the ferocity of the inhabitants of this part of the island was subdued, the utmost severity of the Civil Law was necessary to restrain individuals from plundering each other. Thus the man who intermeddled irregularly with the moveables of a person deceased, was subjected to all the debts of the deceased without limitation. This makes a branch of the law of Scotland, known by the name of *Vitious Intromission;* and so rigidly was

Another observation occurs, connected with the former, that to preserve a strict proportion betwixt a crime and its punishment, is not the only or chief view of a wise legislature. The purposes of human punishments are, first, to add weight to those which nature has provided, and next to enforce municipal regulations intended for the good of society. In this view, a crime, however heinous, ought to be little regarded, if it had no bad effect in society. On the other hand, a crime, however slight, ought to be severely punished, if it tend greatly to disturb the <54> peace of society. A dispute about the succession to a crown, seldom ends without a civil war, in which the party vanquished, however zealous for right and for the good of their country, must be considered as guilty of treason against their lawful sovereign; and to prevent the ruin of civil war, it becomes necessary that such treason be attended with the severest punishment; without regarding that the guilt of those who suffer arose from bad success merely. Hence, in regulating the punishment of crimes, two circumstances ought to weigh, viz. the immorality of the action, and its bad tendency; of which the latter appears to be the capital circumstance, as the peace of society is an object of much greater importance, than the peace, or even life, of a few individuals.

One great advantage, among many, of transferring to the magistrate the power of punishment, is, that revenge is kept within the strictest bounds, and confined to its proper objects. The criminal law was in perfection among the ancient Egyptians. Among them, a woman with child could not be put to death till she was delivered. And our author Diodorus Siculus* observes, That this law was received by many of the Greek states, deeming it unjust that the innocent should suffer with the guilty; and that a child, common to father and mother, should lose <55> its life for the crime of the

---

this regulation applied in our courts of law, that the most trifling moveable abstracted *mala fide,* subjected the intermeddler to the foregoing consequences, which proved, in many instances, a most rigorous punishment. But severity was necessary, in order to subdue the rude manners of our people. In proportion to our improvement in manners, this regulation was gradually softened, and applied by our sovereign court with a sparing hand. It is at present so little in repute, that the vitious intromission must be extremely gross which provokes the judges to give way to the law in its utmost extent; and it seldom happens, that vitious intromission is attended with any consequence beyond reparation, and costs of suit.

* Book I. ch. 6.

mother. The power to punish must have long been the privilege of the magistrate, before a law so moderate and so impartial could take place. We find no similar instance while punishment was in the hands of individuals: Such moderation is incompatible with the partiality of man, and the inflammable nature of resentment. Nor is this the only instance of wisdom and moderation in the criminal law of the country now mentioned. Capital punishments are avoided as much as possible; and in their stead punishments are chosen, that, equally with death, restrain the delinquent from committing the crime a second time. In a word, the ancient Egyptian punishments have the following peculiar character, that they effectually answer their end, with less harshness and severity, than is found in the laws of any other nation ancient or modern. Thus those who revealed the secrets of the army to the enemy, had their tongues cut out. Those who coined false money, or contrived false weights, or forged deeds, or razed public records, were condemned to lose both hands. He who committed a rape upon a free woman, was deprived of his privy members; and a woman committing adultery, was punished with the loss of her nose, that she might not again allure men to wantonness (11). <56>

(11) We have an instance in this law of still greater refinement. The criminal law of other civilized nations, has not, in any instance, a farther aim than to prevent injury and mischief. Egypt is the only country we read of, where individuals were obliged to aid the distressed, under a penalty. In the table of laws recorded by the above-mentioned author, we read the following passage: "If a man be violently assaulted and in hazard of death, it is the duty of every by-stander to attempt a rescue; and if it be proved against such a man, that he was sufficiently able to prevent the murder, his neglect or forbearance is to be punished with death." [[*Historical Library* I.vi; trans. Booth, p. 40.]] It is altogether concordant with the refined spirit of the other laws mentioned by our author, that relieving the distressed should be made the duty of every individual: But to punish with death an act of omission, or a neglect of any duty, far more the neglect of a duty so refined, must arise from the most exalted notions of morality. Government must have arrived at great perfection, before such a regulation could be admitted. None of the present European nations are even at present so far refined as to admit of such a law. There must be some cause, natural or artificial, for such early perfection of the criminal law in Egypt; and as the subject is of importance in tracing the history of mankind, I cannot resist the present opportunity of attempting to investigate the cause.

Hunting and fishing for sustenance, were the original occupations of men. The shepherd life succeeded; and the next stage was that of agriculture. These progressive changes, in the order now mentioned, may be traced in all nations, as far as we have any remains of their original history. The life of a fisher or hunter is averse to society, except among the members of single families. The shepherd-life promotes larger societies; if that can be

I have one thing further to add upon public punishment. Though all civilized nations have <57>agreed to forbid private revenge, and to trust punishment, whether of public or private crimes, <58> in the hands of

---

called a society, which hath scarce any other but a local connection. The true spirit of society, which consists in mutual benefits, and in making the industry of individuals profitable to others as well as to themselves, was not known till agriculture was invented. Agriculture requires the aid of many other arts: the carpenter, the blacksmith, the mason, and other artificers, contribute to it. This circumstance connects individuals in an intimate society of mutual support, which again compacts them within a narrow space. Now in the first state of man, that of hunting and fishing, there obviously is no place for government, except that which is exercised by the heads of families over children and domestics. The shepherd-life, in which societies are formed by the conjunction of families for mutual defence, requires some sort of government; slight indeed in proportion to the slightness of the mutual connection. But it was agriculture which first produced a regular system of government. The intimate union among a multitude of individuals, occasioned by agriculture, discovered a number of social duties formerly unknown. These were ascertained by laws, the observance of which was enforced by punishment. Such operations cannot be carried on, otherwise than by lodging power in one or more persons, to direct the resolutions and apply the force of the whole society. In short, it may be laid down as an universal maxim, That in every society the advances of government toward perfection, are strictly proportioned to the advances of the society toward intimacy of union.

The condition of the land of Egypt makes husbandry of absolute necessity; because in that country, without husbandry there are no means of subsistence. All the soil, except what is yearly covered with the river when it overflows, is a barren sand unfit for habitation, and the people are confined to the low grounds adjacent to the river. The sandy grounds produce little or no grass; and however fit for pasture the low grounds may be during the bulk of the year, the inhabitants, without agriculture, would be destitute of all means to preserve their cattle alive during the inundation. The Egyptians must therefore, from the beginning, have depended upon husbandry for their subsistence; and the soil, by the yearly inundations, being rendered extremely fertile, the great plenty of provisions produced by the slightest culture, could not fail to multiply the people exceedingly. But this people lived in a still more compact state, than is necessary for the prosecution of husbandry in other countries; because their cultivated lands were no less narrow than fertile. Individuals, thus collected within very narrow bounds, could not subsist a moment without regular government. The necessity, after every inundation, of adjusting marches by geometry, naturally productive of disputes, must have early taught the inhabitants of this wonderful country, the necessity of due submission to legal authority. Joining all these circumstances, we may assuredly conclude, that in Egypt government was coeval with the peopling of the country; and this perhaps is the single instance of the kind. Government therefore must have long subsisted among the Egyptians in an advanced state; and for that reason it ceases to be a wonder, that their laws were brought to perfection more early than those of any other people.

This, at the same time, accounts for the practice of hieroglyphics, peculiar to this country. In the administration of public affairs, writing is in a great measure necessary. The Egyptian government had made vigorous advances toward perfection before writing

disinterested judges; yet they differ as to the persons who are allowed to pro-<59>secute before these judges. In Rome, where there was no *calumniator publicus,* no attorney-general, every one was permitted to prosecute crimes that have a public bad tendency, and for that reason are termed *public crimes.* This was a faulty institution; because such a privilege given to individuals, could not fail to be frequently made the instrument of venting private ill-will and revenge. The oath of calumny, which was the first check thought of, was far from restraining this evil. It grew to such a height, that the Romans were obliged to impose another check upon criminal prosecutors, indeed of the severest kind, which shall be given in <60> Voet's words:*

> Ne autem temere quis per accusationem in alieni capitis discrimen irruerit, neve impunita esset in criminalibus mentiendi atque calumniandi licentia, loco jurisjurandi calumniae adinventa fuit in crimen subscriptio, cujus vinculo cavet quisque quod crimen objecturus sit et in ejus accusatione usque ad sententiam perseveraturus, dato eum in finem fidejussore; simulque ad talionem seu similitudinem supplicii sese obstringet, si in probatione defecisse et calumniatus esse deprehensus fuerit.[19]

Had the Roman law continued to flourish any considerable time after this regulation, we may be pretty certain it must have been altered. It was indeed

---

was invented. A condition so singular, occasioned necessarily a strong demand for some method to publish laws, and to preserve them in memory. This produced hieroglyphical writing, if the emblems made use of to express ideas can be termed writing.

Public police appears in ancient Egypt to have been carried to an eminent degree of perfection, in other articles as well as in that of law. We have the authority of Aristotle, *Polit. l. 3. ch.* 15. and of Herodote, *l.* 2. That in Egypt the art of physic was distributed into several distinct parts, that every physician employed himself mostly in the cure of a single disease, and that by this means the art was brought to great perfection.

* Tit. De accusationibus et inscriptionibus, § 13. [[Voet, *Commentarius ad Pandectas,* Bk. 48, Tit. 2: vol. ii, p. 1023.]]

19. "But, so that no-one make the rash decision to accuse someone else, or that the liberty to lie and bring false accusation in criminal cases go unpunished, a signature has been devised in place of swearing, which binds anyone to be aware that, once someone giving surety has been appointed to that end, he will present the offence and press ahead with his accusation as far as [judicial] sentencing; and at the same time he will bind himself to a penalty equal or similar in kind if he is found wanting in his proof and to have brought a false accusation."

a complete bar to accusations true or false; for what man will venture his life and fortune, in bringing to punishment a criminal who hath done him no injury, however beneficial it may be to the state to have the criminal destroyed? This would be an exertion of public spirit, scarce to be expected among the most virtuous people, not to talk of times of universal corruption and depravity.

In modern governments, a better method is invented. The privilege of prosecuting public crimes belongs to the chief magistrate. The King's Advocate in Scotland is *calumniator publicus;* and there is delegated to him from the <61> crown, the privilege of prosecuting public crimes. In England, personal liberty has, from the beginning, been more sacred than in Scotland; and to prevent the oppression of criminal prosecutions, there is in England a regulation much more effectual than that now mentioned. A grand jury is appointed in every county for a previous examination of capital crimes intended to be prosecuted in name of the crown; and they must find a *billa vera,* as it is termed, without which the trial cannot proceed. But the crown is not tied to that form. A criminal trial may proceed on an information, without any previous examination by a grand jury.[20]

With respect to private crimes, where individuals are hurt in their persons, goods, or character, the public, and the person injured, have each of them separately an interest. The King's Advocate may prosecute such crimes alone, as far as the public is concerned in the punishment. The private party is interested to obtain reparation for the wrong done him. Even where this is the end of the prosecution, our forms require the concurrence of the King's Advocate, as a check upon the prosecutor, whose resentment otherwise may carry him beyond proper bounds. But this concurrence must be given, unless the Advocate will take upon him to show, that there is no foundation for the prosecution; for the Advocate cannot bar the private party from the <62> reparation due him by law; more than the private party[21] can bar the Advocate from exacting that reparation or punishment which is a debt due to the public.

20. 1758, 1761: "A grand jury . . . by a grand jury" = "No criminal trial, in the name of the crown, can proceed, till first the matter be examined by the grand jury of the county, and their authority be interposed for the prosecution."

21. 1758, 1761: "by with-holding his consent."

The interposition of the sovereign authority, to punish crimes more severely than by a composition, was at first, we may believe, not common; nor to be obtained at any rate, unless where the atrocity of the crime called aloud for an extraordinary punishment. But it happened in this, as in all similar cases where novelty wears off by reiteration of acts, that what at first is an extraordinary remedy, comes in time to be reckoned a branch of common law. There being at first, however, no rule established for the King's interposition, it was understood to be a branch of his prerogative to interpose or not at his pleasure; and to direct an extraordinary punishment, or to leave the crime to the composition of common law. Though evidently this prerogative could not regularly subsist after criminal jurisdiction was totally engrossed by the public;[22] yet our forefathers were not so clear-sighted. The prerogative now mentioned, was misapprehended for a power of pardoning even after sentence; and the resemblance of the cases made way for the mistake. It appears to me, that the King's prerogative of pardoning arbitrarily, which is asserted by all lawyers, can have no foundation other than this now assigned. <63> Were it limited in criminal as in civil cases, not to give relief but where strict law is over-balanced by equity, the prerogative would have a more rational foundation. But we must prosecute the thread of our history. Though the option of inflicting an adequate punishment, or leaving the crime to common law, was imperceptibly converted into an arbitrary power of pardoning even after sentence; yet the foundation of this new prerogative was not forgot. The King's pardon is held as leaving the crime to common law, by which the person injured is entitled to a composition. And the evident injustice of a pardon upon any other condition, tends no doubt to support this construction: For it would be gross injustice, that the law should suffer a man to be injured, without affording him any satisfaction, either by a public punishment, or by a private composition. This, however, it would appear, has been attempted. But the matter was settled by a law of Edward the Confessor,* declaring, That the King, by his prerogative, may pardon a capital crime; but that the criminal must satisfy the person injured, by a just composition.

* Lambard's Collection, law 18.
22. 1758, 1761: "and a criminal was regularly condemned by the solemn sentence of a judge."

Thus the *Vergelt*, or composition for crimes, which obtained in all cases by our old law, is still in force where the criminal obtains a pardon; and the claim that the relations of the <64> deceased have against the murderer who obtains a pardon, known in the law of Scotland by the name of *assythment*, has no other foundation. The practice is carried farther, and may be discovered even in civil actions. When a process of defamation is brought before a civil court, or a process for any violent inversion of possession, a sum is generally decreed in name of damages, proportioned to the wrong done; even where the pursuer cannot specify any hurt or real damage. Such a sentence can have no other view, but to gratify the resentment of the person injured, who has not the gratification of any other punishment. It is given, as lawyers say, *in solatium;* and therefore is obviously of the nature of a *Vergelt*, or composition for a crime. Damages awarded to a husband, against the man who corrupts his wife, or against the man who commits a rape upon her, are precisely of the same nature.

In taking a review of the whole, the manners and temper of savages afford no agreeable prospect. But man excels other animals, chiefly by being susceptible of high improvements in a well-regulated society. In his original solitary state, he is scarce a rational being. Resentment is a passion, that, in an undisciplined breast, appears to exceed all bounds. But savages are fierce and brutal; and the passion of resentment is in the savage state the chief protection that a <65> man hath for his life and fortune.[23] It is therefore wisely ordered, that resentment should be a ruling passion among savages. Happy it is for civilized societies, that the authority of law hath in a good measure rendered unnecessary this impetuous passion; and happy it is for individuals, that early discipline under the restraint of law, by calming the temper and sweetening manners, hath rendered it a less troublesome guest than it is by nature. <66>

23. 1758, 1761: "But savages . . . life and fortune" = "But savages, unrestrained by law, indulge their appetites without control; and in this state, resentment, were it more moderate, would, perhaps, scarce be sufficient to keep men in awe, and to restrain them, in any considerable degree, from mutual injuries."

Promises and Covenants

Moral principles, faint among savages, acquire strength by refinement of manners in polished societies.*[1] Promises and covenants, in particular, have full authority among nations disciplined in a long course of regular government: But among barbarians it is rare to find a promise or covenant of such authority as to counterbalance, in any considerable degree, the weight of appetite or passion. This circumstance, joined with the imperfection of a language in its infancy, are the causes why engagements are little regarded in original laws.

It is lucky, that among a rude people in the first stages of government, the necessity of engagements is not greater than their authority. Originally, every family subsisted by hunting, and by the natural fruits of the earth. The taming wild animals, and rendering them domestic, multiplied greatly the means of subsistence. The invention of agriculture produced <67> to the industrious a superfluity, with which foreign necessaries were purchased. Commerce originally was carried on by barter or permutation, to which a previous covenant is not necessary. And after money was introduced into commerce, we have reason to believe, that buying and selling also was at first carried on by exchanging goods for money, without any previous covenant. But in the progress of the social life, the wants and appetites of men multiply faster than to be readily supplied by commerce so

---

* See Essays on the Principles of Morality and Natural Religion, part 1. essay 2. ch. 9.

1. 1758, 1761: "Moral principles . . . polished societies" = "Moral duties, originally weak and feeble, acquire great strength by refinement of manners in polished societies. This is peculiarly the case of the duties that are founded on consent."

narrow and confined. There came to be a demand for interposed persons, who take care to be informed of what is redundant in one corner, and of what is wanted in another. This occupation was improved into that of a merchant, who provides himself from a distance with what is demanded at home. Then it was, and no sooner, that the use of a covenant came to be recognised; for the business of a merchant cannot be carried on to any extent, or with any success, without previous agreements.

As far back as we can trace the Roman law, we find its authority interposed in behalf of sale, location, and other contracts deemed essential to commerce. And that commerce was advanced in Rome before action was sustained upon such contracts, is evident from the contract of society or partnership put in that class. Other covenants were not regarded, but left upon the <68> obligation of the natural law. One general exception there was: A promise or paction, of whatever nature, executed in a solemn form of words, termed *stipulatio,* was countenanced with an action. This solemn manner of agreement, testified the deliberate purpose of the parties; and at the same time removed all ambiguity as to their meaning, to which language in its infancy is liable (1). <69>

(1) A naked promise, which is a transitory act, makes but a slender impression upon the mind among a rude people. Hence it is, that after the great utility of conventions came to be discovered in the progress of the social life, we find certain solemnities used in every nation, to give conventions a stronger hold of the mind than they have naturally. The Romans and Grecians, after their police was somewhat advanced, were satisfied with a solemn form of words. Ouvert acts were necessary among other people, less refined. The solemnity used among the Scythians, according to Herodotus, *book* 4. is curious.

> The Scythians (says that author), in their alliances and contracts, use the following ceremonies. They pour wine into an earthen vessel, and tinge it with blood drawn from the parties contractors. They dip a scymeter, some arrows, a bill, and a javelin, in the vessel, and after many imprecations, the persons principally concerned, with the most considerable men present, drink the liquor.

Among other barbarous nations, ancient and modern, we find ceremonies contrived for the same end. The Medes and Lydians, in their federal contracts, observe the same ceremonies with the Grecians; with this difference, that both parties wound themselves in the arm, and then mutually lick the blood.—*Herodotus, book* 1.—The Arabians religiously observe contracts that are attended with the following ceremonies. A person standing between the parties, draws blood from both, by making an incision with a sharp stone in the palm of the hand under the longest fingers; and cutting a thread from the garment of each, dips it in the blood, and anoints seven stones brought there to that end;

Courts of law were a salutary invention in the social state; for by them individuals are compelled to do their duty. This invention, as commonly happens, was originally confined within narrow bounds. To take under the protection of a court, natural obligations of every sort, would, in a new experiment, have been reckoned too bold. It was deemed sufficient to enforce, by legal authority, those particular duties that contribute most to the well-being of society. A regulation so important gave satisfaction; and, while recent, left no desire or thought of any farther improvement. This <70> fairly accounts for what is observed above, that in the infancy of law, promises and agreements which make a figure are countenanced with an action, while others of less utility are left upon conscience. But here it must be remarked, that this distinction is not made where the effect of a promise or agreement is not to create an obligation, but to dissolve it. *Pacta liberatoria* have, in all ages, been enforced by courts of law. The reason commonly assigned, that liberty is more favourable than obligation, is not satisfactory; for no pactions merit more favour than those which promote the good of society, by obliging individuals to serve and aid each other. The following reason will perhaps be reckoned more solid. There is a wide difference betwixt refusing action even where the claim is just, and sustaining action upon an unjust claim. With respect to the former, all that can be complained of is, that the court is less useful than it might be: The latter would be countenancing, or rather enforcing, iniquity. It is not surprising to find courts confined within too narrow bounds, in point of utility: But it would be strange indeed if it were made their duty to enforce wrong of any sort. Thus where a court refuses to make effectual a gratuitous promise, there is no harm done; matters are left where they were before courts were instituted. But it is undoubtedly unjust to demand payment of a <71> debt after it is discharged, though by a gratuitous promise only. And therefore,

---

invoking their gods, Bacchus and Urania, and exhorting the parties to perform the conditions. The ceremony is closed with a mutual profession of the parties, that they are bound to perform.—*Ibid. book* 3.—The Nasamones of Africa, in pledging their faith to each other, mutually present a cup of liquor; and if they have none, they take up dust, which they put into their mouths.—*Ibid. book* 4.—To the same purpose is the striking or joining hands; and a practice so frequent among the Grecians and Romans as to be introduced into their poetry, of swearing by the gods, by the tombs of their ancestors, or by any other object of awe and reverence.

when in this case an action for payment is brought, the court has no choice: It cannot otherwise avoid supporting this unjust claim, but by sustaining the gratuitous promise as a good defence against the action (2).

One case excepted, similar to the Roman *stipulatio,* of which afterward, it appears to me that no naked promise or covenant was, by our forefathers, countenanced with an action. A contract of buying and selling was certainly not binding by the municipal law of this island, unless the price was paid, or the thing sold delivered. There was *locus poenitentiae* even after arles were given; and change of mind was attended with no other penalty, but loss of the arles, or value of them.* Our ancient writers are not so express upon other covenants; but as permutation, or in place of it buying and <72> selling, are of all the most useful covenants in common life, we may reasonably conclude, that if an agreement of this kind was not made effectual by law, other agreements would not be more privileged.

The case hinted above as an exception, is where an agreement is made or acknowledged in the face of court, taken down in writing, and recorded in the books of the court.† For though this was done chiefly to make evidence, the solemn manner of making the agreement probably had the same effect with *stipulatio* in the Roman law, which tied both parties, and absolutely barred repentance. And indeed the recording a transaction would be an idle solemnity, if the parties were not bound by it.

The occasion of introducing this form, I conjecture to be what follows. In difficult or intricate cases, it was an early practice for judges to interpose, by pressing a transaction betwixt the parties; of which there are instances in the court of session, not far back. This practice brought about many agreements betwixt litigants, which were always recorded in the court where the process depended. The record was compleat evidence of the fact; and

---

(2) This difference betwixt an action and an exception, arising from the original constitution of courts of law, is not peculiar to promises and covenants, but obtains universally. Thus, in the Roman law, the *exceptiones doli et metus,* were sustained from the beginning; though for many ages after the Roman courts were established, no action was afforded to redress wrong done by fraud or force. It was the *Praetor* who first gave an action, after it became his province to supply what was defective in the courts of common law.

* Reg. Maj. l. 3. cap. 10.; Fleta, l. 2. cap. 58. § 3. & 5.

† Glanvil, l. 10. cap. 8.; Reg. Maj. l. 3. cap. 4.

if either party broke the concord or agreement, a decree went against him
without other proof.* The <73> singular advantages of a concord or transaction thus finished in face of court, moved individuals to make all their
agreements, of any importance, in that form. And indeed, while writing
continued a rare art, skilful artists, except in courts of justice, were not easily
found readily to take down a covenant in writing.

So much upon the first head, How far naked covenants and promises
were effectual by our old law. What proof of a bargain was required by a
court of justice, comes next to be examined. Evidence may justly be distinguished into natural and artificial. To the former belong proof by witnesses, by confession of the party, and by writ. To the latter belong those
extraordinary methods invented in days of gross superstition, for bringing
out the truth in doubtful cases, such as the trial by fire, the trial by water,
and singular battle.

Before writing was invented, or rather while, like painting, it was in the
hands of a few artists, witnesses were relied on for evidence in all cases.
Witnesses were in particular admitted for proving a debt to whatever extent,
as well as for proving payment. But experience discovered both the danger
and uncertainty of such evidence; which therefore was confined within narrower bounds gradually as the art of writing became more common. It was
first established, that two witnesses were not sufficient <74> to prove a debt
above forty shillings; and that there must be a number of witnesses in proportion to the extent of the debt. Afterward, when the art of writing was
more diffused, the King's courts took upon them to confine the proof of
debt to writing, and the confession of the party, leaving inferior judges to
follow the common law, by admitting debt to be proved by witnesses. This
seems to be the import of Quon. Attach. cap. 81. and the only proper sense
that it can bear. The burghs adhered the longest to the common law,† by
admitting two witnesses to prove debt to any extent (3).

* See Glanvil, l. 8. cap. 1. 2. 3. &c.
† Curia quatuor burg. cap. 3. § 6.
(3) This limitation of proof regards the constitution only of a debt. Payment being
a more favourable plea, was left to the common law; and accordingly, in England, to this
day, parole evidence is admitted to prove payment of money. The rule was the same in
Scotland while our sovereign court, named *the Daily Council,* subsisted, as appears from

The King's courts assumed the like privilege in other actions. Though they admitted witnesses to prove that a contract of sale, for example, or location, was performed in part, in order to be a foundation for decreeing full performance; yet they permitted nothing to be <75> proved by witnesses, but what is customary in every covenant of the sort. If any singular paction was alledged, such an irritancy *ob non solutum canonem,* witnesses were not admitted to prove such pactions, more than to prove a claim of debt. The proof was confined to writ, or confession of the party.*

The second species of natural evidence, is, confession of the party; which, in the strictest sense, must be a confession; that is, it must be voluntary. For, by the original law of this island, no man was bound to bear testimony against himself, whether in civil or criminal causes. So stands the common law of England to this day; though courts of equity take greater liberty. Our law was the same, till it came to be established, through the influence of the Roman law, that in civil actions, the facts set forth in the libel or declaration may be referred to the defendant's testimony, and he be held as confessed if he refuse to give his oath. The transition was easy from civil matters, to such slight delinquencies as are punished with pecuniary penalties in a civil court; and in these also, by our present practice, the person accused is obliged to give evidence against himself.

The discovery of truth by oath of party, denied in civil courts, was, in the ecclesiastical court, obtained by a circuit. An action for <76> payment could not be brought before the ecclesiastical court; but in a religious view a complaint could be brought for breach of faith and promise. The party, as in the presence of God, was bound to declare, whether he had not made the promise. The truth being thus drawn from him, he was of course enjoined, not only to do penance, but also to satisfy the complainer. This was in effect a decree, which was followed with the most rigorous execution for obtaining payment of the debt. And this by the by is the foundation of the privilege our commissary-courts have, of judging in actions of debt when the debt is referred to oath.

---

the records of that court still preserved; and continued to be the rule till the act of sederunt 8th June 1597 was made, declaring the resolution of the court, That thereafter they would not admit witnesses to prove payment of any sum above 100 pounds.

* Glanvil, l. 10. cap. ult.; Reg. Maj. l. 3. cap. 14. § ult.

The third species of natural evidence is writ; which is of two kinds, viz. record of court, and writ executed privately betwixt parties. The first kind, which has already been mentioned, is in England termed *recognisance,* because debt is there acknowledged. And here it must be remarked, that this writ is of itself compleat evidence, so as to admit of no contrary averment, as expressed in the English law. But with respect to a private writ, it is laid down, that if the defendant deny the seal, the pursuer must verify the same by witnesses, or by comparison of seals; but that if he acknowledges it to be his seal, he is not permitted to deny the writ.* The presumption lies, that it was he himself who <77> sealed the writ; unless he can bring evidence, that the seal was stolen from him, and put to the writ by another.

A deed hath sprung from the recognisance that requires peculiar attention. In England it is termed *a bond in judgment,* and with us *a bond registrable.* When, by peace and regular government, this island came to be better peopled than formerly, it was extremely cumbersome to go before the judge upon every private bargain, in order to minute and record the same. After the art of writing was spread every where, a method was contrived to render this matter more easy. The agreement is taken down in writing; and, with the same breath, a mandate is granted to a procurator to appear in court, and to obtain the writ, to be recorded as the agreement of such and such persons. If the parties happen to differ in performing the agreement, the writ is put upon record by virtue of the mandate; and faith is given to it by the court, equally as if the agreement had been recorded originally. The authority of the mandate is not called in question, being joined with the averment of the procurator. And, from the nature of the thing, if faith be at all given to writ, the mind must rest upon some fact, which is taken for granted without witnesses. A bond, for example, is vouched by the subscription of the granter, and the granter's subscription by that of one or <78> more witnesses. But the subscription of a witness must be held as true; for otherwise a chain of proof without end would be necessary, and a writ could never be legal evidence. The same solemnity is not necessary to the mandate, which being a relative deed, is supported by the bond or agreement to which it relates; and therefore, of such a mandate

---

* Glanvil, I. 10. cap. 12.; Reg. Maj. l. 3. cap. 8.

we do not require any evidence but the subscription of the party. The stile of this mandate was afterward improved, and made to serve a double purpose; not only to be an authority for recording the writ, but also to impower the procurator to confess judgment against his employer; on which a decree passes of course, in order for execution. The mandate was originally contained in a separate writing, which continues to be the practice in England. In Scotland, the practice first crept in of indorsing it upon the bond, and afterward of ingrossing it in the bond at the close, which is our present form (4). <79>

With respect to the evidence of English bonds in judgment, and Scots bonds having a clause of registration, there appears no difference: They bear full faith; and without any extraneous evidence are a sufficient foundation for execution. The laws of England and of Scotland appear also to have been originally the same with respect to writs that need an action to make them effectual. The antient form of testing a writ, was by the party's seal; and if the defendant denied the seal to be his, the pursuer as above mentioned was bound to prove the same. The law continued the same in both countries, when subscription became necessary as well as the seal: If the defendant denied the subscription to be his, it was incumbent on the pursuer to bring a proof of it, as formerly of the seal. In England to this day, if the defence *Non est factum* be pleaded, or, in other words, that the writ was not signed and sealed by the defendant, the plaintiff must prove the affirmative. But in Scotland various checks have been introduced to prevent forgery: One of these checks is the subscription of the witnesses, required by act 5. parl. 1681, which vouches the party's subscription. And as a bond thus fortified bears faith in judgment, the defendant is <80> now deprived of his negative defence, *Quod non est factum;* he must sub-

(4) Before the bond could be recorded as a decree in order for execution, it was required, that the procurator should, by a writing under his hand, consent to the decree. And when it became customary to indorse the mandate upon the bond, this consent was also indorsed upon it. But in course of time the consent was neglected, as a step merely of form; and the practice of recording without such consent, was authorised by an act of sederunt 9th December 1670. So that the naming a procurator to confess judgment is now no longer necessary; and indeed the consent of the debtor that a decree should pass against him, is in all views sufficient for execution, without any other ceremony. [[Note added in 1776.]]

mit to the claim, unless he undertake positively to prove that the subscription is not his.[2]

I cannot, upon this occasion, overlook a remarkable impropriety in our old statutes, requiring witnesses to the subscription of an obligor, without enjoining the witnesses to subscribe, in token that they did witness the obligor's subscription. To appoint any act to be done, without requiring any evidence of its having been done, is undoubtedly an idle regulation. The testing clause, it is true, bears, that the obligor subscribed before such and such witnesses. But the testing clause, which in point of time goes before the subscription of the obligor, cannot, otherwise than prophetically, be evidence that the witnesses named saw the obligor subscribe. This blunder is not found in the English law: For though witnesses are generally called, and do often subscribe; yet, according to my information, witnesses are not

---

2. 1758, 1761: "With respect to . . . the subscription is not his." = "Comparing the law of England and of Scotland, upon the evidence of writ, I can discover no discrepance betwixt them. For, first, as to registrable writs, or bonds in judgment, these do and must bear full faith; because, without other evidence, they are a sufficient foundation for execution. Such a writ, when put upon record, produces a decree, which cannot be challenged but in a process of reduction or suspension; and in England it is a rule, that matters of record prove themselves, and admit of no averment against the truth of them [New Abridgment of the Law, vol. 2. p. 306]. In the next place, as to a private writ, used as evidence in a process, it appears from the Regiam Majestatem, compared with Glanvil in the passages above cited, that the law was also the same in both countries. In England, to this day, a party may deny the verity of the writ, by pleading *quod non est factum*. But then it is not enough barely to deny, without undertaking a proof. What I am to suggest, will make it evident, that *non est factum* is a proper exception, which, like all other exceptions, must be verified by evidence. One needs but reflect, that a bond signed sealed and delivered, makes an effectual obligation by the law of England, and is therefore a good foundation for an action. This is in other words saying, that such bond is probative, and requires not the support of extraneous evidence: and if so, it cannot be sufficient for the defendant to rest upon a denial, without attempting, by contrary evidence, to disprove the evidence of the bond. To this end he has an opportunity to produce the instrumentary witnesses. But if these be dead, it is a rule in England, as well as in Scotland, that they prove the verity of the writing; which, in plain sense, comes to this, that every thing said in the bond, is presumed to be true, until the contrary is proved. This is, in every point, agreeable to the law of Scotland; for which, in place of all other authority, I appeal to Lord Stair [Book 4. Tit. 40. § 39, 40], who lays down in express terms, 'That against registrable writs, improbation ought not to be sustained, but only by action; but that against other writs, improbation may be proponed by way of exception.'"

essential by the law of England.[3] This blunder in our law is corrected by the statute 1681; enacting, "That none but subscribing witnesses shall be probative, and not witnesses insert not subscribing." By this regulation the evidence of writ is now with us more compleat than it is in England. The subscriptions of the witnesses are justly held legal evidence of their having <81> witnessed the subscription of the granter of the deed; and the subscriptions must be held to be theirs; otherwise, as above observed, no writ can in any case afford legal evidence. And thus the evidence required in Scotland to give faith to a bond or other deed, is by this statute made proper and rational. It is required that the granter subscribe before witnesses: But we no longer hold the testing clause to be evidence of this fact: the subscription of the witnesses is the evidence, as it properly ought to be.

Of the artificial means used in a process to discover truth, those by fire and water (5) were discharged by Alexander II.* And it is won-<82>derful, that even the grossest superstition could support them so long. But trial by singular battle, introduced by Dagobert king of Burgundy, being more agreeable to the genius of a warlike people, was retained longer in practice.

(5) This sort of artificial trial prevailed in nations that had no communication with each other, which may be accounted for by the prevelancy of superstition. Among the Indians on the Malabar coast, when a man is to clear himself of some heinous crime, as theft, adultery, or murder, he is obliged to swim over the river Cranganor, which swarms with alligators of a monstrous size. If he reach unhurt the opposite bank, he is reputed innocent. If devoured, he is concluded guilty.—*Texeira's History of Persia* [[trans. Stevens, p. 7]].—The trial by fire also is discovered in a country no less remote than Japan.—*Kempfer's History of Japan, book* 3. *ch.* 5.

We have evidence of the same practice in ancient Greece. In the tragedy of Antigone by Sophocles, there is the following passage:

The guards accus'd each other: Nought was prov'd,
But each suspected each; and all denied,
Offering in proof of innocence to grasp
The burning steel, to walk through fire, and take
Their solemn oath they knew not of the deed.

[[Act II, Scene 1: Sophocles, *Works,* trans. Francklin, vol. ii, p. 23. Quotation added 1776.]]

* Cap. 7. of his Statutes.

3. 1758, 1761: "It is sufficient to specify in the declaration, that the bond was signed sealed and delivered. Of the signing and sealing, the bond itself is evidence; and it is legal evidence of the delivery, that the bond is produced by the obligee."

And being considered as an appeal to the Almighty, who would infallibly give the cause for the innocent, it continued long a successful method of detecting guilt; for it was rare to find one so hardened in wickedness, as to behave with resolution under the weight of this conviction. But instances of such bold impiety, rare indeed at first, became more frequent. Men of sense began to entertain doubts about this method of trying causes; for why expect a miraculous interposition of Providence upon every slight dispute, that may be decided by the ordinary forms of law? Custom, however, and the superstitious notions of the vulgar, preserved it long in force; and even after it became a public nuisance, it was not directly abolished. All that could be done, was to sap its foundations (6), <83> by substituting gradually in its place another method of trial.

This was the oath of purgation; the form of which is as follows. The defendant brings along with him into court, certain persons called *Compurgators;* and after swearing to his own innocence, and that he brings the compurgators along with him to make and swear a leil and true oath, they all of them shall swear that this oath is true, and not false.* Considering this form in itself, and that it was admitted where the proof was defective on the pursuer's part, nothing appears more repugnant to justice. For why should a defendant be so loaded, when there is no proof against him? But considering it with relation to the trial by singular battle, to which it was substituted, it appears to me a rational measure. For in effect it was giving an advantage to the defendant which originally he had not, that of choosing whether he would enter the lists in a warlike manner, or undergo the oath of purgation. That the oath of purgation came in place of singular battle, is not obscurely insinuated, Leges Burgor. cap. 24. and <84> is more directly said, Quon. Attach. cap. 61. "If a man is challenged for theft in the King's court, or in any court, it is in his will, whether he will defend himself by battle, or by the cleansing of twelve leil men."† It bears in England the law-

---

(6) Among the Longobards, an accuser could not demand singular battle in order to prove the person accused guilty, till he swore upon the gospel that he had a well-founded suspicion of the person's guilt. And it is added, "Quia incerti sumus de judicio Dei, et multos audivimus per pugnam sine justa causa, suam causam perdere. Sed propter consuetudinem gentis nostrae, Longobardorum legem impiam vetare non possumus." *Laws of the Longobards, l.* 1. *tit.* 9. § 23.

* Quon. Attach. cap. 5. § 7.

† See Spelman's Glossary [[i.e., *Archaeologus*]], tit. Adrhamire.

term of *Wager at Law;* * that is, waging law instead of waging battle; joining issue upon the oaths of the defendant and compurgators, in place of joining issue upon a duel. But the oath of purgation, invented to soften this barbarous custom of duels, being reckoned not sufficient to repress the evil, duels were afterwards limited to accusations for capital crimes, where there are probable suspicions and presumptions, without direct evidence.[†] And consequently, if the foregoing conjecture be well founded, the oath of purgation came also to be confined to the same case. By degrees both wore out of use; and, in this country, there are no remaining traces of the oath of purgation, if it be not in ecclesiastical courts.

It is probable, that as singular battle gave place to the oath of purgation, so this oath gave place to juries. The transition was easy, there being no variation, other than that the twelve compurgators, formerly named by the defendant, were now named by the judge. The va-<85>riation proved notably advantageous to the defendant, though in appearance against him. Singular battle wearing out of repute, the injustice of burdening with a proof of innocence every person who is accused, was clearly perceived; and witnesses being now more frequently employed on the part of the prosecutor to prove guilt, than on the part of the defendant to prove innocence, it was thought proper that they should be chosen by the judge, not by the defendant. If it be demanded, Why not by the prosecutor, as at present? it is answered, That at that time the innovation would have been reckoned too violent. However this be, one thing appears from Glanvil,[‡] That in all questions concerning the property of land, founded on the brieve of right, a privilege was about that time bestowed on the defendant, to have the cause tried by a jury, instead of singular battle. As this was an innovation authorised by reason, and not by statute, it was probably at first attempted in questions upon the brieve of right only; matters of less importance being left upon the oath of purgation. That a jury trial, and the oath of purgation, were in use both of them at the same time, we have evidence from the Regiam Majestatem,[‖] compared with the foregoing quotations. But these two me-<86>thods could not long subsist together. The new method of

* Jacob's Law-Dictionary, *voce* Wager at Law.
† Stat. Rob. III. cap. 16.
‡ L. 2. cap. 7. to the end of that book.
‖ L. 4. cap. 1. § 13. and cap. 4. § 2.

trial by jury, was so evidently preferable, that it would soon become universal, and be extended to all cases civil and criminal: In fact, we find it so extended as far back as we have any distinct records.

From this deduction it appears, that a jury was originally a number of witnesses chosen by the judge, in order to declare the truth.* And hence the process against a jury for perjury and wilful error. This explains also why the verdict of a jury is final, even when they are convicted of perjury. Singular battle, from the nature of the thing, was so; the oath of purgation, substituted to singular battle, was so; and a verdict, substituted to an oath of purgation, fell of course to be so. It likewise explains the practice of England, that the jury must be unanimous in their verdict; for it was required, that the compurgators should be so in their oath of purgation. The same rule probably obtained in Scotland: But at present, and as far back as our records carry us, the verdict is fixed by the votes of the majority.

In later times, the nature and office of a jury were altered. Through the difficulty of procuring twelve proper witnesses acquainted with the facts, twelve men of skill and integrity were chosen, to judge of the evidence produced by <87> the litigants. The cause of this alteration may be guessed, supposing only that the present strict forms of a jury-trial were at first not in use. If jurymen, considered as witnesses, differed, or were uncertain about the facts, they would naturally demand extraneous evidence; of which when brought, it belonged to them to judge. It is likely, that for centuries jurymen acted thus both as witnesses and as judges. They may, it is certain, act so at this day; though, for the reason above given, they are commonly chosen by rotation, without being regarded in the character of witnesses. Hence it is, that a jury is now considered chiefly as judges of the fact, and scarce at all as a body of witnesses. And this explains why the process for perjury against them is laid aside: This process cannot take place against judges, but only against witnesses. <88>

* See Reg. Maj. l. 1. cap. 12.

Property

That peculiar relation which connects a person with a subject, signified by the term *Property*, is one of the capital objects of law. The privileges founded on this relation, are at present extensive, but were not always so. Property originally bestowed no other privilege, but merely that of using or enjoying the subject. A privilege essential to commerce was afterward introduced, viz. to alien for a valuable consideration: And at present the relation of property is so intimate, as to comprehend a power or privilege of making donations to take effect after death, as well as during life. Laws have been made, and decisions pronounced in every age, conformable to the different ideas that have been entertained of this relation. These laws and decisions are rendered obscure, and perhaps scarce intelligible, to those who are unacquainted with the history of property: And therefore we may hope, that this history will prove equally curious and instructive (1). <89>

Man by his nature is fitted for society; and society is fitted for man by its manifold conveniencies. The perfection of human society consists in that just degree of union among individuals, which to each reserves freedom and independency, as far as is consistent with peace and good order.

(1) The term *Property* has three different significations. It signifies properly, as above, a peculiar relation betwixt a person and certain subjects, as land, houses, moveables, &c.; sometimes it is made to signify the privileges a person has with relation to such a subject; and sometimes it signifies the subject itself, considered with relation to the person. I have not scrupled to use the term, in these different senses, as occasion offered.

The bonds of society may be too lax; but they may also be overstretched. A society where every man should be bound to dedicate the whole of his industry to the common interest, would be unnatural and uncomfortable, because destructive of liberty and independence. The enjoyment of the goods of fortune in common, would be no less unnatural and uncomfortable: There subsists in man a remarkable propensity for appropriation; and a communion of goods is not necessary to society, though it may be indulged in some singular cases. And happy it is for man to be thus constituted. Industry, in a great measure, depends on property; and a much greater blessing depends on it, which is the gratification of the most dignified natural affections. What place would there be for generosity, benevolence, or charity, if the goods of fortune were common to <90> all? These noble principles, being destitute of objects and exercise, would for ever lie dormant; and what would man be without them?—a very groveling creature; distinguishable indeed from the brutes, but scarce elevated above them. Gratitude and compassion might have some slight exercise; but how much greater is the figure they make in a state of divided property? The springs and principles of man are adjusted with admirable wisdom to his external circumstances; and these in conjunction form one regular constitution, harmonious in all its parts.

Hunting and fishing were originally the occupations of men, upon which chiefly they depended for food. A beast caught in a gin, or a fish with a hook, being the purchase of art and industry, were from the beginning considered by all as belonging to the occupant: The appetite that man has for appropriation, vouches this to be true. But the extent of the relation thus created betwixt the hunter and his prey, and the power acquired by the former over the latter in common estimation, are questions of more intricacy. That this relation implies a power to use for sustenance the creature thus taken, and to defend the possession against every invader, is clear. But supposing the creature to have been lost, and without violence to have come into the hands of another; I do not clearly <91> see, that the original occupant would have any claim, or that restitution would be reckoned the duty of the possessor. This may be thought sceptical; for to one who has imbibed the refined principles of law, the conception is familiar of a relation betwixt a man and a subject, so intimate as not to be dissolvable without his consent: But, in the investigation of original laws, nothing is more apt to lead into error, than prepossession derived from modern improvements. It appears to me highly probable, that among savages, involved in objects of sense, and strangers to abstract speculation, property, and the rights or moral powers arising from it, never are with accuracy distinguished from the natural powers that must be exerted upon the subject to make it profitable to the possessor. The man who kills and eats, who sows and reaps, at his own pleasure, independent of another's will, is naturally deemed proprietor. The grossest savages understand power without right, of which they are made sensible by daily acts of violence: But property without possession is a conception too abstract for a savage, or for any person who has not studied the principles of law.[1] To this day the vulgar can form no distinct conception of property, otherwise than by figuring the man in possession, and using the subject without controul. If such at present be the vulgar way of thinking, we may reasonably sus-<92>pect a still greater obscurity in the conceptions of a savage (2).

(2) The escheating wreck-goods was probably founded on the imperfect notion of property here set forth. Among the Romans, the escheating wreck-goods was the practice down till the time of Constantine: "Si quando naufragio navis expulsa fuerit ad littus, vel si quando aliquam terram attigerit, ad dominos pertineat: fiscus meus sese non interponat. Quod enim jus habet fiscus in aliena calamitate, ut de re tam luctuosa compendium sectetur."—*L.* II. *Cod. tit.* 6. *lex.* I. [["If a vessel is driven on land by shipwreck, or if it goes ashore at any time, it shall belong to the owners, and my treasury shall advance no claim to it; for what right has the treasury to take advantage of the misfortunes of others, so as to profit by such an unhappy occurrence?" *Codex* II.5.I. Trans. Scott. Note added 1776.]]

1. 1758, 1761: "But property without possession . . . the principles of law" = "but it requires a habit of abstraction, to conceive right or moral power independent of natural power; because in this condition, right, being attended with no visible effect, is a mental conception merely. That a man may be deprived of a subject, and yet retain the property, is a lesson too intricate for a savage. For how can this be, it will be observed, when he has not the use of the subject, and has no power over it? Hence as a subject, in order for enjoyment, must be under the power of the proprietor, and consequently in his possession, I infer, that, in the original conception of property, possession was an essential

Thus originally property was a very precarious right; and would have been of little value, had not Nature provided means for recovering it when possession was lost. Where a man is deprived of his goods by theft or other criminal act, the wrong-doer is in conscience bound to restore. He has indeed acquired the property with the possession; but he is bound to repair the injuries done to the former possessor; and the proper reparation is, to restore the subject to him.

A *bona fide* purchaser is in a very different condition, supposing even the goods purchased by him to have been stolen: He is not liable for the crime of his author; he did no wrong in purchasing, and consequently cannot be subjected to reparation. And in this case the rule obtains, *Quod potior est conditio possidentis.*[2] And that anciently this was the rule, may be gathered from traces of it which to this day remain in <93> several countries. By the

---

circumstance, and that when the latter was lost, the former could no longer subsist. I confirm this inference by the following observation."

2. 1758, 1761: "Thus originally property . . . *est conditio possidentis*" = "But though originally property was lost with the possession, it follows not that it was always acquired with the possession. That property cannot be acquired by theft, or other immoral act, is a sentiment dictated by nature; and which therefore influences even the grossest savages. Hence it behoved to be a rule, that though property is lost by theft, it is not acquired by theft. Here is a clear foundation laid for obliging the thief to restore. He has no title to retain a subject which, though in his possession, is not his property; and he is besides bound in conscience to repair the damage done by him to the person formerly proprietor, by restoring the possession, which of course restores the property. But this claim of restitution, evidently reaches not any person who has acquired the subject by honest means, and who having done no wrong, cannot be liable to make any reparation. To illustrate this subject, I figure the case of a horse carried off by theft, which, after passing through several hands, is fairly purchased in open market. Let us see what arguments are suggested by reason on either side; and after weighing these arguments, let natural justice pronounce sentence. The claimant urges, 'That he was deprived of his horse by theft.' The Purchaser answers, 'That he had no accession to the theft, and that the thief alone is liable.' The claimant again urges, 'That a man may lay hold of his own goods wherever they are found.' Answered, 'The horse was the property of the claimant, while in his possession; but the property was lost with the possession. And supposing the connection of property to subsist independent of possession, this can only hold where there is no separate connection formed. In the present case, the connection of property arising from an honest bargain, and a full price paid, is of the strongest kind.' Betwixt pretentions so equally balanced, how can a judge otherwise interpose, than by pronouncing, *quod potior est conditio possidentis?*"

old law of Germany, the proprietor could demand his goods from the person to whom he delivered them, in order to be restored; because this claim is founded on a contract. But he had no claim against any other honest possessor. And Heineccius observes,* that this continues to be the law of Lubec, of Hamburg, of Culm in Prussia, of Sweden, and even of Holland. Upon the same principle, stolen goods were confiscated.† For it was held, that the fisc is a *bona fide* purchaser, and cannot be reached by an action of restitution or reparation; which indeed must be confessed to be a very great stretch *in favorem fisci.* And this continued to be the law till it was abrogated by the Emperor Charles V.‡ Upon the same principle the Saxon law is founded, That if a thief suffer death, by which the stolen goods are confiscated,|| his heir is not bound to pay the value (3). <94>

* Compend. of the Pandects [[i.e., *Elementa Juriis Civilis*]], part 2. § 86.
† Maevius De jur. Lubec. part 4. tit. 1. § 2.
‡ Constit. Crim. 218.
|| Carpzovius, part 4. const. 32. def. 23.

(3) If the reader, neglecting the opinions delivered by writers on the Roman law, form his judgment on facts and circumstances reported by them, he will, to the foregoing authorities, add the practice of the ancient Romans, which, to the man who lost his goods by theft, afforded a *condictio furtiva* against the thief. This action being merely personal, founded on the delinquency of the defendant, takes it for granted, that the pursuer had by the theft lost his property; and accordingly the purpose of the action is, to compel the defendant to restore the possession to the pursuer, and consequently the property. Afterward, when property was distinguished from possession, and theft was held not sufficient to deprive a man of his property, a *rei vindicatio* was given. This being a real action, takes it for granted that the property remains with the pursuer; and accordingly, it concludes only that the possession be restored to him. After this alteration of the law concerning property, there was evidently no longer occasion or place for the *condictio furtiva;* because a man who has not lost his property, cannot demand that it be restored to him. And yet the later Roman writers, Justinian in particular, not adverting to the alteration, hold, most absurdly, That the *rei vindicatio,* and *condictio furtiva,* are competent, both of them, against the thief, and that the pursuer has his choice of either; which is in effect maintaining, that the pursuer is proprietor and not proprietor at the same time.—*l. 7. pr. De condict. furt.* [[i.e., *Digest* 13.1.7]]; § *ult. Institut. De oblig. quae ex delict.* [[i.e., *Justinian's Institutes* 4.1.19]]—Vinnius, in his commentary on Justinian's Institutes,—*tit. De action.* § 14.—sees clearly the inconsistency of giving to a proprietor the *condictio furtiva.* His words are,

Quomodo igitur fur qui dominus non est, domino cui soli condictionem furtivam competere constat, rem dare poterit? Quod si hoc impossibile est, absurdissimum videtur quod hic traditur, furem sic convenire posse, ut dare jubeatur, et domin-

Were we altogether destitute of evidence, it would remain probable,
however, that in this <95> island the original notions about property did
not widely differ from what prevailed in other <96> countries. But luckily

---

ium rei quod non habet transferre in actorem, eundemque rei petitae dominum.
Nodus hic indissolubilis est, &c. [["So how will a thief who is not the owner be
able to restore an object to the owner who is the only person who can pursue a
claim of restitution for theft? If this is not possible, the tradition that a thief can
agree to be told to restore it and to transfer the ownership of an object—an ownership he does not possess—to the pursuer who is the same owner of the object
which has been claimed, appears to be quite ridiculous. This is an unsolvable
difficulty."]]

Is it not strange, that an inconsistency set in so clear a light, did not lead our author to
conclude, that the sustaining a *condictia furtiva* is compleat evidence, that when this
action was invented the property was by theft understood to be lost?

We find traces of the same way of thinking in other matters. A man who by force or
fear was compelled to sell his subject at an undervalue, had no redress by the common
law of the Romans—[*The reason of this is given in the second Tract.* [[See above pp. 48–
60.]]]—It was the Praetor who first took upon him to restore *in integrum* those who
were thus deprived of their property. The action originally was strictly personal, being
directed against the wrong-doer only; nor could it be extended against a *bona fide* purchaser, as long as property was held to vanish when the possession was lost. For though
no man is bound by a covenant which by force or fear he is compelled to make, yet when
delivery is made, and the subject is acquired by a third party, who purchases *bona fide,*
an action of restitution cannot lie against him. The claimant who lost his property with
the possession, had not a *rei vindicatio;* and a personal action could not lie against a
purchaser who had no accession to the wrong. But after the doctrine prevailed, That
property can subsist independent of possession, it came naturally to be a subject of deliberation, whether in this case a *rei vindicatio* might not lie against the *bona fide* purchaser, as well as where a subject is robbed or stolen. There is fundamentally no difference.
For a contract, however formal, is no evidence of consent where force has been interposed; and delivery without consent transfers not property. In this case, however, which
had the appearance of some intricacy, the Roman Praetor did not venture to sustain a
rei vindicatio in direct terms. But the same thing was done under disguise. The connection of property had by this time taken such hold of the mind, as to make it a rule, that
a man cannot be deprived of his subject by an involuntary sale, more than by theft or
robbery; and to redress such wrong, the *actio metus* was, by the perpetual edict, extended
even against the *bona fide* purchaser.—*l.* 3. *C. His quae vi metusque caus* [[i.e., *Codex*
2.19.3]].—The *actio metus* being in this case made truly a real action, differed in nothing
but the name from a *rei vindicatio;* for, from a purchaser *bona fide,* the subject evidently
cannot be claimed upon any medium, other than that the claimant is proprietor; and
consequently is entitled to a *rei vindicatio.* Hence, in the Roman law, the *actio metus* is
classed under a species denominated *Actiones in rem scriptae,* a species which has puzzled
all the commentators, and which none of them have been able to explain. It is the history

we have very strong evidence that they were the same; not even excepting the case of stolen goods. Our act 26. parl. 1661, vouches it to have been the law of Scotland, that when a thief was condemned, his effects, including the stolen goods, were confis-<97>cated. Nor is this law abrogated totally by the statute. The proprietor cannot demand his goods, unless he prosecute the thief *usque ad sententiam*. Such being the law with regard to stolen goods, we cannot doubt, but that a man purchasing *bona fide* from one not proprietor, was secure against this claim of property. That such was the practice, may be gathered from many passages in our ancient law-books, and from the following fact. A regulation appears to have been early introduced, prohibiting buying and selling except in open market. The purpose undoubtedly was, to repress theft, and to prevent the transference of property by private bargains. It is not safe to venture stolen goods in open market; and if they be disposed of privately, the buyer cannot be secure who purchases *prohibente lege* (4). I have another <98> fact to urge, which is no slight confirmation of what is here suggested. By the oldest law of the Romans, a single year completed the prescription of moveables; which testi-

---

of law only that can give us a clear notion of these actions. All actions pass under that name, which, originally personal, were, by the augmented vigour of the relation of property, made afterward real.

We also discover from the Roman law, that other real rights made a progress similar to that mentioned concerning property. There was, for example, in the Roman law no real action originally for recovering a pledge, when the creditor by accident or otherwise lost the possession. It was the Pretor Servius who gave a real action.—§ 8. *Instit. De action* [[i.e., *Justinian's Institutes* 4.6.8]]; *and Vinnius upon that section* [[i.e., *Commentarius*, pp. 782–85]].

(4) Coke—*Instit.* 2, *p.* 713.—seems not to have understood this matter, when he can find no cause for the regulation, other than the encouragement of fairs and markets, in order to promote commerce. This implies, that formerly a purchase, even in open market, afforded no security against the proprietor; and that the legislature for encouraging fairs and markets could think of no better expedient, than to render property precarious, and to subject individuals to frequent forfeitures. A measure so unjust and so violent is not agreeable to the genius of the law of England. This regulation was introduced to secure property, not to unhinge it: which also appears from the two statutes mentioned by our author, confining the privilege of those who purchase in open market within the narrowest bounds. By the latter, viz. 31st of Elisabeth, no person is in safety to buy a horse, even in open market, unless some sufficient or credible person vouch for the vender. And even in that case, the horse must be restored to the proprietor claiming within six months, and offering the price that was paid by the *bona fide* purchaser.

fies, that property independent of possession was considered to be a right of the slenderest kind. In later times, when the relation of property was so strengthened as to be clearly distinguished from possession, this prescription was extended to ten years; and with us a man, by prescription, is not deprived of the most trifling moveable in a shorter time than forty years.

But if such originally was the law of property, by what over-ruling principle has property acquired strength and energy to follow the subject wherever found, and to exclude even an honest purchaser, where the title of his author is discovered to be lame? This question enters deep into the history of law; and the answer to it must be drawn, partly from natural, partly from political principles. It will appear in the course of this history, that both have concurred to be-<99>stow upon property that degree of firmness and stability which at present it enjoys among all civilized nations. Proceeding regularly, according to the course of time, the first cause which offers itself to view is a natural principle.

Man, by the frame of his body, is unqualified to be an animal of prey. His stomach requires more regular supplies of food, than can be obtained in a state where food is so precarious (5). <100> His necessities taught him the art of taming such of the wild creatures as are peaceable and docile. Large herds were propagated of horned cattle, sheep, and goats; which afforded plenty of food ready at hand for daily use. By this invention, the conveniencies of living were greatly promoted: and in this state, which

(5) When men were hunters, and lived like carnivorous animals upon prey, there could be no regular supplies of food; and after they became shepherds, the former habit of abstinence made their meals probably less frequent than at present, though food was at hand. In old times, there was but one meal a-day; which continued to be the fashion, even after great luxury was indulged in other respects. In the war which Xerxes made upon Greece, it was pleasantly said of the Abderites, who were appointed to provide for the King's table, that they ought to go in general procession and acknowledge the favour of the gods, in not inclining Xerxes to eat twice a-day.—*Herodotus, l. 7.*—In the reign of Henry VI. of England, we have Shakespeare's authority, that the people of England fed but twice a-day—*Vol 5. p. 95. near the top, compared with p. 93 in the middle. Warburton's edition.*—Our historian Hector Boyes exclaims against the growing luxury of his time, that, not satisfied with two meals, some men were so gluttonous as to eat thrice every day. [[See Boece, *Chronicles,* Bk. 17, ch. v: trans. Bellenden, vol. ii, p. 392.]] Custom, no doubt, has a powerful effect in this case, as well as in many others: yet the human frame is not so much under the power of custom, as to make it easy for a man, like an eagle, to fast perhaps a month.

makes the second stage of the social life, the relation of property, though not entirely disjoined from possession, was considerably enlivened. The care and attention bestowed upon a domestic animal from the time of its birth, form in the mind of every one a strong connection betwixt the man and his beast, which, upon any casual interruption of possession, does not so readily vanish, as in the case of a wild beast seized by a hunter.

Thus, by a natural principle, the relation of property was in some measure fortified, and was considered as forming a stricter connection betwixt man and other animals than it did originally. In this condition, a political principle contributed to make the relation appear still more intimate. Experience demonstrated, that it is impracticable to repress theft and robbery, if purchasers be secure on the pretext of *bona fides*. For every purchase must be presumed honest, till the contrary be proved; and nothing is more easy than to contrive a dishonest purchase that shall be secure from detection. To <101> remedy an evil which gave so great scope to stealth and violence, the regulation above mentioned was introduced, prohibiting all buying and selling except in open market. After this regulation, a private purchase afforded no security, nor was the property transferred. The *nexus,* or lien, of property was greatly strengthened, when it was now become law, that no man could be deprived of his property without his own consent; except singly in the case of a purchase *bona fide* in open market. I add upon this head, that the notion of right, independent of natural power, once unfolded, acquired the greatest firmness and stability, by the regular establishment of courts of justice, the great purpose of which is, to afford natural power whenever it is of use to make right or moral power effectual.

The influence of property in its different stages of improvement, is remarkable. The *nexus,* or lien, of property being originally slight, it was not thought unjust to deprive a man of his property by means of a *bona fide* purchase, even where the subject was sold by a robber. The law that restrained purchases except in open market, bestowed a firmness on the relation of property, which made it in some measure prevail over the right of a *bona fide* purchase. This produced the statute above mentioned, 31st of Elizabeth, enacting, that <102> even a *bona fide* purchase in open market shall not transfer the property, provided the proprietor claim within six months, and offer to the purchaser the price he paid. So stands the law of

England to this day; and yet to such stability has the relation of property arrived in course of time, by the favour of all men, that it is doubtful, whether at present the claim of property would not be sustained, even without offering the price. In Scotland, there is a regulation of a very old date, for the security of property. Beside buying in open market, the purchaser is bound to take from the vender security for his honesty, termed *Borgh of haimhald.* By this precaution the purchaser was secure against all the world. But if the goods came to be claimed by the true owner, the cautioner was bound to produce the vender, otherwise to be liable for damages.* But though this continues to be our statute-law, such however is the influence of property, that I doubt whether our judges would not be in hazard of sustaining a *rei vindicatio* against the purchaser in open market, even after using the foregoing precaution. Property, it is certain, is a great favourite of human nature, and is frequently the object of a very strong affection. In the fluctuating state of human affairs before regular governments were formed, property was seldom <103> so permanent as to afford great scope for this affection. But in peaceable times, under a steady administration of law, the affection for property becomes exceeding warm; which fortifies greatly the relation of property. Thus there is discovered a natural resemblance between government and property: from the weak and infantine state in which both are found originally, they have equally arrived at that stability and perfection which they enjoy at present.

Having advanced so far in the history of moveable property, it is time to turn our view to the property of land. In the two first stages of the social life, while men were hunters or shepherds, there scarce could be any notion of land-property. Strangers to agriculture, and to the art of building, if it was not of huts which could be raised or demolished in a moment, men had no fixed habitation, but wandered about in hords, to find pasture for their cattle (6). In this vagrant life, men had scarce any connection with land more than with air or water. A field of grass might be considered as

___

(6) The Scythians drawing no subsistence from the plough, but from cattle, and having no cities nor inclosed places, made their carts serve them for houses: by which it was easy for them to move from place to place. Herodotus, *book* 4. from this observes, that the Scythians are never to be found by an enemy they chuse to avoid.

* Leg. Burg. cap. 128.

belonging to a hord or clan, while they were in possession; <104> and so might the air which they breathed, and the water which they drank: but the moment they removed to another quarter, there no longer subsisted any connection betwixt them and the field that was deserted. It lay open to newcomers, who had the same right as if it had not been formerly occupied. Hence I conclude, that while men were shepherds, there was no relation formed betwixt them and land, in any manner so distinct as to obtain the name of property.*

Agriculture, which makes the third stage of the social life, produced the relation of land-property. A man who has bestowed labour in preparing a field for the plough, and who has improved that field by artful culture, forms in his mind an intimate connection with it. He contracts by degrees a singular affection for a spot, which in a manner is the workmanship of his own hands. He is fond to live there, and there to deposit his bones. It is an object that fills his mind, and is never out of thought at home or abroad. After a summer's expedition, or perhaps years of a foreign war, he returns with avidity to his own house, and to his own field, there to pass his time in ease and plenty. By such trials, the relation of property is disjoined from possession; and to this disjunction, <105> the lively perception of property with respect to an object so considerable, mainly contributes. If a proprietor happen to be dispossessed in his absence, the injustice is perceived and acknowledged. In the common sense of mankind, he continues proprietor, and a *rei vindicatio* will be sustained to him against the possessor, to whom the property cannot be transferred by an immoral act. But what if the subject, after a long interval, be purchased *bona fide,* and peaceable possession attained? I have given my reasons above for conjecturing, that in ancient times such a purchase transferred property, and extinguished the right of the former proprietor. Such undoubtedly was once the condition of moveable property, gradually altered, as observed above, by successive regulations. Land-property continued a much shorter time in this unstable condition. Of all subjects of property, land is that which engages our affection the most; by which means the relation of land-property

---

* See the description given by Thucydides of the original state of Greece, book I. at the beginning.

grew up much sooner to its present firmness and stability, than the relation of moveable property. For many centuries past, it is believed, that in no civilized nation has *bona fides* alone been held to secure the purchaser of land. Where the vender is not proprietor, it is requisite that the purchase be followed with a long and peaceable possession. <106>

It is highly probable, that the strong *nexus* of land-property, which cannot be loosed otherwise than by consent, had an influence upon moveable property, to make it equally stable. But if land-property led the way in this particular, moveable property undoubtedly led the way in what we are now to enter upon, viz. the power of aliening. The connection of persons with moveables is more immediate than with land. A moveable may be locked up in a repository: Cattle are killed every day for the sustenance of the proprietor and his family. From this power, the transition is easy to that of alienation; for what doubt can there be of my power to alien what I can destroy? The right or power of alienation must therefore have been early recognised as a quality of moveable property. The power of disposing moveables by will, to take effect after death, is a greater stretch; and we shall have occasion to see, that this power was not early acknowledged as one of the qualities even of moveable property. We have reason beforehand to conjecture, that a power of aliening land, whether to take effect instantly or after death, was not early introduced; because land admits not, like moveables, a ready delivery from hand to hand. And this conjecture will be verified in the following part of our history. Land, at the same time, is a desirable object; and a power to alien, after it came to be esta-<107>blished in moveable property, could not long be separated from the property of land.

But before we proceed farther in this history, we must take a view of the forms and solemnities that in the common apprehension of mankind are requisite, first to acquire, and then to transfer land-property. For these, if I mistake not, will support the foregoing observations. It is taught by all writers, that occupation is an essential solemnity in the original establishment of land-property. The reason will be evident from what is said above, that property originally was not separated from possession. And the same solemnity is requisite at this day with respect to every uninhabited country:

For where there is no proprietor to alien, there can be no means other than occupation to form the connection of property, whether with land or with moveables. Occupation was equally necessary in old times to compleat the transference of land-property; for if property was thought not to have an existence without possession, occupation was necessary for transferring the property of land, as well as for establishing it originally. But when property came to be considered as a right independent of possession, it was natural to relax from the solemnities formerly requisite in the transference of land-property. It is often difficult, and always troublesome, to introduce a purchaser with his family and goods into the <108> natural possession; and this solemnity was dispensed with, because not essential upon the later system of property. But then, in opposition to a practice so long established, the innovation would have been too violent, to transfer property by the bare will of the former proprietor, without any solemnity in place of possession. Such is our attachment to visible objects, that it would have appeared like magic, or the tricks of a juggler, to make the property of land jump from one person to another, merely upon pronouncing certain words expressing will or consent. Words are often ambiguous, and always too transitory to take fast hold of the mind, without concomitant circumstances. In place, therefore, of actual possession, some ouvert act was held necessary in order to compleat the transmission. This act, whatever it be, is conceived as representing possession, or as a symbol of it; and hence it has acquired the name of symbolical possession. When this form first crept in, some act was chosen to represent possession as near as possible; witness the case mentioned by Selden,* where a grant of land made to the church *anno* 687, was perfected by laying a turf of the land upon the altar. This innovation was attempted with the greatest caution; but after the form became customary, there was less nicety in the choice. The delivery of a <109> spear, of a helmet, or of a bunch of arrows, completed the transmission. In short, any symbol was taken, however little connected with the land: It was sufficient that it was connected with the will of the granter. In the cathedral of York, there is to this day preserved, a horn delivered by Ulphus King of Deira to

* Janus Anglorum, cap. 25.

the monastery of York, as a symbol for completing a grant of land in their
favour (7).

A single observation, with which I shall conclude this branch of the
subject, may serve to give a more enlarged view of it. There is a stricter
analogy betwixt creating a personal obligation and transferring land property, than is commonly imagined. Words merely make no great impression
upon the rude and illiterate. In ancient times, therefore, some external solemnity was always used to fortify covenants and engagements, without
which they were reckoned not binding.* As writing at present is common,
and the meaning of words ascertained, we <110> require no other solemnity
but writ, to compleat the most important transactions. Writ hitherto, with
regard to land-rights, has not in Scotland superseded the use of symbolical
delivery: But when our notions shall be more refined, and substance regarded more than form, it is probable, that external symbols, which have
long been laid aside in personal rights, will also be laid aside in rights affecting land. We return to our history.

Property, which originally bestowed no power of alienation, carries the
mind naturally to the children of the possessor, who continue the possession after his death, and who must succeed if he cannot alien (8). Their
right, being independent of his will, was conceived a sort of property. They
make part of the family, live upon the land, and, in common with their
parents, enjoy its product. When the father dies, they continue in possession without any alteration, but that the family is less by one than formerly.
Such a right in children, which commenced at their birth, and which was
perfected by the father's death, was not readily to be distinguished from

---

(7) It is a common practice among the salmon-fishers to purloin from their masters
part of the fish; and it is very difficult to restrain them, because they scarce think it a
fault. They cannot conceive, that a salmon before delivery belongs to their master. After
delivery, indeed, or after the master's mark is put upon the fish, they readily admit, that
it would be theft to take any away. This shows, that in the natural sense of mankind,
occupation or delivery is requisite to establish property.

(8) Heredes tamen successoresque sui cuique liberi: Et nullum testamentum. *Tacitus
de moribus Germanorum.* [["However, so far as heirship and succession are concerned,
each man's children are his own heirs, and there is no will." *Germania* I.20, trans.
Peterson.]]

* See the essay immediately foregoing.

property. It is in effect the same with the strictest entail that can be contrived.

To those who are ignorant of the history of law, and are rivetted to the present system of <iiii> things, the right here attributed to children may appear chimerical. But it will have a very different aspect, after mentioning a few of the many ancient customs and regulations founded upon it. And, to pave the way, I shall first show, that the notions of the ancients were precisely as here stated; for which I appeal to a learned Roman lawyer, Paulus.*

In suis heredibus evidentius apparet, continuationem dominii eo rem perducere ut nulla videatur hereditas fuisse, quasi olim hi domini essent, qui etiam vivo patre quodammodo domini existimantur. Unde etiam filius familias appellatur, sicut paterfamilias: Sola nota hac adjecta, per quam distinguitur genitor ab eo qui genitus sit. Itaque post mortem patris non hereditatem percipere videntur, sed magis liberam bonorum administrationem consequuntur.[3]

Here we see, even in an author far removed from the infancy of law, the interest which children once had in the estate of their father, termed a sort of property. The only thing surprising in this passage is, that a notion so distinct should remain of the property of children in their father's effects, for such a length of time after the right was at an end. But to proceed, it plainly arose from this right, that among the Romans children got the appellation of *sui et necessarii heredes.* The strict connection betwixt parents <112> and children produced the first term; and the other arose from the singularity of their condition, that the heritage becoming theirs *ipso facto* by the father's death, they were heirs necessarily, without liberty of choice. Nor did this subject them to any risk; because, deriving no right from their

---

* L. 11. De liber. et posthum. hered. [[I.e., *Digest* 28.2.11.]]

3. "In the case of *sui heredes,* it is more clearly evident that the continuation of ownership leads to this, that no inheritance is regarded as having taken place, as if they were already owners, being thought of as in some sense owners even in the lifetime of the father. And so a son-in-power is even called the same as the head of the household with the addition only of a qualification which makes a distinction between the person who fathers and the person who is fathered. Therefore, after the death of the father they are not regarded as taking up an inheritance, but rather get free power of administration of the property." Trans. Watson.

father, they were not bound to fulfil his deeds. In general, while property subsisted without power of aliening, no deed done by the father, whether civil or criminal, could affect the children. And as to crimes, some good authorities are still extant. It was a law of Edward the Confessor, That children born or begot before commission of a crime that infers forfeiture of goods, shall not lose their inheritance.* And it was a law of the Longobards,† That goods are not confiscated where the criminal has near relations. Other regulations, acknowledging this right in children, and authorising particular exceptions from it, will come in more properly after proceeding a little farther in our history.

It is remarked above, that the enlarged notion of property, by annexing to it a power of alienation, obtained first in moveables: And indeed society could scarce subsist without such a power; at least as far as is necessary for exchanging commodities, and carrying on com-<113>merce. But the same power was not early annexed to the property of land; unless perhaps to support the alienation of some small part for value. This we know, that a proprietor of land that had descended to him from his ancestors, could not dispose of it totally, even for a valuable consideration, unless he was reduced to want of bread; and even in that case he was obliged to make the first offer to his heir. This regulation, known among lawyers by the name of *jus retractus,* is very ancient; and we have reason to believe it was universal. It obtained among the Jews.‡ It was the law of Scotland,‖ of which we have traces remaining not above three centuries ago.§ And it appears also to have been the law among other European nations.¶ But this regulation gave place gradually to commerce; and, now for ages, bargains about land have been no less free than bargains about moveables. The power of aliening for a valuable consideration, is now universally held to be inherent in the property of land as well as of moveables.

Donations, or gratuitous alienations, were of a slower growth. These were at first small, <114> and upon plausible pretexts. By degrees they gained

---

* Lambard's collection of old English laws, Edw. the Confessor, l. 19. at the end.
† L. 1. tit. 10. § 1.
‡ Ruth, iv.
‖ Leg. Burg. cap. 45. 94. 95. 96. 115. 125. § 7. 127.
§ See Appendix, No 2.
¶ Laws of the Saxons, § 14. 16.

ground, and in course of time came to be indulged almost without limitation. By the laws of the Visigoths,* it was lawful to make donations to the church. The Burgundians sustained a gift by a man though he had children.† And among the Bavarians, it was lawful for a free man, after dividing his means with his sons, to make a donation to the church out of his own portion.‡ With respect to our Saxon ancestors, the learned antiquary Sir Henry Spelman is an excellent guide. He observes,∥

> That heritable land began by little and little to be aliened by proprietors, first to churches and religious houses by consent of the next heir; next to lay persons; so that it grew at last a matter of course for children, as *heredes proximi,* for kinsmen, as *heredes remotiores,* and for the lord, as *heres ultimus,* to confirm the same. Such consent being understood a matter of course, it grew to be law, That the father, without consent of his heirs, might give part of his land, either to religious uses, or in marriage with his daughter, or in recompence of service.

That such was the practice of England in the days of Henry II. Glan-<115>vil testifieth.§ And that such also was the law of Scotland in the days of David II. is testified by Reg. Maj.¶ But here a limitation mentioned by both authors must be attended to, That such a donation was not effectual unless completed by delivery. The reason assigned is slight and unsatisfactory; but the true reason is, that if the subject was not delivered, the heir, whether we consider the feudal or allodial law, was entitled to take possession after his ancestor's death, without being subjected to pay any of the debts, or perform any of the engagements of his ancestor. And upon that account, there was no security against the heir, but by delivery. This also appears to have been the Roman law.**

Donations *inter vivos,* paved the way to donations *mortis causa.* But this was a wide step that required the authority of a law; for it was hard to conceive that the will of any man should, after his death, and after his own

---

* L. 5 tit. 1. § 1.
† Laws of the Burgundians, tit. 1.
‡ Laws of the Bavar. tit. 1. § 1.
∥ Of ancient deeds and charters [[*English Works,* vol. ii]], p. 234.
§ L. 7. cap. 1.
¶ L. 2. cap. 18.
** Heineccii Antiquitates Romanae, l. 2. tit. 7. § 13.

right was at an end, have so strong an effect, as to prefer any person before the lawful heir. The power of testing was introduced among the Athenians by a law of Solon, giving power to every proprietor who had no children, to regulate his succession by testament. Plutarch, in the life of that lawgiver, has the following passage.

> Magnam quoque sibi existimationem peperit <116> lege de testamentis lata. Antea enim non licebat testamentum condere; nam defuncti opes domumque penes genere proximos manere oportebat. Hic liberum fecit, si liberi non essent, res suas cui vellet dare: praetulitque amicitiam generi, et gratiam necessitati: et effecit, ut pecuniae possessorum propriae essent.[4]

The concluding sentence is remarkable. Alienations *inter vivos* had been long in practice; and it was but one step farther to annex to property a power of alienating *mortis causa*. Athens was ripe for this law; and hence it was natural for Plutarch to observe, that the power of testing made every man proprietor of his own goods. The Decemviri at Rome transferred this law into their Twelve Tables, in the following words, *Pater-familias uti legassit super familiae, pecuniae, tutelaeve suae rei, ita jus esto.*[5] This law, though conceived in words unlimited, was certainly not intended, more than Solon's law, to deprive children of their birthright, which, in that early period, was too firmly established to be subjected to the arbitrary will of the father; and if their interest in the succession had not been greater than that of other heirs, they would not have been distinguished by the appellation of *sui et necessarii heredes.* Further, that among the Romans the power of testing did not originally affect the heirs of the testator's own body, must be evi-<117>dent from the following circumstance, that even after the law of the Twelve Tables, no man had a power to exheredate his own issue, unless in the testament he could specify a just cause, ingratitude, for example,

---

4. "He was also greatly respected for his wide-ranging law concerning testaments. For previously it was not permitted to produce a testament; the wealth and goods of the deceased had to remain with his closest family. He granted the freedom that if he had no children a man could give his goods to whoever he wished, giving preference to friendship over kinship and to kindness over necessity. Thus he ensured that a man's money and property were his own." *Life of Solon,* XXI.

5. "According as a person shall give direction regarding his household chattels or guardianship of his estate, so shall right be." Table V, § 3. Trans. Warmington.

rendering them unworthy of the succession. And the *querela inofficiosi testamenti* was an action introduced in favour of children, for rescinding testaments made in their prejudice, in which no cause of exheredation was assigned, or an unjust cause assigned. It is true, that a man afterward was indulged to disinherit his children without a cause, provided he bequeathed to them the fourth part of what they would have inherited *ab intestato*.* But Justinian[†] restored the old law, declaring, that without a just cause of exheredation specified in the testament, the *querela* shall be competent, notwithstanding his leaving the said fourth part to his son and heir. And this regulation was adopted by the Longobards.[‡]

But though the *sui et necessarii heredes* could not be directly exheredated, it was in the father's power not only by alienations *inter vivos*, but even by contracting debt, to render the succession unprofitable. As soon as the power of aliening becomes a branch of property, every subject belonging to a debtor, land or moveables, must lie open to be attached by his cre-<118>ditors. It is his duty to convert into money the readiest of his subjects for their payment; and if he prove refractory, by refusing to do what in conscience is incumbent upon him, the law will interpose. Justice bestows this privilege upon creditors during their debtor's life; and consequently also after his death; it being inconsistent with justice that the heir should profit by their loss. This new circumstance introduced necessarily an alteration of the law as to the *sui et necessarii heredes:* for now they could no longer be held as necessary heirs, when their being heirs was no longer attended with safety, but might prove ruinous instead of beneficial. The same rule of justice which prevailed in the former case, prevailed also in this, and conferred upon them the privilege of abandoning the succession, in which case their father's debts did not reach them.[‖]

It may appear singular, that while children were thus gradually losing ground, collateral heirs, who originally had no privilege, were in many countries gaining ground. I shall first state the facts, and afterward endeavour to assign the cause. Several nations followed the Grecian plan, in-

---

* L. 8. § 6. De inoff. test. [[I.e., *Codex* 2.18.8.6.]]
† Novel. 115. cap. 3. [[I.e., *Novels* 115.3.]]
‡ L. 2. tit. 14. § 12.
‖ L. 12. De acquir, vel omit. hered. [[I.e., *Digest* 28.2.12.]]

dulging an unlimited power of testing, where the testator had not issue of his own body. Thus, by the Ripuarian law, a man who had no children might dispose of his effects <119> as he thought proper;* and, among the Visigoths, the man who had no descendants might do the same.† But this privilege was more limited among other nations. The power of making a testament, bestowed at large by the Roman law failing children, was afterward confined within narrower bounds. The privilege of children and other descendants to rescind a testament exheredating them without just cause, spread itself upon other near relations; and these therefore might insist in a *querela inofficiosi,* which originally was competent to descendants only.‡ By the laws of the German Saxons, it was not lawful to disinherit the heir.‖ And by the laws of King Alfred, "He who inherits lands derived from his ancestors by writ, shall not have power to alien the same from his heirs, especially if it be proved by writing or witnesses, that the person who made the grant discharged such alienation."§ Thus we see in several instances, the prerogative of a child who is heir, extended in part to other heirs, which, as hinted above, may appear surprising, when the powers of the proprietor in possession over his subject were by this time enlarged, and the right of his children abridged in proportion. <120>

To set this matter in its proper light, I must premise, that originally there was not such a thing as a right of succession, in the sense we now give to that term. Children came in place of their parents: But this was not properly a succession; it was a continuation of possession, founded upon their own title of property. And while the relation of property continued so slight as it was originally, it was perhaps thought sufficient that children *in familia* only should enjoy this privilege. Hence when a man died without children, the land he possessed fell back to the common, ready for the first occupant. But the connection betwixt a man and the land upon which he dwells, having in course of time acquired great stability, is now imagined to subsist even after death. This conception preserves the subject as in a state of

* Lex Ripuariorum, § 48.
† Lex Visigothorum, l. 4. tit. 2. § 20.
‡ L. 1. De inoff. test. [[I.e., *Codex* 2.18.1.]]
‖ Laws of the Saxons, § 14.
§ Lambard's Collection. Laws of King Alfred, l. 37.

appropriation; and consequently bars every person except those who de-
rive right from the deceased. By this means, the right of inheriting the
family estate was probably communicated first to children *forisfamiliate,*
especially if all the children were in that situation; afterward, failing children, to brothers, and so gradually to more distant relations. We have to
this day traces remaining of the gradual progress. In the laws of the Longobards, collaterals succeeded to the seventh degree.* Our countryman
Craig[†] relates it as <121> the opinion of some, that if there be no heirs
within the seventh degree, the king hath right as *ultimus heres.* He indeed
signifies his own opinion to the contrary; and now it is established, That
relations succeed, however distant.

The succession of collaterals, failing descendants, produced a new legal
idea; for as they had no pretext of right independent of the former proprietor, their privilege of succeeding could stand upon no ground but the
presumed will of the deceased, which made them heirs in the proper sense
of the word, succeeding to the right of the deceased, and enjoying his land
by his will. This makes a solid difference betwixt the succession of collaterals, depending on the will of the ancestor, and the succession of descendants, which originally did not depend on his will. But the privilege of
descendants being gradually restrained within narrower and narrower
bounds, was confounded with the hope of succession in collaterals. They
were put upon the same footing, and considered equally as representatives
of the person in whose place they came. This deduction appears natural;
and what I have farther to observe appears no less so, That descendants and
collaterals being thus blended into one class, the privileges of the former
were communicated to the latter.

But the privileges thus acquired by collaterals, were not of long continuance. The powers <122> annexed to property being carried to their utmost
bounds, it came, in most countries which did not adhere to the Roman
law, to be considered as an inherent power in proprietors, to settle their
estates at their pleasure, without regard to their natural heirs, descendants
or collaterals. In this island the power of disposal became unlimited, even

* L. 2. tit. 14. § 1.
[†] L. 2. dieg. 17.

to take effect after death, provided the deed were in the form of an alienation *inter vivos*. The property which children once had in the family estate was no longer in force, except as to one particular, that of barring deeds on deathbed (9). And this, with other privileges of descendants, was <123> communicated to collateral heirs.* In England, the powers of proprietors were so far extended by a law of Henry VIII.,† as to entitle them, without the formality of a deed of alienation, to settle or dispose of their lands by testament; after which, deeds on deathbed could no longer be restrained. In Scotland, the law of deathbed subsists entire, as well as the limitation upon proprietors, that they cannot dispose of their heritable subjects by testament. The former is not now considered as a limitation of the powers of property, but as a personal privilege belonging to heirs: For which reason, a deed on deathbed is not void for want of power: It is an effectual grant till it be voided by the heir upon his privilege. But the latter is plainly a limitation of the powers of property; which shews, that in this country property is more limited than in England. By the old law, a donation had no effect without delivery: For supposing the deed to have contained warrandice, yet this warrandice was not effectual against the heir, who was not bound to pay his father's debts, or fulfil his engagements. Heirs, it is true, are now liable: But then a testament contains no warrandice; and therefore an heritable subject legated by testament is considered, as of old, an incompleat donation, which the heir is <124> not bound to make effectual. But though we admit not of the alienation of an heritable subject by tes-

---

(9) While the law stood as originally, That no man could dispose of his estate in prejudice of his heir, there could not be place for the law of deathbed. This law was a consequence from indulging proprietors to dispose of a part for rational considerations; from which indulgence deathbed was an exception. Hence it appears, that the law of deathbed was not a new regulation introduced into Scotland by statute or custom. It is in reality a branch of the original law, restricting proprietors from aliening their lands in prejudice of their heirs, which original law is still preserved entire in the circumstance of deathbed. Our authors have not been lucky in guessing, when they ascribe the law of deathbed to the wisdom of our forefathers, in order to protect their estates from the rapacity of the clergy. It existed too early among us to make this a probable supposition. In those early times, the prevalence of superstition would have prevented such a regulation, had it been necessary.

* See Glanvil, l. 7. cap. 1.; Reg. Maj. l. 2. cap. 18.
† 34. and 35. Henry VIII. cap. 5. § 4.

tament, alienation is sustained in a form very little different. A disposition of land, though a mere donation, implies warrandice; and therefore such a deed, after the granter's death, supposing it to contain neither procuratory nor precept, will be effectual against his heir. And the difference betwixt this deed and a testament in point of form, is so slight, that it is not to be understood, except by those who are daily conversant in the forms and solemnities of law.

Children by the law of Scotland enjoy another privilege, which is, a certain portion of the father's moveable estate. Of this he cannot deprive them by will, nor by any deed which does not bind himself. This privilege, like that of deathbed, is obviously a branch of the original law; being founded upon the nature of property as originally limited. The power over land is in Scotland not so far extended, as that an incompleat donation will be effectual against the heir, when executed in the form of a testament. The power over moveables is so far extended, as that they can be gifted by testament; but yet not so as to affect the interest which the children have in the moveables. And there is the following analogy between the heir's title to heritage, and that of children to moveables, that <125> both have been converted from rights of property to personal privileges; with this difference only, that the privilege of a child, heir in the land-estate, to bar the father's deathbed-deed, is communicated to other heirs; whereas the privilege of children, respecting the moveable estate, is communicated to descendants only, and not to collaterals.

As a moveable subject is more under the natural power of man than land, so the legal powers of moveable property were brought to perfection more early than of land-property. It may therefore appear whimsical, that the power of aliening moveables should be more limited than that of aliening land. The latter may be aliened from the heir by a deed to take effect after the granter's death: The former cannot be so aliened from the children.[6]

---

6. 1758, 1761: "As a moveable subject . . . from the children" = "Touching the foregoing privilege of children over the moveable estate of their father, one thing must appear whimsical, that the power of aliening moveables should be more limited than that of aliening land. For as a moveable subject is more under the natural power of man than land, so the legal powers of moveable property were brought to perfection more early than of land-property."

Were I to indulge a conjecture in order to account for this branch of our law, it would be what follows. The privilege of children respecting the moveable estate was preserved entire, because it was all along confined to children; but their privilege respecting the real estate having been communicated to collaterals, which put all heirs upon the same level, the character of child was lost in that of heir, and their common privileges sunk together. Thus, though collaterals have profited by being blended <126> in one class with descendants, the latter have been losers by the union.

After so much discourse upon a subject that is subtile and perhaps dry, it will, I presume, be agreeable to the reader, before entering upon the second part, to unbend his mind for a few moments, upon some episodical matters that tend to illustrate the foregoing doctrine. The first shall be the equal division of land-property effectuated in Sparta by Lycurgus. One whose notions are derived from the present condition of land property, must be extremely puzzled about this memorable event; for where is the man to be found, who will peaceably surrender his land to the public without a valuable consideration? And if such a man could be found for a wonder, it would be downright frenzy to expect the same from a whole people: Yet in settling this branch of public police, so singular in its nature, we read not even of the slightest tumult or commotion. The story always appeared to me incredible, till I fell upon the train of thinking above mentioned. In ancient times property of land was certainly not so valuable a right as at present: It was no better than a right of usufruct, a power of using the fruits for the support of the possessor and his family. At the same time, the manner of living anciently was more simple than at present: Men were satisfied with the product of the land they pos-<127>sessed, for their food and raiment. When the foregoing revolution was brought about in Sparta, it is probable, that permutation of commodities, and buying and selling, were not far advanced. If so, it was not refining much to think, that a family is not entitled to the possession of more land than is sufficient for the conveniency of living, especially if any other family of the same tribe be in want. In this view, an equal distribution of land-property, and an agrarian law, might not be so difficult an undertaking, as a person at present will be apt to imagine.

The next episode relates to the Feudal law. Though, by the feudal system, the property remains with the superior, the right given to the vassal being only an usufruct; yet it appears, that both in England and Scotland the vassal was early understood to be proprietor. He could alien his land to be held of himself; and the alienation was effectual to bar the superior even from his casualties of ward, marriage, escheat, &c. This was not solely a vulgar way of thinking; it was deemed to be law by the legislature itself; witness the English statute, *Quia emptores terrarum,* 18 Edward I. cap. 1. & 2.; Statutes Robert I. cap. 25. It may appear not easy to be explained, how a notion should have gained ground so repugnant to the most obvious principles of law. For it might <128> occur, even at first view, that as the property is reserved by the superior, he must be entitled to possess the land, and levy the rents upon all occasions, except where he is excluded by his own deed. And as in every military feu, the superior is entitled to the possession, both while there is no vassal, and while the vassal is young and unable to go to war; how could it be overlooked, that the casualties of non-entry and ward, which are effectual against the vassal, must be equally effectual against every one who comes in his place? I cannot account for this otherwise than by observing, that property originally differed nothing from a right of possession, which gave the enjoyment of the fruits; and therefore, that every man who was in possession, and who had the enjoyment of the fruits, was readily conceived to be proprietor. This was the case of the vassal; and accordingly, when the power of alienation came to be considered as an inherent branch of property, it was thought, that a grant made by the vassal of part of the land, or even of the whole, to be held of himself, must be effectual.

One episode more before we return to the principal subject. So great anxiety in the Roman legislature to restrain men from doing injustice to their own children, has a very odd appearance. "Children are not to be exheredated without a just cause, chiefly that of in-<129>gratitude. The cause must be set forth in the testament: It must be tried before the judge, and verified by witnesses, if denied."[7] Among other nations, natural affection without the aid of law, is a sufficient motive with parents to do full justice to their children. Shall we admit, that natural affection was at a lower ebb among the Romans than among other people? It would seem so. Yet the Romans, in the more early periods of their history, were a brave and

7. Kames here summarizes *Novels* 115.3.

gallant people, fond of their country, and consequently, one should think, of their children. Whence then should proceed want of parental affection? I do not suppose they were left unprovided by nature: But laws and customs have a strong influence to produce manners contrary to Nature. Let us examine the *patria potestas,* as established by the Roman law. By the law of Nature, the *patria potestas* is bestowed on the father for the sake of the child; and tends to produce in time a reciprocal affection, the strongest our nature is capable of. Nature lays the foundation: Continual attention, on the one hand, to promote the good of a beloved object, and, on the other, continual returns of gratitude, augment mutual affection, till the mind be incapable of any addition. If in any instance the event be different, it must be occasioned, either by a wrong application of the *patria potestas,* or by an extreme perverse dispo-<130>sition in the child. But was the *patria potestas* among the Romans established upon the plan of nature? Quite the contrary. It was the power of a tyrant over slaves. A man could put his children to death. He could sell them for a price; and if they obtained their liberty by good luck or good behaviour, he could sell them a second and a third time. These unnatural powers were perhaps not often put in exercise; but they were lawful. This very circumstance is sufficient to produce severity in parents, and fear and diffidence in children. There is not like to be in this case more harmony, than in pure despotism betwixt the awful monarch and his trembling slaves. In short, the Roman *patria potestas,* and the legal restraint proprietors were laid under not to hurt their own children, serve to illustrate each other: There could be no cordiality where such restraints were necessary. We have reason beforehand to conjecture, that the *patria potestas* must have had some such effect; and we have reason to be pleased with our conjecture, when we find it justified by substantial facts.

Putting now an end to episodical amusements, we proceed with new vigour in our historical course. It was interrupted at that part, where, with a very few exceptions, the powers of a proprietor were extended, one should think, their utmost length. Every man had the full enjoy-<131>ment of his own subject, while it remained with him. He might dispose of it for a valuable consideration, without any restraint. He might do the same for love and favour; and his power reached even so far, as to direct what person or persons should have the enjoyment of it after his death. Would any moderate man covet more power over the goods of fortune that fall to his share? No moderate man will covet more. But many are the men whose thirst of power is never to be quenched. They wish to combine their name, family, and estate, in the strictest union; and, leaving nothing to Providence, they wish to prolong this union to the end of time. Such ambitious views, ill suiting the frail condition of humanity, have produced entails in this island; and would have done so in old Rome, had such settlements been found consistent with the nature of property.

Being arrived at entails in our historical course, it will be necessary to discuss a preliminary question, Whether and how far they are consistent with the nature of property? In order to answer this question, some principles of law must be premised. The first respects every subject of property, that the whole powers of property, whether united in one person, or distributed among a plurality, must subsist entire somewhere; and that none of them can be sunk or annihilated, so as to be beneficial to no per-<132>son. The reason will be obvious when we consider, that the goods of fortune are intended for the use of man; and that it is contrary to their nature to be withdrawn from use in whole or in part. A man, if he please, may abandon his subject; but in that case, no will nor purpose of his can prevent the right of the first occupant. No law, natural or municipal, gives such effect to the will of any man. Therefore, if I shall divest myself of any moveable subject, bestowing it upon my friend, but declaring, that though he himself may enjoy the subject, he shall have no power of disposal, such a deed will not be effectual in law. If I be totally divested, he must be totally invested; and consequently must have the power of alienation. The same must hold in a disposition of land. If the granter reserve no right to himself, the entire property must be transferred to the disponee, however express the granter's will may be to confine the disponee's property within narrower bounds.

Secondly, Though none of the powers of property can be annihilated by will or consent, a proprietor however may, by will or consent, limit himself in the exercise of his property, for the benefit of others. Such limitations are effectual in law, and are at the same time perfectly consistent with absolute property. If a man be put in chains, or shut up in a dungeon, his property in a legal sense is as entire as ever; <133> though at present he is deprived of the use or enjoyment of the subjects which belong to him. In like manner, a civil obligation, subjecting the proprietor to damages and forfeiture, may restrain him by terror from the free use of his own subject: But such restraint limits not his right to the subject, more than restraint by walls or chains.

A third principle will bring the present subject fully within view. A practice was derived from Greece to Rome, of adopting a son when a man had not issue of his own body. This was done in a solemn manner before the *Calata Comitia,* who in Rome possessed the legislative authority. The adopted son had all the privileges of one born in lawful wedlock; he had the same interest in the family-estate, the same right to continue the father's possession, and to have the full enjoyment of the subject. A testament, when authorised by the law of the Twelve Tables, received its form from this practice. A testament was understood to be only a different form of adopting a son, which bestowed the same privilege of succeeding to the family-estate after the testator's death, that belonged to the heir adopted in the *Calata Comitia.* A testament is in Britain a *donatio mortis causa,* an alienation to take effect after death; and the legatee does not succeed as heir, but takes as purchaser, in the same manner as if a formal dona-<134>tion were made in his favour, to have a present effect. In Rome, as hinted, a testament was of a different nature. It was not a conveyance of land or goods from one person to another; it entirely consisted in the nomination of an heir, who in this character enjoyed the testator's effects. The person named took the heritage as heir, not as purchaser. This explains a maxim in the Roman law, widely differing from our notions, that a man cannot die *pro parte testatus et pro parte intestatus;* and that if in a testament one be named heir, and limited to a particular subject, he notwithstanding is of necessity heir to the whole.

The privilege of adoption was never known in Britain; nor have we any form of a writ similar to a Roman testament, which a man could use, if he were disposed to exclude his natural heir, and to name another in his place. Testaments we had early; but not in the form of a nomination of heirs. This writ is a species of alienation, whether we consider moveables, which is its sole province in Scotland, or land, to which in England it was extended by the above-mentioned statute of Henry VIII. Therefore, by the common law of this land, there is no method for setting aside the natural heirs, otherwise than by an alienation of the estate *inter vivos* or *mortis causa*. Nor in this case does the disponee take as heir; he takes as pur-<135>chaser; and the natural heirs are not otherwise excluded, than by making the succession unprofitable to them. This may serve to explain a maxim in our old law, which, to those educated in the Roman notions, must appear obscure, if not unintelligible. The maxim is, That God only can make an heir, not man.* The Roman testament laid a foundation for a distinction among heirs. They were either *heredes nati* or *heredes facti*. Our common law acknowledges no such distinction: No man can have the character of an heir but an heir of blood.

We are now, I presume, sufficiently prepared to enter upon the intricate subject of entails. And to prevent the embarrassment of too much matter on hand together, we shall first examine the power of substituting a series of heirs to each other, who are to take the heritage in their order, exclusive of the natural heirs; and then proceed to the limitations imposed upon heirs, which prevent alienation, whether direct by disponing land, or indirect by contracting debt. A maxim in the Roman law, concerning heirs, is necessary in explaining the first point. A Roman testator could name any person to be his heir, but he had not the power to name substitutes; for thus says the maxim, NO MAN CAN NAME AN HEIR TO SUCCEED TO HIS HEIR. The reason will appear when we reflect upon <136> some particulars already explained. The heir, whether *natus* or *factus,* became unlimited proprietor as soon as the predecessor was dead. The inheritance was now his, and entirely at his disposal. If he made a testament, the heir named by him took place of the heir named by his predecessor; and if he died *intestate,* the succession opened to his own natural heirs. For it is the will of the proprietor that must regulate his own succession; and not the will of any other, not even of a predecessor. This maxim then is not founded upon any peculiarity in the Roman law, but upon the very nature of property. While a subject is mine, it is entirely at my disposal; but after bestowing it upon another without any reservation, my power is at an end; and my will,

* Glanvil, l. 7. cap. 1; Reg. Maj. l. 2. cap. 20. § 4.

though expressed while I was proprietor, cannot now have the effect to limit the power of the present proprietor.[8] An heir named in a Roman testament, might, it is true, be subjected personally to whatever burdens or obligations the testator thought proper to impose upon him: But we ought not to lose sight of the difference betwixt a real burden or limitation and a personal obligation. A man, by his own consent, may restrain himself from the use of his property; but the full property nevertheless remains with him.

One exception to this rule was introduced from utility, viz. the pupillar substitution. A <137> proprietor who had a son under age to succeed him as his heir, was impowered to name a substitute, who took the estate as heir to the son, in case the son died so early as to be incapable of making a testament. In all other cases, if a testator, after naming his heir, inclined to make a substitution, he had no other method but to take the heir bound personally to make over the estate to the substitute. This form of a settlement is known by the name of *Fideicommissum.* And after the substitute succeeded by virtue of the *fideicommissary* clause, there was an end of the entail.

The foregoing maxim, That no man can regulate the succession of his heir, holds in property only, not in inferior rights. If a proprietor grant a right burdening or limiting his property, and call to the succession a certain series of heirs, it is clear, that neither the grantee nor any of the heirs named, who accept the right in these terms, have power, without the consent of the granter or his heirs, to alter the order of succession. In the practice even of the Roman law, where the foresaid maxim was inviolable, it was never doubted, that in a perpetual lease, termed *Emphyteusis,* or in any lease, it is in the power of the granter to regulate the succession of the lessee. For the same reason, in our feudal rights, a perpetual succession of heirs established in the original grant, is consistent with <138> the strictest principles of prop-

8. 1758 and 1761 add a note here: "The coins of a Roman emperor had scarce any currency after his death; and therefore the first act of power generally was to recoin the money of the former emperor [Walker's Grecian and Roman history, illustrated by medals, page 15]. It was the present emperor's will only which could give authority to publick money, or to any other publick concern. This serves to illustrate the principle, That a man's will after his death cannot have the effect to regulate conduct, or limit the property of the next successor; particularly, that it cannot have the effect to limit the successor with regard to the choice of his own heir."

erty. The order of succession cannot be altered without consent of the superior; for it would be a breach of agreement, to force upon him as vassal any person who is not called to the succession by the original grant. And thus in Britain it came to be an established practice, by means of the feudal system, not that a man singly can name an heir to his heir; but that, with consent of the superior, he can substitute heirs without end, to take the feudal subject successively one after another (10).

The persons thus called to the succession of the feudal subject, are in Scotland understood to be heirs to the original grantee, whether they be of his blood or not. This way of thinking is borrowed from the Roman law, in which every person is esteemed an heir who is <139> called by will to the succession. He is at least *heres factus,* according to their language, if not *heres natus.* In this we have deviated from our own common law, which acknowledges none to be an heir who is not of the predecessor's blood.

In England different notions have obtained. The maxim, That God only can make an heir, not man, is not so strictly taken, as to exclude every person from the character of an heir, save the heir at law only. From the beginning nothing was more common in feudal grants, than to chuse a certain species of heirs, such as the male descendents of the original vassal, or the heirs of a marriage. These are heirs in the sense of the English law, though they may happen not to be the heirs who would succeed by law. Hence every person who is called to the succession under a general description, such as heirs of the granter's body, or male issue, or heirs of a marriage, or male issue of a marriage, is considered as an heir. The true sense of the maxim appears then to be, That no person can have the character of an heir who is not of the blood of the original vassal: Also, that it is not sufficient to be of the blood, unless he be also called under some general description. Therefore,

(10) According to the original constitution of a feudal holding, a perpetual succession was established on a foundation still more clear and indisputable. A feudal holding, while it was beneficiary and not patrimonial, admitted not, properly speaking, of a succession of heirs. When a vassal died, the subject returned to the superior, who made a new grant in favour of the heir called to the succession in the original grant; and so on till all the heirs were exhausted to whom the succession was originally limited; after which the subject returned simply and absolutely to the superior. The title, therefore, of possession being a new grant from the superior, the persons called to the succession could not properly be considered as heirs but as purchasers.

in England, when a stranger or any man is by name called to the succession, he is understood to be called as a conditional institute; <140> precisely as if one grant were made to Sempronius and the heirs of his body; and another grant of the same subject to Titius and the heirs of his body, to take effect whenever the heirs of Sempronius should fail. Titius, in this case, is not called in the quality of an heir to Sempronius: he is, as well as Sempronius, an institute, or a disponee; only that the right of Sempronius is pure, and that of Titius conditional. This conditional right is in England termed a *Remainder;* and as a remainder-man is not considered to be an heir, he is not liable to fulfil any of the debts or deeds of the first institute, or of his heirs; and when these heirs are exhausted, he takes, not by a service upon a brieve *quod diem clausit supremum,* but as purchaser, by authority of the original grant.

Thus it is, that the Feudal law, by furnishing means for a perpetual succession of heirs as in Scotland, or of heirs and remainder men as in England, hath fostered the ambitious views of men to preserve their names, families, and possessions, in perpetual existence. The feudal system, as originally constituted, was qualified to fulfil such views in every particular. It not only paved the way for a perpetual succession, but secured the heirs by preventing dilapidation.

And this leads naturally to the second point proposed to be handled with respect to entails, viz. The limitations imposed upon heirs to pre-<141>vent aliening or contracting debt. This followed from the very nature of the feudal system; for the vassal's right, being a liferent or usufruct only, gave him no power of alienating the property, which remained with the superior. It was only unlucky for entails, that during the vigour of the Feudal law, constant wars and commotions, a perpetual hurry in attacking or defending, afforded very little time for indulging views of perpetuity. In times only of peace, security, and plenty, do men dream of distant futurity, and of perpetuating their estates in their families. The Feudal law lost ground in times of peace. It was a violent and unnatural system, which could not be long supported in contradiction to love of independence and property, the most steady and industrious of all the human appetites. After a regular government was introduced in Britain, which favoured the arts of peace, all men conspired to overthrow the Feudal system. The vassal was willing

to purchase independence with his money; and the superior, who had no
longer occasion for military tenants, disposed of his land to better advantage. In this manner, land, which is the chief object of avarice, came again
to be the chief subject of commerce: And that this was early the case in
Britain, we have undoubted evidence from the famous statute, *Quia emptores terrarum* above mentioned. By this time the <142> strict principles of
the Feudal law had vanished, and scarce any thing was left but the form
only. Land, now restored to commerce, was mostly in the hands of purchasers who had paid a valuable consideration; and consequently, instead
of being beneficiary as formerly, it had now become patrimonial. The property being thus transferred from the superior to the vassal, the vassal's power
of alienation was a necessary consequence.

But men who had acquired great possessions, and who, in quiet times,
found leisure to think of perpetuating their families, began now to regret
the never-ceasing flux of land-property from hand to hand; and, revolving
the history of former times, to wish for the wonted stability of land-
property, if it could be obtained without subjecting themselves to the slav-
ish dependence of the Feudal law. In particular, when a grant of land was
made to a family, conditioned to return to the granter and his heirs when
the family was at an end, it was thought hard, that the vassal, contrary to
the condition of his right, could sell the land, or dispose of it at his pleasure,
as if he had been a purchaser for a full price. To fulfil the intention of those
who after this manner should make voluntary settlements of land, the English, after the fetters of the Feudal law were gone, found that a statute was
necessary; and to this end the statute *de* <143> *donis conditionalibus* was
made.* It proceeds upon the recital, 1st, Of land given to a man and his
wife, and their issue, conditionally, that if they die without issue, the land
shall revert to the giver and his heirs. 2dly, Of land given in free marriage,
which implies a condition, though not expressed, that if the husband and
wife die without issue, the land shall revert to the giver or his heirs. And,
3dly, Of land given to a man and the heirs of his body, conditionally, that
it shall, in like manner, revert, failing issue. It subsumes, that, contrary to
the conditions expressed or implied in such grants, the feoffees had power

* 13 Edward I. cap. 1.

to alien the land, to the disappointment not only of the heirs, as to their right of succession, but also of the donor, as to his right of reversion. Therefore it is enacted, "That the will of the donor shall be from henceforth observed, so that the donees shall have no power to alien the land, but that it shall remain to the issue chosen in the deed, and when they fail, shall revert to the donor or his heirs." And thus in England, a privilege was bestowed upon proprietors of land, to establish perpetuities by depriving the heirs of the power of aliening, which could not be done by common law.

In Scotland we had no statute authorising entails till the 1685,[9] though before that time we <144> had entails in plenty, many of which are still subsisting. It was the opinion of our lawyers, as it would appear, that by private authority an entail can be made so as to bar alienation. To this end, clauses prohibitory, irritant, and resolutive, were contrived, which were reckoned effectual to preserve an entailed subject to the heirs in their order, and to void every deed prejudicial to these heirs. Whether this be a just way of thinking I proceed to examine.

To preserve the subject in view, I take the liberty shortly to recapitulate what is said above on this point. While the Feudal law was in vigour, there was no occasion for prohibitory clauses: The vassal's right being usufructuary only, carried not the power of alienation, nor of contracting debt, so as to be effectual against the heir of the investiture. But the Feudal law is in England quite extirpated; nor doth it subsist in Scotland except merely as to the form of our title-deeds. Land with us has for several ages been considered as patrimonial. A vassal has long enjoyed the power of contracting debt, and even of alienating *mortis causa*. To restrain him therefore in any degree from the exercise of his property, can only be effectuated by statute or by consent. The former requires no discussion. It is evident, that the restraints imposed by statute, of whatever nature, must be effectual; because every deed <145> done in contempt of the law, is voidable, if not null and void. The latter requires a more particular examination, before we can form an accurate judgment of its effects. For the sake of perspicuity, we shall adapt our reasoning to an entail made in the common form, with a long series of heirs, guarded only with a prohibitory clause, directed

9. Kames refers to the act "concerning tailzies" dated 30 May 1685.

against every one of the heirs of entail, in order to restrain them from aliening and from contracting debt. It is plain, that every single heir, who accepts the succession, is bound by this prohibition, as far as he can be
bound by his own consent. His very acceptance of the deed, vouched by
his serving heir and taking possession, subjects him to the prohibition; for
justice permits no man to take benefit by a deed without fulfilling the provisions and burdens imposed on him in the deed. Admitting then, that the
heir is bound by his acceptance, let us enquire, whether that be sufficient
to make the entail effectual. He transgresses the prohibition, and sells the
estate: Will not the purchaser be secure, leaving to the heirs of entail an
action against the vender for damages? Whatever may be thought of a purchaser who buys knowingly from an heir of entail, in whom it is a breach
of duty to sell, a *bona fide* purchaser must undoubtedly be secure. Or let
us suppose the estate to be adjudged for payment of debt. It is necessity
and not choice <146> that makes a creditor proceed to legal execution: And
supposing him to be in the knowledge of the restraint, there can be no
injustice in his taking the benefit of the law to make his claim effectual.
Hence it is plain, that a prohibition cannot alone have the effect to secure
the estate against the debts and deeds of the tenant in tail.

   To supply this defect, lawyers have invented a resolutive or irritant clause,
for voiding the right of a tenant in tail, who, contrary to a prohibition,
aliens or contracts debt. That a resolutive or irritant clause cannot have the
same effect with a legal forfeiture, is even at first view evident. A forfeiture
is one of the punishments introduced for repressing certain heinous crimes;
and it is inconsistent with the nature of the thing, that a person should be
punished who is not a criminal. An alienation by a tenant in tail, in opposition to the will of the entailer, is no doubt a wrong: But then it is only
a civil wrong inferring damages, and not a delinquency to infer any sort of
punishment; far less a punishment of the severest kind, which at any rate
cannot be inflicted but by authority of a statute. If now a resolutive or
irritant clause cannot have any effect as a punishment, its effect, if any, must
depend on the consent of the tenant in tail, who accepts the deed of entail
under the conditions and provisions contained in it. Such <147> implied
consent, taken in its utmost latitude, cannot be more binding than an express consent signified by the heir in writing, binding himself to abandon

his right to the land, upon the first act of transgression, or of contravention as we call it, whether by aliening or contracting debt. This device to secure an entailed subject, though it hath exhausted the whole invention of the learned in our law, is however singularly unlucky, seeing it cannot be clothed in such words, as to hide, or even obscure, a palpable defect. The consent here is in its nature conditional: "I shall abandon if I transgress or contravene any of the prohibitions." Therefore, from the very nature of the thing, there can be no abandon till there first be an act of contravention. This is no less clear than that the crime must precede the punishment. Where then is the security that arises from a resolutive clause? A tenant in tail agrees to sell by the lump: A disposition is made out—nothing wanting but the subscription: The disponer takes a pen in his hand, and begins to write his name. During this act there is no abandon nor forfeiture, because as yet there is no alienation. Let it be so, that the forfeiture takes place upon the last stroke of the pen: But then the alienation is also completed by the same stroke; and the land is gone past redemption. The defect is still more palpable, if possible, in <148> the case of contracting debt. No man can subsist without contracting debt more or less; and no lawyer has been found so chimerical as to assert, that the contracting debt singly will produce a forfeiture. All agree, that the debtor's right is forfeited no sooner than when the debt is secured upon the land by an adjudication. But what avails the forfeiture after the debt is made real and secured upon the land? In a word, before the adjudication be completed, there can be no forfeiture, and after it is completed the forfeiture comes too late.

But this imperfection of a resolutive or irritant clause, though clear and certain, needed scarce to have been mentioned; because it will make no figure in comparison with another, which I now proceed to unfold. Let us suppose, contrary to the nature of things, that the forfeiture could precede the crime; or let us suppose the very simplest case, that a tenant in tail consents to abandon his right without any condition; what will follow? It is a rule in law, which never has been called in question, That consent alone without delivery cannot transfer property. Nay, it is universally admitted, that consent alone cannot even have the effect to divest the consenter of his property, till another be invested; or, which comes to the same, that one infeftment cannot be taken away but by another. If so, what avails a resolutive clause more than <149> one that is simply prohibitory? Suppose the consent to abandon, which at first was conditional, is now purified by an act of contravention; the tenant in tail is indeed laid open to have his right voided, and the land taken from him: But still he remains proprietor, and his infeftment stands good till the next heir be infeft; or at least till the next heir obtain a decree declaring the forfeiture. Before such process be commenced, every debt contracted by the tenant in tail, and every disposition granted by him, must be effectual, being deeds of a man, who at the time of executing was proprietor. In fine, a consent to abandon, supposing it purified, can in no view have a stronger effect, than a contract of sale executed by a proprietor who is under no limitation. All the world know, that this will not bar him from selling the land a second time to a different person, who getting the first infeftment will be secure; leaving no remedy to the first purchaser, but an action of damages against the vender. In like manner, a tenant in tail, after transgressing every prohibition contained in the entail, and after all the irritancies have taken place, continues still proprietor, until a decree declaring the irritancy be obtained; and such being the case, it follows of necessary consequence, that every debt contracted by him, and every deed <150> done by him, while there is yet no declarator, must be effectual against the entailed estate.

I am aware, that in the decision, 26th February 1662, Viscount of Stormont *contra* heirs of line and creditors of the Earl of Annandale, prohibitory and resolutive clauses engrossed in the infeftment were sustained, as being equivalent to an interdiction; every man being presumed to know the condition of the person with whom he deals. But it appears probable, that this judgment was obtained by a prevailing attachment to entails, which at that time had the grace of novelty, and were not seen in their proper light. There is certainly no ground for bestowing the force of an interdiction upon prohibitory and resolutive clauses in an entail. An interdiction is a writ of the common law, prohibiting the proprietor to sell without consent of his interdictors, and prohibiting every person to deal with him without such consent. It is notified to all and sundry by a solemn act of publication, which puts every person *in mala fide* to deal with a proprietor who is interdicted; and it is a contempt of legal authority to transgress the prohibition. But where lies the contempt of legal authority in a fair purchase from an heir of entail? An entailer may give law to his heirs, but what authority has he over strangers to prohibit them to lend money to his heir, or to purchase from him? An interdiction be-<151>side is appointed to be published, without which it has no force: But before the 1685, there was no law for publishing the conditions of an entail.[10] It has indeed been urged, that there is no necessity for publication, because every man is presumed to be acquainted with the circumstances of those with whom he contracts. I deny there is any such legal presumption. In fact, nothing is more common than to execute a contract of sale, without seeing any of the title-deeds of the subject purchased; and a discovery afterward of the entail will not oblige the purchaser to relinquish a profitable bargain. At any rate, the contract of sale must operate to him, if not a performance of the bargain, at least a claim of damages against the vender, either of which destroys the entail. What if the creditors of the tenant in tail, or perhaps of the entailer, have arrested the price in the hands of the purchaser? He cannot afterward hurt the arresters by passing from the contract of sale. Let us put another case, That entailed lands, after being sold and the purchaser infeft, have passed through several hands by similar purchases. It surely will not be affirmed, that the last purchaser, in possession of the land, must be presumed to know that the land was derived from a tenant in tail. This would be stretching a presumption very far. But I need not go farther than the contracting of debt, to show the weakness <152> of the argument from presumed knowledge. Persons without their consent become creditors every day, who furnish goods or work for ready money, and yet obtain not payment; sometimes against their will, as when a claim of damages is founded upon a wrong done. When one becomes cautioner for his friend, it is not usual to consult title-deeds. In short, so little foundation is there for this presumption of knowledge, that the act 24. parl. 1695, made for the relief of those who contract with heirs-apparent, is founded upon the direct opposite presumption.

10. 1758, 1761: "But where lies . . . conditions of an entail." = "Prohibitory and resolutive clauses in an entail, being provisions in a private deed, have no authority except against the heir who consents to them; because none except the heir are supposed to know, or bound to know them: and therefore, such clauses notwithstanding, every person is in *optima fide* to deal with the tenant in tail."

Some eminent lawyers, aware of the foregoing difficulties, have endeavoured to support entails, by conceiving a tenant in tail to be in effect but a liferenter, precisely as of old when the Feudal law was in vigour. What it is that operates this limitation of right, they do not say. Nor do they say upon what authority their opinion is founded: Not surely upon any entail that ever was made. If the full property be in the entailer, it must be equally so in every heir of entail who represents him; because, such as he has it, it is conveyed to the heirs of entail whole and undivided, without reserving any share to himself or to a separate set of heirs. But the very form of an entail is sufficient to confute this opinion: For why so many anxious prohibitory and irritant clauses, if a tenant in <153> tail were restrained from aliening by the limited nature of his right? Fetters are very proper where one can do mischief; but they make a most ridiculous figure upon the weak and timorous, incapable of doing the least harm.

What is said on this head may be contracted within narrower bounds. It resolves into a proposition, vouched by our lawyers, and admitted by our judges in all their reasonings upon the subject of entails, viz. That a resolutive clause when incurred, doth not *ipso facto* forfeit the tenant in tail, but only makes his right voidable, by subjecting him to a declarator of forfeiture; and that there is no forfeiture till a decree of declarator be obtained. Such being the established doctrine with respect to irritant clauses, I never can cease wondering, to find it a general opinion, that an entail with such clauses is effectual by the common law. For what proposition can be more clear than the following, That as long as a man remains proprietor, his debts must be effectual against his land as well as against himself? What comparison can be more accurate, than betwixt a tenant in tail who has incurred an irritancy, and a feuer who has neglected to pay his feu-duties for two years? Both of them are subjected to a declarator of irritancy, and both of them will be forfeited by a decree of declarator. But an adjudication upon the feuer's debt, before commencing the <154> declarator, will be effectual upon the land. This was never doubted; and there is as little reason to doubt, that an adjudication upon the debt of a tenant in tail, must, in the same circumstances, be equally effectual. If there be a difference, it favours the latter, who cannot be stript of his right till it be acquired by another; whereas a bare extinction of the feuer's right is sufficient to the superior. I cannot account for an opinion void of all foundation, otherwise than from the weight of authority. Finding entails current in England, we were by force of imitation led to think, they might be equally effectual here; being ignorant, or not adverting, that in England their whole efficacy is derived from statute.

I shall conclude this tract with a brief reflection upon the whole. While the world was rude and illiterate, the relation of property was faint and obscure. This relation was gradually unfolded, and in its growth toward maturity accompanied the growing sagacity of mankind, till it became vigorous and authoritative, as we find it at present. Men are fond of power, especially over what they call their own; and all men conspired to make the powers of property as extensive as possible. Many centuries have passed since property was carried to its utmost length. No moderate man can desire more than to have the free disposal of his goods <155> during his life, and to name the persons who shall enjoy them after his death. Old Rome, as well as Greece, acknowledged these powers to be inherent in property; and these powers are sufficient for all the purposes to which goods of fortune can be subservient: They fully answer the purposes of commerce; and they fully answer the purposes of benevolence. But the passions of men are not to be confined within the bounds of reason: We thirst after opulence; and are not satisfied with the full enjoyment of the goods of fortune, unless it be also in our power to give them a perpetual existence, and to preserve them for ever to ourselves and our families. This purpose, we are conscious, cannot be fully accomplished; but we approach to it the nearest we can, by the aid of imagination. The man who has amassed great wealth, cannot think of quitting his hold; and yet, alas! he must die and leave the enjoyment to others. To colour a dismal prospect, he makes a deed, arresting fleeting property, securing his estate to himself, and to those who represent him, in an endless succession: His estate and his heirs must for ever bear his name; every thing to perpetuate his memory and his wealth. How unfit for the frail condition of mortals are such swoln conceptions? The feudal system unluckily suggested a hint for gratifying this irrational appetite. Entails in England, authorised by statute, <156> spread every where with great rapidity, till becoming a public nuisance, they were checked and defeated by the authority of judges without a statute. It was a wonderful blindness in our legislature, to encourage entails by a statute, at a time when the public interest required a statute against those which had already been imposed upon us. A great proportion of our land is already, by authority of the statute 1685, exempted from commerce. To this dead stock portions of land are daily added by new entails; and if the British legislature interpose not, the time in which the whole will be locked up, is not far distant. How pernicious this event must prove, need not to be explained. Land-property, naturally one of the great blessings of life, is thus converted into a curse. That entails are subversive of industry and commerce, is not the worst that justly can be said of them: They appear in a still more disagreeable light, when viewed with relation to those more immediately affected. A snare they are to the thoughtless proprietor, who, even by a single act, may be entangled past hope of relief: To the cautious they are a perpetual source of discontent, by subverting that liberty and independence, to which all men aspire, with respect to their possessions as well as their persons. <157>

❧ TRACT IV ❧

Securities upon Land
for Payment of Debt

Land is not only the most valuable subject of commerce, but the most commodious by admitting a variety of real rights.[1] Thus the property of land is split, between superior and vassal, debtor and creditor, and between one having a perpetual, one a temporary right.

In Scotland we distinguish, and not without reason, rights affecting land into two kinds, viz. property, and a right burdening or limiting property. The property of a subject cannot otherwise be bounded but by rights burdening or narrowing it; and it is restored to its original unbounded state, as soon as the burdening right is extinguished: But a burdening right, being in its nature bounded, becomes not more extensive by the extinction of other rights affecting the same subject. The English differ in their notions of land-rights, at least in their terms. Without distinguishing property from other rights, they conceive every right affecting land, the most extensive and the most limited, to be <158> an estate in the land. A fee-simple, a fee-tail, a liferent, a rent-charge, a lease for life, pass all equally under the denomination of an estate.[2]

---

1. 1758, 1761: "Land is not only . . . a variety of real rights." = "The multiplied connections among individuals in society, and their various transactions, have bestowed a privilege upon land-property, not only of being transferred from hand to hand whole and entire, but of being split into parts, and being distributed among many. Land is the great object of commerce, and it is useful not only by its product, but by affording the highest security that can be given for payment of debt."

2. 1758: paragraph continues: "And in this sense it is very consistent, that different persons may, at the same time, possess estates in the same land."

The grafting on land rights of such different kinds, favourable indeed to commerce, makes law intricate, and purchases insecure: But these inconveniencies are unavoidable in a commercial country. Land is not divisible indefinitely; for the possession of a smaller quantity than what occupies a plough or a spade, is of no use: And he who possesses the smallest profitable share, may be engaged in transactions and connections, not fewer nor less various than he who possesses a large territory. It may be his will to make a settlement, containing remainders, reversions, rent-charges, &c.; and it is the province of municipal law, to make effectual, as far as utility will admit, private deeds and conventions of every sort. This is so evident, that whereever we read of great simplicity in the manner of transmitting land-property, we may assuredly pronounce, that the people are not far advanced in the arts of life.

The foregoing cursory view of land-rights, leads to the subject proposed to be handled in this essay. The Romans had two forms of a right upon land for security of money. The one, distinguished by the name of *antichresis,* resembles the English mortgage, and our wadset; the creditor being introduced into posses-<159>sion to levy the rents for extinguishing the sum that is due him. The other, termed a *hypothec,* is barely a security for money, without power to levy the rents for payment. As to the former, whether any solemnity was requisite to compleat the right, I cannot say, because that sort of security is but slightly mentioned in Justinian's compilations: Neither is it told us whether any form was requisite to compleat the latter. One thing seems evident with respect to a hypothec, that an act of possession, whether real or symbolical, cannot be required as a solemnity. But as it is difficult to conceive, that a right can be established upon land by consent alone, without some ouvert act, therefore in Holland there is required to the constitution of a hypothec upon land or houses, the presence of a judge.* And in Friesland, to complete a general hypothec, so as to give it preference, registration is necessary.†

By the Roman law, to make a hypothec effectual, when payment could not be obtained from the debtor, the creditor was impowered to expose the

---

* Voet, tit. De pignor. et hypoth. § 9. & 10. [[I.e., *Commentarius ad Pandectas,* Bk. 20, Tit. 1, §§ 9–10: vol. i, pp. 852–54.]]

† Ibid. § 10. [[I.e., *Commentarius ad Pandectas,* Bk. 20, Tit. 1, § 10: vol. i, pp. 853–54.]]

land to sale after repeated denunciations. He needed not the authority of
a judge; and as he himself was the vender, he for that reason could not be
also the purchaser. But Voet* observes, that in Holland the authority <160>
of a judge being necessary, and the judge being the vender, the creditor may
be the purchaser.

It appears to have been of old, both in England and Scotland, a lawful
practice, to force payment of debt, by taking at short hand from the debtor
a pledge, which was detained by the creditor till the debtor repledged the
same, by paying the debt, or finding security for the payment. This rough
practice was in England prohibited by the statute 52d Henry III. cap. 1.
enacting, "That no man take a distress of his neighbour without award of
court." In Scotland it was restrained by several statutes. In the first statutes
Robert I. cap. 7. it is enacted, "That in time coming no man take a poynd
for debt within another man's land, unless the king's baillie, or the baillie
of the ground be present." And in the statutes of David II. cap. 6. "That
if a man dwelling in one shire desire to take a poynd in another shire, it
must be done in presence of the sheriff or his depute." Again, in the statutes
of Robert III. cap. 12. it is enacted in general, "That no man shall take a
poynd without the King's officers or the lord's officers of the land, unless
within his own land, for his farms or proper debts." See to the same purpose,
Reg. Maj. l. 4. cap. 22.

But these regulations did not extend to poinding within a royal borough.
For though a bur-<161>gess might not poind a brother-burgess without
licence from the provost,[†] yet from a stranger found within the borough
he might take a poind or pledge at short hand;[‡] and the stranger was obliged
to repledge in common form, by finding a surety for the debt.[||] This is ev-
idently the foundation of a privilege which burgesses enjoy at this day, viz.
arresting strangers for debts contracted within the borough.

Neither did these regulations extend to rents or feu duties, for which in
England the landlord may to this day distrain at short hand. And in this
part of the island, as a proprietor might poind at short hand for his house-

---

* Tit. De destruct. pignor. § 3. [[I.e., *Commentarius ad Pandectas,* Bk. 20, Tit. 5, § 3:
vol. i, pp. 906–7.]]

† Leg. Burg. cap. 4.

‡ Cap. 34. & 58.

|| Cap. 35. & 37.

mail,* and for his rents in the country,† so this privilege is expressly reserved to him in the above-mentioned statute of Robert III. This privilege of the landlord may be traced down to the present time; with some restrictions introduced by change of manners. Craig observes,‡ That the landlord for three terms rent can poind by his private authority; and‖ that for the price of the seisin-ox, which the vassal pays for his entry, the superior may distrain without process. Nor at present is the landlord or superior <162> subjected to the ordinary solemnities. It is required, indeed, that the arrears be constituted by a decree in his own court, which has been introduced in imitation of poinding for other debts; but after constituting the arrears by a decree, he may proceed directly to poind without giving a charge.§

Nor is it difficult to discover the foundation of this privilege. It will appear in a clear light by tracing the history of leases in this island. Lands originally were occupied by bond-men, who themselves were the property of the landlord, and consequently were not capable to hold any property of their own: But such persons, who had no interest to be industrious, and who were under no compulsion when not under the eye of their master, were generally lazy, and always careless. This made it eligible to have a free-man to manage the farm; who probably at first got some acres set apart to him for his maintenance and wages. But this not being a sufficient spur to industry, it was found a salutary measure to assume this man as a partner, by communicating to him a proportion of the product in place of wages; by which he came to manage for his own interest as well as that of his master. The next step had still a better effect, entitling the master to a yearly quantity certain, and the overplus to remain with the <163> servant (1.). By this contract, the benefit of the servant's industry accrued wholly to himself;

---

(1) Servis, non in nostrum morem, descriptis per familiam ministeriis, utuntur. Suam quisque sedem, suos penates regit. Frumenti modum dominus, aut pecoris, aut vestis, ut colono injungit. *Tacitus de moribus Germanorum.* [["Their slaves are not organised in our fashion: that is, by a division of the services of life among them. Each of them remains master of his own house and home: the master requires from the slave as serf a certain quantity of grain or cattle or clothing." *Germania* I.25, trans. Peterson.]]

  * Cap. 57.
  † First Stat. Robert I. cap. 7.
  ‡ L. 1. dieg. 10. § 38. in fine.
  ‖ L. 2. dieg. 7. § 26.
  § Act 4. parl. 1669.

and his indolence or ignorance hurt himself alone. One farther step was necessary to bring this contract to its due perfection, which is, to give the servant a lease for years, without which he is not secure that his industry will turn to his own profit. By a contract in these terms, he acquired the name of *tenant;* because he is entitled to hold the possession for years certain. According to this deduction, which is supported by the nature of the thing, the tenant had a claim for that part only of the product to which he was entitled by the contract. He had no real lien to found upon in opposition to his landlord's property. The whole fruits as *pars soli* belonged to the landlord while growing upon the ground; and the act of separating them from the ground, could not transfer the property from him to his tenant: Neither could payment of the rent transfer the property of the remaining fruits, without actual delivery. It is true, the tenant, impowered by the contract, could lawfully apply the remainder to his own use: But still, while upon the ground, it was the landlord's property; and for that <164> reason, as we shall see afterward, it lay open to be attached for payment of the landlord's debts.

But in course of time our notions varied considerably. The tenant who is in possession of the land, who sows and reaps, and who after paying the rent disposes of the product at his pleasure, will naturally be considered as proprietor of the product; especially after the act 18. parl. 1449, securing him against a purchaser of the land. The vulgar are led by impressions of sight, with very little regard to abstract objects. I lay the greater weight on this observation, because the same means produced a capital revolution in our law, viz. the transference of the property from the superior to his vassal. Of which afterward, Tract 5.[3] The landlord's property however continued inviolable, so far as his rent extended. To this limited effect he was held proprietor; and therefore there was nothing singular in allowing him to levy

3. 1758, 1761: "But in course of time . . . Tract 5" = "Matters, it is true, were greatly altered by the act 18. p. 1449, making the tenant secure against a purchaser of the land. This statute was understood to give the lessee a real lien upon the land, or to make a lease, when compleated by possession, a real right, as we term it in Scotland; for a lease, considered as a covenant merely, can only be effectual betwixt the contracters. The real right thus established in the tenant, behoved to regulate the property of the fruits. The maxim, *Quia fatum cedit solo,* which formerly gave the property to the landlord, was thought to apply now in favour of the tenant; and thus, after the rent was paid, the remaining fruits came to be considered as the tenant's property."

his rents by his own authority, whether from his tenants or from his feuers, who differ not from tenants but in the perpetuity of their leases. It was no more than what follows from the very nature of property; for no man needs the authority of a judge to lay hold of his own goods. There could not be a scruple about this privilege, while rents were paid in kind; and landlords, authorised by custom, proceeded in the same train when money-rent was intro-<165>duced, without adverting to the difference. But after the landlord's rent was paid, it soon came to be reckoned an intolerable grievance, or rather gross injustice, that the landlord's creditor should be admitted to poind the remainder, which was in effect the tenant's property. A remedy was provided as to personal debt, by the act 36. parl. 1469, restricting poindings for such debts, to the extent of the arrears due by the tenant, and to the current term. With regard to debts secured upon the land, the legislature did not interpose; for it was judged, that the creditor who had a real lien upon the land, had the same title to the fruits for payment of his interest, that the landlord had for payment of his rent. It was not adverted to, that a creditor is not bound to take possession of the land for his payment; that the landlord is entitled to levy the rent if the creditor forbear; and that it is unjust to oblige the tenant to pay the same rent twice. But what was neglected or avoided by the legislature, was provided for by custom; justice prevailing over ancient usage. And now, tenants are by practice secure against poinding for real debts, as well as they are by statute against poinding for personal debt. In England, it appears, that to this day the creditor in a rent-charge may levy a distress to the extent of what is due to him, without confining the distress to the rent due by the te-<166>nant.* And indeed this is necessary in England, where it is not the practice to take the land itself in execution. But of this afterward.

It was necessary to explain at large the privilege that landlords have at common law to force payment of their rents; because it is a fundamental doctrine with relation to the present subject. I now proceed to consider the case of a creditor who hath obtained a security upon land for debt due to him. Lord Stair observes,† that the English distinguish rent into rent-service, rent-charge, and rent-seck. *Rent-service* is that which is due by the

* See 2d William and Mary, cap. 5.
† Institut. p. 268.

Reddendo of a charter of land, such as a feu or blench duty. *Rent-charge* is that which is given by the landlord to a creditor, containing a clause of distress impowering the creditor to distrain the land at short hand for payment of the debt.* A deed of the same nature without a clause of distress, is termed *Rent-seck.*

A rent-charge must be completed by the writ alone without possession; because the creditor, till interest be due, cannot lawfully take possession, or levy rent. And it is evident, that possession cannot be necessary to establish a right upon land, while such right admits not of pos-<167>session. A rent-seck is in a different case, as may appear from the following considerations. The tenants are not personally liable to the creditor; and the deed, which contains no clause of distress, affords no title to take payment from them. If therefore they be unwilling to pay their rents to the creditor, he has no remedy but a personal action against the granter of the deed. A tenant, it is true, acknowledging a rent-seck, by delivering but a single penny in part payment, puts the creditor in possession of levying rent; after which, if the tenant refuse to pay, it is construed a disseisin, to entitle the creditor to an assize of nouvel disseisin.† But before seisin or possession so had by the creditor, I see not that in any sense the rent-seck can be construed a real right. A hypothec is a real right, because the creditor can sell the land if the debtor fail to make payment. A rent-charge is a real right, because the creditor can levy rent when his term of payment comes. But no right can be conceived to be real, or a branch of property, which gives the creditor no power whatever over the land. And upon this account, if the land be sold before a creditor in a rent-seck is acknowledged by the tenants, the purchaser, I presume, will be preferred.

I have just now hinted at the means for recovering payment, afforded by law to the cre-<168>ditor in a rent-seck. The creditor in a rent-charge, standing on the same footing with the landlord, hath a much easier method. Where the rent payable to the landlord is a certain quantity of the fruits of the ground, the creditor lays hold of the rent at short hand, which concludes the process with respect to the tenant. The operation is not altogether so simple in case of money-rent. The creditor in this case lays hold of any

* New abridgement of the law, tit. *Annuity and Rent-charge.*
† Jacob's Law-dictionary, tit. *Rent.*

goods upon the land, corn or cattle, considered as the landlord's property: But then, as the goods distrained belong in reality to the tenant, free of all embargo as soon as the rent is paid, the tenant is entitled to repledge the same, or to demand restitution, upon making payment of the rent, or giving security for it. The creditor in thus distraining for obtaining payment, has not occasion for a decree; nor is it even necessary that he distrain in presence of an officer of the law. But this form, though easy in one respect to the creditor as well as to the landlord, is not however effectual to draw payment, unless the tenant concur by repledging and substituting security in place of the goods. If the tenant be unable to find a surety, or perversely neglect his interest, there was no remedy till the 2d of William and Mary, cap. 5. by which it is enacted, "That in case the tenant or owner of the goods, do not within five days replevy the same with sufficient security <169> for the rent, the creditor shall have liberty to sell for payment of the rent." Thus the form of distraining upon a rent-charge was made compleat: But a rent-seck remained a very precarious security, for the reasons abovementioned, till the 4th George II. cap. 28. by which it is enacted "That the like remedy by distress, and by impoinding and selling the goods, shall be in the case of rent-seck, that is provided in the case of rent reserved upon lease."

That a power to fell the goods distrained, so necessary to make rent effectual, was not introduced more early, must appear surprising. But the English are remarkably addicted to old usages. Another thing is not less surprising in this form of execution, for which no remedy is provided, that it may be followed out by private authority, when in all other civilized countries execution is not trusted to any but the officers of the law.

I have another observation to make upon this subject, That in the infancy of government shorter methods are indulged to come at right, than afterward when, under a government long settled, the obstinacy and ferocity of men are subdued, and ready obedience is paid to established laws and customs. By the Roman law, a creditor could sell his pledge at short hand. With us, of old, a creditor could even take a pledge at short hand; and which was worse <170> than either, it was lawful for a man to take revenge at his own hand for injuries done him.* None of these things, it is

* See Tract 1.

presumed, are permitted at present in any civilized country, England excepted, where the ancient privilege of forcing payment at short hand, competent to the landlord and to the creditor by a rent-charge, is still in force.

And now to come to our own securities upon land for payment of debt,
we find, in the first place, That originally our law was the same with that
of England, as to the form of making rent-services effectual, viz. taking a
distress at short hand, to be repledged by the tenant on finding security for
the arrears. We have regulations laid down as to the method of taking a
distress: the goods must remain in the same barony till they be repledged,
or in the next adjacent barony, and within the same sheriffdom, but not in
castles or fortalices;* regulations which obviously are borrowed from 52d
Henry III. cap. 4. In the next place, When we consider that the system of
our laws and government is fundamentally the same with that of England,
and that nothing is more natural than to adopt the manners and customs
of a more potent neighbour, it is extremely probable, that a rent-charge was
in practice here as well as in England. Luckily we have direct <171> evidence
of the fact. Several of these securities are preserved to this day; though they
have been long out of use, having given place to what is called *an infeftment
of annualrent,* a land security established in the feudal form. Copies of two
rent-charges are annexed;† one by Simon Lockhart of Lee, by which, for a
certain sum delivered to him,

> he grants and sells to William de Lindsay rector of the church of Ayr, ten
> pounds Sterling yearly rent, to be taken out of the lands of Caitland and
> Lee; binding himself and his heirs to pay the said annuity at two terms in
> the year Pentecost and Martinmas; and binding the above lands of Cait-
> land and Lee, with all the goods and chattles upon the same, to a distress,
> at the instance of the said William Lindsay, his heirs and assignees, in case
> he (the granter) and his heirs shall fail in payment.

This bond is dated in the year 1323. The other is a bond of borrowed money
for L. 40, dated anno 1418, by James Douglas Lord Baveny to Sir Robert
Erskine Lord of that Ilk, in which the debtor becomes bound,

---

* First. Stat. Robert I. cap. 7.
† App. No. 3.

That all the lands and barony of Sawlyn shall remain with the creditor, with all freedoms, eases, and commodities, courts, plaints, and escheats, till he the creditor, his heirs, executors, and assignees, be fully paid of the said sum. And <172> failing payment out of the said lands of Sawlyn, the debtor obliges and binds all his lands of the lordship of Dunsyre, to be distrained, as well as the lands of Sawlyn, at the will of the creditor, his heirs or assignees, till they be paid of the forementioned sum; in the same manner that he or they might distrain their proper lands for their own rents, without the authority of any judge, civil or ecclesiastical.

The bond last mentioned is a happy instance, as it affords irrefragable evidence, that a rent-charge in this country, was in all respects the same as in England; and particularly, that the creditor enjoyed that singular privilege of the landlord, to distrain at short hand without the authority of a judge. It serves at the same time to explain the above-mentioned regulations of Robert I. and of Robert III. about poinding, which, from analogy of the law of England, and from the positive evidence of this deed, must appear now to relate to personal debts only, and by no means to rent-charges more than to rent-services (2). <173>

Whether our law be improved by substituting an infeftment of annualrent in place of a rent-charge, may be doubted. I propose to handle this subject at leisure, because it is curious. While land was held as a proper benefice for services performed to a superior, the whole forms relating to such a grant, and the whole casualties due to the superior, were agreeable to the nature of the tenure: But when land returned to be a subject of commerce, and, like moveables, to be exchanged for money, forms and casualties, arising from the feudal connection between the superior and vassal, could regularly have no place in these new transactions, with which they were inconsistent in every respect. When a man makes a purchase of land and pays a full price, the purpose of the bargain is, That he shall have the unlimited property, without being subjected in any manner to the

---

(2) A clause burdening a disposition of land with a sum to a third party, is, in our practice, made effectual by poinding the ground. A right thus established resembles greatly a rent-charge. The power which in this case the creditor hath to poind the ground, can have no other foundation to rest on than a clause of distress, which is expressed in a rent-charge, and is implied in the right we are speaking of.

vender: And yet such is the force of custom, that titles must be made up in the feudal form, because no other titles to land were in use. And thus the purchaser, contrary to the nature of the transaction, was metamorphosed into a vassal, and consequently subjected to homage, fealty, non-entry, liferent-escheat, &c. upon account of that very land which he purchased <174> with his own money. Such an inconsistency, it is true, could not long subsist; and form by degrees yielded to substance. When land came universally to be patrimonial, and no longer beneficiary, the forms of the Feudal law indeed remained, but the substance wore out gradually. This change produced blench duties, an elusory sum for non-entry in place of the full rents, collateral succession without limitation; and failing heirs, the King, and not the superior, as last heir: Which regulations, with many others upon the same plan, are wide deviations from any tenure that in a proper sense can be termed beneficiary. When the substantial part of the Feudal law has thus vanished, it is dismal to lie still under the oppression of its forms, which occasion great trouble and expence in the transmission of land-property.

Our forefathers, however, in adhering to the feudal forms after the substance was gone, merit less censure than at first sight may appear just from the foregoing deduction. So many different persons were connected with the same portion of land, stages of superiors being commonly interjected betwixt the vassal in possession and the crown, that in most instances it would have been difficult to throw off the feudal holding, and to make the right purely allodial. This affords a sufficient excuse for not attempting early to set land free from feudal titles. And <175> when time discovered that the feudal forms could be squeezed and moulded into a new shape, so as to correspond in some measure with a patrimonial estate, it is not wonderful that our forefathers acquiesced in the forms that were in use, improper as they were.

But it will be a harder task to justify our forefathers for deserting the established form of a rent-charge, substituting in its place an infeftment of annualrent, than which nothing in my apprehension can be more absurd. For here a man, who hath no other intention but to obtain a real security for his money, is transformed, by a sort of hocus-pocus trick, into a servant or vassal, either of his debtor or of his debtor's superior. And to prevent a mistake, as if this were for the sake of form only, I must observe, that the creditor is even held to be a military vassal, bound to serve his superior in war; if the contrary be not specified in the bond.* The superior again, after the creditor's death, was entitled to the non-entry duties; and it required an act of parliament[†] to correct this glaring absurdity. It must be confest to be somewhat ludicrous, that the heir of a creditor, acting for form's sake only the part of a vassal, and by the nature of his right bound neither for service nor duty to his imagined superior, should yet be punished with the loss of <176> the interest of his money for neglecting to enter heir, which might be hurtful to himself, but could not in any measure hurt his debtor acting the part of a superior. In a word, it is impossible to conceive any form less consistent with the nature and substance of the deed to which it relates, than an infeftment of annualrent is. The wonder is, how it ever came to be introduced in opposition to the more perfect form of a rent-charge. I can discover no other cause but one, which hath an arbitrary sway in law as well as in more trivial matters, and that is the prevelancy of fashion. We had long been accustomed to the Feudal law, and to consider a feudal tenure as the only compleat title to land: No man thought himself secure with a title of any other sort: Jurisdictions and offices must be brought under a feudal tenure; and even creditors, influenced by the authority of fashion, were not satisfied till they got their securities in the same form.

And this leads me to another absurdity in the constitution of an annualrent-right, less conspicuous indeed than that mentioned; and that is the order or precept to introduce the creditor directly into possession; though, by the nature of his right, and by express paction, he is not entitled to take possession, or to levy rent, till the first term's interest become due. Seisin, it is true, is but a symbolical possession; but then, <177> as symbolical possession was invented to save the trouble of apprehending possession really, it is improper, nay it is absurd, to give symbolical possession before the person be entitled to possess. A seisin indeed will be proper after

* Stair, p. 268.
† Act 42. parl. 1690.

interest becomes due: But a seisin at that time is unnecessary; because the creditor can enter really into possession by levying rent; and surely real possession can never be less compleat than symbolical possession.

It tends not to reconcile us to an infeftment of annualrent, that, considered as a commercial subject, it is not less brittle than deformed. In its transmission as well as establishment, it is attended with all the expence and trouble of land-property, without being possessed of any advantage of land-property. It is extinguished by levying rent, by receiving payment from the debtor, and even by a voluntary discharge. In short, a personal bond is not extinguished with less ceremony. This circumstance unqualifies it for commerce; for there is no safety in laying out money to purchase it. Nor does the symbolical possession by a seisin give it any advantage over a rent-charge. The seisin does not publish the security: Registration is necessary; and a rent-charge, which requires not infeftment, is as easily recorded as a security established by infeftment. <178>

To compleat this subject, it is necessary to take a view of the execution that proceeds upon an infeftment of annualrent; and comparing it with the ancient form of execution upon a rent-charge, to remark where they agree, and where they differ. In the first place, the creditor in a rent-charge could not bring an action of debt against the tenants for their rents. His claim properly lay to the goods upon the land, which he was entitled to carry off, and to detain till the rent was paid to him. The law stands the same to this day as to the personal action arising from an infeftment of annualrent. This security binds not the tenants to pay to the creditor: He has no claim against them personally for their rents, unless there be in the deed an assignment to the mails and duties.*

But in the following particulars, execution upon an infeftment of annualrent, or other *debitum fundi,* differs from execution upon a rent-charge. First, An infeftment of annualrent has not been long in use; and at the time when this security was introduced, more regularity and solemnity were required in all matters of law than formerly. Poinding could not now proceed

---

* Darie, 24th March 1626, Gray *contra* Graham; Fountainhall, 5th July 1701, Kinloch *contra* Rochead.

upon a personal debt, till first a decree was obtained against the debtor; and an infeftment of annualrent, if it did not contain an <179> assignment to mails and duties, afforded not an action against the tenants. Some other form therefore was necessary, more solemn than that of poinding by private authority. The form invented was to obtain the King's authority for poinding the ground, which was granted in a letter under the signet, directed to messengers, &c. I discover this to have been the practice in the time of our James V. or VI. it is uncertain which; for the letter is dated the 30th year of the reign of James, and no other king of that name reigned so long.* But with respect to the landlord's privilege of distraining the ground, it being afterward judged necessary, that a decree, in his own court at least, should be interposed, the form was extended to an infeftment of annual-rent. There was indeed some difficulty in what manner to frame a libel or declaration, considering that the creditor has not a personal action against the tenants, and can conclude nothing against them that has the appearance of a process. This difficulty is removed, or rather disguised: The landlord and his tenants are called; for there can be no process without a defendant: There is also a sort of conclusion against them, very singular indeed, viz. "The said defenders to hear and see letters of poynding and apprising, directed by decreet of the said Lords, for poynding <180> the readyest goods and gear upon the ground of the said lands," &c. A decree proceeding upon such a libel or declaration, if it can be called a decree, is in effect a judicial notification merely to the landlord and his tenants, that the creditor is to proceed to execution. In a word, the singular nature of this decree proves it to be an apish imitation of a decree for payment of debt; without which, as observed above, poinding for personal debt cannot proceed.

In the second place, The property of the goods distrained was not by the old form transferred to the creditor: The tenant might repledge at any time, upon paying his rent to the creditor, or finding surety for the payment. I have no occasion here to take notice of the English statute that empowered the creditor to sell the goods distrained; because the rent-charge was laid aside in Scotland, long before the said remedy was invented. This old form

* See a copy of this letter in the Appendix, No 4.

must yield to our present form of poinding upon *debita fundi,* borrowed from poinding for payment of personal debt; which is, that the goods are sold, if a purchaser can be found; otherwise adjudged to the creditor upon a just appretiation. 'Tis to be regretted, that we have dropt the most salutary branch of the execution, which is that of selling the goods. But still, it is more commodious to adjudge the goods to the credi-<181>tor upon a just appretiation, than to make payment depend on the tenant; whereby matters may be kept in suspence for ever.

In the next place, The most remarkable difference is, that execution upon a *debitum fundi* is much farther extended than formerly. Of old, execution was directed against the moveables only, that were found upon the land; but in our later practice, it is directed both against the moveables and against the land itself, in their order. It appears probable, that this novelty has been introduced, in imitation of execution for payment of personal debt, though there is no analogy betwixt them.

This subject is an illustrious instance of the prevalency of humanity and equity, in opposition to the rigour of common law. By common law, the creditor who hath a rent-charge or an infeftment of annualrent, may sweep off the tenant's whole moveables, for payment of the interest that is due upon his bond, and is not limited to the arrears of rent. The palpable injustice of this execution with regard to the tenant, has produced a remedy; which is, that though goods may be impoinded to the extent of the interest due, yet these goods may be repledged by the tenant, upon payment of the arrears due by him and the current term. In poinding for payment of personal debt, the attaching the tenant's goods even for the current <182> term, is in disuse; and has given place to arrestment, which relieves the tenant from the hardship of paying his rent before the term. The tenant remains still exposed to this hardship, when a decree for poinding the ground is put in execution. But it is unavoidable, at least where the infeftment of annualrent is in the old form, viz. a species of wadset containing no personal obligation for payment upon which an arrestment can be founded. In this case, there is a necessity for indulging the poinding of goods for the current rent; for otherwise, supposing the rents to be punctually paid, there would be no access to the moveables at all. This restriction in a poinding of the

ground, paved the way for poinding the land itself; which was seldom necessary of old, when the moveables upon the land could be poinded without
limitation.

By the *Levari facias* in England, rents payable to the debtor can be seized
in execution. This being a more summary method than arrestment for attaching rents, is the reason, I suppose, that arrestment is not used in England. For if rents can be thus taken in execution, other debts must be
equally subjected to the same execution.

I shall conclude with pointing out some mistakes in writers who handle
the present subject. Few things passing under the same name, differ <183>
more widely than the two kinds of poinding above-mentioned. Poinding
for payment of personal debt, proceeds upon a principle of common justice, viz. That if a man will not dispose of his effects for payment of his
debts, the judge ought to interpose, and wrest them from him. Poinding
for payment of debt secured upon land, is an exertion of the right of property. The effects are poinded or distrained by the landlord's order or warrant; and the execution can reach no effects but what are understood to be
his property. His property, it is true, is limited, and cannot be exerted farther
than to make the claim of debt effectual; and upon that account the tenant
may repledge, upon satisfying the claim. But if he do not repledge, the
effects are in Scotland adjudged to the creditor for his payment, without
any reversion to the tenant; because, in legal execution, matters ought not
for ever to be in suspense. Hence execution upon personal debt is directed
against the debtor, and the property is transferred from him to his creditor.
Execution upon debt affecting land, is directed against the land and its
product; and transfers not property, but only removes the limitations that
were upon the landlord's property, by extinguishing the tenant's right of
reversion. Though these matters come out in a clear light, when traced to
their origin, yet the two poindings are often <184> confounded by our authors. Lord Stair* mentions the brieve of distress as the foundation of both
sorts of poinding, and remarks, that by the act 36. parl. 1469, the irrational
custom of poinding the tenant's goods without limitation was restrained

* Book 4. tit. 23. § 1.

as to both. And he is copied by Mackenzie.* This is erroneous in every particular. The brieve of distress was nothing else but the king's commission to a judge named, to determine upon a certain claim of debt. This brieve entitled the bearer to a decree, supposing his claim well founded; and consequently to poind for payment of the sum decreed. And the act now mentioned, introduceth a regulation which respects solely the execution upon a debt of this kind; and relates not at all to execution upon debts affecting land.

In the same paragraph, the author first mentioned adds, That there was no longer any use for the brieve of distress, after the said statute. This must be a careless expression; for our author could not seriously be of that opinion. Execution upon personal debt after this statute continued as formerly, except that as to tenants it was limited to their arrears including the current term. And with regard to the brieve of distress considered as an authority from the king to judge of personal debt, there was a <185> very different cause for its wearing out of use, which is, that judges took upon them to determine upon claims of personal debt, without any authority.†

One mistake commonly produceth another. Our author, taking it for granted, that poinding upon *debita fundi* is regulated by the act 1469, as well as poinding upon personal debt, draws the following consequence,‡ That there is a reversion of seven years when lands are apprised upon a *debitum fundi,* as well as when they are apprised upon a personal debt; observing at the same time, that the extension of the reversion to ten years, by the act 62. parl. 1661, relates to the latter only, and that the former remains upon the footing of the act 1469. It will be evident from what is just now said, that apprisings upon *debita fundi* have no reversion as to land more than as to moveables; the act 1469, which introduced the privilege of a reversion, relating only to execution for payment of personal debt.

This author is again in a mistake, when he lays down, That apprising of land upon a *debitum fundi* is laid aside, and that the land must be adjudged

---

* Instit. book 2. tit. 8. § 14.
† See as to this point, Tract 8. Of Brieves.
‡ Book 4. tit. 23. § 8.

by a process before the court of session.* <186> It is clear, that the act 1672,[4] introducing adjudications, goes not one step farther, than to substitute them in place of apprisings for payment of personal debt; and therefore, that execution upon a decree for poinding the ground, remains to this day upon its original footing. <187>

---

* Book 4. tit. 23. § 8. tit. 35. § 27. tit. 51. § 2. and 13.
4. Kames refers to the Act "concerning adjudications" dated 6 September 1762.

Privilege of an Heir-apparent
in a Feudal Holding to Continue
the Possession of His Ancestor

Cujacius gives an accurate definition of a feudal holding in the following words: "Feudum est jus in praedio alieno, in perpetuum utendi, fruendi, quod pro beneficio dominus dat ea lege, ut qui accipit, sibi fidem et militiae munus, aliudve servitium exhibeat."*[1] The feudal contract is distinguished from others, by the following circumstance, That land is given for service, instead of wages in money. This contract at its dawn was limited to a time certain. It was afterward made to subsist during the vassal's life; and in progress of time was extended to the male issue of the original vassal. It was not the purpose of this contract to transfer the property, but only to give the vassal the profits of the land during his service; or, in other words, to give him the usufruct. To transfer the property would have been inconsistent with the nature of the cove-<188>nant; because wages ought not to be perpetual, when the service is but temporary. Hence it necessarily followed, when the male issue of the original vassal called to the succession, were exhausted, that the land returned to the superior, to be employed by him, if he pleased, for procuring a new vassal. And the effect was the same, when any of these heirs refused in his course to undertake the service. Such

---

* Ad lib. 1. Feud. tit. 1. § 10.

1. "A feu is a right in the estate of another, held and enjoyed in perpetuity, which the lord gives as a favour legally, so that he who accepts it owes him fealty, as well as military and other services."

being the nature and intendment of the feudal contract, it is evident, that while a feu was for life only, it was the superior's privilege as proprietor, without any formality, to enter to the possession of the land upon the death of his vassal. Nor was this privilege lost by making feus hereditary. Every heir hath a year to deliberate, whether it will be his interest to undertake the service. During this period, being entitled to no wages since he submits not to the service, the possession and profits of the land must of course remain with the superior. And even supposing the heir makes an offer of his service without deliberating, he cannot take possession at short hand, of land which is not his own. It is necessary, from the nature of the thing, that the superior, accepting his offer, give orders to introduce him to the land; and this act is termed *renovatio feudi.*

This is not the only case, where the superior is entitled to an *interim* possession. A young <189> man is held not capable to bear arms, till he be twenty-one years compleat; and for that reason, the heir of a military vassal, while under age, is not entitled to possess the land. The superior, during that interval, holds the possession and reaps the profits; for a servant has not a claim to wages, while he is incapable to do duty.

Bating these interruptions of possession preparatory to the heir's entry, which at the same time are casual and for the most part momentary, the vassal and his male descendents continue in possession, and enjoy the whole profits of the land. When a vassal dies, the estate descends to his heir, and from one heir to another in a long train. But possession and enjoyment, which are ouvert acts, and the most beneficial exertions of property, make a strong impression on the vulgar; and naturally produce a notion, that the land belongs in property to the family in possession. Hence it came that the property, or the most beneficial part of it, was in popular estimation transferred from the superior to the vassal. The intermission of military service in times of peace, favoured this notion; which at last, through the influence of general opinion, was adopted by the legislature.

This heteroclite notion of the property being split into parts, and the most substantial part transferred to the vassal, produced another, viz. <190> that after the vassal's death, the heir, and not the superior, is entitled to possess the land. This notion prevailed so much, as to procure in England

a law during the reign of Henry II. which shall be given in the words of a
learned author.*

> If any one shall die holding a frank pledge (*i.e.* having a free tenure), let
> his heirs remain in such seisin, as their father had on the day he was alive
> and died, of his fee, and let them have his chattels, out of which they may
> make also the devise or partition of the deceased (that is, the sharing of
> his goods according to his will), and afterwards may require of their lord,
> and do for their relief and other things, which they ought to do as touching
> their fee, (*i.e.* in order to their entering upon the estate).

This law was undoubtedly intended for the benefit of those only who were
of full age, capable of the services which a vassal in possession is bound to
perform. For it would be absurd, that an heir under age, who is incapable
of doing service, should notwithstanding be entitled to the wages. Glanvil,
who wrote in this King's reign, makes the distinction, but without referring
to any statute.† And we have Bracton's authority for the same.‡ <191>

That the king's vassals were not comprehended under this regulation, is
evident from the statute 52d Henry III. cap. 16. where a distinction is made
betwixt the king's vassals and those who hold of a subject. The first section
of this statute declares it to be law, That the heir-apparent, in land held of
a subject, is entitled to continue the possession of his ancestor; and provides
certain remedies against the superior who endeavours to exclude the heir
from possession.

> If any heir, after the death of his ancestor, be within age, and the lord have
> the ward of his lands and tenements, if the lord will not render unto the
> heir his land (when he cometh to full age) without plea, the heir shall
> recover his land by assize of mortancestor, with the damages he hath sus-
> tained by such with-holding, since the time that he was of full age. And
> if an heir, at the time of his ancestor's death, be of full age, and he is heir-
> apparent, and known for heir, and he be found in the inheritance, the chief
> lord shall not put him out, nor take nor remove any thing there, but shall
> take only simple seisin therefor, for the recognition of his seigniority, that

---

* Selden's Janus Anglorum, chap. 17.
† L. 7. cap. 9. l. 9. cap. 4.
‡ [[*De Legibus,*]] L. 4. p. 252.

he may be known for lord. And if the chief lord do put such an heir out
of the possession maliciously, whereby he is driven to purchase a writ of
mortancestor, or of cousenage, then he shall reco-<192>ver his damages,
as in assize of nouvel disseisin.

Here we find it clearly laid down, that the heir, being of full age, is entitled
to continue the possession of his ancestor, and that the superior is entitled
to simple seisin only, by which is meant the relief.* And it is equally clear,
that though the superior is entitled to possess the land, while the heir of
his military vassal is under age; yet that this heir, arriving at full age, is
entitled to recover the possession, without necessity of a service or any other
formality; evident from this, that if the superior be refractory, the heir has
a direct remedy by an assize of mortancestry, which is a species of the assize
of nouvel disseisin.

But the second section of this statute is in a very different strain. The
words are,

> Touching heirs which hold of our Lord the King in chief, this order shall
> be observed, That our Lord the King shall have the first seisin of their
> lands, likeas he was wont to have beforetime. Neither shall the heir, or any
> other, intrude into the same inheritance, before he hath received it out of
> the King's hands, as the same inheritance was wont to be taken out of his
> hands and his ancestors in time past. And this must be understood of lands
> and fees, the which are accustomed to be in the King's hands, by reason
> of <193> knight's service, or serjeantry, or right of patronage.

Here we see the old law preserved in force, as to the king's military vassals,
that they have no title to continue the possession of their ancestors; that
after the death of such a vassal, the possession returns to the king as proprietor; and that the heir cannot otherwise attain the possession, but by a
brieve from the chancery. The difference here established, betwixt the king's
military vassals and those who hold of subjects, is put beyond all doubt by
the statute 17th Edward II. cap. 13.

> When any (that holdeth of the King in chief) dieth, and his heir entereth
> into the land that his ancestor held of the king the day that he died, before

---

* Coke, 2 Instit. 134.

that he hath done homage to the King, and received seisin of the King, he shall gain no freehold thereby; and if he die seised during that time, his wife shall not be endowed of the same land; as it came late in ure by Maud, daughter to the Earl of Hereford, wife to Maunsel the marshal, which, after the death of William Earl Marshall of England his brother, took his seisin of the castle and manour of Scrogoil, and died in the same castle, before he had entered by the King, and before he had done homage to him: whereupon it was agreed, that his wife should not be endowed, because that her husband had not entered by the King, but rather by <194> intrusion. Howbeit this statute doth not mean of soccage and other small tenures.

We have no reason to doubt, that this statute, concerning the king's military vassals, continued in force till the 12th Charles II. cap. 24. when military tenures, of whomever held, were abolished.

It appears from our law-books, that the privilege bestowed upon heirs by the statute of Henry II. of continuing the possession of their ancestors, obtained also in Scotland.* This privilege made a great change in the form of feudal titles; and in particular, with respect to land held of a subject, superseded totally the brieve of inquest, and the consequential steps of service and retour. For where an heir is privileged by law to continue or apprehend at short hand the possession of his ancestor, he has no occasion for a service and retour, of which the only purpose is to procure possession. We followed also the English law with respect to military tenures held of the king. The 2d statute Robert I. cap. 7. which is our authority, is copied almost *verbatim* from the statute of Henry III. above mentioned. But we did not rest there; for we see from the statutes of Robert III.† that the old law was totally restored, enti-<195>tling every superior to the possession at the first instance, and leaving the heir to claim the possession from his superior.

But the authority of these statutes was not sufficient to stem altogether the torrent of popular opinion. By this time, the property, in common apprehension, was transferred from the superior to the vassal; and after the vassal's death, his heir, it was thought, had a better title than the superior

* Reg. Maj. I. 2. cap. 40. cap. 71. § 1.; Second stat. Rob. I. cap. 6. § 1. 2. 3.
† Cap. 19. and 38.

to possess the land. The general bias accordingly, in spite of these statutes, continued in favour of the heir's possession; and an additional circumstance had great weight in his favour: a young man *in familia,* is considered as in possession even during his father's life; and after his father's death, there is no change with regard to him: he has no occasion to apprehend possession: he remains or continues in it, and cannot be thrust out at short hand without some sort of process. Nor in a favourite point were our forefathers nice in distinguishing betwixt heirs. If a son *in familia* was entitled to continue in possession, it was reckoned no wide stretch, that a son *forisfamiliated* should be entitled to step into the possession: nor was it reckoned a wide stretch to communicate this privilege to other heirs, though less connected with the ancestor. Thus, as to the mere right of possession, the heir in Scotland has, for many centuries, been prefer-<196>red before the superior. I must observe, however, that this privilege, acquired by custom against the authority of statute-law, has not the effect to vest the property in the heir, nor to give him a freehold, as termed in England. This would be to overturn the statute altogether, which we have not attempted. The statute is so far only encroached upon in practice, as to privilege the heir to step into the void possession; reserving the superior's privilege to turn him out of possession by a proper process, unless he make up his title by a service, and demand regularly possession or seisin from the superior.

The difference then betwixt our present practice, and what it was before the days of Henry II. appears to be what follows. The heir originally had no right to possess, till he was entered by the superior. If the heir entered at his own hand, he was guilty of intrusion, and could be summarily ejected. At present we consider, as originally, the land to be the superior's property, and that the heir has not a freehold till he be regularly entered: but then we consider him as entitled, at the first instance, to the possession; that his possession is lawful; and that the superior cannot turn him out at short hand or by a summary ejection, but must insist in a regular process of removing, after a declarator of non-entry is obtained. <197>

From what is above laid down, it is evident, that in no case have we adopted the English maxim, *Quod mortuus sasit vivum.* Formerly the English law, with regard to military tenures held of the crown, was the same with what obtains here in all tenures, viz. That the heir has no freehold, till he sue out his livery, after a service upon the brieve *Diem clausit supremum,* which corresponds to our brieve of inquest. But now that in England military tenures are abolished, heirs require not service and infeftment; the maxim holds universally there as in France, *Quod mortuus sasit vivum.*

It may be thought at first view, a very slight favour to prefer the heir *in possessorio,* when it requires only a process to thrust him out of possession. But not to mention that he has a defence at hand, which is an offer to enter heir, it belongs more to the present subject to observe, that this privilege of possession is attended with very remarkable advantages, arising from the bias of popular notions to which the law hath submitted. The superior is entitled to a year's rent in name of relief, or *primer seisin* as termed in England; and if the superior were entitled to the possession, this relief would be the full rent. But by the heir's privilege of possession, the superior for the year's rent is reduced to a claim; and this claim, like all other casualties of superiority, being unfavourable, is measured <198> by the new extent; which, by construction of law, or rather of practice, is in this case held to be the rent of the land. And the same rule is observed in the claim of non-entry. This claim of non-entry also is founded upon the superior's legal privilege of possession. The rents claimed are understood to be the rents of the superior's land, levied by the heir without a title, and for which therefore he is bound to account. But the burden of accounting is made easy to him, the new extent being in this case, as in the former, put for the real rent.

There is scarce one point in our law so indistinctly handled by writers, and upon which there is such contrariety of decisions, as the following, What right an heir possessed of his ancestor's estate has to the rents, before he is infeft. In many cases it has been judged, that the rents are his, in the same manner as if he were regularly entered. In other cases, not fewer in number, it has been judged, that tenents paying their rents to him *bona fide* are secure; but that he has no legal claim to the rents, and therefore has no action against the tenants to force them to pay. Pursuant to the latter opinion, the growing rents, after the predecessor's death, have been considered as a part or accessory of the *hereditas jacens,* and therefore to be carried by an adjudication deduced against the heir, upon a special charge to <199>

enter:* and yet it weighs on the other side, that an apprising upon a special charge was never thought to carry bygone rents; for a good reason, which applies equally to an adjudication, viz. That an apprising upon a special charge ought not to have a more extensive effect, than an apprising deduced against the heir after he is infeft, which assuredly doth not carry any arrears. To relieve from this uncertainty, we must search for some principle that may lead to a just conclusion.

The superior, during the heir's non-entry, is undoubtedly proprietor of the land. Hence it follows, that at common law the rents belong to the superior, and that the heir in possession is liable to account to him for the rents. But our law, or rather our judges, indulging the general prepossession in favour of the heir, have been long in use of limiting this claim to the new extent, which once having been the full rent of the land, is presumed to continue so, in order to relieve the heir from a rigorous claim. What then is to become of the difference betwixt this supposed value of the rents, and what they extend to in reality? This difference must undoubtedly remain with the heir, as what he gains from the superior, by the favour of the <200> law. Let us suppose a declarator of non-entry is commenced, which entitles the superior, in equity as well as at common law, to the full rents; and that upon a transaction with the heir, he accepts of the one half: the other half must belong to the heir by this transaction. It ought to be the same before a declarator; for a legal composition has the same effect with one that is voluntary. This reasoning appears to be solid; and therefore we need not hesitate to conclude, that the heir in possession is entitled to levy the rents, in order to account for the same to the superior, according to the new extent before declarator, and according to the full rents after. And indeed, without a circuit, the power of levying the rents may reasonably be thought a necessary consequence of the right of possession; for without it possession is a mere shadow.

This point being established, there no longer remains any doubt. If the heir apparent, seizing the possession or continuing the possession of his ancestor, have right to the rents without a formal entry, it follows that these

* 13th February 1740, Dickson of Kilbucho *contra* Apparent-heir of Poldean.

rents are not to be considered as *in hereditate jacente* of the ancestor, to be carried by an adjudication upon a special charge. They must be attached by arrestment as the property of the heir-apparent. What of these rents remain in the hands of the <201> tenants without being levied by the heir-apparent, must after his decease belong to his next of kin; and the next heir, though he complete his right to the land by infeftment, will have no claim to these rents.

However clear this doctrine may be in principles, it has been much controverted in practice. On the 28th January 1756 Houston *contra* Nicolson of Carnock, the executor of the heir apparent was preferred. On the 5th December 1760, Hamilton *contra* Hamilton, the heir was preferred. But upon a solemn hearing in presence, 24th July 1765, Lord Banff *contra* Joass, the executor was preferred. By this decision, the executor of the heir-apparent in the case Hamilton *contra* Hamilton was encouraged to bring an appeal; and the result was, to reverse the judgment of the court of session in that case, and to prefer the appellant. So that the matter is at last justly settled on the principles above laid down.[2]

This is a curious branch of the history of the Feudal law in Britain, and of a singular nature. The Feudal law was a violent system, repugnant to natural principles. It was submitted to in barbarous times, when the exercise of arms was the only science and the only commerce. It is repugnant to all the arts of peace, and when mankind came to affect security more than danger, nothing could make it tolerable, <202> but long usage and inveterate habit. It yielded to the prevailing love of liberty and independency; and, through all Europe, it dwindled away gradually, and became a shadow, before any branch of it was abrogated by statute. When it was undermined by so powerful a cause, would one imagine that it could ever recover any ground it had once lost? And yet here is a remarkable instance of its recovering ground. This phenomenon must have had some singular cause, which probably is now lost for ever; for we have no regular records of any antiquity, and our ancient historians seldom take notice of civil transactions that have any relation to law. <203>

2. Paragraph added 1776.

Regalities, and the
Privilege of Repledging

Among all the European nations who embraced the feudal system, it is remarkable, that the crown vassals rose gradually into power and splendor, till they became an over match for the sovereign. It is still more remarkable, that the same crown-vassals, those of Germany excepted, after attaining this height of power and splendor, sunk by degrees; and at present are distinguished from the mass of the people, by name more than by any solid pre-eminence.

The growing power of the crown-vassals, may easily be accounted for: It was the result of making feus hereditary. Experience discovered, what might have been discovered without experience, that to make the bread of a man's family depend on his life, is apt to damp the bravest spirits. This engaged first one prince and then another, to promise a renovation of the feu to the heir, if the vassal should lose his life in battle; till these engagements became <204> universal. The sovereigns in Europe, having no standing army, could not hope to carry on war successfully, without the goodwill of their vassals; to whom therefore it became necessary to give all encouragement and indulgence. If one prince led the way, others were obliged to follow. At length, no powers were to be withheld from the crown-vassals, who had already become too powerful. In England, palatinates were erected, exempted from the jurisdiction of the King's judges, with power of coining money, levying war, &c. In Scotland, regalities were created with the highest civil and criminal jurisdiction, and with all other powers annexed to palatinates in England.

Whether regalities originally were exempted from the jurisdiction of the King's judges, is uncertain. I incline to think they were not; at least, that it has been a matter of doubt. For there are several instances of grants by the King to lords of regality, exempting them from the jurisdiction of the King's judges; which would be an idle clause if all were exempted.[1] One instance there is at hand, viz. a charter by King Robert II. to his brother James de Douglas de Dalkeith, Knight, of the baronies of Dalkeith, Caldercleer, Kinclaven, &c. to be held in one entire and free barony, and in free regality, with the four pleas of the crown. This charter is in the 16th year of the King's reign, supposed <205> to be in the 1386. And in the year immediately following, there is a grant under the great seal to the same James de Douglas, reciting the said charter, and "discharging all the King's justiciars, sheriffs, and their ministers, from all intromission and administration of their offices within the said lands." And it appears by indenture betwixt King Robert I. and his parliament 1326, authorising a tax to be levied for the King's use during his life, that many of the great lords enjoyed the foresaid privilege, maintaining, that the King's officers could not act within their lands. And therefore, these lords take upon themselves, to levy what part of the tax was laid upon their lands, and to pay the same to the King's officers.* This exclusive privilege, in whatever manner introduced, came to be fully established in lords of regality, as will appear from the act 5. parl. 1440, and act 26. parl. 1449: the former regulating the justiceairs on the north and south sides of the Scots sea; and, with the same breath, appointing lords of regality to hold justiceairs within their regalities: the latter appointing regalities to be subjected to the King's justice, while they remain in the King's hands.

And here by the way it may be remarked, that the act 43. parl. 1455, is no slight instance of the authority of the great barons. Those <206> who had obtained regalities, were fond to confine to themselves the power and privileges depending thereon: And to prevent future rivalship, they wrested from the crown one capital branch of its prerogative, that of erecting regalities; the said act declaring, "That in time coming no regalities be granted

---

* See this indenture in the Appendix, No. 5.
1. "which would . . . exempted" added in 1776.

without deliverance of parliament"; that is, without consent of the Lords who had already obtained regalities; for in them was centered the power of the parliament. The circumstances of those times unfold the political view of this statute; for the public good is a motive of no great influence in rude ages. In Scotland, the great families, by monopolizing the higher powers and privileges, secured to themselves dignity and authority. In England, the same spirit procured the statute *de donis conditionalibus;* which, by the power of making entails, and attaching unalienably a great estate to a great family, laid a still more solid foundation for dignity and authority.

The downfal of great families was occasioned by circumstances more complex. These are many in number, but the chief appear to be, the transference of property from the superior to the vassal, the free commerce of land, and the firm establishment of the right of primogeniture. With respect to the two circumstances first mentioned, it is a maxim in politics, That power in <207> a good measure depends on property. The great lords originally had great power, because their vassals had the use only of the lands they possessed, not the property. But popular notions prevailing over strict law, the vassal came to be considered as proprietor, and law accommodated itself to popular notions. And thus the property of the feudal subject was imperceptibly transferred from the superior to his vassal; which made the latter in a good measure independent. The free commerce of land, repugnant to the genius of the Feudal law, brought the great lords lower and lower. Peace and commerce afforded money, and introduced luxury. The grandees, despising the frugality of their ancestors, could no longer confine their expences within their yearly income. They were obliged to dispose of land for payment of their debts; and the industrious, who had money, were fond to purchase land, which, for the sake of independency, they chose to hold of the crown. Thus, by multiplying the crown-vassals without end, their connections were broken, and their power reduced to a shadow.

While the crown-vassals were declining, the crown was gaining ground daily by the privilege of primogeniture. To explain this circumstance, for it requires explanation, it must be observed, that in succession, primogeniture has no privilege by the law of Nature. And though <208> a crown may be an exception, where the succession is confined to a single person;

yet primogeniture in this case, cannot take fast hold of the mind, in opposition to the general rule of succession, which in private estates bestows an equal right on all the males. We see a notable example of this in Turkey, where primogeniture has no privilege, except with regard to the imperial dignity. Influenced by the general rule of an equal succession, the younger sons of the Emperor consider themselves to be upon a level with the first-born; and their title to the empire equal to his. By this means, where one is preferred by will, or the eldest where there is no will, the other sons are apt to pronounce it an act of injustice, depriving them of their birth-right. Hence perpetual jealousies and civil discord, which commonly terminate in the establishment of one of the sons, at the expence of the lives of his brethren. And considering the matter impartially, this is less the effect of brutal manners, than of an infirm political constitution (1). <209>

From the history of Europe we learn, that in the descent of the crown, hereditary right was of old little regarded: Nor is this wonderful, considering, that till the Feudal law was established, primogeniture did not bestow any privilege in point of succession. The feudal system, by confining to a single heir every feudal subject, made way for the eldest son. Then it was, and no sooner, that succession to the crown, and to private estates, were governed by the same rules; which gave force to the right of primogeniture, as if it were a law of nature. But as it required many ages to obliterate former notions, and to give that preference to primogeniture which now is never called in question, the crown-vassals were in the meridian of power long before the kingly authority had gained much ground. Kings being indebted for their advancement to the will of the people more than <210> to the

(1) It was a regulation in Persia, that the King was obliged to name his successor, if he chose to make war in person. Darius had three sons by the daughter of Gobryas, his first wife; all born before he was King. After his accession to the throne, he had four more by Atossa, the daughter of Cyrus. Of the former, Artabazanes was the eldest: of the latter, Xerxes: and these two were competitors for the succession. Artabazanes urged, that he was the eldest of all the sons of Darius, and that by the custom of all nations the eldest has right to the crown. On the other hand, it was urged by Xerxes, that he was the son of Atossa, the daughter of Cyrus, who had delivered the Persians from servitude, and that he was born after Darius was king; whereas Artabazanes was only the son of Darius a private man. These reasons appeared so just, that Xerxes was declared the successor.—*Herodotus, book 7.*—The privilege of primogeniture could not be firmly established in Persia, when it gave way to such trivial circumstances.

privilege of blood, they were little better than elective monarchs. But from the time that primogeniture came to be a general law in succession, European princes, depending now no longer on the choice of their people, acquired by degrees that extent of power, which naturally belongs to a hereditary monarch. The crown-vassals at the same time gradually declining by the commerce of land, and by the transference of their property to their vassals, are reduced within proper bounds, and have now no power but what tends to support a monarchical government.

Germany is in a singular case. Composed of many great parts, which were never solidly united under one government, or under one royal family, it fluctuated many centuries betwixt hereditary and elective monarchy. This advanced the power of the great lords, and reduced the monarchy to be purely elective. The electors became sovereign princes; and the power of the Emperor is almost annihilated.

The jurisdiction of the crown-vassals, comparing the present with former times, is a beautiful example of this decline. It sunk gradually with their power and property. What they lost on the one hand, was on the other acquired by the King and his judges; and at present, with the other privileges of crown-vassals, their jurisdiction is reduced to an empty name. The extent <211> of this jurisdiction in its different periods, and its gradual abridgment, being chiefly the purpose of the present essay, I find it necessary to take a circuit, in order to set the matter in its proper light.

As no branch of public police is of greater importance than that of distributing justice, it is necessary that the jurisdiction of every judge be ascertained, with respect to causes as well as persons. Concerning the latter, a plain and commodious rule is established through most civilized nations. The territory is divided into districts; and in each a judge is appointed, who has under his jurisdiction the people residing in his district. Thus, with regard to jurisdiction, the people are distinguished by their place of residence, which so far regulates the powers of the several judges. And were it possible to distinguish causes by a rule equally precise, disputes among judges about their powers would scarce ever occur.

But this institution is the result of an improved police: Our notions were originally different, and were necessarily different. Before agriculture was invented, people in a good measure depended on their cattle for sustenance.

In these early times, the few inhabitants that were in a country, being classed in tribes or clans, led a wandering life from place to place, for the convenience of pasture. Every clan or <212> tribe had a head, who was their general in war, and their judge in peace. And thus every chieftain was the judge over his own people, without regard to territory, which in a wandering state could not be of any consideration. After the invention of agriculture, which fixed a clan to a certain spot, the same principle prevailed, and neighbouring clans, to prevent disputes about jurisdiction, settled upon the following regulation, That the people of a clan, where-ever found, should be judged by their own chieftain.

During the third and fourth centuries, we find this regulation steadily observed in France, after it was deserted by the Romans and abandoned to the barbarians. It was an established rule among the Burgundians, Franks, Goths, and ancient inhabitants, That each people should be governed by their own laws, and by their own judges, even after they were intermixed by marriages and commerce. Nor was this an incommodious institution, in a country possessed by nations or clans, differing in their language, differing in their laws, and differing in their manners. There can be no doubt, that the same practice prevailed in this country, both before and after our several tribes or clans were united under one general head. The laws of the different clans have been digested into one general law, known by the name of *The Common law of Scotland;* but the chieftain's privilege <213> of judging his own people, continued long in force, and traces of it remain to this day. Clans were distinguished from each other, so as to prevent any confusion in exercising the privilege. They differed in their language, or in their dress; and when these differences were not found, those who lived together and pastured in common were reckoned to be of one clan. After agriculture was introduced, clans were distinguished, partly by a common name, and partly by living within a certain territory.

This regulation was favoured by the Feudal law, which made an additional bond of union betwixt the chieftain and his people, by the relation of superior and vassal. And the jurisdiction being thereby connected with land-property, is with respect to the title, termed territorial jurisdiction; though, with respect to its exercise, it is personal, without relation to territory. On the other hand, jurisdiction granted by the crown to persons or families, without relation to land-property, such as an heritable justiciary or an heritable sheriffship, is personal with respect to the title, but territorial with respect to its exercise. The first barons were no doubt the chieftains of clans; and the right of jurisdiction specified in the charters of creation, must not be constructed an original jurisdiction flowing from the king, but the jurisdiction that these chieftains enjoyed from the beginning o-<214>ver their own people. In imitation of these first barons, every man who got his lands erected into a barony, was held to be a chieftain, or the head of a clan; and the jurisdiction conferred upon him, though depending entirely on the grant, was, by the connection of ideas, considered to be the same that belonged originally to chieftains. And hence it is, that these territorial judges had the power of reclaiming their own people from other judges, and judging them in their own courts.

Upon the same principle, the royal boroughs had the power of reclaiming their own burgesses, not only from territorial judges, but even from the king's judges.* Pleas of the crown were excepted; because the royal boroughs had no jurisdiction in such crimes.[†] And here it must be remarked, that royal boroughs had a peculiar privilege, necessary for preserving peace, That in processes against strangers before the bailies, for a riot or breach of the peace committed within the town, reclaiming to the lord's court was not admitted.[‡]

But among a rude people delighting in war, where the authority of the chieftain depends on the good-will of his clan, this privilege was often exerted to protect criminals, instead of be-<215>ing exerted to bring them to justice. Endeavours were early used to correct this corrupt practice, by enacting, That a chieftain or baron should be bound to give a pledge or surety in the court where the criminal is attached, to do justice upon him in his own court within year and day:[||] and from this time, upon account of the pledge or surety given, the privilege of reclaiming obtained the name of repledging.

This regulation, though a wise and useful precaution, proved but an imperfect remedy. Nor was better to be expected; for the privilege of repledging was an unnatural excrescence in the body-politic, which admitted

---

* Leg. Burg. cap. 61.
[†] Ib. cap. 7.
[‡] First stat. Rob. I. cap. 16. § 3.
[||] Quon. attach. cap. 8.

of no effectual cure, other than amputation. The statutes of Alexander II. cap. 4. are evidence, that the power of repledging was prostituted in a vile manner, not only to protect the lord's own men from justice, but also to protect others for hire. And accordingly, by that statute, and by the first statutes Robert I. cap. 10. the power of repledging is confined within narrower bounds than formerly. But this power, after all the limitations imposed, being found still prejudicial to the common interest, an attack was prudently made upon it in its weakest part, viz. that of the royal boroughs, which produced the act 1. parl. 1488, ordaining burgesses to submit to <216> trial in the justice-air, without power of repledging. And to make this new regulation palatable, it was made the duty of the king's justice, to give an assize to a burgess of his own neighbours, if a sufficient number were present in court.

From what is said above, there can be no doubt that barons had a power of repledging from the king's courts, as well as from each other. The privilege, however, was of no great moment; because every partial judgment of the baron in favour of any of his own people, lay open to immediate redress, by an appeal to the king's court. An appeal lay even to the sheriff, against every sentence pronounced in the baron-court.* In this respect the power of repledging that the lords of regality enjoyed, was a privilege of much greater moment; because from a court of regality there lay no appeal but to the parliament.

Lords of regality had undoubtedly the power of repledging, when their people were apprehended out of their territory and brought before another court. And it is the only case in which there was occasion to exercise the privilege: for their jurisdiction being exclusive even of the king's courts, none of their people could be legally attached within their territory by an <217> extraneous judge; such an attachment would be void as *ultra vires,* and a declarator would be competent without necessity of repledging.

The first manifest symptom of the declining power of the crown-vassals, was the jurisdiction of the king's courts extended over regalities, so as to produce a cumulative jurisdiction. As this privilege was introduced by practice, not by statute, the encroachment was gradual, one instance following

* Reg. Maj. l. 1. cap. 3.

another, till the privilege was established. It is probable, that the power of repledging paved the way to this encroachment. For among a rude people, unskilled in the refinements of law, the encroachment would scarce be perceived, while the substantial prerogative remained with the chieftains, that of judging their own people; and whether that prerogative was maintained by a proper declinator, or by the power of repledging,[2] would be reckoned a mere *punctilio*. The people of a regality, originally exempted from all jurisdiction save that of their own lord, were thus imperceptibly subjected also to the king's courts. But still a regality being co-ordinate with the king's supreme courts, its decrees, as formerly, were subjected to no review except in parliament.

By the establishment of the court of session, which is the supreme court in civil matters, the regality-courts were rendered so far subordinate. <218> But in matters criminal, the jurisdiction, as co-ordinate with that of the justiciary-court, was preserved entire, together with the power of repledging even from that court.*

The sovereign courts, acquiring great splendor under good government, annihilated the baron's power of repledging. But the lords of regality did not so readily succumb under the weight of an enlarged prerogative; and though their privileges were in a great measure incompatible with the growing power of the crown, as well as with the orderly administration of justice; yet such was their influence in parliament, that the attempt to rob them of their privileges by an express law, was found not advisable. It was more prudent, to lie in wait for favourable opportunities to abridge them. The first opportunity that offered, respected church regalities annexed to the crown after the Reformation. The heritable bailies of these regalities being an inconsiderable body and in a singular case, it was not difficult to obtain a statute against them. And accordingly, though their power of repledging from the sheriff, both in civil and criminal matters, was reserved entire; yet it was enacted,† "That they should have no power of repledging from the court of <219> justiciary, except in the case of prevention by the first citation": which was abrogating their privilege of repledging from the

* Skene de verb. signif. tit. (Iter) § 12.
† Act 29. parl. 1587.
2. 1758, 1761 add: "so well known in the practice of Scotland,"

justiciary-court. This being a direct attack upon regality-privileges, though in some measure disguised, it was necessary to soften its harshness; which was done by substituting, in place of the power of repledging, a privilege in appearance greater, but in effect a mere shadow. It was, that the heritable bailie might sit with the king's justice and judge with him, and in case of conviction receive a proportion of the eschear.

This statute paved the way for abridging the privileges of laic regalities; as any handle is sufficient against a declining power.[3] The privilege of re-pledging was however kept alive, though it wore fainter and fainter every day; and at the long-run was indulged for fifteen days only, after the crime was committed. This we learn from the statutes appointing justiciars in the Highlands,* in which the rights and jurisdiction of lords of regality are reserved, and particularly "their right of prevention for fifteen days"; im-porting, That if the person was cited before the justice court within fifteen days of committing the alledged crime, the lord of regality might repledge; for if he was the <220> first attacher, even after the fifteen days, it cannot be doubted, but that he had the exclusive privilege of proceeding in the trial, and of passing a definitive sentence.

Thus we see the power of repledging reduced to a shadow, though in other respects the regality-court still maintained its rank, as co-ordinate with the court of justiciary; acknowledging no superior but the parliament. But as the regality-court had by this time lost all its original authority, its privileges were little regarded. The judges of the court of justiciary grad-ually increasing in power and dignity, heightened by contrasting them with regality-bailies, gave regality courts a severe blow, anno 1730, by admitting an advocation from the regality court of Glasgow (2); which was in effect declaring a regality-court subordinate to the court of justiciary in criminal matters, as it had all along been to the court of session in civil matters. This, it is true, was a church regality, annexed to the crown upon the Reforma-

(2) The act 3. Geo. II. cap. 32. impowering the judges of the court of justiciary, or any of them, to stay for thirty days the execution of any sentence of a regality-court importing corporal punishment, encouraged probably the court of justiciary to assume this power.

* Act 39. parl. 1693, act 37. parl. 1695, and act 8. parl. 1702.

3. 1758, 1761 add: "The speciality in the statute was forgot, or not regarded, and it was extended against all regalities of whatever sort."

tion; and the singularity of the case alarmed not much those who were possessed of laic-regalities. But the court of session gave re-<221>galities the dead-blow without necessity, after heritable jurisdictions were abolished by a late statute. For by virtue of the powers delegated to this court, to try the rights of those who should claim heritable jurisdictions and to estimate the same in money, they found* the justiciary belonging to the Earl of Morton over the islands of Orkney and Zetland, "to be an inferior jurisdiction only, and not co-ordinate with the court of justiciary." This judgment did not rest upon any limitation in the Earl's right, which was granted by parliament in the most ample terms; but upon the following ground, That the court of justiciary as constituted by act 1672,[4] is the supreme court in criminal, as the court of session is in civil matters, which consequently must render all heritable jurisdictions subordinate; courts of justiciary as well as courts of regality. But there is not in that statute, a single clause which so much as hints at a greater power in the court of justiciary than it formerly enjoyed. Thus it frequently happens, that the reason expressed is not always that which produces the judgment, but perhaps some latent circumstance operating upon the mind imperceptibly. Here the act 1672 was given as the cause of the judgment; though probably what at bottom moved the <222> judges, was a very different consideration. The new form of the court of justiciary, by substituting five lords of session as perpetual members instead of justice-deputes who were ambulatory, bestowed a dignity upon this court, to which it was formerly a stranger. This circumstance, joined with the growing power of the crown, which communicates itself to the ministers of the crown, advanced this court to a degree of splendor, that quite obscured bailies of regality. We have reason to believe, that this elevation of the court of justiciary, touching the mind imperceptibly, was really what influenced the judges; for it is difficult to conceive an equality of jurisdiction in two courts, that are so unequal in all other respects. And thus, by natural causes that govern all human affairs, territorial jurisdiction in Scotland was reduced to a mere shadow, which made it no harsh measure, to abolish it altogether by statute. <223>

* January 21. 1748.
4. Kames refers to the Act "concerning the regulation of the judicatories" dated 30 August 1672.

Courts

In most countries originally, the inhabitants were collected into clans or tribes, governed each by a chieftain, in whom were accumulated the several offices of general, magistrate, and judge. These clans or tribes, for a long course of time, subsisted perfectly distinct from each other, without any connection or intercourse among individuals of different clans. The invention of agriculture, extending connections beyond the clan, had a tendency to blend different clans together. Individuals of different clans, came to be more and more blended by intermarriages, and consequently by blood. Commerce arose, and united under its wings, not only distant individuals, but different nations. The clan connection, giving way by degrees, no longer subsists in any civilized country, being lost in the more extended connections that have no relation to clanship.

This change of connection among individuals, introduced a change in jurisdiction. After clans <224> were dissolved, and individuals were left free to their private connections, the jurisdiction of the chieftain could no longer subsist. Instead of it, judges were appointed, to exercise jurisdiction in different causes, and in different territories.

In a very narrow state, one judge perhaps may be sufficient to determine all controversies that belong to a court of law. But where the state is of any extent, many judges are required for an accurate and expeditious distribution of justice. If there must be a number, distribute among them the different branches of law, instead of giving to each a jurisdiction in controversies of whatever kind. It is here as in a manufacture: an artificer confined to one branch becomes more expert than if employed successively in many. But in law this regulation hath its limits: courts may be distinguished into civil, criminal, and ecclesiastical; but more minute divisions would be inconvenient, because the boundaries could not be accurately ascertained.

For the reason now given, it becomes also proper, in an extensive society, to appoint a judge for every district. Such judges can have no interference, as their jurisdictions are distinguished by natural marches and boundaries.

But judges subjected to no review, soon become arbitrary. Hence the necessity of superior <225> courts, to review the proceedings of the inferior. Where the superior court is a court of appeal only, it has no regular continuance, and is never convened but when there is occasion. This was formerly the case in Scotland, as we shall see by and by. It is an improvement to make this court perform, not only the duty of a court of appeal, but also that of an original court: in which case, it must have stated times of sitting and acting, commonly called terms. And such is the present condition of the superior courts in this island.

These observations lead to a distinction of courts into their different kinds. In the first place, courts are distinguished by the nature of the causes appropriated to each: they are either civil, criminal, or ecclesiastical. This is the primary boundary, which separates the jurisdiction of different courts.

The next boundary is territory. Courts of the same rank which judge the same causes, are separated from each other by the marches of their respective districts.

Courts superior and inferior which judge the same causes, admit not any local distinction; because a court superior or supreme has a jurisdiction that extends over the territories of several inferior courts. In this case, there can be no separation, other than the first citation. <226>

Beside these, there is in well-regulated states, a court of a peculiar constitution, that has no original jurisdiction, but is established as a court to review the proceedings of all other courts. This may properly be called a court of appeal; and such is the constitution of the House of Lords in Britain.

In the order here laid down, I proceed to examine the peculiar constitution of the courts in this country. And first, of the difference of jurisdiction with regard to causes. A man may be hurt in his goods, in his person, or in his character. The first is redressed in the court of session, and in other inferior civil courts; the second in the criminal court; and the third in the commissary court. Beside these, the court of exchequer is established, for managing subjects and making effectual claims, belonging to the crown. The court of admiralty has an exclusive jurisdiction, at the first instance, in all maritime and seafaring causes, foreign and domestic, whether civil or criminal, and over all persons within this realm, as concerned in the same. There are also many particular jurisdictions established with respect to certain causes, which must be tried by the judges appointed, and by none other.

The court of session hath an original jurisdiction in matters of property, and in every thing that comes under the notion of pecuniary in-<227>terest. Matters of rank and precedency, and of bearing arms, belong to the jurisdiction of the Lord Lyon. To determine a right of peerage, is the exclusive privilege of the House of Lords. Nor has the court of session an original jurisdiction, with respect to the qualifications of those who elect or are elected members of parliament. The reason is, that none of the foregoing claims make a pecuniary interest. The court of session, therefore, assumed a jurisdiction which they had not, when they sustained themselves judges in the dispute of precedency betwixt the Earls of Crawford and Sutherland. It was a still bolder step, to sustain themselves judges in the peerage of Oliphant, mentioned in Durie's decisions; and in the peerage of Lovat, decided a few years ago.

The matters now mentioned, are obviously not comprehended under the ordinary jurisdiction of the court of session; and the court had no occasion to assume extraordinary powers, when a different method is established for determining such controversies. But what shall we say of wrongs, where no remedy is provided? Many instances of this kind may be figured, which, having no relation to pecuniary interest, come not regularly under the cognisance of the court of session. The freeholders of a shire, for example, in order to disappoint one who claims to be inrolled, forbear to meet at the <228> Michaelmas head-court. This is a wrong, for which no remedy is provided by law; and yet our judges, confining themselves within their ordinary jurisdiction, refused to interpose in behalf of a freeholder who had suffered this wrong, and dismissed the complaint as incompetent before them.* Considering this case attentively, it may be justly doubted, whether such confined notions with respect to the powers of a supreme court, be not too scrupulous. No defect in the constitution of a state deserves greater reproach, than the giving licence to wrong without affording redress. Upon this account, it is the province, one should imagine, of the sovereign, and supreme court, to redress wrongs of every kind, where a peculiar remedy is not provided. Under the cognisance of the privy council in Scotland came many injuries, which, by the abolition of that court, are left without any peculiar remedy; and the court of session have with reluctance been obliged to listen to complaints of various kinds, that belonged properly to the privy council while it had a being. A new branch of jurisdiction has thus sprung up in the court of session, which daily increasing by new matter, will probably in time produce a general maxim, That it is the province of this court, to redress all wrongs for which no other <229> remedy is provided. We are, however, as yet far from being ripe for adopting this maxim. The utility of it is indeed perceived, but perceived too obscurely to have any steady influence on the practice of the court; and for that reason their proceedings in such matters are far from being uniform. In the foregoing case of the freeholders of Cromarty, we have one instance where the court would not venture beyond their ordinary limits; though thereby a palpable wrong was left without a remedy. I shall mention another instance, equally with the former beyond the ordinary jurisdiction of the court, where the judges ventured to give redress. A small land-estate, consisting of many parcels, houses, acres, &c. was split among a number of purchasers, who in a body petitioned the commissioners of supply, to divide the valuation among them, in order to have it ascertained what part of the land-tax each should pay. The commissioners, unwilling to split the land-tax into so small parts, refused the petition. Upon a complaint to the court of session against the commissioners, the convener was appointed to call a general meeting, in order to divide the valuation among the complainers.† This was not even a matter of judgment, but of pure authority,

---

* 20th December 1753, Mackenzie of Highfield *contra* freeholders of the shire of Cromarty.

† 4th August 1757, Malcolm and others *contra* commissioners of supply for the stewartry of Kirkoudbright.

assumed from the necessity of the thing, <230> there being no other remedy provided; for otherwise the court of session hath not by its constitution any authority over the commissioners of supply. A wrong done by the commissioners, in laying a greater proportion of the land-tax upon a proprietor of land than belongs to him, may be rectified by the court of session, as the supreme court in pecuniary matters; but this court has no regular authority over the commissioners, to direct their proceedings beforehand. In a question betwixt the procurator fiscal of the Lyon-court and Murray of Touchadam, 26th July 1775, it was admitted, that the court of session cannot interpose in the giving arms to a family, being purely ministerial. But if there be any dispute about arms between two persons, such as the giving arms to one which are contended to belong to another, the court of session must interpose, there being no other court for deciding such disputes.[1]

Upon a new subject, not moulded into any form nor resolved into any principle, men are apt to judge by sentiment more than by general rules; and for that reason, the fluctuation or even contrariety of judgments upon such subjects, is not wonderful. This is peculiarly the case of the subject under consideration: for beside its novelty, it is resolvable into a matter of public police; which, admitting many views not less various than intricate, occasions much <231> difficulty in the law questions that depend on it. Such difficulties, however, are not insuperable. Matters of law are ripened in the best manner, by warmth of debate at the bar, and coolness of judgment on the bench; and after many successful experiments of a bold interposition for the public good, the court of session will clearly perceive the utility of extending their jurisdiction to every sort of wrong, where the persons injured have no other means of obtaining redress.

This extraordinary power of redressing wrongs, far from a novelty, has a name appropriated to it in the language of our law. For what else is meant by the *nobile officium* of the court of session, so much talked of, and so little understood? The only difficulty is, How far this extraordinary jurisdiction or *nobile officium,* is, or ought to be, extended. The jurisdiction of the court of session, as a court of common law, is confined to matters of pecuniary interest; and it possibly may be thought, that its extraordinary

---

1. "In a question . . . deciding such disputes." added 1776.

jurisdiction ought to be confined within the same bounds. Such is the case of the court of exchequer; for its extraordinary or equitable powers, reach no farther than to rectify the common law, as far as relates to the subjects that come under its jurisdiction as a court of common law. But the power to redress wrongs of all kinds, must sub-<232>sist somewhere in every state; and in Scotland subsists naturally in the court of session. And with respect to the wrongs in particular that came under the jurisdiction of the privy council, our legislature, when they annihilated that court, must have intended, that its powers should so far devolve upon the court of session; for the legislature could not intend to leave without a remedy, the many wrongs that belonged to the jurisdiction of the privy council.

The rule I am contending for, appears to be adopted by the English court of chancery in its utmost extent. Every sort of wrong occasioned by the omission or transgression of any duty, is redressed in the court of chancery, where a remedy is not otherwise provided by common or statute law. And hence it is, that the jurisdiction of this court, confined originally within narrow bounds, has been gradually enlarged over a boundless variety of affairs.

The jurisdiction of the court of session in matters of property, is not only original, but totally exclusive of all other supreme courts. The property of the slightest moveable cannot be ascertained by the justiciary, by the exchequer, by the admiralty, or by the commissaries. The case is not precisely the same in other matters of pecuniary interest. The commissaries of Edinburgh, as well as inferior commissaries, have, with the court of session, a cumulative jurisdic-<233>tion in all such matters referred to oath of party. And in all maritime and seafaring causes, the high court of admiralty has, by act 16. parl. 1681, an exclusive jurisdiction at the first instance. Formerly the jurisdiction of the court of session in such causes, was cumulative with that of the admiral. One peculiarity there was in this cumulative jurisdiction, that where a maritime cause was brought before the session at the first instance, the judge of the admiral-court took his place among the Lords of Session, and voted with them.* But by the statute now mentioned, the powers and privileges of the admiral-court are greatly enlarged; and

---

* Sinclair, 9th March 1543, Lord Bothwell *contra* Flemings.

with relation to this court, the session at present is a court of appeal; precisely as the House of Lords is with relation to the session. Hence it seems to follow, that the court of session cannot regularly suspend the decree of an inferior admiral; which would be the same, as if a cause should be appealed from the sheriff to the House of Lords. With regard to the admiral-court, it must be also observed, that by prescription it hath acquired a jurisdiction in mercantile affairs; an incroachment which has no foundation, other than the natural connection that subsists between maritime affairs and those that are mercantile. But the privileges of this court <234> as to the former, are not extended over the latter: The court pretends not to an exclusive jurisdiction in mercantile affairs; with respect to which it is an inferior jurisdiction, subjected, like the sheriff-court, to the orders and review of the court of session, by advocation, suspension, and reduction, in the ordinary course. And we shall have occasion to see afterward, that the privileges of the admiral-court, with regard to mercantile causes, are not so entire as even those of the sheriff; it being the privilege of every person to decline the admiral-court in these causes.

Having described the causes proper to the court of session, in contradistinction to the other supreme courts, I proceed to causes, proper to it, in contradistinction to inferior courts. These may be comprehended under one rule, That all extraordinary actions, not founded on common law, but invented to redress any defect or wrong in the common law, are appropriated to the court of session, being in civil causes the sovereign and supreme court. Inferior courts are justly confined within the limits of common law; and if extraordinary powers be necessary for doing justice, these cannot safely be trusted but with a sovereign and supreme court. Upon this account, the court of session only, enjoys the privilege of voiding bonds, contracts, and other private deeds. For <235> the same reason, declarators of right, of nullity, and in general all declarators, are competent nowhere but in this court. An extraordinary removing against a tenant, who having a current tack is due a year's rent, is peculiar to this court, as also a proving the tenor or contents of a lost writ. And lastly, all actions between subject and subject founded solely upon equity, belong to the court of session, and to none other.

With respect to criminal jurisdiction, our old law was abundantly circumspect. Jealous of inferior courts, it confined their privileges within narrow bounds; and experience, the best test of political institutions, hath justified our law in this particular. All public crimes, i.e. all crimes by which the public is injured, and where the King is the prosecutor, are confined to the court of justiciary. With the political reason there is joined another, that it is not consistent with the dignity of the crown, to prosecute in an inferior court. All private crimes, however enormous, may be prosecuted before the sheriff. For if the private prosecutor who is injured chuse this court, the law ought to give way. The only case where a baron is trusted with life and death, is where a thief is catched with the stolen goods; and, in this case, the law requires, that the thief be put to death within three suns. The law so far gives way <236> to the natural impulse of punishing a criminal; an indulgence not much greater than is given to the party injured; for he himself may put the thief to death, if catched breaking his house. But after passion subsides, every one is sensible, that now there ought to be a regular trial.* The sheriff has the same power with respect to slaughter, that the baron has with respect to theft. A man taken in the act of murder, or with *red hand,* as expressed in our law, must have justice done upon him by the sheriff within three suns. If this time be allowed to elapse, the criminal cannot be put to death without a citation and a regular process, which must be before the justiciary, unless the relations of the deceased undertake the prosecution.

By the act 1681, mentioned above, an exclusive jurisdiction is given to the high admiral, "in all maritime and seafaring causes, foreign and domestic, whether civil or criminal; and over all persons within this realm, who are concerned in the same." With respect to the civil branch of this jurisdiction, I have had occasion to mention, that by prescription it is extended to mercantile causes. But though the civil jurisdiction of this country, is so far encroached on by the court of admiralty, the criminal judges, I presume, will be more watchful <237> over the powers trusted with them. Prohibited goods were seized at sea, and after they were put in a boat to be carried to land, the seizure-makers were attacked by those who had an interest in the goods; and in the scuffle a man was put to death. A criminal prosecution being brought before the court of justiciary, the judges doubted whether it did not belong to the admiral to try this crime, as committed at

---

* A baron is deprived of all jurisdiction in capital cases, by act 20° Geo. II. 43.

sea. After mature deliberation, the court sustained its own jurisdiction, upon the following grounds. It is not every civil cause arising at sea, that is appropriated to the admiral, but only maritime and seafaring causes. Nor is every crime committed at sea appropriated to him. The admiral has not a jurisdiction by the statute, unless such crime relate to maritime or sea-faring matters. Every crime committed against navigation, such as a mutiny among the crew, orders disobeyed, a ship prevented by violence from sail-ing, beating wounding or killing persons in such fray, piracy, and in general all crimes where the *animus* of the delinquent is to offend against the laws of navigation, are maritime or seafaring crimes, and come under the ex-clusive jurisdiction of the admiral. But if murder, adultery, forgery, or high treason, be committed on board a ship, the cognition belongs to the judge ordinary: The commissaries of Edinburgh will divorce, and the court of ju-<238>sticiary, or commissioners of *Oyer* and *Terminer,* will punish. The only argument for the admiral that seems plausible is, That he is declared the King's justice general upon the seas, and in all ports, harbours, creeks, &c. But to what effect? The answer to this question will clear the difficulty. He is not made justice-general with respect to all crimes whatever, but singly with respect to crimes concerning maritime or seafaring matters.

That a criminal jurisdiction belongs to the court of session is certain. The precise nature of it is not altogether certain. Instead of pretending to decide in a matter that appears somewhat dubious, I venture no farther than to give two different views of this jurisdiction, leaving every man to judge for himself. The first is as follows. In certain criminal matters, the court of session, by the force of connection, have been in use to exercise a criminal jurisdiction. Upon witnesses who prevaricate before them, they are in use to animadvert by a corporal punishment;* which is inherent in every court, civil or criminal. Again, in the case of forgery tried by the court of session, the court itself commonly inflicts the punishment where it is within the pain of death, without remitting the delinquent to the justiciary.† The punish-<239>ment, being a direct consequence of the civil sentence finding the defendant guilty of the forgery, belongs naturally to the court of session;

---

* Gosford, 6th July 1669, Heirs of Towie, *contra* Barclay.
† Durie, 14th July 1638, Dunbar *contra* Dunbar.

unless where the crime deserves death, the inflicting of which punishment, would be an encroachment too bold upon the criminal court. A slight punishment may be considered as accessory to the civil judgment; but a capital punishment makes too great a figure in the imagination to be considered in that light.

I proceed to the second view of this jurisdiction. It is not accurate to say, That the two courts of session and justiciary, are distinguished by the causes appropriated to each; and that the former is a civil court, the latter a criminal court. The justiciary is confined to crimes; but the court of session is not confined to civil actions. It may justly be held, that this court hath a jurisdiction in all crimes, unless where the proof depends totally or chiefly on witnesses. Not to mention punishments that are accessory to judgments in civil cases, such as punishment of forgery; many crimes public and private are prosecuted in this court, baratry, for example, and usury, even where it is prosecuted by the King's Advocate *ad vindictam publicam*.* These, and such like causes, are undertaken by the court, where the evi-<240>dence is chiefly by writ, and not by witnesses. The processes of fraudulent bankruptcy, and of wrongous imprisonment, are by statute† confined to this court; and for the reason now given, stellionate will also be competent before it. It is clear indeed, that this court cannot judge in any criminal action that must be tried by a jury; because its forms admit not this method of trial. Purpresture must be tried by a jury; and for that reason only, cannot be brought before it. And for the same reason, a capital punishment is denied to this court; for a capital punishment cannot be inflicted without a jury.

Ecclesiastical courts, beside their censorial powers with relation to manners and religion, have an important jurisdiction in providing parishes with proper ministers or pastors; and they exercise this jurisdiction, by naming for the minister of a vacant church, that person duly qualified who is presented by the patron. Their sentence is ultimate, even where their proceedings are illegal. The person authorised by their sentence, even in opposition to the presentee, is *de facto* minister of the parish, and as such is

* Haddington, 2d March 1611, Officers of State *contra* Coutie and others.
† Act 5. parl. 1696; Act 6. parl. 1701.

entitled to perform every ministerial function. One would imagine, that this should entitle him to the benefice or stipend; for a person invested in any office, is entitled of course to the emoluments. And yet the court of session, <241> without pretending to deprive a minister of his office, will bar him from the stipend, if the ecclesiastical court have proceeded illegally in the settlement. Such interposition of the court of session, singular in appearance, is however founded on law, and is also necessary in good policy. With respect to the former, there is no necessary connection betwixt being minister of a parish, and being entitled to a stipend; witness the pastors of the primitive church, who were maintained by voluntary contributions. It belongs indeed to the ecclesiastical court to provide a parish with a minister; but it belongs to the civil court to judge whether that minister be entitled to a stipend; and the court of session will find, that a minister wrongously settled has no claim to a stipend. With respect to the latter, it would be a great defect in the constitution of a government, that ecclesiastical courts should have an arbitrary power in providing parishes with ministers. To prevent such arbitrary power, the check, provided by law, is, That a minister settled illegally shall not be entitled to a stipend. This happily reconciles two things commonly opposite. The check is extremely mild, and yet is fully effectual to prevent the abuse.

The commissary-court is a branch of the ecclesiastical court, instituted for the discussion of certain civil matters, which among our supersti-<242>tious ancestors seemed to have an immediate connection with religion; divorce, for example, bastardy, scandal, causes referred to oath of party, and such like.

What shall be thought in point of jurisdiction, with respect to an injury where a man is affronted or dishonoured, without being hurt in his character or good fame; as, for example, where he is reviled, or contemptuously treated. For redressing such injuries, I find no court established in Britain: We have not such a thing as a court of honour. Hence it is, that in England words merely of passion are not actionable; as, You are a villain, rogue, varlet, knave. But if one call an attorney a knave, the words are actionable, if spoken with relation to his profession whereby he gets his living.* I am

* See Wood's Instit. book 4. ch. 4. p. 536.

not certain, that in England any verbal injury is actionable, except such as may be attended with pecuniary loss or damage. If not, we in Scotland are more delicate. Scandal, or any imputation upon a man's good name, may be sued before the commissaries, even where the scandal cannot be the occasion of any pecuniary loss; it is sufficient to say, I am hurt in my character. If I can qualify any pecuniary damage, or probability of damage, such scandal is also actionable before the court of session. <243>

When the several branches of jurisdiction, civil, criminal, and ecclesiastical, were distributed among different courts, great care seems to have been taken, that courts should be confined each precisely within its own limits. Bastardy, for example, could not be tried any where but in the ecclesiastical court; and so strictly was this observed, that if a question of bastardy occurred incidentally in a process depending before another court, the cause was stayed till the question of bastardy was tried in the proper court. This was done by a brieve from chancery, directed to the bishop, to try the bastardy as a prejudicial question.* The expence and delay of justice, occasioned by such scrupulous confinement of courts within precise limits, produced in Scotland an enlargement of jurisdiction, by impowering every court to decide in all points necessary to a final conclusion of the cause. This regulation is but late, though we had been long tending toward it. In the service of an heir, it was, and perhaps is, the practice, that if bastardy be objected, the judge to whom the brieve is directed is bound to stay his proceedings, till the question of bastardy be determined by the commissaries. But in the reduction of such a service, if bastardy be objected, the court of session remit not the question of bastardy to be tried by the commissa-<244>ries: they themselves take cognisance of it, singly to the effect of finishing the reduction. And this has been practised above a century.[†] The following case is of the same kind. A process of aliment was brought before the court of session, at a woman's instance against her alledged husband. He denied the marriage, and she offered a proof. It was thought by the court, that marriage here was not properly an incidental question; that it was the fundamental proposition, and the aliment merely a consequence.

---

* Reg. Maj. l. 2. cap. 50.
[†] See Durie, 23d July 1630, Pitsligo *contra* Davidson.

For this reason, they stayed the process of aliment, till the pursuer should instruct her marriage before the commissaries: Fountainhall, 29th December 1710, Forbes; 25th January 1711, Cameron *contra* Innes. But that this was too scrupulous, I have authority to say from a similar case determined lately. A child was produced in the seventh month after marriage; and the woman confessed, that her husband was not the father, but a man she named. In a process of aliment against this man, he denied that he was the father, and insisted upon the presumption *quod pater est quem nuptiae demonstrant.* Here legitimacy was the fundamental point, of which that of aliment was a consequence. Yet the court, who were bound to give judgment on the aliment, had no difficulty to discuss the preliminary question a-<245>bout the bastardy. And it was the general voice, that though, upon the medium of the child's being a bastard, they should decern for the aliment, this would not bar the child afterward from bringing a process before the commissaries, to ascertain its legitimacy.* Nor is it inconsistent, that two courts should give contrary judgments to different effects; for both judgments may stand and be effectual. Such contrariety of judgments one would wish to avoid; but it is better to submit to that risk, than to make it necessary that different courts should club their judgments to the finishing a single cause; which has always been found a great impediment to justice. It is upon the same principle, that inferior judges, though they have no original jurisdiction in forgery, can try that crime incidentally when stated as a defence.

And this leads me to consider more particularly a conflict betwixt different jurisdictions, where the same point is tried by both. This happens frequently, as above mentioned, with respect to different effects. But I see not that there can be in Britain a direct conflict betwixt two courts, both trying the same cause to the same effect. Opposite judgments would indeed be inextricable, as being flatly inconsistent; one of the courts, for example, ordering a thing to <246> be done, and the other court discharging it to be done. This has happened betwixt the two houses of parliament: it may again happen; and I know of no remedy in the constitution of our government. But in this island, matters of jurisdiction are better ordered than

---

* January 1756, Smith *contra* Fowler.

to afford place for such an absurdity. An indirect conflict may indeed happen, where two courts handling occasionally the same point, in different causes, are of different opinions upon that point. Such contrariety of opinion ought as far as possible to be avoided for the sake of expediency; as tending to lessen the authority of one of the courts, and perhaps both. But as such contrary opinions are the foundation of judgments calculated for different ends and purposes, these judgments when put to execution can never interfere. For example, being in pursuit of a horse stolen from me; and in the hands of a suspected person finding a horse that I judge to be mine, I use the privilege of a proprietor, and take away the horse by violence. A criminal process is brought against me for robbery; against which my defence is, that the horse is mine, and that it is lawful for a man to seize his own goods wherever he finds them. This obliges the criminal judge to try the question of property, as a preliminary point. It is judged, that the evidence I have given of my property, is not sufficient: the result is a sen-<247>tence to restore the horse, and to pay a fine. I obey the sentence in both particulars. But as the question of property was discussed with a view solely to the criminal prosecution, nothing bars me from bringing afterward a claim of property before a civil court; and if I prevail, the horse must again be put in my possession. This is not a conflict of execution, but only of opinion, which disturbs not the peace of society. The horse is declared mine; this secures to me the property; but does not unhinge the criminal sentence, nor relieve me from the punishment.

Another case of a similar nature really existed. Before the justices of peace a complaint was brought by General St Clair, with concourse of the procurator-fiscal, against John Ranken officer of excise, charging,

> That the said John Ranken did, without any legal order, forcibly break open the doors or windows of the house of Pitteadie, belonging to the General; and, after rummaging, left the house open, so as any person might have access to steal or carry away the furniture; and concluding that he should be fined and punished for the said riot and trespass.

The defendant acknowledged,

> That upon a particular information of prohibited goods, he, by virtue of a writ of assistance from the court of exchequer, did force open a window

<248> of the house, and made a search for prohibited goods, but found none; that in acting *virtute officii,* he was liable to no court but the exchequer.

The justices rejected the declinator, imposed a fine upon the defendant, and ordered him to be imprisoned till payment. In this case there is no difficulty. The officers of the revenue are not exempted from the courts of common law; and on a complaint against any one of them for a riot or other malversation, the justices must sustain themselves competent, and of course judge of the defence as well as of the libel. But I put a straiter case, That the officer had found prohibited goods, and sent them to the custom-house. According to the foregoing sentence of the justices, they must, in the case now supposed, have proceeded to order restitution of the goods, *quia spoliatus ante omnia restituendus.* But before restitution, a process is brought in exchequer for forfeiting these goods as prohibited. In this process the seizure is found regular, and the goods are adjudged to belong to the king. This judgment, which transfers the property to the king, relieves of course the officer from obeying the sentence of the justices ordering him to restore the goods; for if the goods belong not to the plaintiff, he cannot demand restitution. But then if the officer have been fined by the justices, their sentence so far must be effectual. The judg-<249>ment of the court of exchequer, cannot relieve him from the fine.

By an act 12th George I. cap. 27. § 17. intitled, "An act for the improvement of his Majesty's revenues of customs and excise, and inland duties," it is enacted,

> That for the better preventing of frauds in the entering for exportation any goods whereon there is a drawback, bounty, or premium, it shall be lawful for any officer of the customs, to open any bale or package; and if upon examination the same be found right entered, the officer shall, at his own charge, cause the same to be repacked; which charge shall be allowed to the officer, by the commissioners of the customs, if they think it reasonable.

Upon this statute, a process was brought before the court of session, against the officers of the customs at Port-Glasgow, for unpacking many hogsheads of tobacco entered for exportation, without repacking the same. The defendants betook themselves to a declinator of the court, contending, That this being a revenue-affair, it should not be tried but in the court of exchequer. The court of session had no opportunity to judge of this declinator, because the matter was taken away by a transaction. But the following reasons make it clear, that this declinator has no foundation. 1*mo,* Where an action of debt, from whatever cause arising, is brought <250> before the court of session, there can be no doubt of the competency of the court; because its jurisdiction, with regard to such matters, extends over all persons of whatever denomination. The court therefore must be competent. And if so, every thing pleaded in way of defence must also come under the cognisance of the same court, according to the modern rule, viz. That it is competent to judge of points proponed as a defence, to which the court is not competent in an original process. 2*do,* With respect to the claim under consideration, it is not competent before the court of exchequer, but only before the court of session; by the act 6*to Ann,* constituting the exchequer, the Barons are the sole judges in all demands by the king upon his subjects, concerning the revenues of customs, excise, &c.; but they have no jurisdiction where the claim is at the instance of the subject against the king. And for that reason, the claims against the forefeited estates, are by statute appointed to be determined by the court of session.

Having said what was thought proper upon courts as distinguished by the different causes appropriated to each, and as thereby different in kind; I proceed to consider courts of the same kind, as distinguished by territorial limits. As the jurisdiction of a territorial judge extends over all persons and over all things within his <251> territory, I shall first take under view personal actions, and next those that are real. With relation to the former, it is a rule that *Actor sequitur forum rei.* The reason is, that the plaintiff must apply to that judge who hath authority over his party, and can oblige him to do his duty; which must be the judge of that territory, within which the party dwells and has his ordinary residence. The inhabitants only are subjected to a territorial judge, and not every person who may be found occasionally within the territory; such a person is subjected to the judge of the territory where his residence is; and it concerns the public police, that jurisdictions be kept as distinct as possible. But as it may frequently be doubtful where the residence or domicil of a party is, a plain rule is established in practice, That a man's domicil is construed to be his latest residence for forty days before the citation. This however is not so strictly understood, as that a man can have but one domicil. There is no inconsistency in his having at the same time different domicils, and in being subjected to different jurisdictions, supposing these domicils to be situated in different territories.* It was accordingly judged, that a gentleman, who had his country house in the shire of Haddington and at the same time lived frequently with his mother-in-<252>law in Edinburgh and had a seat in one of the churches there, was subjected to both jurisdictions.† On the other hand, a man who has no certain domicil, must be subjected to that judge within whose territory he is found. This is commonly the case of soldiers; and hence the maxim, "Miles ibi domicilium habere videtur, ubi meret, si nihil in patria possideat."‡2 In a reduction accordingly of a decree against a soldier, pronounced by the bailies of a town where the regiment was for the time, and he personally cited; it being urged that he was not forty days there, and therefore not subjected to the jurisdiction; the Lords considering that soldiers have no fixed dwelling, repelled the reasons of reduction.‖

To this rule, that *Actor sequitur forum rei,* there are several exceptions, depending on circumstances that entitle the claimant to cite his party to appear before the judge of a territory where the party hath not a residence. A covenant, a delict, nativity, have each of them this effect. A covenant bestows a jurisdiction on the judge of the territory where it is made, provided the party be found within the territory, <253> and be cited there.§ The reason is, that if no other place for performance be specified, it is implied in the covenant, that it shall be performed in the place where it is made; and it is natural to apply for redress to the judge of that territory where the failure happens, provided the party who fails be found there. For the same reason, if a certain place be named for performance, this place only is regarded, and not the place of the covenant; according to the maxim,

---

* See l. 6. § 2. l. 27. § 2. Ad municipalem. [[I.e., *Digest* 50.6.2.]]

† Fountainhall, 15th July 1701, Spottiswood *contra* Morison.

‡ l. 23. § 1. Ad municipalem.

‖ Fountainhall, 12th November 1709, Lees *contra* Parlan.

§ See l. 19. De judiciis. [[I.e., *Digest* 5.1.19.]]

2. "A soldier is regarded as having his domicile where he serves, if he has no possessions in his *patria.*" *Digest* 50.1.23.1. Trans. Watson.

"Contraxisse unusquisque in eo loco intelligitur, in quo ut solveret se obligavit."*[3] The court of session, accordingly, though they refused to sustain themselves judges betwixt two foreigners, with relation to a covenant made abroad, thought themselves competent, where it was agreed the debt should be paid in this country.[†]

A criminal judge, in the same manner, hath a jurisdiction over all persons committing delicts within his territory, provided the delinquent be found within the territory, and be cited there, or be sent there by the authority of a magistrate to whom he is subjected *ratione domicilii*.[‡] Nor can the delinquent decline the court, upon a pretext which in ordinary cases <254> would be sufficient, viz. that he hath not a domicil within the territory, nor hath resided there forty days.[||] This matter is carried so far, as to prefer the *forum delicti* before that of the domicil; according to a maxim, That crimes ought to be tried and punished where they are committed; and that a judge hath no concern with any crime but what is committed within his own territory. Hence it is, that a baron having unlawed his tenant for blood, the decree was declared null; because the fact was not done upon the baron's ground; nor did the party hurt live within his territory; nor did he make his complaint there.[§] In like manner, the Lords turned into a libel, the decree of an inferior court fining a party for a riot committed in a different territory.[¶] In these cases the prosecution was at the instance of the procurator-fiscal. But where the party injured is the prosecutor, I see no reason why he may not have his choice of either *forum,* viz. of the delict, or of the delinquent.**[**] <255>

With relation to jurisdiction, civil, criminal, and ecclesiastical, I have had occasion to observe, how strictly each court was confined originally within its own province. The same way of thinking obtained with relation

---

* l. 21. De obligat. et action.

[†] Haddington, 23d November 1610, Vernor *contra* Elvies.

[‡] l. 3. pr. De re militari. [[I.e., *Digest* 48.16.3.]]

[||] Gosford, 18th November 1673, Gordon *contra* Macculloch.

[§] Durie, 28th July 1630, Freeland *contra* Sheriff of Perth.

[¶] Fountainhall, 14th February 1708, Procurator-fiscal of Dumblane *contra* Wright.

** See to this purpose, l. 1. C. Ubi de crimin. agi oporteat. [[I.e., *Codex* 3.15.1.]]

3. "Every person is considered to have concluded a contract in the place where he had bound himself to pay." *Digest* 44.7.21. Trans. Watson.

to territorial jurisdiction. To found an action, it was not sufficient that the
defendant lived within the territory: if the cause of action did not also arise
within the territory, the judge was not competent. In remedying disorders
and inconveniencies, men seldom confine themselves within proper bounds.
The jurisdiction exercised by chieftains over their own people was found
so inconvenient, especially when different clans came to be mingled together by blood and commerce, that in reforming the abuse judges were
confined within the strictest limits, with respect to territory as well as causes.
And indeed, the thought was natural, that it is the duty of every judge to
watch over the inhabitants of his territory, and to regulate their conduct
and behaviour while subjected to his authority; but that he hath no concern
with what is done in another territory. This I say is a thought that figures
in theory; and might answer tolerably well in practice, while men were in
a good measure stationary, and their commercial dealings confined to the
neighbourhood. But it became altogether impracticable, after men were put
in motion by extensive commerce. <256> The impediment to the distribution of justice, occasioned by this narrow and confined principle of the
common law, was in England soon felt, and an early remedy provided. The
court of the constable and marshal was established for trying all actions
founded upon contracts, delicts, or other facts, that had their existence in
foreign parts; and as the common law of England did not reach such cases,
these actions were tried *jure gentium*. This court was much frequented while
the English continued to have a footing in France. After they were forced
to abandon their conquests there, the court, from want of business, dwindled away to nothing. To support a court with so little prospect of business,
was thought unnecessary; and a contrivance was found out, to bring before
the courts of Westminster the few causes of this nature that occurred. A
fiction is an admirable resource for lawyers, in matters of difficulty. The
cause of action is set forth in the declaration, as having happened in some
particular place within England. It is not incumbent on the pursuer to prove
this fact; nor is it lawful for the defendant to traverse it.* But inferior courts
enjoy not the privilege of this fiction; and therefore in England, to this day,

---

* See Arth. Duck de authoritate juris Civilis, l. 2. cap. 8. pars 3. § 15. 16. 17. and 18.

an inferior court is not competent in any process, where the cause <257> of action doth not arise within the territory of that court.* It is not sufficient that the party against whom the claim lies is subjected personally to the jurisdiction. And if he retire into foreign parts, there is no power by the common law to cite him to appear before any court in England. There is not in the practice of England any form of a citation, resembling ours at the market-cross of Edinburgh, pier and shore of Leith.[4] The defect of the English law with respect to persons out of the kingdom, is supplied by 5th Geo. ll. cap. 25.[5]

We probably had once the same strict way of thinking with respect to territorial judges; but in later times we have relaxed greatly and usefully from such confined notions. As to an action of debt, for example, what can it signify in point of jurisdiction, where the cause of action arose? The debtor's *mora* in the territory where he resides, is a just foundation for a decree against him by the judge of that territory.[6] Crimes indeed admit of a different consideration: a judge or magistrate must preserve the peace within his own territory; but reckons himself not concerned with crimes committed any where else. Upon that account, a criminal prosecution at the instance of the public, comes regularly before that judge within whose <258> territory the crime was committed. But, as above suggested, where the prosecution is at the instance of the party injured, he may bring the

* Abridgment of the Law, vol. 1. p. 562. 563. and 564.

4. See Stair, *Institutions,* p. 660: "All Executions [of Summons] at Merkat Crosses, or at the Peer of *Lieth* must be by Messengers, and must bear his going to the *Merkat Cross in due time of day,* when people may take notice; And before he read the Summons, he must with audible voice, cry three *Oyesses;* The design whereof is to convocat people, to hear and give notice; And then he must read the Letters, and require the Witnesses being present; And must affix a Copy on the *Cross* or *Peer.*"

1758, 1761 add a footnote: "This defect in the common law may occasion so gross injustice, that the court of chancery, I can have no doubt, will find a remedy. The person abroad cannot be legally cited, but notice may be given him by authority of the court; and if he appear not in his own defence, a decree will, I presume, be given, for making the claim effectual out of his funds personal and real."

5. "The defect of the English law . . . 5th Geo. II. cap. 25." added 1776.

6. 1758, 1761: "The debtor's *mora* . . . of that territory" = "This circumstance therefore is quite disregarded. If the party against whom the claim lyes, be subjected personally to the court, we reckon the jurisdiction well founded."

prosecution before that judge to whom the delinquent is subjected *ratione domicilii.* For where a prosecution is chiefly intended to gratify the resentment of the party injured, it naturally belongs to him to chuse the *forum.*

I proceed to the third exception, that of nativity; and in what cases it makes a *forum,* deserves peculiar attention; because writers seem not to have any accurate notions about it. Jurisdiction was of old, for the most part, personal, founded upon the clan-connection; every person belonging to a clan, being subjected to the jurisdiction of the chieftain, and to none else. While such was the law, nativity or the *locus originis* was the only circumstance that founded a jurisdiction. Commerce gave a new turn to this matter, by the connections it formed among different nations, and by the confluence it produced in places of trade from all different countries. The clan-jurisdiction becoming by these means inexplicable, gave place to territorial jurisdiction; after which the *locus originis* became a mighty slight affair. The law of nations indulges individuals to change their country, and to fix their residence where they can find better bread than at home. Such migrations are frequent in all trading countries; <259> and it would be unreasonable to subject a man to the laws of his native country, after he has deserted it, and is perhaps naturalized in the country where he is settled for life. It is indeed not an absurd rule, that, even in this case, the duty he owes to his native country, ought to restrain him from carrying arms against it; and I observe, that this has been reckoned the law of nations. But supposing him so far bound, it is a much wider step to subject him to the courts of his native country, where he has no residence, where he has no effects, and to which he has no intention ever to return. I might add, were it necessary, that the effect of nativity even with regard to treason, is at present scarce thought rational, without other circumstances to support it; and that it is a punishment too severe, to put to death as guilty of high treason the subjects of a foreign prince taken in war, merely because they were born in the country where they are prisoners. Voet* cites many authorities to prove, that birth singly doth not produce a *forum competens, excepto solo majestatis crimine.* And therefore, upon the whole, the following conclusion seems to be well founded, That nativity, with respect to the present subject, stands

* De judiciis, § 91.

upon the precise same footing with contracts and delicts; and that like the *locus contractus,* and *locus delicti,* the *locus ori-*<260>*ginis* will found a jurisdiction, provided the party be found within the territory. None of them have any other effect, than to subject the party to a jurisdiction where he hath not a residence (1).

I am aware, that in practice actions are commonly sustained against natives of this country, even when they are abroad *animo remanendi;* and in this case that an edictal citation at the market-cross of Edinburgh, pier and shore of Leith, is held sufficient. It is not however positively asserted, that such persons, like inhabitants, are subjected to the courts of this country. The pretext commonly is, that the decree is intended for no other purpose but to attach <261> the debtor's effects in Scotland, and his person when found in his native country. Several of these cases, which cannot be justified by principles, are collected in the Dictionary.* So much appears from them, that the court of session did not pretend to assume a jurisdiction over the subjects of a foreign prince, upon account singly of their being natives of Scotland; and that, in order to found such jurisdiction, it was thought necessary to have reference to effects situated here, either really or by supposition. But there is no accuracy in this way of thinking. If nativity, singly considered, make a *forum,* the jurisdiction requires no support from collateral circumstances. If nativity singly make not a *forum,* no other circumstance can be held sufficient, unless actual presence. Without this circumstance, the judge cannot give authority even to the first act of jurisdiction, viz. a citation. And therefore, all that can in this case be done, is to proceed as against foreigners whose effects are found within Scotland.

(1) To carry this matter a step farther, I put the case, That a man born in Scotland and having a land-estate there, goes abroad, is naturalized in a foreign country, acquires a fortune, and settles there with his family, *animo remanendi.* Will not he and his descendants, while they retain their family-estate in Scotland, be considered as Scotsmen? I incline to the affirmative, and that they will be subjected to the courts here, precisely like natives. And if this doctrine hold where a Scotsman settles in Holland, France, or Germany, it must *a fortiore* hold where he settles in England, which with Scotland makes one kingdom. But an Englishman, by purchasing a land estate here, becomes not *eo ipso* a Scotsman, to be subjected personally to the courts of this country. In particular, he is not liable to answer a citation at the market-cross of Edinburgh, pier and shore of Leith. Such weight is still laid upon the *locus originis.*
* [[Kames, *Decisions of the Court of Session.*]] Vol. 1. p. 327.

The foregoing exceptions to the rule of law *quod actor sequitur forum rei,* are constraints upon the defendant, by obliging him to answer in another jurisdiction than where he has fixed his residence. Prorogation of jurisdiction is an exception of a different nature, for it puts the party under no constraint. Where a man is <262> called before an incompetent court, he may offer a declinator; and it is only in case he forbear to make this objection, that the decree is held good against him, by his acquiescence in the jurisdiction. How far and in what cases such prorogation can have effect, is not clearly laid down by our writers. Lawyers are apt to be misled, by following implicitly what is said in the Roman law upon this subject. For these reasons, I shall handle the subject at large; and endeavour to fix, the best way I can, how far decrees are by our law effectual upon the footing merely of prorogation. This subject is treated by Roman writers with great accuracy.* "Si se subjiciant alicui jurisdictioni et consentiant; inter consentientes, cujusvis judicis qui tribunali praeest, vel aliam jurisdictionem habet, est jurisdictio."[7] Thus, though consent, by the Roman law, cannot make a man a judge who is not otherwise a judge; it has however the effect to bestow upon a judge a new jurisdiction, and to enable him to determine in a case, to which, abstracting from consent, he is incompetent. Upon this principle, a civil judge may determine in a criminal matter, a criminal judge in a matter that is civil; and a judge, whose jurisdiction is limited with respect to sums, may give judgment without li-<263>mitation.[†] And hence the doctrine laid down by commentators, may be easily understood. They mention four different ways by which a jurisdiction may be limited; it may be limited as to time, as to place, as to persons, and as to causes. With respect to the two first, it is evident from the law above cited, that jurisdiction cannot be prorogated. A judge, after his commission is at an end, has no manner of jurisdiction; and as little jurisdiction has he, beyond the bounds of his territory. But as to persons and causes the matter is otherwise. For though consent cannot advance a private man to be a judge; yet, supposing him

---

* l. 1. De judiciis.

† See as to this last point, l. 74. § 1. De judiciis. [[I.e., *Digest* 5.1.74.1.]]

7. "If people submit themselves and agree to someone's jurisdiction, any judge who is in charge of a seat of judgment or has other jurisdiction has jurisdiction over those agreeing." *Digest* 5.1.1. Trans. Watson.

once a judge, consent will, in the Roman law, enable him to pronounce sentence against a person not otherwise subjected to his jurisdiction, and in a cause where he has no original jurisdiction.

Our law, with relation to persons, is the same. For though it be a rule in both laws, that the authority of a judge is confined within his territory, and that no person living in another territory is bound to obey his summons; yet, by our law as well as that of the Romans, if a man cited irregularly chuse to appear, or if he appear without citation, and plead defences, the jurisdiction is thereby prorogated, and the decree hath its full effect. But with respect to causes, our law differs widely. A civil cause <264> brought before the justiciary, will not produce an effectual decree, even with the express consent of the defendant. In like manner, if a process for contravention of laburrows, which is peculiar to the court of session, be brought before an inferior court, the acquiescence of the defendant, submitting to the jurisdiction and pleading defences, will not prorogate the jurisdiction. The decree is null by exception.* And the like judgment was given with respect to an extraordinary process of removing, founded on the lessee's failure to pay his rent.† With respect to causes where the judge is incompetent, it is a rule with us, That consent alone cannot found a jurisdiction, nor impower the judge to give sentence. Causes against members of the college of justice when sued before an inferior court, are not an exception from this rule. It is their privilege, to have every civil action against them tried in the court of session; and the defendant may advocate upon his privilege, if he chuse not to submit to the inferior judge. Acquiescence, however, in the inferior judge is not a prorogation of jurisdiction, but merely the waving a privilege; for a court, which hath a radical jurisdiction, stands in no <265> need of a prorogation to establish its authority. An action of debt, for example, is competent before the sheriff against every inhabitant within his territory, not excepting members of the college of justice. The only difference is, that these enjoy the peculiar privilege of removing the cause, if they think proper, to the court of session. But if they chuse not to use their privilege, the sheriff goes on against them as

---

* Haddington, 6th July 1611, Kennedy *contra* Kennedy.
† Falconar, 22d December 1681, Beaton *contra* his tenants.

against others, by virtue of his original jurisdiction. The same is precisely the case of the judge-admiral, with relation to mercantile causes. These are not contained in his charter; in these however he hath obtained a jurisdiction by prescription; not so perfectly indeed, as to oblige any one to submit to this assumed jurisdiction. If he submit, the decree will be effectual; and even a decree in absence will be effectual. But a defendant, who is not willing to submit to such jurisdiction, may bring the cause before the court of session by advocation, singly upon privilege, without being obliged to assign any other reason.

Having discussed personal actions, which with relation to territorial jurisdiction are first in order, I proceed to real actions. A real action is, where the conclusion of the declaration or libel respects things only, and not persons; as, for example, a declarator of property or servitude, a declarator of marches, and such like. And <266> the question is, What is the proper court for trying such causes, when the subject or thing is locally within one territory, and the possessor within another? This is not an intricate question. The answer obviously is, That where the conclusion regards the subject, that judge must be chosen who hath authority over it, viz. the judge of that territory where it is situated; for territorial jurisdiction is connected with things as well as with persons. But a difficulty occurs in this case. The possessor ought in justice to be called, in order to defend his interest; and yet he cannot be summoned by a judge within whose territory he resides not. My notion in this matter may, I am afraid, appear singular. I acknowledge, that those persons only who have a domicil within the territory, are subjected to the authority of the court; and that it is in vain for a judge to command any thing to be done or forborn, by a person who is not under his authority. Such person cannot even be cited to appear in court; because no person is bound to obey the commands of a judge who hath no authority over him. The matter, however, is not without remedy. Instead of a citation, which implies jurisdiction, why may not an intimation or notification suffice, in a case where there is no personal conclusion against the party?* Such notification <267> may be given by any one, especially by the judge. Such notification withal, in material justice, is equivalent to a regular citation;

* See a form of process annexed to the Reg. Majest. ch. 4. § 4. & 5.

because it hath all the advantages of a citation, by affording the party full opportunity to defend his interest. If this form of process be unexceptionable in point of rationality, it is in a good measure necessary in point of expediency. For how otherwise shall any real claim be made effectual, where the antagonist and the subject in debate are not both within the same territory? If I shall follow the domicil of my party, a decree against him may be a foundation for damages, but will not put me in possession of the subject. This branch of my claim cannot by any other judge be made effectual, than by the judge of the territory where the subject is. From this hint it is evident, that if a notification be not sufficient, the supreme court must be applied to in every case of this nature, which would be a great defect in public police. Nor would even this be always an effectual remedy; for what if my party be abroad *animo remanendi,* or perhaps a foreigner? In this case, there is no resource but the notification; and in this case, luckily for my argument, the notification is held sufficient. The process I have in my eye, is that which commonly passes under the name of arrestment *jurisdictionis fundandae gratia.* The judge within whose territory the <268> goods of a foreign debtor are, having a jurisdiction over these goods though not over the proprietor, can adjudge them to a creditor for his payment. In this process of adjudication or forthcoming, the person in whose hands the goods are found, is trusted with the notification; though, in my apprehension, the process would be more regular and more solemn, were the notification directed by authority of the court. This process, when it respects moveables, is generally preceded by an arrestment of the goods, in order to prevent their being withdrawn and carried out of the territory; and as by this means the jurisdiction is secured, the arrestment is termed an arrestment *jurisdictionis fundandae gratia;* improperly indeed: the arrestment, far from founding the jurisdiction, supposes the jurisdiction antecedently founded; for by what authority could the arrestment be used, if the goods were not already subjected to the jurisdiction? And so little essential is an arrestment to this process, that if the creditor rely on the person in whose hands the goods are, he may carry on the process to its final issue, without using an arrestment.

In following out any real action, where the dispute is with one of our own country who resides not within the jurisdiction, I see no good cause why the form now mentioned may not be used as well as in the case of foreigners. And <269> I must observe, that we approach extremely near to this form, by obtaining the interposition of the court of session, or rather of the King, for citing the party to appear within the jurisdiction where the subject lies. The warrant for citation, in this case, is termed a *letter of supplement,* which is never given in a personal action; for there the rule obtains, *Quod actor sequitur forum rei.* And it appears to me, that this form of a supplement has crept in, not from necessity, because I hold a private notification to be sufficient, but from the prepossession of custom; a regular citation, as the first step of process, being so general, as to be thought necessary in all cases. Custom is so naturally productive of a bias, and takes so firm hold of the mind, that it requires the utmost fortitude of reason to overcome it. Were I not afraid of refining too much, I should venture to say further, that though every inhabitant in Scotland is bound to appear in the court of session when regularly called; yet I deny it to be in the power of this court, to oblige them to appear in any court to which they are not subjected. If my creditor shall bring a process against me for payment before a sheriff within whose territory I have no residence, the court of session cannot give warrant for a letter of supplement to oblige me to defend myself there; and were my presence equally necessary in a real action, <270> a letter of supplement could not be issued in a real action more than in one that is personal. But my presence is not necessary, where there is no personal conclusion against me. Common justice indeed requires a notification; and the intention of a letter of supplement is not to be a warrant for citation, but only for notification.

To view this matter in its different circumstances, we shall invert the case, by supposing the debtor to be within the jurisdiction, not his effects. Upon a minute of sale of land, the vender is sued within the sheriffdom where he resides, to grant a disposition. Damages may be awarded for not fulfilling the covenant; but the land cannot be adjudged to the pursuer, because it is not under the sheriff's jurisdiction. The sheriff hath by prescription obtained a privilege of pronouncing a decree of adjudication *contra hereditatem jacentem;* but if the real estate be not locally within his territory, he cannot pronounce such a decree. Hence a remarkable difference appears, betwixt a judicial transference of property or any real decerniture, and a personal decerniture respecting a particular subject. The former is *ultra vires* where the subject is not locally within the territory: not so the latter; for it is enough that the defendant have his residence within the territory. A judge may interpose his authority, and com-<271>mand the defendant to fulfil his bargain by conveying land or moveables to the pursuer: To found the judge's authority in this case, it is not necessary that the subject be within the territory. But what if the defendant be refractory? The judge may punish him with imprisonment, or condemn him in damages. There the judge must stop; for he has no authority over the subject. Upon this footing, a burgess of Edinburgh suing another brother burgess in the town-court, to remove from certain lands *extra territorium,* the Lords thought the process regular.* And upon the same footing, a Scotsman being convened before the court of session for forging a title to a land-estate in Ireland, the court tried the forgery, because the defendant was subjected to their jurisdiction; and the forgery being proved, the forged deed was ordained to be cancelled.† A debtor, within threescore days of his notour bankruptcy, goes to England with a favourite creditor, and there assigns to him, for his security and payment, a number of English debts. In a reduction upon the act 1696,[8] against the assignee, he pleads, that the court of session hath no jurisdiction over English debtors, and that this court cannot reduce an assignment which conveys subjects not under its jurisdiction. Ac-<272>cording to the principles above laid down, the following answer appears to be good, That it was wrong in the assignee to concur with the bankrupt in a stratagem to defraud the other creditors, who, in the case of bankruptcy, are entitled to a proportion of the debtor's effects; that the assignee is subjected to the court of session and to their orders; and that it is the duty of the court, to ordain the assignee to make over to the creditors the debts in question, in order to an equal distribution; or rather to subject him to the creditors for a sum equivalent to these debts, deducting what of these debts he shall convey to the creditors within a limited time.

In the beginning of this discourse, I have given a sketch of the different powers of our supreme courts, with respect to causes. Upon the present

---

* Colvil, 7th March 1759, Johnston *contra* Johnston.
† Falconer, 14th February 1683, Murray *contra* Murray.
8. It is not clear which Act Kames is referring to here.

head it is proper to be observed, that these courts are also, in some measure, distinguished with respect to territory. The territorial jurisdictions of the justiciary and exchequer are not confined to land, but reach over all friths, and also over the sea adjoining to the land: These jurisdictions reach over Scotland, and the portions of water now mentioned are conceived to make part of Scotland. The jurisdiction of the court of session is no less extensive, considered as territorial; and it enjoys beside a jurisdiction over all the natives of Scot-<273>land wherever existing, provided they have not deserted their native country, but are abroad occasionally only.* The admiral-court again hath a jurisdiction with regard to all maritime and seafaring matters, civil and criminal, happening in whatever part of the world, provided the person against whom the complaint is laid be found in this country.

With respect to our courts considered as superior and inferior, I begin with observing, that the ordinary method of seeking redress of injustice done by an inferior court, is by appealing to one that is superior. That this particularly was the method in Scotland, is clear from our most ancient law-books. It is laid down,

> That a party may appeal from one court to another, as oft as judgment is given against him, finding burghs lawful for every doom gainsaid; from court to court; till it be decided for or against him in parliament; from which no appeal can be made, because it is the highest court, and ordained for redressing wrongs done by all inferior courts.†

An appeal lay from the sentence of a baron or freeholder, to the sheriff; and from the sentence of magistrates within burgh, to the chamberlain; from the sheriff and chamberlain, to the king's justiciar; and from him, not to the parliament <274> as originally, but to thirty or forty persons named by his Majesty, with parliamentary powers to discuss the appeal.‡

This method for obtaining redress of error in judgment, hath in Scotland gone into disuse, excepting an appeal to the British House of Lords, from the sovereign courts; and to the higher ecclesiastical courts, from those that are inferior. What was the cause of this innovation? We have the au-

---

* See [[Kames,]] Abridgement of statute-law, note 7.
† Mod. Ten. Cur. cap. 16.
‡ Act 95. parl. 1503.

thority of Stair,* that after the institution of the college of justice, appeals gave place to advocations, suspensions, and reductions. But by what means, and after what manner? Appeals are not discharged by any statute; and depending on the will of those who conceive themselves wronged, are too obsequious to passion and prejudice to be tamely surrendered. Being here left in the dark by our writers, we shall try if the want of facts can be supplied by rational conjecture.

In order to talk with perspicuity, I find it necessary to premise a historical account of the supreme courts that in this country have successively been established for civil causes. Through most of the European nations, at a certain period of their history, the king and council composed the only supreme civil court, in which all causes were tried that came not under the jurisdiction of inferior courts. But it must be re-<275>marked, that, in Scotland at least, this was not a court of appeal; for, as above observed, causes originally were removed by appeal from the King's justiciary to the parliament, and afterward to persons appointed by the King with parliamentary powers. This court, having no continuance nor regular times of meeting, was extremely inconvenient; beside that the King, who presided, had little time or inclination for deciding in private affairs. This made it necessary to establish regular courts for different causes; having appointed terms of sufficient length for all matters that should come before them. Thus in England, the king's bench, the exchequer, and the court of common pleas, arose out of the said court, and were all fully established in the reign of Edward I. We did not early apply so effectual a remedy. What first occurred to our legislature, was, to relieve the King and council, by substituting in their place the court of session,† to sit three times in the year, in order "finally to determine all and sundry complaints, causes, and quarrels that may be determined before the King and his council." This court acted but forty days at a time; and the members, who served by rotation, were so numerous, that the round was seldom completed in less time than seven years.‡ This court was far from being a com-<276>plete remedy. Its members and its place of sitting were changeable; and its terms were too

---

* L. 4. cap. § 31.
† Act 65. parl. 1425.
‡ See act 63. parl. 1457.

short. The next attempt to remedy the inconveniencies of the former courts, was the daily council, erected by the act 58. parl. 1503. The statute, on a narrative of the great delay of justice by the short terms of the session, and their want of time, appoints a council to be chosen by the King, to sit continually in Edinburgh the year round, or where else it shall please the King to appoint, to determine all causes that were formerly competent before the session. This court, called *The Daily Council,* from their sitting daily through the year, was also defective in its constitution, having no quorum named, nor any compulsion on the judges to attend. By that defect it frequently happened, that a cause passed successively through the hands of different judges; which was a great impediment to the regular administration of justice; for in a politic body of judges, there is not a greater disease than a fluctuation of the members. This court accordingly was soon laid aside, to make way for the court of council and session, established *in anno* 1532, in the same form that at present subsists, having stated terms of a reasonable endurance, and a certain number of judges, who all of them are tied to punctual attendance. <277>

To return to appeals, I remark, that an appeal was competent against an interlocutory as well as against a definitive sentence;* which might be extremely vexatious, by putting it in the power of the defendant to prolong a cause without end. Figure only a civil action furnishing exceptions partly dilatory and partly peremptory, to the amount of half a dozen, which is no bold supposition; and observe what may follow. In an appeal, the ascent was necessarily gradual to the court next in order; for there was not access to the court in the last resort, till redress was denied by each of the intermediate courts. Thus, from the sentence of a baron-court, or of the bailie-court in a royal borough, there must have been no fewer than three appeals in order to obtain the judgment of the parliament, or of the court of appeal put in place of the parliament. Supposing each of the exceptions to occasion three appeals, there might be eighteen appeals in this cause before a final determination; an admirable device for giving free scope to a spirit of litigiosity. The first attempt I find made for redress, is in the act 105. parl. 1487, bestowing a privilege upon those who are hurt by the partiality of

* Act 41. parl. 1471.

inferior judges, "to summon before the King and council, the judge and party, who shall be bound to bring the rolls of court along with <278> them in order to verify the matters of fact; and if inquity be committed, the process shall be reduced and annulled." It is declared at the same time, that this method of obtaining redress, shall not exclude the ordinary process of appeal, if it shall be more agreeable to the party aggrieved. This regulation is declared to endure till the next parliament only. But though we do not find it renewed in any following parliament, it would be rash to infer that it was laid aside. If it was relished by the nation, which we have great reason to believe, it is more natural to infer, that it was kept in observance without a statute. One thing appears from the records of the daily council still preserved, that very early after the institution of that court, complaints were received against the proceedings and decrees of inferior judges; and, upon iniquity or error found, that the proceedings were rectified or annulled. The very nature and constitution of the court favoured this remedy; especially as the remedy was not altogether new. This court could not receive an appeal, because the privilege was not bestowed upon it; and the whole forms of a process of appeal, were accurately adjusted by parliament immediately after the institution of this court.* Now, no man who had once experienced an easier remedy, would ever patiently <279> submit to the hardship and expence of multiplying appeals through different courts, before he could get his cause determined in the last resort. We may take it for granted, that a direct application to the daily council for redress, would be the choice of every man who conceived injustice to be done him by an inferior judge. He could not bring his cause before this court by appeal, which justified his bringing it by summons or complaint. And in this form he had not any difficulty to struggle with, more than in an appeal; for the former requires no antecedent authority from the court, more than the latter. This assumed power of reviewing the decrees of inferior judges, was soon improved into a regular form. Decrees of registration were from the beginning suspended and reduced in this court; and by its very institution, it was the proper court for such matters. The same method came to be followed, in redressing iniquity committed by inferior judges. In place of a complaint, a regular pro-

* Act 95. parl. 1503.

cess of reduction was brought; and because this process did not stay execution, the defect was supplied by a suspension.

This deduction affords an answer to a question that has puzzled our antiquaries, viz. How it comes that we hear not of appeals after the institution of the college of justice. Stair, in the passage quoted above, says slightly, That <280> after the institution of this college, they fell in desuetude, and gave place to advocations, suspensions and reductions. We find this to be a mistake. And indeed had they not been antecedently in disuse, it would be difficult to account how it should have happened, that in none of the records of this court, is there a single word of appeals. On the contrary, in its first form of process, we find reduction of inferior decrees among those processes that are to be called in a certain order.*

It may be observed by the way, that the process of reduction, first practised in the daily council, and afterward in the present court of session, put an end to the difference betwixt the sheriff and baron courts in point of superiority. When appeals went into disuse, the sheriff lost his power of reviewing the sentences of the baron-court; and these courts came to be considered as of equal rank, because the proceedings of both were equally subjected to the review of the court of session.

To redress errors in judgment by appealing to a superior court, is undoubtedly the more natural remedy; because, in case of variance, it resembles in private life an appeal to a common friend, or to a neutral person. But reductions and suspensions have more the air of a complete legal police. These actions proceed upon au-<281>thority of letters from the King, who is conceived to be watchful over the welfare of his people, and attentive that justice be done them. When an act of injustice is done by an inferior court, he brings the cause before his own court, where justice will be impartially distributed.

Connection leads me to an advocation, or a *Certiorari* as termed in England; which is the form of redressing iniquity or error committed by an inferior judge, before the final sentence is pronounced. An advocation originally was not granted but for a delay or refusal of justice. So says Voet in express terms.† And that this also was the use of an advocation here, appears

* Act 45. parl. 1537.
† De judiciis, § 143. [[I.e., *Commentarius ad Pandectas*, Bk. 5, Tit. 1, § 143: vol. i, pp. 364–65.]]

from Reg. Maj. l. 3. cap. 20. 21. The King and council was at first the only court that had the privilege of advocating causes *ob denegatam justitiam.* This privilege was not communicated to the court of session instituted in the 1425; which by act 62. parl. 1457, was confined to original actions founded on brieves; and complaints against judges for delay of justice, continued as formerly to be tried before the King and council, act 26. parl. 1469, act 62. parl. 1475. From the former of these it appears, that, upon a complaint of injustice or partiality, letters of advocation were issued to bring the judge before the King and council, to answer to the complaint, and to punish him if the com-<282>plaint was verified. But as to the cause itself,[9] the party wronged got no redress; being left to seek redress in the ordinary form of law by an appeal. The rules of law, originally simple, turn more and more intricate in the progress of society; and the King, occupied with affairs of state or with his pleasures, has little skill and less inclination to hold courts.[10] The privilege of advocation, which had been denied to the court of session, was now permitted to the daily council; but still to be exercised within its original limits. Balfour* mentions a case so late as the 1531, where it was decided, that after litiscontestation a cause could not be advocated; for litiscontestation removed any pretext of a complaint for delay of justice. But the present court of session, applied early the remedy of an advocation, to correct unjust or erroneous proceedings in inferior courts, termed *iniquity* in the law-language of Scotland. An appeal by this time was in disrepute; and it being established that iniquity could be redressed by a reduction after a final sentence, it was thought natural to prevent an unjust sentence, by advocating the cause before hand. And the court was encouraged to proceed in that manner, it being a shorter and less expensive method of obtaining redress, than by an appeal. Thus came about, that an advocation, in-<283>vented as a remedy for delay of justice, was extended to remove causes to the court of session, where there was any suspicion of partiality in the inferior judge, or where there occurred any per-

* p. 342. cap. 12.

9. 1758, 1761 add: "so strictly was the rule observed of confining an advocation to the denial or delay of justice, that"

10. 1758, 1761: "The rules of law . . . to hold courts" = "Matters of government, by the increase of commerce and connections with foreign states, becoming gradually more intricate and involved, the administration of justice by the King and council, came to be pretty much neglected."

sonal objection; till it obtained that iniquity singly was a sufficient ground. This improvement, however beneficial to the public, was not at first relished by our legislature. It was ordained by act 39. parl. 1555, "That causes be not advocated by the Lords from the judge-ordinary, except for deadly feud, or where the judge is a party, or the causes of the Lords of Session, their advocates, scribes, and members." But this statute, occasioned by some remaining influence of former practice, had no great authority, and soon slipt into disuse. Advocations upon iniquity, gaining ground daily, banished appeals against interlocutory sentences; and, being more easy and expeditious, became the only remedy.

After appeals in civil actions yielded to advocations, reductions, and suspensions, the power of advocation was for many years reckoned an extraordinary privilege, competent to the court of session only. Stair observes,* "That no court in Scotland has this privilege but the court of session." It was so in his time; but the improvement did not stop there; it made its way into the court of justiciary, and <284> even into the admiral-court; and from the following historical deduction, it will appear by what means that happened. The writ of *Certiorari* in England, is the same with our advocation. The court of chancery, being the supreme civil court, and the king's-bench, being the supreme criminal court, can both of them issue a *Certiorari*. No other court in England enjoys the privilege. Some method for redressing iniquity committed by an inferior judge, is no less necessary in criminal than in civil actions. The only difference is, that in a criminal action the remedy must be applied before the matter be brought before the jury; for we shall see by and by that a verdict is inviolable. An appeal to a superior court, was originally the only method, in criminal as well as in civil actions. The inconveniencies of that method rendered it generally unpopular, and made it give place to advocation in civil causes, which was reckoned a great improvement. The English *Certiorari* showed the advantages of the same remedy in criminal causes. But how to come at this remedy, was a matter of difficulty. The privilege of advocation, according to the established notion, was confined to the court of session. The justiciary court did not pretend to this privilege; and the court of session could not

* L. 4. tit. 1. § 35.

properly interpose in matters which belonged to another supreme court. The known ad-<285>vantages of an advocation as an expeditious method for obtaining redress of wrong judgment, surmounted this difficulty. The court of session received complaints of wrong done by inferior criminal judges; and, upon finding a complaint well founded, took upon them to remove the cause by advocation to the justiciary. They also ventured to remove criminal causes from one court, to another that was more competent and unsuspected.* The mean figure made in those days by the court of justiciary, consisting but of a single judge, with assessors chosen from time to time to hold circuit-courts, encouraged the court of session to claim this extraordinary privilege. And through the same influence, they interposed in ecclesiastical matters also. They advocated a cause for church-censure, from the dean of the chapel-royal, and remitted it to the bishop and clergy.† And a minister who was pursued before a sheriff as an intruder into a church, having presented a bill of advocation to the court of session, the cause was advocated to the privy council.‡ <286>

The court of justiciary, after it was new modelled by the act 1672,[11] made a much greater figure than formerly. It did not however begin early to feel its own weight and importance. Particularly it did not at first assume the privilege of advocation, though now that appeals were totally in disuse, that privilege belonged to it as the supreme court in criminal actions, as well as to the court of session in those that are civil. The court of session continued to exercise the power of advocation in criminal matters as formerly; for which we have Mackenzie's evidence in his Criminals, title *Advocations,*[12] and that of Dirleton in his Doubts, upon the same title. But the court of justiciary afterward took this privilege to itself; and it hath a signet of its own, which gives authority to its advocations. This privilege, as is usual, was assumed at first with some degree of hesitation. It was doubted, whether a single judge could pass an advocation, or even grant a sist on a

---

* See Durie, 9th January 1629, Baron of Burghton *contra* Kincaid; Stair, 21st February 1666, —— *contra* Sheriff of Inverness.

† Stair, 19th December 1680, Macclellan *contra* Bishop of Dumblane.

‡ Fountainhall, 5th June 1696, Alexander *contra* Sheriff of Inverness.

11. Kames refers to the Act "concerning the regulation of the judicatories" dated 30 August 1672.

12. Mackenzie, *Laws and Customes,* Part II, Tit. 17, § 3.

bill of advocation. Some thought the matter of so great importance, as to require a *quorum* of the judges. But the practice of the court of session, made this doubt vanish. There are many instances, as early as the 1699 and 1700, of advocations being passed by single judges, and now it is no longer a matter of doubt. It remains only to be added, that the judge-admiral, following the example of the <287> two supreme courts of session and justiciary, is in the practices of advocating causes to himself from inferior admiral-courts.

The privilege of advocation in the court of justiciary, introduced that of suspension; which is now customary with regard to any error in the proceedings of an inferior judge. This court, as far as I know, has never sustained a reduction of a criminal sentence pronounced by an inferior judge; and it appears to me doubtful, whether the court will ever be inclined to extend its jurisdiction so far. My reason of doubt is, that a regular process of reduction is not proper for a court which hath no continuance, and which is held occasionally only. And were it proper, the privilege would be of very little use. An error in an interlocutory sentence of an inferior judge, may be corrected by an advocation. The execution of a sentence of con-demnation may be prevented by a suspension. If the person accused be acquitted by the verdict of the jury, the matter cannot be brought under review by reduction. If he be dismissed from the bar upon any informality in the process, he is liable to a new prosecution. I can discover then no necessity for a reduction, except singly with regard to pecuniary matters, as where damages and expences are unjustly refused. If in such cases the court of session could not interpose, it would be necessary for <288> the court of justiciary to undertake the reduction. But as the court of session is reck-oned competent to pecuniary matters, from whatever cause they arise, civil or criminal, the justiciary-court acts wisely in leaving such reduction to the court of session. This draws after it another consequence, by a natural con-nection. The court of session, which, by way of reduction, judges of fines, expences, and damages, refused in an inferior criminal court, assumes nat-urally power to judge of the same articles by way of suspension, when an exorbitant sum is given. These considerations lay open the foundation of a practice current in the court of session. Of riots, batteries, and bloodwits, depending before the sheriff or other inferior judge, advocation is left to the court of justiciary; but as the punishment of such delinquencies is commonly a pecuniary fine, the court of session sustains its jurisdiction in the second instance by reduction or suspension.* From what is now said, it must follow, that the courts of session and justiciary, have in some particulars a cumulative jurisdiction. In a criminal prosecution before the sheriff, the person accused is, for example, acquitted, and obtains immoderate expence against the prosecutor, without any good foundation. In this, and many <289> cases of the same kind which may be figured, the party aggrieved has his option to apply to either court for a suspension.

Upon the power of reviewing the proceedings of inferior courts, whether by the old form of appeal or by the later forms of advocation and reduction, what I have said relates singly to iniquity committed by the judge. Iniquity alledged committed by a jury in giving their verdict, was reserved to be handled separately. In judging of proof, every thing sworn by a witness in judgment, was held by our forefathers to be true; a position which indicates great integrity and simplicity of manners, but little knowledge of mankind. So far was this carried, that, till within a century and a half, a defendant was not suffered to alledge any fact contrary to those contained in the declaration or libel. The reasoning of our judges was to the following purpose. "The pursuer hath undertaken to prove the facts mentioned in his libel. If he prove them, they must be true; and therefore any contradictory fact alledged by the defendant must be false." Hence the rule in our ancient practice, That what is determined by an assize must be held for truth, and cannot thereafter pass to another assize, Quon. attach. cap. 82. This is declared to be the rule in verdicts, even upon civil actions, Reg. Maj. l. 1. cap. 13. § 3. To sup-<290>port this practice, another reason concurred. Litiscontestation originally was a judicial contract binding the parties to submit to the facts that should be proved, and barring every objection to the proof.[13] But as brieves not pleadable, such as a brieve of inquest, of tutory, of idiocy, are carried on without a contradictor, and consequently without litiscontestation, more liberty was taken. To rectify a wrong verdict in such a case, a remedy was provided by act 47. parl. 1471, which was a complaint to the

---

* Fountainhall, 4th March 1707, Alves *contra* Maxwell.
13. "To support this . . . objection to the proof" added 1776.

King and council of the falsehood or ignorance of the inquest; and if the
verdict was found wrong, it was voided, and the parties concerned were
restored to their original situation. The legislature did not venture upon
any remedy, where the verdict proceeded upon a pleadable brieve. This was
left upon the common law, which preserves the verdict entire, even where
it is proved to be iniquitous; being satisfied to keep jurymen to their duty
by the terror of punishment. In a process of error, they were summoned
before a great inquest, and, if found guilty of perjury, they were punished
with escheat of moveables, infamy, and a year's imprisonment.[*][14] The summons of error is limited to three years, not only where the purpose is to
have the assizers punished, but also as to the conclusion of annulling the
verdict or <291> its retour upon a brieve not pleadable.[†] But the reduction
of the verdict or retour, upon a brieve of inquest, was afterwards extended
to twenty years.[‡] No verdict pronounced in a criminal cause ever was re-
viewable. For though the jury should be found guilty of perjury by a great
assize, yet their verdict is declared to be *res judicata,* whether for or against
the pannel.[||] The same rule obtained with regard to verdicts in civil cases
upon pleadable brieves; and continued to be the rule till jury-trials in civil
cases were laid aside.

As the disuse of jury-trials in civil causes is another revolution in our
law, not less memorable than that already handled concerning appeals, the
connection of matter offers me a fair opportunity to trace its history, and
to discover, if I can, by what influence or by what means this revolution
happened. To throw all the light I can upon a dark part of the history of
our law, I take help from a maxim adopted by our forefathers, which had
a steady influence in practice. The maxim is, That though questions in law
may be trusted to a single judge, matters of proof are safer in the hands of

* Reg. Maj. l. 1. cap. 14.
† Act 57. parl. 1494.
‡ Act 13. parl. 1617.
|| Act 63. parl. 1475.
14. 1758, 1761 add: "This is a singular regulation, which deviates from just principles,
and has not a parallel in the whole body of our law. It is both common and rational, to
redress a wrong with relation to the party aggrieved, without proceeding to punish the
wrong-doer, where he can excuse or extenuate his fault. But it is not less uncommon
than irrational, to punish a delinquent, without affording any relief to the party injured."

a plurality. It was probably thought, that in determining questions of law there is little trust reposed in a judge, because he is tied down to a precise rule; but that as there can be no pre-<292>cise rule in matters of proof, it ought to be referred to a number of judges, who are a check one upon another. Whatever be the foundation of this maxim, it undoubtedly prevailed in practice. In all courts, civil and criminal, governed by a single judge, we find juries always employed. Before the judge matters of law were discussed, and every thing preparatory to the verdict; but to the jury was reserved cognisance of the facts. On the other hand, juries never were employed in any British court, where the judges were sufficiently numerous to act as jurymen. A jury was never employed in parliament, nor in processes before the King and council. And in England, when the court last named was split into the king's bench, the exchequer, and the common-pleas, I am verily persuaded, that the continuance of jury-trials in these new courts, was owing to the following circumstance, that four judges only were appointed in each of them, and but a single judge in the circuit courts. Hence I presume, that juries were not employed in the court of session, instituted *anno* 1425. And the nature of its institution adds force to the presumption. Its members were chosen out of the three estates;[15] and it was established to relieve the King and council of a load of business growing daily on them. There is little reason to doubt, that this new court, consisting of many members, would adopt the forms of the two courts <293> to which it was so nearly allied.[16] One thing we are certain of, without necessity of recurring to a conjecture, that the daily council, which came in place of the session and equally with it consisted of many judges, had not from the beginning any jury-trials, but took evidence by witnesses, and in every cause gave judgment upon the proof, precisely as we do at this day. These facts considered, it seems a well-founded conjecture, that so large a number of judges as fifteen, which constitute our present court of session, were appointed with a view to the practice of the preceding courts, and in order to prevent the necessity of trying causes by juries. The daily council was composed of

15. The "three estates" represented in the Scottish Parliament were the prelates, the lairds, and the burgh commissioners.

16. 1758, 1761 add: "And that this was really the case may be gathered not obscurely from Balfour* [*Page 443. cap. 5.]"

bishops, abbots, earls, lords, gentlemen, and burgesses; in order probably that every man might be tried by some at least of his own rank; and in examining the records of this court, we find at first few sederunts but where at least twelve judges are present. The matter is still better ordered in the present court of session. Nine judges must be present to make a *quorum;* and it seldom happens in examining any proof, that the judges present are under twelve in number. This I am persuaded is the foundation of a proposition that passes current without any direct authority from the regulations concerning the jurisdiction of this court, viz. that it is the grand jury of the nation *in civilibus.* In fact, <294> it is the inviolable practice, to give judgment upon the testimony of witnesses in a full court, where there must always be at least a *quorum* present; which is no slight indication that the court in this case acts as a jury. For why otherwise should it be less competent to a single member of the court, to judge of a proof than to judge of a point of law? This account of the court of session, as possessing the powers both of judge and jury, cannot fail to be relished, when it is discovered, that this was far from being a novelty when the court was instituted. The thought was borrowed from the court of parliament, the members of which, in all trials, acted both as judges and jurymen. One clear instance we have on record, *anno* 1481, in the trial of Lord Lile for high treason. The members present, the King only excepted, formed themselves into a jury, and brought in a regular verdict, declaring the pannel not guilty. A copy of the trial is annexed, Appendix, No. 6.

I cannot here avoid declaring my opinion, that in civil causes it is a real improvement, to trust with established judges the power of deciding on facts as well as on law. A number of men trained up to law, and who are daily in the practice of weighing evidence, may undoubtedly be more relied on for doing justice, than the same number occasionally collected <295> from the mass of the people, to undertake an unaccustomed task, that of pronouncing a verdict on an intricate proof.

Supposing the foregoing account why juries are not employed in the court of session to be satisfactory, it will occur, that it proves nothing with respect to inferior courts where the judges are commonly single. I admit the observation to be just; and therefore must assign a different cause for the disuse of jury-trials in inferior courts. Were the ancient records preserved of these inferior courts, it would I presume be found, that civil causes were tried in them by juries, even after the institution of the college of justice; and we are not at freedom to doubt of the fact, after considering the act 42. parl. 1587, appointing molestations to be tried by a jury before the sheriff. In the records indeed of the sheriff's court of Edinburgh, there is no vestige remaining of a jury-trial in a civil action. This however is not a puzzling circumstance, because the records of that court are not preserved farther back than the year 1595. I had little expectation of more ancient records in other sheriffdoms; but conjecturing that the old form of jury-trials might wear out more slowly in shires remote from the capital, I continued to search; and in the record luckily stumbled on a book of the sheriff's court of Orkney, beginning 3d July 1602, and <296> ending 29th August 1604 (2). All the processes engrossed in this book, civil as well as criminal, are tried by juries. That juries wore gradually out of use in inferior courts, will not be surprising when it is considered, that an appetite for power, as well as for imitating the manners of our superiors, do not forsake us when we are made judges. It is probable also, that this innovation was favoured by the court of session, willing to have under their power of review, iniquitous judgments with relation to matters of fact; from which review they were debarred when facts were ascertained by the verdict of a jury. <297>

From the power which courts have to review the decrees of inferior judges, I proceed to the power which courts have to review their own de-

(2) In a book of the baron-court of Crainshaw, there is a process in a court held the 4th of April 1611, in the following words:

> Because it is often and diverse times complained upon by the parishioners, that their corns were evil eaten and destroyed by geese and swine of the laird, therefore thought it meet that an inquest should be chosen to that effect, and that they should reason the matter, laying aside all particulars, whether they should be kept or put away.

An inquest is accordingly chosen: and their verdict follows: "The haill inquest chused Walter Edingtown chancellor, who found, after reasoning and voting of the inquest, that they should be both keeped still." The process is abundantly ludicrous. It verifies the fact however, that jury-processes continued in inferior courts after they were laid aside in the court of session. In this baron-court jury-trials became gradually less frequent; and there is no appearance of any after the 1632. [[Note added 1776.]]

crees. The court of justiciary enjoys not this power; because the verdict is ultimate, and cannot be overturned. This obstacle lies not in the way of the court of session; and as the forms of this court give opportunity for such review, necessity brought it early into practice; for the short sederunts of parliament would have rendered appeals, when multiplied, an impracticable remedy. It was necessary therefore to find a remedy in the court itself; which was obtained by assuming a power to reduce its own decrees. And an appeal came to be necessary in those cases only where the ultimate judgment of the court is unjust. This is the very reason, according to Balfour, which moved the court of session to reduce its own decrees.* The admiralty is the only other court in Scotland that hath a privilege to review its own decrees; and this privilege is bestowed by the act 16. parl. 1681.

Having discussed what occurred upon our courts in the three first views, I proceed to consider a court of appeal; upon which I observe in general, that in its powers it is more limited than where it enjoys also an original jurisdiction. The province of a court of appeal, strict-<298>ly speaking, is not to try the cause, but to try the justice of the sentence appealed from. All that can be done by such a court, is to examine whether the interlocutor or sentence be justly founded upon the pleadings. If any new point be suggested, the court of appeal, having no original jurisdiction, must remit this point to be tried in the court below. A court, which along with its power of receiving appeals hath also an original jurisdiction in the same causes, can not only rectify any wrong done by the inferior court, but has an option, either to remit the cause thus amended to the court below, or to retain it to itself and proceed to the final determination.

The House of Lords is undoubtedly a court of appeal with respect to the three sovereign courts in this country. There are appeals daily from the court of session. Appeals from the court of justiciary have hitherto been rare, and probably will never become frequent; the proceedings of this court, being brought under precise rules, afford little matter for an appeal; which at the same time would be but a partial remedy, as the verdict of the jury can never be called in question. An appeal, however, from this court is competent, as well as from the session; of which there is one noted instance. The King's advocate and the procurator for the Kirk prosecuted the

---

* p. 268.

magistrates of Elgin before <299> the justiciary, for an atrocious riot; specifying, That being entrusted by the ministers of Elgin with the keys of the little kirk of Elgin, they instead of restoring them when required, had delivered them to Mr. Blair Episcopal minister, by which the established ministers were turned out of possession. In this case, the following circumstance came to be material to the issue, Whether the said little kirk was or was not a part of the parish church. The affirmative being found by the court of session, to which the point of right was remitted as preliminary to the criminal trial, the magistrates entered an appeal from the court of session; and upon that pretext, craved from the court of justiciary a delay till the appeal should be discussed. The prosecutors opposed this demand; they founded on an order of the House of Lords, 19th April 1709, resolving, "That an appeal neither stays process nor sists execution, unless the appeal be received by the House, an order made for the respondent to answer, and the order duly served on the respondent"; and urged, that this not being done in the present case, the court ought to proceed. The court accordingly proceeded in the trial, and pronounced sentence, 2d March 1713, "ordaining the defendants to deliver up the keys of the little kirk, with L. 20 of fine, and L. 30 of expences." The defendants appealed also from this sentence <300> of the court of justiciary, and the sentence was reversed.

The distinctions above handled, comprehend most of the courts that are to be found any where, but not the whole. We have many instances in Britain, of a new jurisdiction created for a particular purpose, and for no other. This commonly happens, where a fact is made criminal by statute, and to be tried by certain persons named for that precise purpose; or where a new and severe punishment is directed against what was formerly reckoned a venial transgression; as for instance, the statute 1st George I. cap. 18. against the malicious destroying growing trees, which impowers the justices of peace to try this crime. This also sometimes happens in civil causes; witness the jurisdiction given by act of parliament to the justices of peace in revenue-matters. With relation to such courts, the question of the greatest importance is, Whether they be subject to any review. The author of A new abridgement of the law,* talking of the king's-bench, has the following passage.

* Vol. 1. p. 592.

Also it hath so sovereign a jurisdiction in all criminal matters, that an act of parliament, appointing all crimes of a certain denomination to be tried before certain judges, doth not exclude the jurisdiction of this court, without express <301> negative words. And therefore it hath been resolved, that 33d Henry VIII. cap. 12. which enacts, *That all treasons within the King's house shall be determined before the Lord Steward,* doth not restrain this court from proceeding against such offences. But where a statute creates a new offence, which was not taken notice of by the common law, erects a new jurisdiction for the punishment of it, and prescribes a certain method of proceeding; it seems questionable how far this court has an implied jurisdiction in such a case.

The distinction here suggested, with some degree of hesitation, is, in my apprehension, solidly founded on a clear rule of law. A right established in any court, or in any person, is not presumed to be taken away; and therefore cannot otherwise be taken away but by express words. On the other hand, a right is not presumed to be given, and therefore cannot be given, but by express words. Treason of all sorts, where-ever committed, is under the jurisdiction of the king's-bench; and a statute impowering the Lord Steward to try treason committed within the King's house, bestows upon him, in this particular, a cumulative jurisdiction with the king's-bench; but not an exclusive jurisdiction, because the words do not necessarily imply so much. A new offence created by a statute, must be considered in a <302> different light. If the trial of such offence be committed to a particular judge, there is no foundation in law for extending the privilege to any other judge; because the words do not necessarily import such extension. The justiciary therefore, or sheriff, have no power to inflict the statutory punishment upon those who maliciously destroy growing trees. They have no such jurisdiction by the statute; and they cannot have it by common law, because the punishment is not directed by common law.

One question there is relative to courts of all kinds, How is the extent of their jurisdiction to be tried, and who is the judge in this case? This is a matter of no difficulty. It is inherent in the nature of every court, to judge of its own jurisdiction, and, with respect to every cause brought before it, to determine whether it comes or comes not under its cognisance. For to say, that this question, even at the first instance, must be determined by

another court, involves the following absurdity, that no cause can be taken
in by any court, till antecedently it be found competent by the judgment
of a superior court. This therefore is one civil question, to which every
court, civil, criminal, or ecclesiastical, must be competent. As this preliminary question, before entering upon the cause, must be determined if
disputed, or be taken for granted if not disputed, the power to <303> judge
of it must necessarily be implied, whereever a court is established and a
jurisdiction granted. A judgment, however, of a court upon its own powers, ought never to be final; which in effect would empower a court, however limited in its constitution, to arrogate to itself an unbounded jurisdiction, which would be absurd. This doctrine shall be illustrated, by
applying it to a very plain case, debated in the court of session. In the
turnpike-act for the shire of Haddington, 23d George II. the trustees are
empowered to make compositions with individuals for their toll. Any
abuse withall of the powers given by the act, is subjected to the cognisance of the justices of peace, who are authorised to rectify the same ul-
timately and without appeal. The trustees made a transaction with a
neighbouring heritor, allowing those who purchased his coal and salt the
use of the turnpike-road free of toll; but obliging him to pay L. 3 Sterling
yearly, whenever he should open coal in a different field specified. This
bargain, an exemption in reality, not a composition, was complained of
as an abuse; and as such was, by the justices of peace, declared void,
and the toll ordered to be levied. The question was, Whether this sentence could be reviewed by the court of session. The question admits of
a clear solution, by splitting the sentence into its two constituent parts,
the first re-<304>specting the jurisdiction, the other respecting the cause.
With regard to the last only, are the sentences of the justices of peace
declared final. With regard to the first, ascertaining their own jurisdiction,
their judgment is not final. The cause therefore may be brought before
the court of session to try this preliminary point; and if, upon a review,
it be judged that the justices have exceeded the limits of their jurisdiction,
the judgment they have given in the cause must also be declared void, as
ultra vires.

On the other hand, if the opinion of the justices about their own jurisdiction be affirmed, the court of session must stop short; and however

wrong the judgment upon the cause may to them appear, they cannot interpose, because the judgment is final.

I shall finish this discourse with a comparative view of our different chief courts in point of dignity and pre-eminence. The court of session is sovereign and supreme: Sovereign, because it is the King's court; and it is the King who executes the acts and decrees of this court: Supreme, with respect to inferior courts having the same or part of the same jurisdiction, but subjected to a review in this court. The court of justiciary, in the foregoing respects, stands precisely upon the same footing with the court of session. The court of exchequer is sovereign, but not supreme: I know no inferior <305> court with which it has a cumulative jurisdiction, and whose proceedings it can review: causes cannot be brought before the exchequer from any inferior court, whether by reduction, advocation, or appeal. The admiral-court is by the act 1681, declared sovereign; and accordingly every act of authority of this court goes in the King's name. It is also supreme with respect to inferior admiral-courts, whose sentences it can review. But with regard to the courts of session and justiciary, it is an inferior court, because its decrees are subjected to a review in these courts. The commissary-court of Edinburgh is properly the bishop's court, and not sovereign. With respect to its supremacy, it stands upon the same footing with the admiral-court. <306>

Brieves

Jurisdiction was originally extremely simple. The chieftain who led the hord or clan to war, was naturally appealed to in all controversies among individuals.

Jurisdiction included not then what it doth at present, viz. a privilege to declare what is law, and authority to command obedience. It included no more but what naturally follows when two persons differ in matter of interest, which is to take the opinion of a third.

Thus a judge originally was merely an umpire or arbiter, and litigation was in effect a submission; on which account litiscontestation is, in the Roman law, defined a *judicial contract.**

The chieftain, who upon the union of several clans for common defence got the name of King, was the sole judge originally in matters of importance (1). Slighter controversies were <307> determined by fellow-subjects; and persons distinguished by rank or office, were commonly chosen umpires.

But differences multiplying by multiplied connections, and causes becoming more intricate by the art of subtilizing, the sovereign made choice

(1) Caesar describing the Germans and their manners: "Quum bellum civitas aut illatum defendit, aut insert; magistratus, qui ei bello presint, ut vitae necisque habeant potestatem, diliguntur. In pace nullus communis est magistratus, sed principes regionum atque pagorum inter suos jus dicunt, controversiasque minuunt." *Commentaria, lib. 6.* [["When a state makes or resists aggressive war, officers are chosen to direct it, with the power of life and death. In time of peace there is no general officer of state, but the chiefs of districts and cantons do justice among their followers and settle disputes." Caesar, *De Bello Gallico,* VI.23. Trans. Edwards.]]

* See p. 21. [[Note added 1792.]]

of a council to assist him in his awards; and this council was denominated, *the King's Court;* because in it he always presided. Through most of the European nations, at a certain period of their progress, we find this court established.

In the progress of society, matters of jurisdiction becoming still more complex and multiplying without end, the sovereign, intent on the greater affairs of government, had not leisure nor skill to decide differences among his subjects. Law became a science. Courts were instituted; and the several branches of jurisdiction, civil, criminal, and ecclesiastical, were distributed among these courts: Their powers were ascertained, and the causes that could be tried by each. These were likewise called the King's courts; not only as being put in place of the King's court properly so called, but also as the King did not renounce the power of <308> judging in person, but only freed himself from the burden of necessary attendance.

But the sovereign, jealous of his royal authority, bestowed upon these courts no other power but that of jurisdiction in its strictest sense, viz. a power to declare what is law. He reserved to himself all magisterial authority, even that which is necessary for explicating the jurisdiction of a court. Therefore, with relation to sovereign courts, citation and execution proceed in the King's name, and by his authority.

As to inferior courts, all authority is given to them that is necessary for explicating their jurisdiction. The trust is not great, considering that an appeal lies to the sovereign court; and it is below the dignity of the crown, to act in an inferior court.

In the infancy of government, the danger was not perceived, of trusting with the King both the judicative and executive powers of the law. But it being now understood, that the safety of a free government depends on balancing its several powers, it has become an established maxim, That the King, with whom the executive part of the law is trusted, has no part of the judicative power.

It seems now agreed, that our kings having delegated their whole judicial power to the judges of their several courts, they, by the constant and uninterrupted usage of many ages, have now <309> gained a known and stated jurisdiction, regulated by certain established rules, which our kings themselves cannot make any alteration in, without an act of parliament.*

The same is understood to be the law of Scotland, though as late as Craig's time it was otherwise. That author† mentions a case, where it was declared to be law, that the King might judge even in his own cause.

Religion and law, originally simple, were strangers to form. In process of time, form usurped on substance, and law as well as religion were involved in formalities. What is solemn and important, produceth naturally order and form among the vulgar, who are addicted to objects of sense. For this reason, forms in most languages are named *solemnities,* being connected with things that are solemn. But by gradual improvements in society, and by refinement of taste, forms come insensibly to be neglected, or reduced to their just value; and law as well as religion are verging toward their original simplicity. Thus, opposite causes produce sometimes the same effect. Law and religion were originally simple, because man was so. They will again be simple, because simplicity contributes to their perfection. <310>

After courts were instituted, the various causes at that time known were distributed among them. But new grounds of action occurring, it became often doubtful in what court a new action should be tried. An expeditious method was invented, for resolving such doubts. The King was the fountain of jurisdiction, and under his prerogative fell naturally the power of delegating to what judge he thought proper, any cause of this kind that occurred. This was done by a brieve from the chancery, directed to some established judge, ordering him to try the particular cause mentioned in the brieve. The King at first was under no restraint as to the choice of the judge; provided only, the party who was to be defendant, was subjected to the jurisdiction of the judge named in the brieve. This limitation was necessary; because the King's brieve contained not a warrant for citing the party to appear before the judge; and the judge's warrant could not reach beyond his territory. But in time, reason produced custom, and custom became law. Matters of moment were always delegated to a supreme judge; and, in general, the rule was, to avoid mixing civil and criminal jurisdiction.

---

* New abridgement of the law, vol. 1. p. 554.
† L. 3. dieg. 7. § 12.

In the most general sense of the word, every one of the King's writs, commanding or prohibiting any thing to be done, is termed a *brieve*. Brieves, with respect to judicial proceedings, <311> are of two kinds. One is directed to the sheriff, or a messenger in place of the sheriff, ordering him to cite the party to appear in the King's court, to answer the complaint made against him. This brieve is in the English law termed an *original;* and corresponds to our summons including the libel. The other kind is that above mentioned, directed to a judge, delegating to him the power of trying the particular cause set forth in the brieve.

Of the first kind of brieve, that for breaking the King's protection, is an instance.* Of the other kind, the brieve of bondage, the brieve of distress, the brieve of mortancestry, the brieve of nouvel disseisin, of perambulation, of terce, of right, &c. are instances.

Of the last-mentioned brieve the following was a peculiar species. When in the King's court a question of bastardy occurred, to which a civil court is not competent, a brieve was directed from the chancery to the bishop, to try the bastardy as a prejudicial question.† If such a case happened in an inferior court, the court, probably by its own authority, made the remit to the spiritual court. And the same being done at present in the King's courts, there is no longer any use for this brieve. <312>

The brieve of bondage might be directed either to the justiciar, or to the sheriff.‡ The brieve for relief of cautionry, might be directed to the justiciar, sheriff, or provost and bailies within burgh.‖ The brieves of mortancestry, and of nouvel disseisin, could only be directed to the justiciar.§

The brieve of distress, corresponding to the English brieve *Justicies,* must be examined more deliberately, because it makes a figure in our law. While the practice subsisted of poinding *brevi manu* for payment of debt, there was no necessity for the interposition of a judge to force payment.¶ When courts therefore were instituted, a process for payment of debt was not

---

* Quon. attach. cap. 54.
† Reg. Maj. l. 2. cap. 50.
‡ Quon. attach. cap. 56.
‖ Idem, cap. 51.
§ Idem, cap. 52. & 53.
¶ *See Tract 4. *History of securities upon land for payment of debt.*

known. The rough practice of forcing payment by private power being prohibited, an action became necessary; and the King interposed by a brieve, directing one or other judge to try the cause: "The brieve of distress for debts shall be determined before the justiciar, sheriff, bailies of burghs, as it shall please the King by his letter to command them particularly within their jurisdiction."* And it may be remarked by the way, that when a decree was recovered under the authority of this <313> brieve, the judge directed execution by his own authority, adjudging to the creditor for his payment, the land of the debtor if the moveables were not sufficient. With regard to the sheriff at least, the fact is verified by the act 36. parl. 1469. This brieve explains a maxim of the common law of England: "Quod placita de catallis, debitis, &c. quae summum 40 s. attingunt vel excedunt, secundum legem et consuetudinem Angliae sine brevi regis placitari non debent."† The indulging a jurisdiction to the extent of 40 s. without a brieve, arose apparently from the hardship of compelling a creditor to take out a brieve for a sum so small. In England the law continues the same to this day; for the sheriff, without a brieve, cannot judge in actions of debt beyond 40 s. But in Scotland, an original jurisdiction was by statute bestowed upon the Lords of Session, to judge in actions of debt;‡ and the sheriff and other inferior judges, copying after this court, have by custom and prescription acquired an original jurisdiction in actions of debt, without limitation; and the brieve of distress is no longer in use, because no longer necessary.

After the same manner, most of these brieves have gone into desuetude; for to nothing are we more prone than to enlargement of power. <314> A court that has often tried causes by a delegated jurisdiction, loses in time sight of its warrant, and ventures to try such causes by its own authority. Some few instances there are of such brieves still in force; viz. those which found the process of division of lands, of terce, of lyning within burgh, and of perambulation. For this reason I think it wrong in the court of session to sustain a process of perambulation at the first instance, which ought to be carried on before the sheriff, upon the authority of a brieve from the chancery. And what the rather inclines me to be of that opinion,

* Reg. Maj. l. 1. cap. 3.
† New abridgement of the law, vol. 1. p. 646.
‡ Act 61. parl. 1457.

is, that all the brieves of this sort preserved in use, regard either the fixing of land-marches, or the division of land among parties having interest, which never can be performed to good purpose, except upon the spot.

Soon after the institution of the college of justice, it was made a question, Whether that court could judge in a competition about the property of land, without being authorised by a brieve of right. But they got over the difficulty upon the following consideration: "That the brieve of right was long out of use; and that this being a sovereign and supreme court for civil causes, its jurisdiction, which in its nature is unlimited, must comprehend all civil causes from the lowest to the highest."* <315>

As the King's writs issuing from chancery did pass under either the great or the quarter seal, such solemnity came to be extremely burdensome, and was severely felt in the multiplication of law-proceedings. This circumstance had great influence in antiquating the brieves that conferred a delegated jurisdiction, and in bringing all causes under some one original jurisdiction. The other sort of brieve, which is no other than the King's warrant to call the defendant into the King's court, has been very long in disuse; and instead of it a simpler form is chosen, which is a letter from the King, passing under the signet, directed to the sheriff, or to a messenger in place of the sheriff, ordering him to cite the party to appear in court. This change happened probably without an express regulation: a few singular instances which were successful, discovered the conveniency; and instances were multiplied, till the form became universal, and brieves from the chancery were totally neglected. One thing is certain, that letters under the signet for citing parties to appear in the King's courts, can be traced pretty far back. In the chartulary of Paisley, preserved in the Advocate's library,† there is a full copy of a libelled summons in English, dated the 2d February 1468, at the instance of George Abbot of Paisley, against the bailies of <316> the burgh of Renfrew, with respect to certain tolls, customs, privileges, &c. for summoning them to appear before the King and his council, at Edinburgh, or where it shall happen them to be for the time, ending thus: "Given under

---

* Ult. February 1542, Wemyss *contra* Forbes, observed by Skene [[*De Verborum Significatione*]], *voce Breve de recto.*
† p. 246.

our signet at Perth, the second of December, and of our reign the eight year." And there are extant letters under the signet,* containing a charge to enter heir to the superiority, and infeft the vassal within twenty days; and, if he fail, summoning him to appear before the Lords of Council the seventh of July next, to hear him decerned to tyne his superiority, and that the vassal shall hold of the next lawful superior. "Given under our signet at Stirling, the second of June, and of our reign the first year." It is to be observed, at the same time, that this must have been a recent innovation; for so late as the year 1457, the ordinary form of citing parties to appear before the Lords of Session, was by a brieve issued from chancery.†

It is probable, that originally every sort of execution that passed upon the decrees of the King's courts, was authorised by a brieve issuing from chancery; for if a brieve was necessary to bring the defendant into court, less solemnity would not be sufficient in executing the decree pronounced against him; and that this in <317> particular was the case when land was apprised for payment of debt, is testified by 2d Statutes Robert I. cap. 19. At what time this form was laid aside, or upon what occasion, we know not. For as far back as we have any records, we find every sort of execution, personal and real, upon the decrees of the King's courts, authorised by letters passing the signet.

Of old, a certain form of words was established for every sort of action; and if a man could not bring his case under any established form, he had no remedy. In the Roman law, these forms are termed *formulae actionum.* In Britain, copying from the Roman law, all the King's writs or brieves, those at least that concern judicial proceedings, are in a set form of words, which it was not lawful to alter. But in the progress of society,[1] new cases occurring without end to which no established form did correspond, the Romans were forced to relax from their solemnities, by indulging *actiones in factum;* in which the fact was set forth without reference to any form. The English follow this practice in their *actions upon the case.* It is probable, that, in Scotland, the warrant for citation passing under the signet, was at

---

* 2d June 1514.
† See act 62. parl. 1457.
1. 1758, 1761: "progress of society" = "progress of law."

first conceived in a set form; in imitation of the brieve to which it was substituted. But if so, the practice did not long continue. These forms have been very long neglected, every man being at <318> liberty to set forth his case in his own words; and it belongs to the court to consider, whether the libel or declaration be *relevant;* or, in other words, whether the facts set forth be a just cause for granting what is requested by the pursuer. <319>

Process in Absence

In Scotland, the forms of process against absents, in civil and criminal actions, differ too remarkably to pass unobserved. Our curiosity is excited to learn whence the difference has arisen, and upon what principle it is founded; and for gratifying curiosity in this particular, I can think of no means more promising, than a view of some foreign laws that have been copied by us.

But in order to understand the spirit of these laws, it will be necessary to look back upon the origin of civil jurisdiction, of which I have had occasion, in a former tract, to give a sketch;* viz. that at first judges were considered as arbiters, without any magisterial powers: That their authority was derived from the consent of the litigants: That litiscontestation was in reality a contract; and therefore, that the decrees of judges had not a stronger effect than an award pronounced by an arbiter properly so called. Upon this system of jurisdiction, there <320> cannot be such a thing as a process in absence; for a judge, whose authority depends on consent, cannot give judgment against any person who submits not to his jurisdiction. But civil jurisdiction, like other human inventions, weak and imperfect at its commencement, was improved in course of time, and became a more useful system. After a public was recognised, with a power in the public to give laws to the society and to direct its operations, the consent of litigants was no longer necessary to found jurisdiction. A judge is held to be a public officer, having authority to settle controversies among individuals, and to oblige them to submit to his decrees. The defendant, bound to submit to

---

* History of the Criminal Law.

the authority of the court, cannot hurt the pursuer by refusing to appear; and hence a process in absence against a person who is legally cited.

In the primitive state of Rome, jurisdiction was altogether voluntary. A judge had no coercive power, not even that of citation. The first dawn of authority discovered in old Rome with relation to judicial proceedings, is a power which was given to the claimant to drag his party into court, *obtorto collo,* as expressed in the Roman law; which was a very rude form, suitable however to the ignorance and rough manners of those times. This glimpse of authority was improved, by transferring the power of for-<321>cing a defendant into court from the claimant to the judge; and this was a natural transition, after a judge was held to be a public officer, vested with every branch of authority that is necessary to explicate his jurisdiction. Litiscontestation ceased to be a contract. But as our notions do not instantly accommodate themselves to the fluctuation of things, litiscontestation continued to be handled by lawyers as a contract, long after jurisdiction was authoritative, and neither inferred nor required consent. Litiscontestation, it is true, could no longer be reckoned a contract; but to deviate as little as possible from ancient maxims, it was defined to be a *quasi* contract; which in plain language is saying, that it hath nothing of a contract except the name. We return to the history. The power of citation assumed by the judge, was at first, like most innovations, exercised with remarkable moderation. In civil causes, four citations were necessary in order to oblige the defendant to put in his answer. The fourth citation was peremptory, and carried the following certification: "Etiam absente diversa parte, cogniturum se, et pronunciaturum."* What followed is distinctly explained.

Et post edictum peremptorium impetratum, cum dies ejus supervenerit, tunc absens citari debet: et sive responderit sive <322> non responderit, agetur causa, et pronunciabitur: non utique secundum praesentem, sed interdum vel absens, si bonam causam habuit, vincet.†

---

* [["To examine and decide the case even while the other party is still absent."]] l. 71. De judiciis. [[I.e., *Digest* 5.1.71. Trans. Watson.]]

† [["And after a peremptory edict has been obtained, on the day named in it, the absent party should be summoned and, whether he does or does not respond, the case will proceed and a verdict will be given, not necessarily in favor of the party who is present, but sometimes even the absent party will win, if he had a good case."]] l. 73. De judiciis. [[I.e., *Digest* 5.1.73. Trans. Watson.]]

In criminal actions, the form of proceeding against absents, appears not, among the Romans, to have been thoroughly settled. Two rescripts of the Emperor Trajan are founded on, to prove that no criminal ought to be condemned in absence. And because a proof *ex parte* cannot afford more than a suspicion or presumption, the reason given is, "Quod satius est impunitum relinqui facinus nocentis, quam innocentem damnare."[1] On the other hand, it is urged by some writers, that contumacy, which itself is a crime, ought not to afford protection to any delinquent; and therefore that a criminal action ought to be managed like a civil action. Ulpian, to reconcile these two opposite opinions, labours at a distinction: admits, as to lesser crimes, that a person accused may be condemned in absence; but is of opinion, that of a capital crime no man ought to be condemned in absence.* Marcian seems to be of the same opinion.† And it is laid down, that the criminal's whole effects, in this case, were inventaried and sequestred; to the effect, that if within the year he did not appear <323> to purge his contumacy, the whole should be confiscated.‡

This form of proceeding, as to civil actions at least, appears to have a good foundation both in justice and expediency. If my neighbour refuse to do me justice, it is the part of the judge or magistrate to compel him. If my neighbour be contumacious and refuse to submit to legal authority, this may subject him to punishment, but cannot impair my right. In criminal causes, where punishment alone is in view, there is more ground for hesitating. No individual hath an interest so substantial, as to make a prosecution necessary merely on his account; and therefore writers of a mild temper, satisfy themselves with punishing the person accused for his contumacy. Others, of more severe manners, are for proceeding to a trial in every case that is not capital.

That a difference should be established between civil and criminal actions in the form of proceeding, is extremely rational. I cannot, however, help testifying some degree of surprise, at an opinion that gives peculiar indulgence to the more atrocious crimes. I should rather have expected,

---

* l. 5. De poenis. [[I.e., *Digest* 48.19.5.]]

† l. 1. pr. et § 1. De requir. vél absen. damnan. [[I.e., *Digest* 48.17.1.]]

‡ viz. in the title now mentioned.

1. "Because it is preferable that a guilty man is not punished than that an innocent man is condemned." *Digest* 48.19.5. Trans. Watson.

that the horror we naturally have at such crimes, would have disposed these writers to break through every impediment, in order to reach a condign punishment; leaving <324> crimes that make a less figure, to be prosecuted in the ordinary form. Nature and plain sense undoubtedly suggest this difference. But these matters were at Rome settled by lawyers, who are led more by general principles, than by plain feelings. And as the form of civil actions was first established, analogy moved them to bring pecuniary mulcts, and consequently all the lesser crimes, under the same form.

I reckon it no slight support to the foregoing reflection, that as to high treason, the greatest of all crimes, the Roman lawyers, deserting their favourite doctrine, permitted this crime to be prosecuted, not only in absence of the person accused, but even after death.*

As far back as we can trace the laws of this island, we find judges vested with authority to explicate their jurisdiction. We find, at the same time, the original notion of jurisdiction so far prevalent, as to make it a rule, that no cause could be tried in absence; which to this day continues to be the law of England. This rule is unquestionably a great obstruction to the course of justice. For instead of trying the cause, and awarding execution when the claim is found just, it has forced the English courts upon a wide circuit of pains and penalties. The refusing to submit to the justice of a court invested with legal authority, is a crime of the <325> grossest nature, being an act of rebellion against the state. And it is justly thought, that the person who refuses to submit to the laws of his country, ought not to be under the protection of these laws. Therefore, this contempt and contumacy, in civil actions as well as criminal, subjects the party to divers forfeitures and penalties. He is held to be a rebel or outlaw: He hath not *personam standi in judicio;* he may be killed *impune;* and both his liferent and single escheat fall.

In Scotland, we did not originally try even civil causes in absence, more than the English do at present. The compulsion to force the defendant to appear, was attachment of his moveables, to the possession of which he was restored on finding bail to sist himself in court. If he remained obstinate and offered not bail, the goods attached were delivered to the claimant,

---

* l. 11. Ad leg. Jul. Majest. [[I.e., *Digest* 48.4.11.]]

who remained in possession till the proprietor was willing to submit to a trial. This is plainly laid down in the case of the brieve of right, or declarator of property: If the defendant remain contumax, and neither appear nor plead an essoinzie, the land in controversy is seized and sequestered in the King's hands, there to remain for fifteen days; if the defendant appear within the fifteen days, he recovers possession on finding caution to answer as law will; otherwise the land is adjudged to the pursuer; <326> after which the defendant has no remedy but by a brieve of right.* Neither appears there to be any sort of cognition in other civil causes, such as actions for payment of debt, for performance of contracts, for moveable goods; where the first step was to arrest the defendant's moveables, till he found caution to answer as law will.† And in these cases, as well as in the brieve of right, the goods attached were, no doubt, delivered to the claimant, to be possessed by him while his party remained contumacious.

After the Roman law prevailed in this part of the island, the foregoing practice wore out, and, with regard to civil actions, gave place to a more mild and equitable method, which, without subjecting the defendant to any penalty, is more available to the pursuer. This method is to try the cause in absence of the defendant, in the same manner as was done in Rome, of which mention is made above. The relevancy is settled, proof taken, and judgment given, precisely as where the defendant is present. The only inconvenience of this method upon its introduction, was the depriving the pursuer of the defendant's testimony, when he chose to refer his libel to the defendant's oath. This was remedied by holding the defendant as <327> confessed on the libel. To explain this form, I shortly premise, that by the old law of this island, it was reckoned a hardship too great, to oblige a man to give evidence against himself; and for that reason the pursuer, even in a civil action, was denied the benefit of the defendant's evidence. In Scotland, the authority of the Roman law prevailing, which, in the particular now mentioned, was more equitable than our old law, it was made a rule, that the defendant in a civil action is bound to give evidence against himself; and if he refuse, he is held as confessing the fact alledged by the pursuer.

* Reg. Maj. l. 1. cap. 7.
† Quon. attach. cap. 1. cap. 49. § 3.

This practice was copied in a process where the defendant appears not; and from this time the contumacy of the defendant who obeys not a citation in a civil cause, has been attended with no penal consequence; for a good reason, that the pursuer hath a better method for attaining his end, which is, to insist that the defendant be held as confessed on the libel. Nor is this a stretch beyond reason; for the defendant's acquiescence in the claim may justly be presumed, from his refusing to appear in court.

But this new form is defective in one particular case. We hold not a party as confest, unless he be cited personally. What if one, to avoid a personal citation, keep out of the way? is there no remedy in this case? why not recur <328> to the ancient practice of attaching his effects, till he find caution to answer?

The English regulation, that there can be no trial in absence, holds in criminal as well as in civil causes, not even excepting a prosecution for high treason. But as this crime will never be suffered to go unpunished, a method has been invented, which by a circuit supplies the defect of common law. If a party accused of treason or felony, contemptuously keep out of the way; the crime, it is true, cannot be tried; but the person accused may be outlaw'd for contumacy; and the outlawry brings about the end proposed by the prosecution; for though outlawry, by common law, hath no effect, as above observed, beyond that of a denunciation upon a horning with us; yet the horror of such offences hath introduced a new regulation, that outlawry in the case of felony, subjects the party to that very punishment which is inflicted upon a felon convict; and the like in treason, corruption of blood excepted. There is no occasion to make any circuit with relation to other crimes. For the punishment of outlawry by common law equals the punishment of any crime, treason and felony excepted.

Hence the reason why death before trial, is, in England, a total bar to all forfeitures and penalties, even for high treason. The crime <329> cannot be tried in absence; and after death there can be no contempt for not appearing.

Lawyers have not always a happy talent for reformation; for they seldom search to the root of the evil. In the case before us, a superstitious attachment to ancient forms, hath led English lawyers into a glaring absurdity. To prevent the hazard of injustice, there must not be a trial in absence of the person accused. Yet no difficulty is made to presume an absent man guilty without a trial, and to punish him as if he had been fairly tried and condemned. This is in truth converting a privilege into a penalty, and holding the absent guilty, without allowing them the benefit of a trial. The absurdity of this method is equally glaring in another particular. It is not sufficient that the defendant appear in court; it is necessary that he plead, and put himself upon a trial by his country. The English adhere strictly to the original notion, that a process implies a judicial contract, and that there can be no process unless the defendant submit to have his cause tried. Upon this account it is an established rule, that the person accused who stands mute or refuses to plead cannot be tried. To this case a peculiar punishment is adapted, distinguished by the name of *peine fort et dure;* the person accused is pressed to death. And there are instances on record, of persons submitting to this punish-<330>ment, in order to save their land-estates to their heirs, which in England are forfeited in some cases of felony, as well as in high treason. But here again high treason is an exception. Standing mute in this case is attended with the same forfeiture, which is inflicted on a person attainted of high treason.

We follow the English law so far as that no crime can be tried in absence. Some exceptions to this rule were once indulged, which shall be mentioned by and by. But we at present adhere so strictly to the rule, that a decree in absence, obtained by the procurator-fiscal before an inferior court for a bloodwit upon full proof, was reduced; "the Lords being of opinion, that a decreet in absence could not proceed; and that the judge could go no further, than to fine the party for contumacy, and to grant warrant to apprehend him, till he should find caution to appear personally."*

It is certainly a defect in our law, that voluntary absence should be a protection against the punishment of atrocious crimes. Excepting the crime of high treason, in which the English regulation hath now place with us, the punishment of outlawry, whatever the crime be, never goes farther than single and liferent escheat. <331>

As to the trial of a crime after death, which the Roman law indulged in the case of treason, there are two reasons against it. The chief is, that

* Dalrymple, 19th July 1715, Procurator-fiscal *contra* Simpson.

whether the crime be committed against the public or against a private person, resentment, the spring and foundation of punishment, ought to be buried with the criminal; and, in fact, never is indulged by any person of humanity, after the criminal is no more. The other is, that the relations of the deceased, unacquainted with his private history, have not the same means of justification, which to himself, it may be supposed, would have been an easy task. Upon this account, the indulging criminal prosecutions after death, would open a door to grievous oppression. In a country where such is the law, no man can be secure, that his heirs shall inherit his fortune. With respect, however, to treason, it seems reasonable, that in some singular cases it ought to be excepted from the rule. If a man be slain in battle, fighting obstinately against an established government, there is no inhumanity in forfeiting his estate after his death; nor can such a privilege in the crown, confined to the case now mentioned, be made an engine of oppression, considering the notoriety of the fact. And indeed it carries no slight air of absurdity, that the most daring acts of rebellion, viz. rising in arms against a lawful sovereign and opposing <332> him in battle, should, if death ensue, be out of the reach of law; for dying in battle, honourably in the man's own opinion and in that of his associates, can in no light be reckoned a punishment. This in reality is a great encouragement to persevere in rebellion. A man who takes arms against his country, where such is the law, can have no true courage, if he lay them down, till he either conquer or die. This justifies the Roman law, which countenanced a trial of treason after death, confined expressly to the case now mentioned.

> Is, qui in reatu decedit, integri status decedit. Extinguitur enim crimen mortalitate, nisi forte quis majestatis reus fuit; nam hoc crimine, nisi a successoribus purgetur, hereditas fisco vindicatur. Plane non quisquis legis Juliae majestatis reus est, in eadem conditione est; sed qui perduellionis reus est, hostili animo adversus rempublicam vel principem animatus: caeterum si quis ex alia causa legis Juliae majestatis reus sit, morte crimine liberatur.*

* [["He who dies while under accusation dies with his status unimpaired; for the charge is extinguished by death. Unless perchance he has been charged with treason; for

The Roman law was copied, indiscreetly indeed, by our legislature, authorising, without any limitation, a process for treason after the death of the person suspected.* But the legislature, reflecting upon the danger of trusting with the crown a privilege so extraordinary, <333> did, by an act in the year 1542, which was never printed, restrain this privilege within proper bounds. The words are:

> And because the saids Lords think the said act (viz. the act 1540) too general and prejudicial to all the Barons of this realm; therefore statutes and ordains, that the said act shall have no place in time coming, but against the airs of them that notourly commits, or shall commit crimes of lese-majesty against the King's person, against the realm for everting the same; and against them that shall happen to betray the King's army, allenarly, it being notourly known in their time; and the airs of these persons to be called and pursued within five years after the decease of the said persons committers of the said crimes; and the said time being by-past, the saids airs never to be pursued for the same. (1) <334>

A process of treason against an absent person regularly cited, rests upon a different footing. It is some presumption of guilt, that a man accused of a crime, obstinately refuses to submit himself to the law of his country; and yet the dread of injustice, or of false witnesses, may, with an innocent person, be a motive to keep out of the way. This uncertainty about the

---

with this offense his inheritance is claimed by the imperial treasury, unless he is cleared by his successors. Clearly, not everyone charged with treason under the *lex Julia* is on the same footing, but he who is charged with *perduellio,* animated by a hostile spirit against the state or the emperor [is liable even after death]; he who is charged under the *lex Julia* on treason on other grounds is cleared of the charge on his death.")] L. ult. Ad. leg. Jul. majest. [[I.e., *Digest* 48.4.11. Trans. Watson.]]

(1) In the year 1609, Robert Logan of Restalrig was, after his death, accused in parliament, as accessory to the Earl of Gowrie's conspiracy, and his estate was forfeited to the crown; though, in appearance at least, he had died a loyal subject, and in fact never had committed any ouvert act of treason. Strange, that this statute was never once mentioned during the trial, as sufficient to bar the prosecution! Whether to attribute this to the undue influence of the crown, or to the gross ignorance of our men of law at that period, I am at a loss. Of one thing I am certain, that there is not to be found on record, another instance of such flagrant injustice in judicial proceedings.

* Act 69. parl. 1540.

motive of the person accused, ought to confine to the highest court every trial in absence, that of treason especially, where the person accused is not upon an equal footing with his prosecutors. And probably this would have been the practice in Scotland, but for one reason. The sessions of our parliament of old, were generally too short for a regular trial in a criminal cause. Upon this account, the trial of treason after death, was, from necessity rather than choice, permitted to the court of justiciary. And this court which enjoyed the greater privilege, could entertain no doubt of the less, viz. that of trying treason in absence. This latter power however being called in question, the legislature thought proper to countenance it by an express statute; not indeed as to every species of treason in general, but only in the case of "treasonable rising in arms, and open and manifest rebellion against his Majesty."* <335>

From this deduction it will be manifest, that the act 31. parl. 1690, rescinding certain forfeitures in absence pronounced by the court of justiciary before the said statute 1669, proceeds upon a mistake in fact, in subsuming, "That before the year 1669, there was no law impowering the Lords of Justiciary to forfeit in absence for perduellion." And yet this mistake is made an argument, not indeed for depriving the court of justiciary of the power in time coming, but for annulling all sentences for treason pronounced in absence by this court before the 1669. These sentences, it is true, proceeding from undue influence of ministerial power, deserved little countenance. But if they were iniquitous, it had been suitable to the dignity of the legislature to annul them for that cause, instead of assigning a reason that cannot bear a scrutiny. However this be, I cannot avoid observing, that the jurisdiction of the court of justiciary to try in absence open and manifest rebellion, is far from being irrational. And it is remarkable, that this was the opinion of our legislature, even after the revolution; for though they were willing to lay hold of any pretext to annul a number of unjust forfeitures, they did not however find it convenient to abrogate the statute 1669, but left it in full force. Comparing our law in this particular with that of England, it appears to me, that the giving a <336> fair trial is preferable

* Act 11. parl. 1669.

before the English method of annexing the highest penalties to an outlawry for treason, without any trial.

It remains only to be observed, that the English treason-laws being now extended to Scotland, the foregoing regulations for trying the crime of treason in absence of the party accused or after his death, are at an end; and that the rule holds now universally that no crime can be tried in absence. In England, no crime was ever tried in absence, far less after death. The parliament itself did not assume that power; an attainder for high treason in absence of the delinquent, proceeds not upon trial of the cause, but is of the nature of an outlawry for contumacious absence. Nor is this form varied by the union of the two kingdoms; for the British parliament, as to all matters of law, is governed by the forms established in the English parliament before the union. And I conjecture from the humanity of our present manners, that the treason laws will never be extended in Britain as they have been in Scotland, to forfeit an heir in possession for a crime said to have been committed by an ancestor. I am not of opinion that such a forfeiture is repugnant to the common rules of justice, when it is confined to the case above mentioned; and yet it is undoubtedly more beneficial for the inhabitants of this island, that by the mildness of our laws <337> some criminals may escape, than that an extraordinary power, which in perilous times may be stretched against the innocent, should be lodged even in the safest hands. The national genius is far from favouring rigorous punishments, or any latitude in criminal prosecutions; of which there cannot be more illustrious evidence than the late acts of parliament, discharging all forfeiture of lands or hereditaments, even for high treason, after the death of the pretender and his two sons.* <338>

---

* 7th Ann. 20. and 17th Geo. II. 39.

Execution against Moveables and Land
for Payment of Debt

Against a debtor refractory or negligent, the proper legal remedy is to lay hold of his effects for paying his creditors. This is the method prescribed by the Roman law,* with the following limitation, that the moveables, as of less importance than the land, should be first sold. But the Roman law was defective in one particular, that the creditor was disappointed if no buyer was found. The defect is supplied by a rescript of the Emperor,† appointing, that failing a purchaser the goods shall be adjudged to the creditor by a reasonable extent.

Among other remarkable innovations of the Feudal law, one is, that land was withdrawn from commerce, and could not be attached for payment of debt. Neither could the vassal be attached personally, because he was bound personally to the superior for service. The moveables therefore, which were always the chief <339> subject of execution, came now to be the only subject. In England, attachment of moveables for payment of debt, is warranted by the King's letter directed to the sheriff, commonly called a *Fieri facias;* and this practice is derived from common law without a statute. The sheriff is commanded "to sell as many of the debtor's moveables as will satisfy the debt, and to return the money with the writ into the court at Westminster." The method is the same at this day, without any remedy where a purchaser is not found.

Land, when left free to commerce by dissolution of the feudal fetters, was of course subjected to execution for payment of debt. This was early

* l. 15. § 2. De re judic. [[I.e., *Digest* 42.1.15.2.]]
† l. 15. § 3. De re judic. [[I.e., *Digest* 42.1.15.3.]]

introduced with relation to the King. For from the *Magna Charta,** it appears to have been the King's privilege, failing goods and chattels, to take possession of the land till the debt was paid. And from the same chapter it appears, that the like privilege is bestowed upon a cautioner, in order to draw payment of what sums he is obliged to advance for the principal debtor. By the statute of merchants,† the same privilege is given to merchants; and by 13th Edw. l. cap. 18. the privilege is communicated to creditors in general; but with the following remarkable limitation, that they are allowed to possess the half only of the land. <340> By this time it was settled, that the military vassal's power of aliening, reached the half only of his freehold;‡ and it was thought incongruous, to take from the debtor by force of execution, what he himself could not dispose of even for the most valuable consideration. The last-mentioned statute enacts,

> That where debt is recovered, or acknowledged in the King's court, or damages awarded, it shall be in the election of him that sueth, to have a *Fieri facias* unto the sheriff, to levy the debt upon the lands and chattels of the debtor; or that the sheriff shall deliver to him all the chattels of the debtor, (saving his oxen and beasts of his plough) and the one half of his land, until the debt be levied upon a reasonable extent; and if he be put out of the land, he shall recover it again by writ of nouvel disseisin, and after that by writ of redisseisin if need be.

The writ authorised by this statute, which, from the election given to the creditor, got the name of *Elegit,* is the only writ in the law of England that in any degree corresponds to our apprising or adjudication. The operations, however, of these two writs are far from being the same. The property of land apprised or adjudged is transferred to the creditor in satisfaction of his claim, if the debtor forbear to make payment for ten <341> years; but an *Elegit* is a legal security only, having no effect but to put the creditor in possession till the debt be paid, by levying the rents and profits. This is an inconvenient method of drawing payment (1). But at the time of the stat-

---

* Cap. 8.

† 13th Edward I.

‡ See abridgement of statute law, tit. *Recognition.*

(1) For beside the inconvenience of obtaining payment by parcels, it is not easy for the creditor in counting for the rents, to avoid a law-suit, which in this case must always be troublesome and expensive. It may also happen, that the rent exceeds not the interest

ute, it was probably thought a stretch, to subject land at any rate to a creditor for his payment; and the English, tenacious of their customs, never think of making improvements, nor even of supplying legal defects; of which this statute affords another instance, more inconvenient than that now mentioned. In England at present, land generally speaking is totally under the power of the proprietor; and yet the ancient practice still subsists, confining execution to the half, precisely as in early times when the debtor could dispose of no more but the half. Means however are contrived, indirect, indeed, to supply this palpable defect. Any other creditor is authorised to seize the half of <342> the land left out of the first execution, and so on without end. Thus, by strictly adhering to form without regarding substance, law, instead of a rational science, becomes a heap of subterfuges and incongruities, which tend insensibly to corrupt the morals of those who make law their profession.

And here to prevent mistakes, it must be observed, that the clause in the statute, bearing, "That the sheriff by a *Fieri facias* may levy the debt upon the land and chattels of the debtor," authorises not the sheriff to deliver the land to the creditor, but only to sell what is found upon the land, such as corn or cattle, and to levy the rents which at the time of the execution are due by the tenants.

Letters of poinding in Scotland, correspond to the writ of *Fieri facias* in England; but the defect above mentioned in the *Fieri facias,* is supplied in our execution against moveables according to its ancient form, which is copied from the Roman law. The execution was in the following manner:

> The goods upon the debtor's land, whether belonging to the master or tenant, are carried to the market-cross of the head burgh of the sheriffdom, and there sold for payment of the debt. But if a purchaser be not found, goods are apprised to the value of the debt, and deliver-<343>ed to the creditor for his payment.*

---

of the money: must the creditor be satisfied with the possession, without ever hoping to acquire the property? The common law assuredly affords him no remedy. But it is probable, that upon application by the creditor, the court of chancery, on a principle of equity, will direct the land to be sold for payment of the debt.

* Quon. attach. cap. 49.

And here it must be remarked, that bating the rigour of selling the tenant's goods for the landlord's debt, this method is greatly preferable to that presently in use, which enjoins not a sale of the goods, but only that they be delivered to the creditor at apprised values. This is unjust; because instead of money, which the creditor is entitled to claim, goods are imposed on him, to which he has no claim. But this is a trifle compared with the wrong done to the debtor by another branch of the execution that has crept into practice. In letters of poinding, a blank being left for the name of the messenger, the creditor is impowered to chuse what messenger he pleases, and of consequence to chuse also the appretiators; by which means he is in effect both judge and party. In a practice so irregular, what can be expected but an unfair appretiation, always below the value of the goods poinded? And for grasping at this undue advantage, the creditor's pretext is but too plausible, that contrary to the nature of his claim, he is forced to accept goods in lieu of money. Thus our execution against moveables in its present form, is irregular and unjust in all views. Wonderful, that contrary to the tendency of all public regulations toward perfection, this should have gradually declined from <344> good to bad, and from bad to worse! And we shall have additional cause to wonder, when in the course of this enquiry it appears, that the indulging to the creditor the choice of the messenger and appretiators, has, with respect to execution against land, produced effects still more pernicious than that under consideration.

Our kings, it is probable, borrowed from England the privilege of entering upon the debtor's land, for payment of debt. That they had this privilege appears from 2d Statutes Robert I. cap. 9. which is copied almost word for word from the 8th chapter of the *Magna Charta*. Cautioners had the same privilege,* which was extended, as in England, to merchants.† This execution did not entitle the creditor to have the land sold for payment of the debt, but only to take possession of the land, and to maintain his possession till the debt was paid, precisely as in England. But as it has been the genius of our law in all ages to favour creditors, a form of execution against land for payment of debt, more effectual than that now mentioned or to

---

* Ibid. cap. 10.
† Ibid. cap. 19.

this day is known in England, was early introduced into this part of the island, which is to sell land for payment of the debt, in the same manner that moveables were sold. The brieve of distress, failing moveables, is extended to the debtor's land, which is appoint-<345>ed to be sold by the sheriff for payment of the debt.* Nor was this execution restricted to the half as in England; for our forefathers were more regardful of the creditor than of the superior. And though this originally might be a stretch, it happens luckily to be perfectly well accommodated to the present condition of land-property, which is not more limited than the property of moveables.

A defect will be observed in Alexander's statute, that no provision is made where a purchaser is not found; the less excuseable that the legislature had before their eyes a perfect model, in the form prescribed for attachment of moveables.

There are words in this statute to occasion a doubt, whether attachment of land for payment of debt, was not an earlier practice in our law. The words are:

> The debtor not selling his lands within fifteen days, the sheriff and the King's servants shall sell the lands and possessions pertaining to the debtor, *conform to the consuetude of the realm,* until the creditor be satisfied of the principal sum, with damage, expence, and interest.

But these words, *conform to the consuetude of the realm,* seem to refer to the form of selling moveables. For I see not what regulation was introduced by the statute, if it was not the selling land for <346> payment of debt. And considering the circumstances of these times, when the Feudal law was still in vigour and the commerce of land but in its infancy, we cannot rationally assign an earlier date to this practice.

In England, the statute of merchants was necessary to creditors, who at that period had not access to the land of their debtors. But as in Scotland every creditor had access to the land of his debtor, it will be expected that some account should be given, why the statute of merchants was introduced here. What occurs is, that the chief view of the Scotch statute of merchants was to give access to the debtor's person, which formerly could

---

* Stat. Alex. II. cap. 24.

not be attached for payment of debt. And when such a novelty was introduced, as that of giving execution against the person of the debtor, against his moveables, and against his land, all at the same time, it was probably thought sufficient, to give security upon the land for payment of the debt, without proceeding to a sale.

It appears from our records, that sometimes land was sold for payment of debt by authority of the above-mentioned statute of Alexander II. and sometimes that security only was granted upon the land by authority of the statute of merchants. Of the latter, one instance occurs upon record, in a seisin dated 29th January 1450; and many such instances are upon re-<347>cord down to the time that general apprisings crept into practice.

It is observed above, that the statute of Alexander II. is defective, in not providing a remedy where a purchaser is not found. But this defect was supplied by our judges; and land, failing a purchaser, was adjudged to the creditor by a reasonable extent; which was done by analogy of the execution against moveables. Of this there is one instance in a charter dated 22d July 1450, a copy of which is annexed.* And thus we find, that what is properly called a decreet of apprising, was introduced into practice before the statute 1469, though that statute is by all our authors assigned as the origin of apprisings. But it appears from the statute itself, compared with former practice, that nothing else was in view, but to limit the effect of the brieve of distress with respect to tenants, that there should not be execution against their goods for the landlord's debt, but to the extent of a term's rent. And because it was reckoned a hardship on a debtor to have his land taken from him, when there were moveable goods upon the land; therefore a sweetening privilege is bestowed on him, of redeeming the land within seven years. This regulation had an unhappy consequence, probably not foreseen: it rendered ineffectual the most useful <348> branch of the execution, viz. the selling land for payment of the debt; for no person will chuse to purchase land under reversion, while there is any prospect of coming at land without an embargo. This statute, therefore, instead of giving a beginning to apprisings of land, did in reality reduce them to a form less perfect than they had originally.

* App. No. 7.

One salutary regulation was introduced by this statute. By the former practice, no bounds being set to the time of completing the execution, it was left to the discretion of the sheriff, to delay as long as he pleased for a purchaser. To supply this defect, it was enacted, "That if a purchaser be not found in six months, the sheriff must proceed to apprise land, and to adjudge it to the creditor."

In no particular are the different manners of the two nations more conspicuous, than in their laws. The English have from the beginning preserved their forms entire, with little or no variation. The Scots have been always attempting or indulging innovations. By this propensity for improvements, many articles of our law are brought to a reasonable degree of perfection. But at the same time, we are too apt to indulge relaxation of discipline, which has bred a profusion of slovenly practice in law matters. The following history will justify the latter part of this reflection. <349>

During a vacancy in the office of sheriff, or when the sheriff was otherwise employed, it appears to have been early the practice of the King's courts, to name a substitute for executing any particular affair; and this substitute was called *the sheriff in that part.* Within thirty years of the statute 1469, there are examples of letters of apprising, directed to messengers at arms, as *sheriffs in that part.* These letters, we may believe, were at first not permitted without a sufficient cause; but slighter and slighter causes being sustained, heritable sheriffs took the alarm, and obtained an act of parliament,* "discharging commissions to be given in time coming for serving of brieves, or apprising of lands, but to the judge-ordinary, unless *causa cognita* upon calling the judge-ordinary to object against the cause of granting." But this statute did not put an end to the abuse. The practice was revived of naming messengers at arms as sheriffs in that part, for executing letters of apprising; and at length it became an established custom, to direct all letters of apprising to these officers.

Apprising of land, being an execution by the sheriff, behoved of consequence to be within the county. But the substitution of messengers who are not connected with any particular county, paved the way to the infringement of <350> a regulation derived from the very nature of the ex-

* Act 82. parl. 1540.

ecution. The first instance on record, of permitting the court of apprising to be held at Edinburgh, is in the year 1582. The reason given for a step so irregular was, that the debtor's lands lay in two shires. And as Edinburgh by this time had become the capital of the kingdom, where the King's courts most commonly were held, and where every landed gentleman was supposed to have a procurator to answer for him; it was reckoned no wide stretch, to hold courts of apprising at Edinburgh for the whole kingdom. From this period downward, instances of holding courts of apprising at Edinburgh, multiply upon us; and this came to be considered as a matter of right, without necessity of assigning any cause for demanding a dispensation, or at least without necessity of verifying the cause assigned.

The substitution of a messenger instead of the sheriff, produced another effect, no less irregular than that now mentioned, and much more pernicious to debtors. In letters of poinding, as observed above, a blank is left for the name of the messenger; the same is the form of letters of apprising; and by this means, in both executions equally, the creditor has the choice of the messenger, and consequently of the appretiators. Thus, by obtaining the court of apprising to be held at Edinburgh, by a judge <351> chosen at will, the creditor acquired the absolute direction of the execution against land; and, precisely as in the execution against moveables, became in effect both judge and party. It will not be surprising, that the grossest legal iniquity was the result of such slovenly practice. Creditors taking the advantage of the indulgence given them, exerted their power with so little reserve, as to grasp at the debtor's whole land-estate, without the least regard to the extent of the debt. In short, without using so much as the formality of an appretiation, it became customary to adjudge to the creditor every subject belonging to the debtor that could be carried by this execution; for which the expence of bringing witnesses to Edinburgh from distant shires to value land, and the difficulty of determining the value of real burdens affecting land, were at first the pretext.

As there is no record of apprisings before the year 1636, we are not certain of the precise periods of these several innovations. The only knowledge we have of apprisings before that time, is from the King's charters passing upon apprisings; which is a very lame record, considering how many apprisings must have been led, that were not completed by charter and seisin. But imperfect as this record may be, we find several charters in the 1607, 1608, <352> 1613, 1614, &c. passing upon general apprisings.

It cannot but appear strange, that such gross relaxation of essential forms, and such robbery under colour of law, were not checked in the bud by the sovereign court. Yet we find nothing of this kind attempted, though the remedy was at hand. There was no occasion for any new regulation; it would have been sufficient to restore the brieve of distress to its original principles. All excesses, however, promote naturally their own cure; which is the most peculiarly remarkable in avarice. General apprisings by their frequency became a public nuisance, past all enduring. The matter was brought under consideration of parliament, and a statute was made, by far too mild. For instead of cutting down general apprisings root and branch, as illegal and oppressive, the exorbitant profits were only pruned off; and it was enacted,* "That the rents intromitted with by the creditor, if more than sufficient to pay his annualrent, shall be applied towards extinction of the principal sum."

It must not escape observation, that by this new regulation, an apprising is in effect moulded into a new form, much less perfect than it was originally: from being a judicial sale, it is reduced to a judicial security, or a *pignus prae*-<353>*torium,* approaching much nearer than formerly to the English *Elegit.*

An attempt was made by act 19. parl. 1672, to restore special adjudications, but unsuccessfully. It might have been foreseen, without much penetration, that no debtor will voluntarily give off land sufficient to pay the debt claimed, and a fifth part more, reserving a power of redemption for five years only, when his refusal subjects him to no harder alternative, than to have his whole lands impledged for security of the neat sum due, with power of redemption for ten years. It had been an attempt more worthy of the legislature, to restore the brieve of distress, by appointing land to be sold upon application of any single creditor, and to apply the price for his payment. But nothing of this kind was thought of, till the year 1681, when a statute was made, authorising a sale of the debtor's whole estate, in case of insolvency. This regulation, which was brought to greater perfection by

* Act 6. parl. 1621.

later statutes, is after all an imperfect remedy; because it only takes place where the debtor is insolvent. And hence it is, that by the present law of Scotland, there is no effectual means for obtaining payment out of the debtor's land estate, while he continues solvent. Being familiarised with this regulation, it doth not disgust us; but it probably will surprise a stranger, to find a country, where <354> the debtor's insolvency affords the only effectual means his creditors have to obtain payment by force of law.

Upon the whole, it is a curious morsel of history that lies before us. In the first stages of our law, we had a form of execution for drawing payment of debt, perfect in its kind, or so nigh perfection, as scarce to be susceptible of any improvement. It has been the operation of ages, to alter, change, innovate, and relax from this form, till it became grievous and intolerable. New moulded by various regulations, it makes at present a better figure. But with all the improvements of later times, the best that can be said of it is, that, though far distant, it approacheth nearer to its original perfection, than at any time for a century or two past. And for the public good, nothing remains but to revive the brieve of distress in its original state, with respect to moveables as well as land; admitting only some alterations that are made necessary by change of circumstances; such as the present independency of tenants, and their privilege to hold property distinct from their landlords. <355>

Personal Execution for Payment of Debt

The subjects that lie open to execution for payment of debt, are, 1st, The debtor's moveables. 2dly, His land. And, 3dly, His person. The two first mentioned being discussed in the tract immediately foregoing, we proceed to the third. Personal execution for payment of debt, was introduced after execution against land, and long after execution against moveables. Nor will this appear singular, when we consider, that the debtor's person cannot, like his land or moveables, be converted into money for the payment of debt. And with regard to a vassal in particular, his person cannot regularly be withdrawn from the service he owes his superior. This would not have been tolerated while the Feudal law was in vigour; and came to be indulged in the decline of that law, when land was improved, and personal services were less valued than pecuniary casualties (1). The first statute in this <356> island introducing personal execution, is 11th Edward I. which, as appears from the preamble, was to secure merchants and encourage trade. It is directed against the inhabitants of royal boroughs, and

> subjects, in the first place, their moveables and burgage-lands to be sold
> for payment of the debt due to the merchant. And failing goods, the body

(1) Among the ancient Egyptians, payment was taken out of the debtor's goods; but the body of the debtor could not be attached. An individual, on account of a private debt, could not be withdrawn from the service he owed to the public, whether in peace or war. Our author Diodorus Siculus mentions, that Solon established this law in Athens, freeing all the citizens from imprisonment for debt.—*Book* 1. *chap.* 6.—And he adds, that some did justly blame many of the Grecian law-makers, who forbade arms, ploughs, and other things necessary for labour, to be taken as pledges, and yet permitted the persons who used these instruments to be imprisoned.

of the debtor is to be taken and kept in prison till he agree with his creditor. And if he have not wherewith to sustain himself in prison, the creditor shall find him in bread and water.

An additional security is introduced by 13th Edward I.

If the debtor do not pay the debt at the day, the magistrates, upon application of the creditors, are obliged to commit him to the town-prison, there to remain upon his own expence until payment. If the debtor be not found within the town, a writ is directed to the sheriff of the shire <357> where he is, to imprison him. After a quarter of a year from the time of his imprisonment, his goods and lands shall be delivered to the merchant by a reasonable extent, to hold them till the debt is levied, and his body shall remain in prison, and the merchant shall find him bread and water.

This latter statute was adopted by us;* and our statute, I presume, is the foundation of the act of warding peculiar to royal boroughs.[1] A copy of this writ is in the appendix, No. 8.[2]

As this was found a successful expedient for obtaining payment of debt, it was afterward extended to all creditors.† And thus in England, the creditor may begin with attaching the person of his debtor, by a writ named *Capias ad satisfaciendum,* the same with an act of warding in Scotland against inhabitants of royal boroughs. But as this act of Edward III. was not adopted by our legislature, there is to this day with us no authority for a *Capias ad satisfaciendum,* except in the single case of an act of warding.

It is a celebrated question in the Roman law, touching obligations, *ad facta praestanda,* Whether the debtor be bound specifically to perform, or whether he be liable *pro interesse* only. It is at least the more plausible opinion, that a <358> man is bound according to his engagement; and after all, why indulge to the debtor an option to pay a sum, instead of performing that work to which he bound himself without an option? The person accordingly who becomes bound *ad factum praestandum,* is not with us indulged in an alternative. A refusal, when he is able to perform, is understood

* 2d Stat. Robert I. cap. 19.
† 25th Edward III. cap. 17.
1. 1758, 1761 add: "for this execution is precisely in terms of the statute."
2. "A copy . . . appendix, No. 8." added 1776.

an act of contumacy and disobedience to the law. This is a solid foundation for the letters of four forms, which formerly were issued upon obligations *ad facta praestanda*. And the tenor of these letters is abundantly moderate; for it is worthy to be remarked, that there is not in them a single injunction but what is in the obligor's power to perform. The ultimate injunction is, "To perform his obligation, or to surrender his person to ward, under the penalty, that otherwise he shall be denounced rebel." If the obligor surrendered his person to prison, the will of the letters was fulfilled, and no further execution did proceed. If he was contumacious by refusing both alternatives, his disobedience to the law was justly held an act of rebellion, to subject him to be denounced or declared rebel.* This execution was rather too mild; for the man who refuseth to perform his engagement when it is in his power, may <359> in great justice be declared a rebel, without admitting any alternative, such as delivering his person to ward.

Obligations for payment of money, were viewed in a different light. If a man failed to pay his debt, the failure was presumed to proceed from inability, not obstinacy. Therefore, unless some criminal circumstance was specified, the debtor was not subjected to any sort of punishment. His land and moveables lay open to be attached by poinding, apprising, and arrestment, which were in this case the only remedies provided to the creditor. The English have adopted very different maxims. Imprisonment upon failure of payment, whether considered as a punishment or a compulsion, cannot be justified but upon the supposition of contumacy and unwillingness to pay: on the supposition of inability without any fault on the debtor's part, it is not only unjust to punish him with loss of liberty, but an absurd regulation, tending to no good end. Therefore the *Capias ad satisfaciendum* in England, must be founded upon the presumption of unwillingness to pay. This appeared to us a harsh presumption, as it is frequently wide of the real fact; and therefore we forebore to adopt the English statute. But experience taught our legislature, that failure of payment proceeds from obstinacy or idleness, as often as from inability; nay, debt-<360>ors were often found secreting their effects, in order to disappoint their creditors; and there was encouragement to deal in such fraudulent practices, when

---

* See in the Appendix, No. 9. a copy of Letters of four forms.

debtors were in all events secure against personal execution. These considerations produced the act of sederunt 1582. It is set forth in the preamble,

> That the defect of personal execution upon liquid grounds of debt was heavily complained of; because, after great charge and tedious delay in obtaining decreet, the creditors were often disappointed of their payment, by simulate and fraudulent alienations made by the debtors, of their lands and goods, whereby execution upon such decreets was altogether frustrated:

—therefore appointed, "That letters of horning, as well as of poinding, shall be directed upon decreets for liquid sums, in the same manner as formerly given upon decreets *ad facta praestanda*." And this act of sederunt is ratified by the act 139. parl. 1584.

There is not in the law of any country a more pregnant instance of harshness, I may say of brutality, than in our present form of personal execution for payment of debt; where the debtor, without ceremony, is declared a rebel, merely upon failure of payment. To punish a man as a rebel, who, by misfortune or be it bad oeconomy, is rendered insolvent, betokens savage and barbarous manners. One would <361> imagine love of riches to be the ruling passion, in a country where poverty is an object of punishment. It is true, the cruelty of this execution is softened in practice, as it could not possibly stand in vigour against every principle of humanity. It is a subject, however, of curiosity, to enquire how this rigorous execution crept in. The act 1584, just now mentioned, gives no countenance to it; for the letters of four forms to be issued by that statute upon decrees for payment of debt, are far from being so rigorous as our hornings are at present. These letters, as above explained, impose no other hardship upon the debtor, than to oblige him to surrender his person in ward if he doth not pay. This indeed is a stretch, but a moderate one, which the uncertainty whether failure of payment proceeds from unwillingness or inability, may justify. But upon such an uncertainty, to declare a debtor rebel unless he pays, is a brutal practice, which can admit of no excuse. If indeed the debtor, failing to pay, will not go to prison, for this contempt of authority he may be justly declared rebel. The question then is, What it was that produced an alteration so rigorous in the form of this execution, that a debtor, instead of being denounced rebel on failing to go to prison, is denounced rebel on

failing to make payment, when it is often not in his power to make payment. <362>

In handling this curious subject, we must be satisfied to grope our way
in the dark paths of antiquity, almost without a guide. And the first thing
we discover is, that letters of four forms were not the only warrant for personal execution upon *facta praestanda*. By the act 84. parl. 1572, touching
the designation of a manse and glebe to the minister, letters of horning are
ordered to be directed by the privy-council, to charge the possessor to remove within ten days, under the pain of rebellion; without any alternative,
such as that of surrendering his person in ward. And indeed such alternative
would be absurd, where a fact is commanded to be done that cannot con-
veniently admit of delay. Obligations *ad facta praestanda* arising *ex delicto,*
were, I presume, attended with the like summary execution. And I have
seen one instance of this, viz. letters of horning, *anno* 1573, against a person
who had been guilty of a spuilzie, commanding, that he should be charged
to redeliver the spuilzied goods within eight days, under the penalty or certification of being denounced rebel. Thus, though no execution was
awarded upon civil contracts *ad facta praestanda* other than letters of four
forms; yet, I presume, that upon such obligations arising *ex delicto,* horning,
properly so called, upon one charge (2) was commonly the <363> execution.
And as to obligations introduced by statute, the manner of execution is
generally directed in the statute itself.

I have made another discovery, that the alternative of surrendering the
person in ward, was not always the style of letters of four forms. When
letters of four forms proceeded on a delict, as they sometimes did, I conjecture, that the foregoing alternative was left out. My authority is the act
53. parl. 1572, "ordering letters to be direct by the Lords of Council in all
the four forms, charging excommunicated persons to satisfy the kirk, under
the pain of rebellion," without any such alternative as surrendering the
person in ward.

(2) Letters of horning mean a letter from the King, ordering or commanding the
debtor to make payment, under the pain of being proclaimed a rebel. The service of
this letter upon the debtor, is named a *Charge of horning.* If the debtor disobey the charge,
he is denounced or proclaimed a rebel; and because of old, a horn served the same purpose in proclamations that trumpets do at present, therefore, the said letter has by custom, though improperly, obtained the name of *Letters of horning,* and the service of the
letter has obtained the name of a *Charge of horning.*

Though horning be a generic term, comprehending letters of four forms as well as horning properly so called, as is clear from the above-mentioned statute 1584, appointing a decree for a liquid sum to be made effectual by letters of four forms which there pass under the <364> general name of *horning;* yet, generally speaking, when horning is mentioned in our old statutes, it is understood to be horning on one charge, in opposition to letters of four forms. And it is a rule without exception, that whereever horning is ordained to proceed upon a single charge, the alternative of surrendering the person in ward, is understood to be excluded. For where the common number of charges is remitted in order to force a speedy performance, it would be absurd to put it in the power of the person charged, to evade performance by going to prison.

The operations of our law were originally slow and tedious. There behoved to be four citations before a man could be effectually brought into court, and there behoved to be four charges before a man could be effectually brought to give obedience to a decree pronounced against him. The inconveniency was not much felt in the days of idleness; but when industry prevailed, and the value of labour was understood, the multiplicity of these legal steps became intolerable. The number of citations were reduced to two, authorised by the same warrant, and at last a single citation was made sufficient. It is probable, that the charges necessary to be given upon decrees, did originally proceed upon four distinct letters or warrants; but it being found that one letter or warrant might be a sufficient authority for the four <365> charges, the form was changed according to the model of the letters of four forms latest in use. At the same time, where dispatch was required, as upon obligations *ad facta praestanda* arising *ex delicto,* and upon statutory obligations, one charge instead of four was made sufficient. But these different forms of execution were confined to obligations *ad facta praestanda.* And with relation to all of them, not excepting the most rigorous, it must be remarked, that they did not exceed rational bounds. The obligor was in no case declared a rebel, unless where he was guilty of a real contempt of legal authority, by refusing to do some act which he had power to perform.

We proceed to unfold the origin of personal execution upon bonded debts, which probably will give light to the present enquiry. There is no ground to suppose, that personal execution was known in this island before the reign of Edward I. In England it was introduced by two statutes, which were adopted by us. This hath already been mentioned; as also that in England, by statute of Edward III. every debtor in a sum of money is subjected to personal execution; which was not adopted by us, now though our law gave no authority for personal execution except against inhabitants of royal boroughs, yet a hint was taken to make this execution more general by consent. While money was a scarce commodity, and while the <366> demand for it was greater than could be readily supplied, moneyed men introduced a practice of imposing upon borrowers hard conditions, which were engrossed in the instrument of debt. One of these was, that in case of failing to make payment, personal as well as real execution should issue. And letters of four forms were accordingly issued; though it may be a doubt, whether in strict law a private paction be a sufficient foundation for such execution, which being of the nature of a punishment, cannot justly be inflicted where there is no crime. But by this time we had begun to relish the English notion, that the failing to make payment proceeds commonly from unwillingness, and not from inability; and on that supposition the execution was materially just, though scarce founded on law. This practice, however, gained ground without attention to strict principles; and it came to be established, that consent is a sufficient foundation for personal execution. See Appendix No. 9. Letters of four forms.[3]

But the rigour of money-lenders did not stop here. They were not satisfied with letters of four forms, because the dreadful commination of being declared rebel, might in all events be evaded by the debtor's surrendering his person in ward. Nothing less would suffice, than to have the most rigorous execution at command, such as was in practice upon an obligation *ad* <367> *factum praestandum* arising *ex delicto*. And thus in bonds for borrowed money, it became customary to provide, that, instead of letters of four forms, letters of horning should proceed upon a single charge, commanding the debtor to make payment, under the penalty of being declared a rebel without admitting the alternative of going to prison. At the same time, the debtor commonly was charged to make payment within so few days, as not even to have sufficient time for the performance, however willing or ready he might be. The rigour of these pactions was in part repressed

3. "See Appendix . . . four forms." added 1776.

by the act 140. parl. 1592; particularly with respect to the time of performance; but personal execution upon obligations for debt was left untouched; as was also the form of this execution upon a single charge, attended with the penalty of rebellion upon failing to make payment.

In this manner crept in personal execution on bonded debts, which in practice was so thoroughly established, as to be issued on a bare consent, "that executorials might proceed in form as effeirs." One instance of this appears in the record, viz. letters of four forms, John Lawson *contra* Sir John Stewart and his son, dated the 7th of May 1582, and recorded 16th August after. But probably letters of horning, properly so called, upon a single <368> charge, were never issued unless in pursuance of an explicit consent.

It may justly be presumed, that the practice of personal execution upon bonded debts, paved the way to the above-mentioned act of sederunt 1582. For after personal execution upon decrees of consent for payment of money was once established, it was a natural extension to give the same execution upon decrees for payment of money obtained *in foro contentioso.*

It only remains to be observed, with respect to personal execution upon decrees *in foro contentioso,* that it has always been understood an extraordinary remedy; and therefore that it requires the special interposition of the sovereign authority. This authority is obtained by an order directed to the keeper of the King's signet, issuing from any of his proper courts, such as the session, justiciary, or privy council when it was in being; and the King interposes his authority of course, for executing the ordinances of his own courts. But as he condescends not to execute the ordinances of any other court, therefore no inferior judge or magistrate can give warrant for letters of horning; not even the judge of the court of admiralty, nor the commissaries of Edinburgh, neither of which properly are the King's courts. The method formerly in use for procuring personal execution upon the decrees of such courts, was to <369> obtain from the court of session a decree of interposition, commonly called a *Decreet conform;* which being a decree of a sovereign court, was a proper foundation for letters of horning. But this method gave place to one more expeditious, as we shall see anon.

If this sketch of the origin of personal execution with respect to debt be but roughly drawn, let the deficiency of materials plead my excuse. Luckily there is not the same ground of complaint in the following part of the history, every article of which is clearly vouched. The first statute abridging letters of four forms upon decrees *in foro contentioso,* is the act 181. parl. 1593, "authorising letters of horning containing a single charge of ten days, to proceed upon decreets of magistrates within burgh, without the necessity of letters conform." Letters of horning, properly so called, upon a single charge, being here introduced in place of letters of four forms, the known tenor of such letters removed all ambiguity, and made it evident, that the legislature intended the debtor should be denounced rebel upon failing to make payment, without admitting the alternative of surrendering his person in ward. Here is a monster of a statute, repugnant to humanity and common justice. But by this time, the alternative of being denounced rebel upon failing to make payment, founded on consent, was familiar; and if such execution could be founded <370> on consent, it was reckoned no wide stretch to give the same execution upon a decree *in foro contentioso.* This however is no sufficient apology for extending a harsh practice, which ought rather to have been totally abolished. But the influence of custom is great; and our legislature submitted to its authority without due deliberation; not only in this statute, but afterwards in extending the regulation to the decrees of other inferior courts.* It may justly be a matter of surprise, that statutes so contradictory to equity and humanity were tamely submitted to. To account for this, I must observe, that the same thing happened here that constantly happens with relation to harsh and rigorous laws. Such laws have a natural tendency to dissolution; and even where they are supported by the authority of a settled government, means are never wanting to blunt their edge. Thus, though the law was submitted to, which inflicted the penalties of rebellion on presumed disobedience, when possibly at bottom there was no fault; yet no judge could be so devoid of common humanity, as willingly to give scope to such penalties. A distinction was soon recognised, betwixt treason or rebellion in the proper sense of the word, and the constructive rebellion under consideration, termed *civil rebellion;* and it came to be reckoned oppressive <371> and disgraceful, to lay hold of any of the penalties attending the latter. In this manner civil rebellion

---

* Act 10. parl. 1606; act 6. parl. 1607; act 15. parl. 1609; act 7. parl. 1612.

lost its sting, first in practice, and now with regard to single and liferent escheat, by a British statute.* For though the law was scarce ever put in execution to make these penalties effectual, yet as upon some occasions they were used as a handle for oppression, it was thought proper to abolish them altogether.

In the mean time, letters of four forms continued to be the only warrant for personal execution, upon decrees of the court of session. But this court, esteeming it a sort of impeachment upon their dignity to be worse appointed than inferior courts are with respect to personal execution, took upon them† to abolish letters of four forms, and to appoint the same letters of horning to pass on their own decrees, that by statute were authorised to pass upon decrees of inferior courts. That decrees of the supreme court should at least be equally privileged with those of inferior courts, is a proposition that admits not a doubt. I cannot, however, without indignation, reflect on the preamble of the act of sederunt, asserting, that letters of horning properly so called are a form of execution less burdensome upon debtors than letters of four forms; which is a bold attempt to impose on the common sense of mankind. <372>

To complete this short history, there only remains to be added, that to obtain a warrant for personal execution, it is scarce ever necessary, as our law now stands, to apply to the court of session for a decree of interposition. By the regulations 1563, concerning the commissary-court, a more curt method was introduced for obtaining letters of horning upon the precepts of the commissaries of Edinburgh; which is, that the court of session, upon an application to them by petition, should instantly issue a warrant for letters of horning. And the same method was prescribed, in all the statutes above mentioned that authorised letters of horning upon decrees of inferior courts.

When we compare our form of personal execution with that of England, we perceive a wide difference. In England, the *Capias ad satisfaciendum* is a writ directed to the sheriff, to imprison the person of the debtor till he give satisfaction to his creditor; of which the consequence is, that payment

---

* 20th Geo. II. 50.
† Act of sederunt 1613.

made by the debtor entitles him of course to his liberty. But in Scotland, an act of warding excepted, a debtor is not committed to prison upon account merely of his failing to make payment. He must be denounced rebel before a *Capias* or caption can be issued. Nor is this a *Capias ad satisfaciendum;* it is built upon a different foundation. Imprisonment is one of the penalties of rebel-<373>lion; and our *Capias* is issued against the person, not as debtor but as rebel. The debtor accordingly, by the words of our caption, must remain in prison, "till he be relaxed from the process of horning"; that is, obtain the King's pardon for his rebellion. For this reason it is, that tendering the sum due, is not in strict law sufficient to save the debtor from prison. Nor after imprisonment will he be entitled to his freedom upon tendering the sum, till he also obtain letters of relaxation. The court of session indeed dispensed with this formality in small debts, "declaring the creditor's consent sufficient for the debtor's liberation, when the sum exceeds not 200 merks."* <374>

* Act of sederunt, 5th February 1675.

Execution for Obtaining Payment
after the Death of the Debtor

In handling this subject, I cannot hope fully to gratify the reader's curiosity otherwise than by tracing the history of this branch of law from remote ages. It will be necessary not only to gather what light we can from the rules of common justice, but also to examine the laws of England and of old Rome, which have been copied by us in different periods.

The great utility of money as a commercial standard, made it from the time of its introduction a desirable object. It came itself to be one of the principal subjects of commerce, and of contracts of loan. When money is lent, it is the duty of the debtor to pay the sum at the term covenanted; and to procure money by a sale of his goods, if he cannot otherwise satisfy his creditor. If the debtor be refractory or negligent, it is the duty of the judge to interpose, and to direct a sale of the goods, in order that the creditor may draw his payment out of the price. <375>

In what manner debts are to be made effectual after the debtor's death, by the rules of common justice, is a speculation more involved. One thing is obvious, that if no person claim the property of the goods as heir, or by other legal title, the creditors ought to have the same remedy that they had during their debtor's life. In this case, there is required no stretch of authority. On the contrary, when a debtor's goods after his death are sold for payment of his debts, the law is no further exerted than to supply the defect of will, which, it is presumed, the debtor would have interposed had he been alive; whereas when a debtor's goods, during his life, are sold by public authority, his property is wrested from him against his will.

But now an heir appears, and the property is transferred to him by right of succession. Justice will not allow him to enjoy the heritage of his ancestor, without acknowledging his ancestor's debts. Therefore, if he submit not to pay the whole debts, one of two things must necessarily follow, either that he account to the creditors for the value of the heritage, or that he consent to a sale for their behoof. Justice, as appears to me, cannot be fulfilled but by pursuing the latter method; and my reasons for thinking so are two. The first is, that creditors have an equitable claim to the effects of their deceased debtor, but none against his issue or <376> other relations; and therefore that these effects ought to be surrendered to the creditors for their payment, unless the heir, by making full payment, put an end to their claim. The next is, that sale, the best method for determining the value of a commercial subject, ought to be preferred by judges before the uncertain opinion of witnesses. The *praetium affectionis* of the heir ought not to weigh against the more solid interest of creditors, who are *certantes de damno evitando;* not to mention, that an heir, if he have an affection for the subject, may gratify his affection by offering the smallest sum above what another esteems the intrinsic value.

The Romans, with respect to heirs, had a peculiar way of thinking, which must be explained because it relates to the subject under consideration. An heir, in the common sense of mankind, is that person who, by blood or by will, is entitled to the effects of a person deceased; and the succession of an heir, is a mode established by law, for vesting in a living person effects which belonged to another at his death. Hence it is, that with respect to different subjects, the same person may have different heirs; as for example, an heir of blood may succeed to some subjects, and an heir by will to others. The idea of an heir in the Roman law, is not derived from the right of succeeding to the heritage in general or to any particular subject, <377> but rests upon a very different foundation. The Roman people were distinguished into tribes or *gentes.* A tribe was composed of different *familiae,* and a *familia* of different *stirpes;* and while the republic stood, it was one great branch of their police, to preserve names and families distinct from each other. To perpetuate old families, the privilege of adoption was bestowed on those who had not children. The person adopted, who assumed the name of the family, came in place of a natural son, and had all the privileges that by law belong to a natural son. This branch of the Roman police produced a singular conception of an heir, viz. the bearing the name of the family, and adding a link to the family-chain. The succession of an heir among the Romans had no relation to property, was not considered as a right of succeeding to subjects, but as a right of succeeding to the person deceased, of coming in his place, of representing him, and of being as termed in the Roman law, *eadem persona cum defuncto.* In a word, an heir in the Roman law is he who represents the deceased personally; and the representing the deceased with respect to subjects of property, doth not less or more enter into the Roman definition of an heir. Nor was it at all necessary that this circumstance should enter the definition: it was sufficient that every benefit of succession was the unavoidable consequence <378> of personal representation; which obviously is the case; for if an heir is *eadem persona cum defuncto,* succession in the eye of law makes no change of person, and consequently no change of property. Hence the maxim in the Roman law, that *Nemo potest mori pro parte testatus et pro parte intestatus;* if an heir was adopted or named, his personal representation of the testator entitled him of course to every subject and every privilege that belonged to the testator.

This singular notion of an heir among the Romans, gave creditors a benefit that they have not by common justice. The death of their debtor, if he was represented by an heir, made no alteration in their affairs. A debtor who had a representative, died not in a legal sense; his existence was continued in his heir, without change of person. The heir accordingly was subjected to all the debts, whether he had or had not any benefit by the succession; and if the heir proved dilatory or refractory, his whole effects might be sold for payment, as well what belonged properly to himself, as what he acquired by succession. This undoubtedly was a stretch beyond the rules of common justice; for creditors ought not to gain by the death of their debtor, and an heir ought not to suffer by his succession. But to palliate this injustice, an heir had a year to deliberate whether he should accept of the succession; if he made it his <379> choice to accept and to run all hazards, which sometimes produced loss instead of gain, that loss, resulting from his own choice, was reckoned no such hardship as to deserve a remedy. But this notion of an heir, beneficial to the creditors in one respect, was hurtful to them in another: for where the heir's proper debts exceeded his own funds, his creditors had access to the funds of the ancestor, which were now become their debtor's property by succession. Here was real injustice done to the ancestor's creditors; which in course of time was remedied by the Praetor. He decreed a *separatio bonorum,* and authorised the ancestor's funds to be sold for payment of his debts.*

The gross injustice of subjecting an heir to the debts of the ancestor without limitation, produced in time another remedy, viz. the benefit of inventory, by which, upon making an exact list of the ancestor's effects, an exception in equity was given to the heir, to protect him from being liable personally to more than the value of the goods contained in the list. Whether this value was to be ascertained by the opinion of witnesses, or whether the heir was bound to sell the goods for payment of the ancestor's debts, is not clear. But the latter seems to have been the rule, as may be gathered, not only from the reason of the thing, but <380> from the constitution of Justinian introducing the benefit of inventory.† And in our practice, though an heir who has the benefit of inventory, is not liable personally beyond the value of the goods in the inventory, to be ascertained by a proof, yet if the creditors chuse to take themselves to the goods for their payment, it is in their power to bring the same to sale, and to lay hold of the price for their payment.

But however far the Roman law strayed from justice where the debtor's heritage was claimed by an heir, the same complaint does not lie in the case of insolvency, where the heir abandoned the succession; for the debtor's goods were in this case sold for payment of his debts, in the same manner as when he was alive. It is true, that among the Romans, remarkable originally for virtue and temperance, it was ignominious for a citizen to have his effects sold by public authority. To prevent such disgrace, it was common to institute a slave as heir, who, after the testator's death, being obliged to enter, the hereditary subjects were sold as his property, and the real debtor's name was not mentioned.‡

---

* l. 1. § 1. De separationibus. [[I.e., *Digest* 42.6.1.1.]]

† l. 22. § 4. et 8. C[[odex]]. De jure delib.

‡ Instit. De hered. qualit. et diff. § 1. [[i.e., *Institutes* 2.19.1]]; Heineccius Antiquit. l. 2. tit. 17. 18. 19. § 11.

We proceed to the English law, which in all probability was anciently the same with our <381> own. And to understand the spirit of that law, it must be premised, that while the Feudal law was in its purity, a vassal had no land property; he had only the profits of the land for his wages; and when he died, his service being at an end, there could no longer be a claim for wages. The subject returned to the superior, and he drew the whole profits, till the heir appeared; who was entitled by the original covenant, upon performing the same service with his ancestor, to demand possession of the land as his wages. If his claim was found just, the possession was delivered to him by a very simple form, viz. an order or precept from the superior to give him possession; and this was called *renovatio feudi.* There is nothing to be laid hold of in any branch of this process, for making the heir liable to the ancestor's debts. By performing the feudal services, every heir is entitled to the full enjoyment of the land in name of wages; and his right being thus limited, he hath no power of disposal, nor of contracting debt to affect the subject farther than his own interest reaches. The next heir who succeeds is not liable to the predecessor's debts; because the land is delivered to the next heir, not as the predecessor's property, but as the property of the superior; and possession is given to the next heir, as wages for the service he hath undertaken to perform. From this short sketch it <382> must be evident, that, while the Feudal law subsisted in its purity, a vassal's debts after his death, however effectual against his moveables, could not burthen the land, nor the heir who succeeded to the land.

But after land was restored to commerce, and a vassal was understood to be in some sort proprietor so as even to have power of alienation; it was a natural consequence, that the land, as his property, should be subjected for payment of his debts, not only during his life, but even after his death. And if a man's moveables can, after his death, be attached for payment of his debts, why not his land; supposing him equally proprietor of both? Accordingly by the law of England, "Judgments of all kinds, whether *in foro contentioso,* or by consent, may be made effectual by an *Elegit,* after the debtor's death, as well as during his life, without necessity of taking a new judgment against the heir."* A judgment by the law of England hath still

* New Abridgement of the law, vol. 2. p. 337.

greater force. "Lands are bound from the time of the judgment, so that execution may be of these, though the party aliens *bona fide,* before execution sued out."* If an *Elegit* can attach land conveyed after the judgment to a *bona fide* purchaser, it is not so great a stretch to make it attach land after the <383> debtor's death, in the hand of the heir, or *in hereditate jacente,* if the heir be not entered.

The same method takes place in debts on which there is no judgment against the debtor; with this only variation, that the creditor must begin with taking a decree against the heir, because the authority of a decree is necessary for execution. The decree taken against the heir in this case, resembles a decreet of cognition with us, to be a foundation for attaching the deceased debtor's heritage, but not to have any personal effect against the heir, nor against his proper estate.†

Nor is it difficult to discover the foundation of this practice. It depends on a principle of justice, which is simple and obvious, That every man's proper effects ought to be applied for payment of his debts. His death cannot by any rule of justice withdraw these effects from his creditors; nor can it subject the heir, who ought not to be liable for debts not of his own contracting; unless he converts to his own use the ancestor's effects.[1]

The rule in England, That an heir is not subjected to his ancestor's debts, but only the ancestor's own funds, produced another effect, which is, to vest in the heir the property of the ancestor's heritable estate, even without exerting any act of possession. The very survivance <384> of the heir gives him, in the law-language of England, legal seisin; that is, gives him all the advantages of real possession; and justly, because his *animus possidendi* must always be presumed, where the apprehending possession is attended with no risk. This is the sense of the maxim, *Quod mortuus sasit vivum,* which obtains in France as well as in England; and of which we now see the foundation. This branch of the law of England, is not more beautiful by its simplicity, than by its equity and expediency. Nothing can be more simple or expedient, than by mere survivance to vest in the heir the estate

---

* Ibid. vol. 2. p. 361.

† New abridgement of the law, vol. 3. p. 25.

1. 1758, 1761 add: "which are the only fund destined by law for the payment of the ancestor's debts."

that belonged to the ancestor; and nothing can be more equitable than a *separatio bonorum,* by which the funds of the ancestor are set apart for payment of his debts; without vexing the heir, who in common justice ought not to be liable but for debts of his own contracting.

We have great reason to presume as to this matter, that our law was once the same with that of England, though we have now adopted different maxims, deviating far from natural equity and from the simplicity and expediency of the English law. That our law was the same will not be doubted, when in this country of old we find the same effect given to judgments, that at present is given in England. In the 2d Statutes Robert I. cap. 19. § 12. it is laid down <385> with respect to debts due to merchants, "That in execution against the lands of the debtor, sasine shall be given of all the lands which belonged to the debtor at the time of entering into the recognisance, in whose ever hands they have since come, whether by infeftment or otherwise." This authority, it is true, relates to a decree of consent; but we are not to suppose, that such a decree was more privileged than a judgment *in foro contentioso;* and if so, there could be no difficulty of making a judgment effectual against the debtor's land, in the hands of his heir, or *in hereditate jacente.* And we find traces of this very thing in our old law. In the above-mentioned 2d Statutes Robert I. § ult. it is enacted, "That if a debtor die, the merchant-creditor shall not have his body, but shall have execution against his lands, as there above laid down"; that is, by a brieve out of the chancery directed to the sheriff, to deliver to the creditor all the goods and lands which belonged to the debtor, by a reasonable extent. The like execution is authorised, Leg. Burg. cap. 94. even where the heir is entered. But this is not all; we have positive evidence, that such was the practice in Scotland even after the beginning of the sixteenth century. There is on record a charter of apprising, *anno* 1508, in favour of Richard Kine, who having been decerned to <386> pay L. 20, as cautioner for Patrick Wallance, obtained letters after Patrick's death for apprising his land. Patrick's heirs were edictally cited, and his land was apprised and adjudged to Richard, for payment to him of the said sum; and this was done without any previous decree against the heir, or charge to enter. A copy of this charter is annexed;*

* Appendix, No. 10.

and upon searching the records, more of the same kind will probably be found. In a matter of such antiquity, these authorities ought to convince us, that as to execution against a debtor's land-estate after his death, our old law was the same with the English law, and the same that continues to be the English law to this day.

And if such was the law of Scotland with respect to execution after the debtor's death, upon decrees whether *in foro* or of consent, it cannot be doubted but that the same form of execution did obtain where there was no judgment during the debtor's life; with this variation only, that a decree of cognition was necessary before execution could be awarded.

A man who treads the dark paths of antiquity, ought to proceed with circumspection, and be constantly on the watch. We have entertained hitherto little doubt about the right road; but in prosecuting our journey, appearances are not quite so favourable. We stum-<387>ble unluckily upon the act 106. parl. 1540, which seems to pronounce, that far from proceeding in the right path, we have been wandering this while.[2] The act, it is true, is conceived in terms so ambiguous, as to make it doubtful whether it concerns the creditors of the ancestor or those of the heir. But that it is calculated to benefit the former only, all our authors agree. And we have a still greater authority, viz. the act 27. parl. 1621, which, proceeding upon the narrative that the said statute regards the creditors only of the deceased, extends the same remedy to creditors of the heir. This in effect is declaring, not only that the creditors of the heir before the 1621, had no execution against the ancestor's land unless the heir their debtor was pleased to enter; but also, that not even the creditors of the ancestor had before the act 1540, any execution against the land, unless the heir, who was not their debtor, was pleased to enter.

These are weighty authorities in support of the sense universally given to the statute 1540. And yet that the common law of Scotland should impower every heir of a land estate, by abstaining from the succession, to forfeit the creditors of his ancestor, is a proposition too repugnant to the

2. 1758, 1761 add: "In this statute it appears to be taken for granted, that if the heir avoided entering to the land, the ancestor's creditors had no means to recover payment. Nay, a remedy is provided, by entitling them to apprise the land after charging the heir to enter."

common principles of justice to gain credit. This proposition will appear still more absurd, upon bringing the superior <388> into the question. The land returned to him, if the heir did not submit to be his vassal; but a good understanding betwixt them, perhaps for a valuable consideration, might entitle the heir to hold the land in defiance of all the creditors. To accomplish a scheme so fraudulent, no more was necessary but a private agreement, that the land should return to the superior by escheat, and then be restored to the heir by a new grant. A contrivance so grossly unjust would not have been tolerated in any country. We had apprisings of land as early as the reign of Alexander II. I have demonstrated above, that it is no stretch of legal authority, to issue this execution after the debtor's death more than during his life, and that the heir hath no title to prevent this execution whether he be entered or not entered. Let it further be considered, that by our oldest law the heir was liable even for moveable debts, where the moveables were deficient.* What then was to bar law from taking its natural course? It is certain there lay no bar in the way; and the necessity of such an execution must have been obvious to the meanest capacity, in order to fulfil the rules of common justice; not to mention its utility for supporting credit and extending commerce. <389>

But it is losing time, to argue thus at large about the construction of a statute. The above mentioned charter 1508, makes it clear, that the statute cannot relate to the creditors of the ancestor. By that charter it is vouched, that in the 1508, execution against the debtor's estate proceeded after his death, with as little ceremony as during his life. The practice must have been the same in the 1540; and therefore as the creditors of the deceased had no occasion for a remedy, the remedy provided by the statute must have been intended for the creditors of the heir. To fortify this construction, there is luckily discovered another remarkable fact. Our sovereign court, so far from doubting of the privilege that creditors have to attach the land-estate of their debtor after his death, ventured to authorise an apprising of the predecessor's estate on the debt even of the heir apparent. One instance of this I find in a charter of apprising, 24th May 1547, granted by Queen Mary to the Master of Semple. This charter subsumes,

* Reg. Maj. l. 2. cap. 39. § 3.

That the Earl of Lennox, in order to protect his family-estate from being attached for payment of a debt due by him personally to the Queen, had refused to enter heir to the said estate: That he had been charged to enter heir within twenty-one days, under certification, that the lands should be apprised as if he were really entered; and <390> that he having disobeyed the charge, the lands were accordingly apprised,

&c.* The date of the charge to enter is omitted in the charter; but that it must have been before the statute 1540, is evident from the following circumstances, that the statute is not mentioned in the charter; and that the charge is upon twenty-one days, which shows that it proceeded not on the statute; for by the statute the charge must be on forty days. We have no reason to suppose this to be a singular instance; nor is it mentioned in the charter as singular. Here then is discovered an important link in the historical chain; to wit, that a charge against the heir to enter at the instance of his own creditor, was introduced by the sovereign court, without authority of a statute. And if this hold true, the act 1540, could not be intended for any other effect, but to confirm this former practice, with the single variation, that the charge to enter should be upon forty days in place of twenty-one. This curious fact affords convincing evidence, that before the 1540, the debtor's death did not bar his creditors from access to his estate. For it is not consistent with the natural progress of improvements, that the common law should be stretched in favour of the creditors of the heir-apparent; while the predecessor's own creditors, whose connection <391> with his estate is incomparably stronger, were left without a remedy. These creditors must have been long secure, before a remedy would be thought of for remoter creditors, viz. those of the heir-apparent.

But in combating the authority of the said act 1621, we must not rest satisfied with such proofs as may be reckoned sufficient in an ordinary case. I add therefore other proofs, that will probably be thought still more direct. In the first edition of the Statutes of James V. bearing date 8th February 1541, the title prefixed to the statute under consideration is in the following words: "The remeid against them that lye out of their lands, and will not enter in defraud of their creditors."[3] This clearly shows what was under-

---

* See a copy of this charter, Appendix, No. 11.

3. *The new actis and constituvtiones of parliament maid be the rycht excellent prince Iames the Fift Kyng of Scottis,* p. 23.

stood to be the meaning of the statute at the time it was enacted, viz. that it respects the creditors solely of the heir-apparent. And the same title is also prefixed to the next edition, which was in the 1566. The other proof I have to mention, appears to be altogether decisive. Upon searching the records, it is discovered, that the first charges given by authority of the statute, were at the instance of creditors of heirs-apparent; one of them as early as the year 1542. This I take to be demonstrative evidence of the intendment of the statute; for we cannot indulge so wild a thought, as that our judges, the very <392> persons probably who framed this statute, were ignorant of its meaning.

As the foregoing arguments and proofs seem to be invincible, we must acknowledge, however unwillingly, that our legislature, in making the act 1621, were in one particular ignorant of the law of their own country. They are not however altogether without excuse. I shall have occasion immediately to show, that long before the year 1621, the old form of execution against land after the death of the debtor, simple and easy as it was, had been abandoned, and another form substituted, no less tedious than intricate; which, considered in a superficial view, might lead our legislature into an opinion, that the creditors of the heir-apparent were not provided for by the statute 1540. In fact they adopted this erroneous opinion, which moved them to make the act 1621.

No sort of study contributes more to the knowledge of law, than to trace it through its different periods and changes. Upon this account, the foregoing enquiry, though long, will not be thought tedious or improper. In reality it is not practicable, with any degree of perspicuity, to handle the present subject, without first ascertaining the true purpose of the act 1540. For according to the interpretation commonly received, how ridiculous must the attempt appear, of tracing from the beginning <393> the form by which debts are made effectual after the death of the debtor, where the heir renounces or avoids entering; while it remains an established opinion, that creditors were left without a remedy till the statute was made.

Having thus paved the way by removing a great deal of rubbish, I proceed to unfold the principles that govern our present form of attaching land and other heritable subjects, after the death of the debtor.

There is great reason to presume, that our notion of an heir was once the same with what is suggested by the common principles of law, viz. one who by will or by blood is entitled to succeed to the heritage of a person deceased, wholly or partially. Nay, we have the same notion at present with respect to all heirs who succeed in particular subjects, such as an heir of conquest, an heir-male, an heir of entail, an heir of provision. Nor is there the least reason or occasion to view even an heir of line in a different light. For what more proper definition of an heir of line, than the person who succeeds by right of blood to every heritable subject belonging to the deceased, which is not by will provided to another heir? And yet, with respect to the heir of line, we have unluckily adopted the artificial principle of the Roman law, of a personal representation, and of identity of person; according to the Roman fiction, <394> that the heir is *eadem persona cum defuncto*. The Roman law, illustrious for its equitable maxims, deserves justly the greatest regard. But the bulk of its institutions, however well adapted to the civil polity of Rome and the nature of its government, make a very motley figure when grafted upon the laws of other nations. In this country, ever famous for love of novelty, the prevailing esteem for the Roman law, has been confined within no rational bounds. Not satisfied with following its equitable maxims, we have adopted its peculiarities, even where it deviates from the common principles of justice. The very instance now under consideration, without necessity of making a collection, is sufficient to justify this reflection. No man can hesitate a moment, to prefer the beautiful simplicity and equity of our old law concerning heirs, before the artificial system of the Romans, by which an heir cannot demand what of right belongs to him, without hazarding all he is worth in this world. No regulation can be figured more contradictory to equity and expediency; and yet such has been the influence of the Roman law, that as far as possible, we have relinquished the former for the latter; that is, with respect to general heirs; for as to heirs of conquest, heirs of provision, and all heirs who succeed to particular subjects, their condition is so opposite to that of an heir in the Roman law, <395> that it is impossible, by any stretch of fancy, to apply the Roman fiction to them.

This unlucky fiction, which supposes the heir and ancestor to be the same person, hath produced that intricate form presently in use, for obtaining payment of debt after the death of the debtor. The creditors originally had no concern with the heir; their claim lay against their debtor's effects, which they could directly attach for their payment, whether *in hereditate jacente,* or in the hands of the heir. But when the maxim of representation and identity of person came to prevail, the whole order of execution was reversed. By the heir's assuming the character of representative, and by becoming *eadem persona cum defuncto,* the ancestor's effects are withdrawn from his creditors, and are vested in the heir as formerly in the ancestor. In a strict legal sense, a debtor who has a representative dies not: his existence is continued in his heir, and the debtor is not changed. In this view the heir comes in effect to be the original debtor; and the creditors cannot reach the effects otherwise than upon his failure of payment, more than if he were in reality, instead of fictitiously, the original debtor.

The foregoing case of an heir's taking the benefit of succession, is selected from many that belong to this subject, in order to be handled <396> in the first place; for being the simplest, it furnishes an opportunity to examine with the greater perspicuity, what it was that moved our forefathers, to give up their accustomed form of execution for that presently in use. This new form of execution against the heir when entered, was probably established long before the sixteenth century. We discover from our oldest law books, and in particular from the *Regiam Majestatem,* that our forefathers began early to relish the maxims of the Roman law. And though in this book we discover no direct traces of the fiction that makes the heir and the ancestor to be the same person; it is probable, however, considering the swift progress of the Roman law in this country, that the fiction obtained a currency with us not long after the *Regiam Majestatem.* Hence it is likely, that the old form of apprising the land for the predecessor's debt without regarding the heir, must have been long in disuse, where the property is by service transferred to the heir; and who thereby is subjected personally to all the predecessor's debts. This case undoubtedly gave a commencement to the form presently in use; which requires, that the estate be attached, not as belonging to the ancestor the original debtor, but as belonging to the heir. In this view, a decree goes against the heir, making him liable for the debt; upon which follows an adju-<397>dication against the estate, as his property, for payment of his debt. But though the new form commenced so early, we have reason to believe it was not so early completed. Where an heir lies out unentered and intermeddles not with the ancestor's effects, he cannot be held as *eadem persona cum defuncto;* and an estate to which the heir lays no claim, is naturally considered as still belonging to the ancestor. For these reasons, there was in this case nothing to obstruct the ancestor's creditors from attaching the estate by legal execution, more than if their debtor were still alive. Accordingly, from the charter of apprising above mentioned granted to Richard Kine, we find, that where the heir did not enter, the old form of attaching land was in use as late as the 1508. Nor have we reason to suppose that this was the latest instance of the kind; for where the creditors of the ancestor are willing to confine their views to his estate without attacking the heir, there cannot be a more ready method for answering their purpose than that of apprising the land, which might be done with as little ceremony as when the debtor was alive. A decree it is true was necessary for this execution, as no execution can proceed without the authority of a judge; but it was a matter of no difficulty to obtain a decree, if not already obtained against the debtor himself. The form is, to call the <398> heir in a process, not concluding against him personally, but only that the debt is true and just. The heir has no concern here but merely to represent a defendant, and therefore a decree goes of course, declaring the debt to be just. This declaratory decree, commonly called a *decreet of cognition,* was held, and to this day is held, a sufficient foundation for execution.

Considering that in the beginning of the sixteenth century, creditors after their debtor's death had access to attach his land in the manner now mentioned, and considering that a general charge was in practice before this time, as will by and by be proved; it appears to me evident, that this writ was invented for no other purpose but to reach the heir, and to subject him personally to the debts of his ancestor; which may be gathered even from the writ itself. The heir was subjected if he entered, and this was a contrivance to reach him, if possible, where he was not entered. This writ, as will be shown by and by, produced the present form of execution for obtaining payment after the debtor's death, and thereby occasioned a considerable revolution in our law, which makes it of importance to trace its history with all possible accuracy.

To have a just notion of letters of general charge, we must view an heir apparent with re-<399>lation to the superior. The heir apparent has a year to deliberate whether he should enter to the land, and subject himself to all the duties incumbent on the vassal. And he may also continue to deliberate after the year runs out, until he be compelled in the following manner to declare his will. The superior obtains a letter from the king, giving authority to charge or require the heir to enter within forty days, under the penalty of forfeiting his right to the feudal subject. This furnished a hint to creditors who wanted to make the heir liable. A similar form was invented, which had the sanction of the sovereign court without a statute. A creditor obtains a letter from the king, giving authority to charge or require the heir to enter within forty days; and to certify him, that his disobedience shall subject him personally to the creditor, in the same manner as if he were entered. This letter, commonly called *Letters of general charge,* being served on the heir, obliges him to come to a resolution. If he obey the charge by entering, he is of course subjected to all his ancestor's debts. If he remain in his former situation without entering, the charge is a medium upon which he may be decerned personally to make payment to the creditor in whose favour the letter is given; and therefore to avoid being liable, he has no other method but to renounce the succession, <400> which is done by a formal writing under his hand, put into the process or into the register.

At what time the general charge was introduced, cannot with accuracy be determined. That it was known long before the statute 1540, appears from a decision cited by Balfour, dated *anno* 1551,* in which it is mentioned as a writ in common and general use; not as recent or newly invented. Its antiquity is further ascertained by an argument, which, though negative, must have considerable weight. The court of session, the same that is now in being, was established *anno* 1532; and though the most ancient records of this court are not entire, we have however pretty great certainty of its regulations, such of them at least as are of importance; for these, where the records are lost, may be gathered from our authors, and from other authentic evidence. But as there is not in any author, or in any writing, the smallest hint that this writ was introduced by the court of session; we have reason to conclude, that it had a more early date.

The better to understand what follows, we must take a deliberate view of this new writ. To supply defects in the common law, is undoubtedly the province of the sovereign court, and is one of its most valuable prerogatives.

* Tit. Heirs and Successors, chap. 17.

But regulations of this sort ought not only to <401> be founded on expediency, but also on material justice. Unhappily, neither of these grounds can be urged, to justify letters of general charge. For first, this writ was in no view necessary; the common law giving ready access to a debtor's effects after his death for payment of his debts, as well as during his life; beyond which a creditor can have no just claim. In the next place, this writ, with respect to the heir-apparent, is oppressive and unjust; for while the effects of the debtor lie open to execution, what earthly concern has the creditor with an heir who hath not claimed the succession, nor intermeddled with the effects? and why should any attempt be indulged, to subject a man to the payment of debt not of his own contracting? This heteroclite writ, procured in all appearance by the undue influence of creditors, hath in its consequences proved even to them an unhappy contrivance. It evidently produced our present form of obtaining payment after the debtor's death; which, as observed, being unjust as to the heir, has recoiled against the creditors, by involving them in an execution, intricate, tedious, and expensive; opposite in every particular to the simple and beautiful form established at common law. I proceed to show in what manner the general charge produced that change. <402>

Upon reflection it will appear, that after the charge is given and the forty days elapsed, the creditor charging has it no longer in his power to attach by real execution the estate as belonging to the ancestor. If the heir obey the charge by entering, he occupies the place of the ancestor: He is in a legal sense the ancestor;[4] and execution proceeds against him and his effects, precisely as if he were really, and not by a fiction, the original debtor. This bars all access to the original form of execution; the ancestor is withdrawn as if he had never been, and the estate cannot now be apprised as his property. If the heir remain in his former situation, without declaring his mind, he becomes personally liable, precisely as if he had entered. This situation, equally with the former and for the same reason, bars the creditor from having access to the estate by the old form of execution: as soon as the debt is transferred against the heir, he becomes *eadem persona cum defuncto*. With

---

4. 1758, 1761 add: "Such necessarily must be the effect of the change of circumstances occasioned by this charge."

regard to this debt, he is considered to be the original debtor; and as the creditor no longer enjoys the character of the ancestor's creditor, he cannot have access to the estate as belonging to the ancestor; neither can he have access to it as creditor to the heir, who himself hath no right until he enter. If the heir renounce, the estate returns to the superior, who must have the land if he have not a vassal, and <403> by this means also the creditor is excluded from all access to the land; because it is now no longer the property either of the ancestor or of the heir. These consequences of a charge, where the heir enters not, appear to be strong obstacles against the creditor wanting to attach the land. In what manner they were surmounted, I proceed to show.

I begin with the case where the heir-apparent, after he is charged, remains silent, and neither enters nor renounces. The charge, for the reason above mentioned, subjects him personally to the creditor at whose instance he is charged; and by the same means he may be subjected to all the creditors. So far good. The creditors upon this medium may proceed to personal execution. But as to real execution, the difficulty is great, for, as above observed, the debt by the charge being laid upon the heir, there cannot be access to the land otherwise than as belonging to him. But then, how can land be adjudged from a debtor who is not vested in the property? The reader will advert, that he is engaged in a period long before the statute 1540, affording relief to the proper creditors of the heir by means of a special charge. As the heir is thus subjected to his ancestor's debts, it becomes his duty to enter to the land, in order to give his creditors access to it for their payment. And if he <404> prove refractory, it becomes the duty of the sovereign court to perform for him, by selling the land, or by adjudging it to the creditors for their payment. The latter was done. But as before attempting an extraordinary remedy, good order requires the debtor's obstinacy to be ascertained, a second letter is obtained from the King, giving authority to charge or require the heir, to enter to the land within forty days; and to certify him, that after the lapse of this term he shall be held, with respect to the creditors, as actually entered. This method solves all difficulties. The creditors proceed to apprise the land from the heir, now their debtor, in the same manner as if he had a complete title to the same by a solemn entry.

In the case of a renunciation, the obstacle is much greater than in that last mentioned. A renunciation to be heir, according to the nature of feudal property, is a total bar to the ancestor's creditors, which could not have been surmounted, and ought not to have been surmounted, while the Feudal law was in vigour. In the original feudal system an heir hath no claim to the land which his ancestor possessed, unless he undertake to serve the superior in quality of a vassal; and therefore if he refuse to submit to this service, the superior enters to possess the land, which antecedently was his property. But a renunciation to be heir, <405> though obtained at the suit of a creditor, being however an express declaration by the heir that he will not submit to be vassal, must in strict law restore the land to the superior, and cut out all the creditors. This, as observed, would originally have been thought no hardship. But by this time land in a great measure was restored to commerce: The bulk of it had passed from hand to hand for a full price; and such a purchase, contrary to the original constitution of the Feudal law, transferred the property to the purchaser, though according to the form of our land-rights he is obliged to assume the character of a vassal. Therefore, whatever effect a renunciation might have while a vassal's right was merely usufructuary, it was rightly judged, that it ought not to have the same effect where the vassal is proprietor. Equity pleaded strongly for the creditors, that the superior, *certans de lucro captando,* ought not to be preferred to them, *certantes de damno evitando.* These considerations moved the sovereign court, to think of some remedy for relieving the creditors. It would have been too bold an attack on established law, to declare, that in this case a renunciation should not operate in favour of the superior, but only of the creditors. The court took softer measures. The law was permitted to have its course, in restoring the land to the superior. But action was sustained to the cre-<406>ditors against the superior, to infeft them in the land for security and payment of their debts; and the decree given in this process obtained the name of "an adjudication upon a renunciation to be heir," "or an adjudication *cognitionis causa*"; which being afterwards modelled into a different form, passes now commonly under the name of "an adjudication *contra hereditatem jacentem.*"* Here was invented a new

* See [[Kames,]] Statute Law abridged, note 1.

sort of execution against land, similar in its form to no other sort in practice. And it may be thought strange, why the court, in imitation of the established form of apprising, did not rather direct the land to be sold for payment of the creditors. In matters of great antiquity where history affords scarce any light, it is difficult to give satisfaction upon every point. I can form no conjecture more probable, than that in contriving a remedy against the hardships of the common law, the court thought that it was venturing far enough to afford the creditors a security upon land, which once indeed belonged to their debtor, but was now legally transferred to the superior with whom they had no connection.

With respect to other heritable subjects, allodial in their nature as not held of any superior, heirship moveables, for example, bonds secluding executors, and dispositions of land with-<407>out infeftment, the heir's renunciation created no difficulty. Subjects of that kind are by the renunciation left *in medio* without an owner; and it is an obvious as well as a natural step, to adjudge them to a creditor for his payment. By such adjudication the court doth nothing but what the debtor himself ought to have done when alive; and which it is presumed he would have done, had he not been prevented by death. This adjudication, it is probable, was the first that came into use, and paved the way to an adjudication of land, when it returned to the superior by the heir's renunciation.

If the general charge be of an ancient date, we cannot have much difficulty about the aera of the special charge. For as the general charge is a very imperfect remedy without the special charge, the invention of the latter could not be at any distance of time from the establishment of the former. And a fact is mentioned above, which puts this matter beyond conjecture. Before the statute 1540, we find relief by a special charge afforded even to the proper creditors of the apparent heir; which proves to conviction, that the same relief must have been afforded long before to the creditors of the ancestor, after the heir is made liable by a general charge.[5] According to the natural course of human improvements, the creditors of the deceased proprietor, must have been long <408> privileged with a special

---

5. 1758, 1761 add: "For, as above observed, it is not supposable, that a remedy, afforded to the proper creditors of the heir-apparent, would be denied to the creditors of the deceased proprietor, who are more connected with the estate."

as well as with a general charge, before it would be thought proper to extend the privilege of a special charge to the creditors of his heir apparent.

It appears from Craig,* that an adjudication *cognitionis causa* is the remedy which of all came latest. We have this author's express authority for saying, that in his time it was a recent invention. Nor is this at all wonderful. For a renunciation to be heir, must to the ancestor's creditors have been a puzzling circumstance, when its legal effect is to restore the land to the superior, who is liable for none of the vassal's debts.

Taking under review the foregoing innovations, to which we were insensibly led by the prevailing influence of the Roman law, it is probable, that the fiction of identity of person was first applied by our lawyers to the case where an heir regularly enters to the estate of his ancestor. Being in this case beneficial to creditors, who have the heir bound as well as the estate, it gained credit, and obtained a currency. Nor was it attended with any inconvenience to creditors, at least, while they had access to apprise, as formerly, the estate of their debtor, where the heir abstained from entering. This, one should think, was affording to creditors every privilege they could justly de-<409>mand for obtaining payment. But this did not satisfy them. To have the heir bound personally, in place of his ancestor, was an enticing prospect; and the general charge was invented, in order to make him liable even where he has not taken the benefit of the succession. This legal step, it must be acknowledged, is well contrived to answer its purpose. The heir, urged by a general charge, hath no way to evade the certification of being personally liable, other than the hard alternative of renouncing altogether the succession. This new form was much relished. Creditors did not incline to confine themselves to the estate of the ancestor their debtor, while any hope remained of subjecting the heir personally, by means of a general charge. And accordingly for a century and a half, or perhaps more, it has been the constant method to set out with a general charge, where the heir is not entered. If this method to subject the heir personally prove successful, the creditors, as made out above, must bid adieu to the estate considered as *in hereditate jacente* of their original debtor. Having chosen the heir for their debtor, they cannot now attach the estate otherwise than in

* lib. 3. dieg. 2. § 23.

quality of his creditors. Thus it has happened, that for many years there has been no instance of following out the old form by apprising or adjudging the land after the debtor's death, with-<410>out regarding the heir. Whether it may be thought too late now to return to this old form, governed by the principles of justice as well as of expediency, I take not upon me to determine.

The difference betwixt the law of Scotland and of England as to the present subject, will be clearly apprehended from what follows. A pure donation, which doth not subject the donee to any obligation, transfers property without the necessity of acceptance; and upon that account, infants and absents are benefited by such deeds, without knowing any thing of the matter. But a deed laying the donee under any burden, bestows no right without actual acceptance; if it did, any man might be subjected to the severest burdens without his consent. Thus, in England, the rule obtains, *Quod mortuus sasit vivum;* because an heir, though vested in his ancestor's heritage, is not subjected personally to his ancestor's debts. In Scotland, the effects of the ancestor are not transmitted to the heir, but by some voluntary act importing his consent to subject himself to his ancestor's debts. For by our law a strict connection is formed, betwixt the right that the heir has to the ancestor's estate and the obligation he is under to pay the ancestor's debts, the latter being a necessary consequence of the former. It may indeed happen, that the <411> heir is made liable to pay the ancestor's debts, without being vested in the estate; but this is to be considered as a penalty for refusing to enter heir when he is charged, or for intermeddling irregularly with the ancestor's effects, which are singular cases.

The foregoing history is so singular, as not perhaps to have a parallel in the law of any country. Here, from the dead law of an ancient people, we find a metaphysical fiction adopted, without any foundation in the common rules of justice, and repugnant to the common law of this island; and yet so fervently embraced, as to have made havock of every part of our law that stood in opposition. I have pointed out some of the many inconveniencies that its reception produced, with regard to creditors, and consequently to credit. I have shown what subterfuges and fictitious contrivances were necessary, in order to give it a currency. I have shown how tedious, how intricate, and how expensive a form it hath occasioned, for recovering payment of debt. But I have not yet shown it in its worst light; the evils I have mentioned, are mere trifles compared with those that follow. No person who hath given any attention to the history of our law, can be ignorant of the numberless artifices invented by heirs in possession of the family-estate, to screen themselves from paying the fa-<412>mily debts. The numberless regulations made in vain, age after age, to prevent such artifices, will satisfy every one, that there must be an error in the first concoction, by which a remedy is rendered extremely difficult. How comes it that we never hear of such frauds in England? The reason is obvious. The just and natural rule of a *separatio bonorum*, which obtains there, makes it impracticable for the heir to defraud his ancestor's creditors. They have no concern with the heir, but take themselves to the ancestor's estate for their payment. In Scotland, the ancestor's estate cannot be reached even by his own creditors, otherwise than by attacking the heir, unless he be pleased to abandon it to them. But this seldom was done of old. The heir had a more profitable game to play, even where the estate was overburdened with debts. His method commonly was, to renounce to be heir in order to evade a personal decerniture. He did not, however, abandon the estate; it was not difficult to procure some artificial or fictitious title to the estate; under cover of which, possession was apprehended; and this was a great point gained. If this title, after a dependence perhaps for years, was found insufficient to bar the creditors, another title of the same kind was provided, and so on without end. It is true, the heir's renunciation entitles the creditors to attach the estate by adjudica-<413>tions *cognitionis causa;* but then the heir, as has been observed, was provided with some collateral title, not only to colour his possession, but also to compete with the creditors. In the mean time, the rents were a fund in his hands to take off any of the preferable creditors that were like to prove too hard for him. And such purchase was a new protection to the unconscientious heir, against the other creditors. In fact, the most considerable estates in Scotland, are possessed at this day by such dishonest titles; the legislature, however willing, never having been able to invent any complete remedy against such pernicious frauds. The foregoing observations will enable us to trace these frauds to their true source. They may be justly ascribed to the fiction of identity of person; because by means of this fiction chiefly, opportunity was furnished for committing them.

Had this matter been unfolded to our legislature, a very simple and very effectual remedy must have occurred to them. If the heir refused to subject himself to the debts of his ancestor, nothing else was necessary but to restore the ancient law, authorising the ancestor's heritage to be sold for payment of his debts. But this regulation had been long in disuse, and we were no less ignorant of it, than if it never had existed. <414>

And, as an evidence of the weakness of human foresight, I must observe, that a statute made without any view to the frauds of heirs, proved more successful against these frauds, than all the regulations purposely made; and that is the statute for selling the estates of bankrupts. An heir has now little opportunity to play the accustomed game, when it is in the power of creditors to wrest the estate out of his hands by public auction. And the experience now of fifty years, has vouched this to be a complete remedy. For we hear not at present of any frauds of this kind, nor are we under any apprehension of them. So far from it, that we are receding more and more, every day, from the rigid principle of an universal representation, and approaching to the maxim of equity, which subjects not the heir beyond the value of the succession. For what other reason is it, that the act 1695,[6] introducing some new rigid passive titles is totally neglected, though it is undoubtedly an additional safeguard to creditors against the frauds of heirs? We are not now afraid of these frauds: They are prevented by the equitable remedy of selling the ancestor's estate; and judges, if they have humanity, will be loath to apply a severe remedy, when a mild one is at hand, which is also more effectual. It is remarkable, that though the statute for selling the estates of bankrupts proved an effectual <415> remedy, yet this virtue in the statute was not an early discovery. It was not discovered at the time of the act 1695; and when that statute was made, it must in a person of sagacity have provoked a smile, to find our legislature, with their eyes open, contriving an imperfect remedy, when they had already, with their eyes shut, stumbled on one that was perfect. <416>

6. Kames refers to the Act "for obviating the frauds of apparent heirs" dated 10 July 1695.

Limited and Universal
Representation of Heirs

By the law of nature, an heir, beyond what he takes by the succession, is not subjected to the debts of his ancestor. In the Roman law an artificial notion was adopted, that the heir is the same person with the ancestor. Hence an heir in the Roman law succeeds to all the effects of the ancestor, and is subjected to all his debts. This was carried so far with regard to children, that they were heirs *ex necessitate juris;* and upon that account were distinguished by the name of *sui et necessarii heredes.* Natural principles afterward prevailed; and children, in common with other heirs, were privileged to abstain from the succession. This was done by a *separatio bonorum,* and by abandoning the estate of the ancestor to his creditors. But still if the heir took possession of the ancestor's effects, or in any manner behaved as heir; he, from that moment, was understood to be *eadem persona cum defuncto,* and consequently was subjected universally to <417> all the ancestor's debts. At last the benefit of inventory was afforded, which protected the heir from being liable farther than *in valorem.* This privilege tempered the severity of the foregoing artificial principle; and, in some measure, restored the law of nature, which had been overlooked for many ages.

In England, the artificial principle of identity of person never took place. An heir by the English law is not bound to pay his ancestor's debts, even when he takes by succession. The creditors have the privilege of attaching their debtor's effects possessed by the heir, in the same manner as when these effects were in the debtor's own possession, during his life. The heir is personally liable to the extent only of what he intermeddles with. The

English law, indeed, deviates from natural justice, in making a distinction betwixt heritable and moveable debts, subjecting the heir to the former only, and the executor to the latter. This is evidently unjust as to creditors; for they may be forfeited by their debtor's death, though he die in opulent circumstances; which as to personal creditors must always happen, when his moveable funds are narrow and his moveable debts extensive. Such a regulation is the less to be justified, that it furnisheth an opportunity for fraud. For what if a man, with a view to disappoint his personal creditors after his death, <418> shall lay out all his money upon land? I know of no remedy to this evil, unless the court of chancery, moved by a principle of equity, venture to interpose.

By the Feudal law, when in purity, there could not be such a thing as representation; because the heir took the land, not as coming in place of his ancestor, but by a new grant from the superior. But when land was restored to commerce, and was purchased for a full price, it was justly reckoned the property of the purchaser, though held in the feudal form. Land by this means is subjected to the payment of debt, even after it descends to the heir. And in Scotland, probably, the privilege at first was carried no farther than in England, to permit creditors, after the death of their debtor, to attach his funds in possession of the heir.

But as Scotland always has been addicted to innovations, the Roman law prevailed here, contrary to the genius of our own law; and the fiction was adopted of the heir and ancestor being the same person. The fiction crept first into the reasonings of our lawyers figuratively, in order to explain certain effects in our law; and gained by degrees such an ascendant, as, in our apprehension, to form the very character of an heir. Yet, considering that we acknowledge heirs of different kinds, an heir of line, an heir-male, an heir of provision, &c. one <419> should not imagine that our law lay open to have this fiction grafted upon it. In the Roman law there was but one heir who succeeded *in universum jus defuncti,* and who, by a very natural figure, might be styled *eadem persona cum defuncto.* But can we apply this figure, with any propriety, to an heir who succeeds not *in universum jus,* but is limited to a particular subject? This opens a scene which I shall endeavour to set in a just light, by examining how far the figure has been carried with us, and what bounds ought to be set to it.

Our law, in all probability, was once the same with that of England, viz. that the heir, who succeeds to the real estate, is liable to real debts only; the moveable debts being laid upon the executor. But this did not long continue to be our law. It must sometimes have happened, notwithstanding the frugality of ancient times, that the personal estate was not sufficient for satisfying the personal debts. It was justly thought hard, that the heir should enjoy the family estate, while the personal creditors of his father, or other ancestor, were left without remedy. Equity dictates, that after the moveables are exhausted, the personal creditors shall have access to the land for what remains due to them. This practice is with us of an early date. We find it established in the reign of David II. as appears from the Regiam Ma-<420>jestatem.* And it was improved to the benefit of creditors by act 76. parl. 1503, enacting, "That if the personal creditors are not paid out of the moveables within the year, they shall, without further delay, have access to the heir." Upon the same foundation, and by analogy of the statute, the executor is made liable for the heritable debts. This came in late; for Sir Thomas Hope† observes, "That the Lords of old were not in use to sustain process against the executor for payment of an heritable debt." And overlooking the equity of the innovation, he censures and condemns it; for a very insufficient reason indeed; because (says he) there is no law to give the executor relief against the heir, as the heir has against the executor when he pays a moveable debt"; as if this relief did not follow from the nature of the thing. Reviewing this historical deduction, I perceive not in it the slightest symptom of identity of person. This fiction admits not a distinction betwixt heritable and moveable subjects; identity of person bestows necessarily upon the heir every subject that belonged to the ancestor. Neither admits it any distinction among debts; for if the deceased was liable to all debts without distinction, so must the heir. In place of which <421> we find the heir of line subjected by the common law to heritable debts only; and not to moveable debts, otherwise than upon a principle of equity, which, failing moveables, subjects the land-estate, rather than forfeit the creditors.

* lib. 2. cap. 39. § 3.
† Minor Practicks, § 104.

Thus the heir of line is subjected universally to his ancestor's debts, without any foundation in the common law; and stood even without any foundation in the fiction itself. For as an heir of line is clearly not *eadem persona cum defuncto,* except as to the heritable estate, it is equally clear, that by this fiction he ought not to be subjected universally to any debts but what are heritable. As to moveable debts, equity dictates that creditors be preferred to every representative of their deceased debtor; and therefore that the land-estate should be subjected to the personal creditors, when the moveables are not sufficient. But this maxim of equity can never be extended farther against the heir, than to make him liable for moveable debts as far as he is benefited by the succession; because equity, which relieves from oppression, can never be made the instrument of oppression.

Next as to a limited heir succeeding to one subject only, is there any reason for making him liable universally to the ancestor's debts? If he represent the ancestor, it is not universally, but only as heir in a particular subject. <422> And therefore he ought to be liable for debts only which affect that subject, or for debts of the same kind with the subject, or at farthest for debts of every kind to the extent of the subject. I know not that it has been held by any able writer, far less decided, that an heir provided to a particular subject is liable universally to the ancestor's debts, Dirleton gives his opinion to the contrary.* His words are:

> Heirs of provision and tailzie who are to succeed only *in rem singularem* albeit *titulo universali: Quaeritur* if they will be liable to the defunct's whole debts, though far exceeding the value of the succession; or if they should be considered as *heredes cum beneficio inventarii,* and should be liable only *secundum vires,* there being no necessity of an inventory, the subject of their succession being only, as is said, *res singularis?* Answer. It is thought that if one be served general heir-male without relation to a singular subject (as to certain lands) he would be liable *in solidum;* but if he be served only special heir in certain lands, he should be liable only *secundum vires.*

The heir of line, or heir-general, is then the only person to whom the character of identity of person can with any shadow of reason be applied.

* Doubts. Tit. Heirs of Tailzie.

Nor to him can it be applied in the un-<423>limited sense of the Roman law; but only as to the heritable estate and heritable debts. To all that is carried by a general service he has right, without limitation; and it is plausible if not solid, that he ought to be liable without limitation to all heritable debts, such as come under a general service. We follow the same rule betwixt husband and wife, when we subject him to her moveable debts in general, and give him right to all her moveable effects in general. And this at the same time appears to be the true foundation of the privilege of discussion, competent to heirs whose right of succession is limited to particular subjects. The general heir, or heir of line, who is not thus limited but succeeds in general to all subjects of a certain species, is the only heir who ought to bear the burden of the debts.

It may be thought more difficult to say, why an heir of line, making up titles by a service to a land-estate which was the property of his ancestor, should be subjected universally to his ancestor's debts; when this very title, viz. his retour and seisin, contains an inventory *in gremio;* not being in its nature a general title, but only a title to one particular subject.

To explain this matter, it will be necessary to carry our view pretty far back in the history of our law. Among all nations it is held as a principle, that property is transferred from the <424> dead to the living, without any solemnity. Children and other heirs are entitled to continue the possession of their ancestor; and where the heir is not bound for his ancestor's debts, such possession is understood to be continued by will alone, without any ouvert act. In Scotland, the heir originally was not liable for the debts of his ancestor, nor at present is he liable in England. Hence it is, that as to rent-charges, bonds secluding executors, and other heritable subjects, which may be termed *allodial* because not held of any superior, these were transferred to the heir of blood directly on his survivance; and, with regard to these, the same rule obtained here, that obtains universally in England and France, *Quod mortuus sasit vivum.* Land and other subjects held of a superior, are with us in a very different condition. The vassal, by the principles of the Feudal law, is not proprietor; and strictly speaking transmits no right to his heir. The subject must be claimed from the superior; and the heir's title is a new grant from him. Thus then stood originally the law of Scotland. Heritable subjects vested in the heir merely by survivance. The single exception was a feudal holding, which required, and still requires a new grant from the superior. If the heir of line had this new grant, he needed no other title to claim any heritable subject which belonged to his ancestor. But <425> heirs were put in a very different situation, by the fiction of identity of person adopted from the Roman law. The heir by claiming the succession being subjected personally to his ancestor's debts, must have an election to claim or to abandon as it suits his interest. This of necessity introduced an *aditio hereditatis,* as among the Romans, without which the heir can have no title to the effects of his ancestor. If he use this form, he becomes *eadem persona cum defuncto* with regard to benefits as well as burdens. If he abstain from using it, he is understood to abandon the succession, and to have no concern either with benefits or burdens. The only point to be considered was, what should be the form of the *aditio.* By this time the property being transferred from the superior to his vassal, it was justly thought, that the vassal's heir who enjoyed the land-estate of his ancestor, could not evade payment of his debts. For this reason, an infeftment being the form established for transmitting the property to the heir, the same form was now held as a proper *aditio hereditatis* to have the double effect, not only of vesting the heir with the property as formerly, but also of subjecting him to the ancestor's debts. This title, it is true, being in its nature limited, ought not to subject him beyond the value of the subject. But then the identity of the ancestor and his heir being once <426> established, it was thought, as in the Roman law, to have an universal effect, and to be an active title to every subject that could descend to the heir of line. And our former practice tended mainly to support this inference; for it was still remembered, that formerly all allodial heritable subjects were vested in the heir of line, upon his survivance merely. The infeftment being thus held an *aditio hereditatis,* not only with respect to the land-estate, but with respect to all other heritable subjects, it was of course an universal passive title; for if the heir succeeded to all heritable subjects without limitation, it seemed not unreasonable that he should be subjected to all debts without limitation. These conclusions, it must be owned, were far from being just or accurate. It appears extremely plain, that if a man die possessed of a subject held of a superior, and of other heritable subjects that are allodial, the heir ought to be privileged to make a title to one or other at his pleasure,

and to be subjected accordingly to the debts; that if he use a general service, he must lay his account to be liable universally; but that if he confine
himself to a special service, he is not to be liable beyond the value of the
subject. But our ancient lawyers were not so clear-sighted. They blindly
followed the Roman law, by attributing to identity of person the most
extensive effects possible. <427> An infeftment in the land-estate established the identity, which, it was thought, did on the one hand entitle the
heir of line to all the heritable subjects, and on the other did subject him
to all the debts. And this affords a clear solution of the difficulty above
mentioned. If the identity of person take at all place, it applies to none
more properly than to an heir of blood, who enters by infeftment; especially as he generally is of the same name and family with his ancestor,
lives in the same house, possesses the same estate, and carries on the line
of the same family.

But now supposing the foregoing deduction to be just, is there not great
reason to alter our present practice, and to hold a special service to be, as
it truly is in its nature and form, a limited title? Let us suppose that the heir
of line, unwilling to represent his ancestor universally, chuses to abandon
all the heritable subjects, except a small land-estate, to which he makes up
titles by a special service; why should he be liable universally in this case:
The natural construction of such a service is, that the heir intends to confine
himself to the subject therein mentioned, and to abandon the ancestor's
other estate, since he forbears to take out a general service. Such construction will better the condition of heirs, by removing some part of the risk
they run, and will not hurt creditors as far <428> as their claim is founded
on natural equity, viz. to have their debtor's effects applied for payment of
his debts.

And I must observe with some satisfaction, that we have given this very
construction to an infeftment on a precept of *Clare constat;* it being an
established rule, That such infeftment is not a title to any other subject but
that contained in the precept. And for this very reason, neither doth it make
the heir liable for the debts of his ancestor farther than *in valorem.* Lord
Stair,* it is true, considers a precept of *Clare* as an universal passive title.

* Instit. p. 467. at the bottom.

But the court of session entertained a juster notion of that precept. A remarkable case is observed by Lord Harcus,* to the following purpose.

A man infeft upon a precept of *Clare constat* as heir to his father, being pursued for payment of a debt that was due by his father; pleaded an absolvitor upon the following medium, That he had no benefit by the succession, the subject to which he had connected by a precept of *Clare* being evicted from him.

It was answered,

That his entering heir by the precept of *Clare constat,* made him *eadem persona cum defuncto;* that it was a behaviour as heir, which subjected him to all his predecessor's debts, without regard to <429> the estate, whether it was swallowed up by an earthquake, or evicted by a process.

The Lords "judged the defender not liable as heir, in respect the land was evicted from him." It was said, "That had there been a general service, or a special service which includes a general, the matter would have been more doubtful; especially if there were other subjects to which a general service gives right." The plain inference from this judgment is, that if eviction of the land-estate relieve the heir from being liable to pay the family debts, the estate must be the measure of his representation, and consequently that he is not liable beyond the value.

This subject will perhaps be thought unnecessary, now that the benefit of inventory is introduced into our law. It is indeed less necessary than formerly, but not altogether useless. In many instances heirs neglect to lay hold of this benefit; and frequently the forms required by the statute are unskilfully or carelessly prosecuted, so as to leave the heir open to the rigour of law; in which cases it comes to be an important enquiry, how far an heir is liable for the debts of his ancestor. I cannot at the same time help remarking, that it shows no taste for science, to relinquish a subject, however beautiful, merely because it appears not to be im-<430>mediately useful. The history of law can never be useless. And, taking it upon the humblest footing, it enables us to compare our present with our former practice, which always tends to instruction. <431>

* Tit. *Heirs,* March 1683, Farmer *contra* Elder.

Old and New Extent

The Extents old and new make a part of our law that is involved in the dark clouds of antiquity. These extents are not mentioned by our first writers, and later writers satisfy themselves with loose conjectures, the product of fancy without evidence. The design of the present essay is to draw this subject from its obscurity, into some degree of light. It is a matter of curiosity, and possibly may be not altogether unprofitable, with relation especially to our retours, of which these extents make an essential part.

As the English brieve of *Diem clausit extremum* approaches the nearest of any to our brieve of inquest, it may be of use to examine the English brieve, and the *Valent* clause therein contained. Fitz-Herbert, in his New nature of brieves,* explains this brieve in the following words.

> The writ of *Diem clausit extremum* properly lieth, where the King's tenant, who holdeth of him *in capite,* as of his crown, by knights service or in soccage, dieth seised, <432> his heir within age or of full age, then that writ out to issue forth, and the same ought to be at the suit of the heir, &c. for upon that, when the heir cometh of full age, he ought to sue for livery of his lands out of the King's hands.

And the writ is such.

> Rex dilect. sibi W. de K. escheatori suo in Com. Deven. Salut. Quia W. de S. qui de nobis tenuit in capite, diem clausit extremum, ut accipimus; tibi praecipimus, quod omnia terras et tenementa de quibus idem W. fuit seisitus in dominico suo ut de feodo in balliva tua die quo obiit sine dilatione cap. in manum nostram, et ea salvo custodiri fac, donec aliud inde

* p. 558.

praeceperimus, et per sacramentum proborum et legal. hominum de balliva tua, per quos rei veritas melius scire poterit diligent. inquiras, quantum
terrae et tenementorum idem W. tenuit de nobis in capite, tam in domi-
nico quam in servitiis, in balliva tua die quo obiit, et quantum de aliis, et
per quod servic. et quant. terrae et tenementa illa *valent* per annum in
omnibus exitibus; et quo die idem W. obiit, et quis propinquior ejus heres
sit; et cujus aetatis: et inquisic. inde distincte et aperte fact. nobis in cancell.
nostra sub sigillo tuo, et sigillis eorum per quos fact. fuerit, sine dilatione
mittas, et hoc breve. Teste,

&c.[1]

At what time the question about the yearly <433> rent of the land was
ingrossed in this brieve, is uncertain; probably after the days of William
the Conqueror; for as all the lands in England were accurately valued in
that king's reign, and the whole valuations collected into a record, commonly called *Domes-day book,* this authentic evidence of the rent of every
barony, was a rule for levying the king's casualties as superior, without necessity of demanding other evidence. But Domes-day book could not long
answer this purpose; for when great baronies were dismembered, each part
to be held of the crown, this book afforded no rule for the extent of the
casualties to be levied out of the lands of the new vassals. An inquisition
therefore was necessary, to ascertain the yearly rents of the disjoined parcels;
and there could not be a more proper time for such enquiry than when the
heir of a crown vassal was suing out his livery. This seems to be a rational
motive for ingrossing the foregoing question in the brieve. And in England,

---

1. "The King, to his beloved W. de K., his escheator in the county of Devon. Because,
as we understand, W. de S., who held in chief of us, has died, we order you to take into
our hands, without delay, all of the lands and tenements with which the same W. was
siesed in demesne by fee in your bailiwick on the day on which he died, and keep them
in safe custody until we order otherwise; and by the oath of wise and competent men
of your bailiwick, through whom the truth of the matter will be most effectively known,
make diligent enquiry regarding the extent of the lands and tenements which the said
W. held of us in chief, either in demesne or in service, in your bailiwick on the day that
he died, and the extent [of lands and tenements he held] of others, and for what service,
and the annualvalue of those lands and tenements through all of their issues; and on
what day the said W. died, who is his closest heir, and of what age. And this inquisition
having been carried out clearly and openly, send it without delay, along with this writ,
to us in our Chancery under your seal and the seals of those by whom it was done.
Witnessed by . . ."

this enquiry was necessary upon a special account. It was not the custom there to give gifts of the casualties of superiority. Officers were appointed in every shire to take possession in name of the king of the lands of his deceased vassals, and to keep possession till the heirs were entered. These officers, called *escheators,* were accountable to the crown for the rents and issues, and for the other casualties; and the rent <434> of the land ascertained by the retour, was the rule to the treasurer for counting with escheators.

There are two values or extents in the Scotch brieve,[2] only one in the English brieve. I shall endeavour to trace the occasion of the difference, after premising a short history of our taxes; carrying the matter no farther back than we have evidence.

Taxes were no part of the constitution of any feudal government. The king was supported by the rents of his property-lands; and by the occasional profits of superiority, passing under the name of *casualties.* These casualties, such as ward, non-entry, marriage, escheat, &c. arose from the very nature of the holding; and beyond these the vassal was not liable to be taxed; some singular cases excepted established by custom, such as, for redeeming the king from captivity, for a portion to his eldest daughter, and a sum to defray the expence of making his eldest son a knight. For this reason, it is natural to conjecture, that the first universal tax was imposed upon some such singular occasion. The first event we can discover in the history of Scotland to make such a tax necessary, happened in the reign of William the Lyon. This king was taken prisoner by the English at Alnwick, 12th July 1174; and in December that year, he obtained his liberty from Henry II. upon a treaty, <435> in which he and his nobles subjected this kingdom to the crown of England.* Hector Boece our fabulous historian says, That upon this occasion, William paid to Henry an hundred thousand merks.[3] But this seems to be asserted without any authority; the dependency of Scotland on the crown of England, was a price sufficient for William's liberty, without the addition of a sum of money; and the silence of all other historians, joined

* Rymer, vol. 1. p. 39.
2. 1758, 1761: "There are . . . English brieve." = "We find not different values or extents in the English brieve, like what we find in the Scotch brieve."
3. Boece, *Chronicles,* Bk. 13, ch. v: trans. Bellenden, vol. ii, p. 203.

with the improbability that a sum so immense could be paid, leave this author without excuse.

Richard I. who succeeded Henry, bent upon a voyage to the holy land, stood in need of great sums for the expedition. William laid hold of this favourable conjuncture, met Richard at York, and, upon paying ten thousand merks Sterling, obtained from him a discharge of the treaty made with his father Henry; which was done by a solemn deed, dated the 25th December 1190, still extant.*

The sum paid to King Richard upon this occasion was too great to be raised by the King of Scotland out of his own domains. It must have been levied by a tax or contribution; and there was a just cause for the demand, as the money was to be applied for restoring the kingdom to its former independency. But of this fact we have better evidence than conjecture. The <436> monks of the Cistertian order having contributed a share, obtained from King William a deed, declaring, That this contribution should not be made a precedent in time coming.† "Ne quod in tali eventu semel factum est, qui nec prius evenit, nec in posterum Deo miserante futurus est, ullo modo in consuetudinem vel servitutem convertatur; ut videlicit per quod ipsi, pro redimenda regni libertate gratis fecerunt, servitus iis imponatur."⁴ This, in all probability, is the first tax of any importance that was levied in Scotland; and though our historians are altogether silent as to the manner, the deed now mentioned proves it to have been levied by voluntary contribution, and not by authority of parliament, which in those days probably had not assumed the power of imposing taxes.

The next tax we meet with, is in the days of Alexander II. son to the above-mentioned William. This king made a journey the length of Dover, and his ready money being exhausted, he procured a sum by pledging some lands, to redeem which he levied a tax. This appears from a deed, *anno regni* 15°, in which he declares, that the monastery of Aberbrothock, having aided him on this occasion, it should not turn to their prejudice.‡ <437>

---

* Ibid. vol. i. p. 64.

† Appendix to Anderson's Essay on the independency of Scotland, No. 21.

‡ Chartulary of Aberbrothock, fol. 74.

4. ". . . lest in an event, something which has happened once, which has never occurred previously and, by the mercy of God will not occur in the future, be altered in

Alexander III. married Margaret, daughter to Henry III. of England, and was in perfect good understanding with that kingdom during his whole reign. He was but once obliged to take up arms, and the occasion was, to resist an invasion by Acho King of Norway, who landed at Ayr, August 1263. Nor was this war of any continuance: Acho was defeated on land, and his fleet suffered by a storm, which obliged him to retire not many months after his landing. Alexander, some years after, viz. 25th July 1281,* contracted his daughter Margaret to Eric the young King of Norway, and bound himself for a tocher of 14,000 merks Sterling; a fourth part to be instantly advanced, a fourth part to be paid 1st August 1282, a fourth part 1st August 1283, and the remaining fourth 1st August 1284; but providing an option to give land for the two latter shares, at the rate of 100 merks of rent for 1000 merks of money.

This sum, which Alexander contracted in name of portion with this daughter, amounted to about 28,000 l. Sterling of our present money;† too great a sum to be raised out of his own funds; and as by law he was intitled to demand aid from his vassals upon this occasion, the sum must have been levied by some sort of tax or contribution. He had recent authority <438> for laying this burden upon his subjects, viz. that of his father-in-law Henry III.;‡ and if his subjects were to be burdened equally, it was necessary to ascertain the value of all the lands in the kingdom. Possibly he might take a hint of this valuation from the statute 4th Edward I. *anno* 1276, directing a valuation to be made of the lands, castles, woods, fishings, &c. of the whole kingdom of England. And the rent ascertained by such valuation got the name of *extent;* because the lands were estimated at their utmost value or extent.‖ One thing is certain, that there was a valuation of all the lands of Scotland in the reign of Alexander III. the proof of which shall be immediately produced; and there is not upon record any event to be a motive for an undertaking so laborious other than that of levying the said sum.

---

any way into a custom or service for them; so that, for example, through something which is imposed on them as a service, they acted freely to restore the liberty of the kingdom."

  * Rymer, vol. 2. p. 1079.

  † Ruddiman's preface to Anderson's Diplomata Scotiae.

  ‡ Spelman's Glossary [[i.e., *Achaeologus*]], *voce* Auxilium.

  ‖ Cowel's Dictionary, *voce* Extent.

Alexander III. left no descendants but a grand-daughter, commonly called the *Maid of Norway;* and she having died unmarried and under age, Scotland was miserably harrassed by Edward I. of England, who laid hold of the opportunity of a disputed succession to enslave this kingdom. Robert Bruce, unwearied in opposition, got peaceable possession of the crown, *anno* 1306; and though he seized on the lands belonging to Baliol and the Cummins, and <439> made considerable profit by lessening the weight of money in the re-coinage; yet, by a long train of war and intestine commotions, the crown-lands were so wasted, that toward the end of his reign it became necessary to petition the parliament for a supply. Upon the 15th July 1326, the parliament being convened at Cambuskenneth, the laity agreed to give him during his life the tenth penny of all their rents, *tam infra burgos et regalitates quam extra,* "according to the old extent of the lands and rents in the time of Alexander III." This curious deed, a copy of which is annexed,* contains an exception in these words:

> Excepta tantummodo destructione guerrae, in quo casu fiet decidentia de decimo denario praeconcesso, secundum quantitatem firmae, quae occasione praedicta de terris et redditibus praedictis levari non poterit, prout per inquisitionem per vicecomitem loci fideliter faciendam poterit reperiri.[5]

Here is complete proof of a valuation in the reign of Alexander III. named in the indenture, the *Old extent.* And as the necessity of a supply affords intrinsic evidence that the tax was levied, we have no reason to doubt, but that every man whose rents had fallen by the distresses of war, took the benefit of the foregoing clause, to get his lands revalued by the sheriff, that he might pay no more than a just proportion of the tax. <440>

We have now materials sufficient for an explanation of the *Valent* clause in our retours. At what time it came into practice, is altogether uncertain. If this clause was not made a part of the brieve of inquest before the days of Alexander III. there was little occasion for it, after the extent made in

---

* Appendix, No. 5.

5. "Making exceptions only for the destruction of war, in which case there shall be a decrease of the tenth penny granted before according to the size of the farm, which, by reason of the aforegoing, cannot be raised from the aforesaid lands and rents, as can be discovered by an inquest to be made faithfully by the sheriff of the place."

that reign, till the great baronies were split into parts, and the king's vassals were multiplied. One thing we may rely on as certain, that before the 1326, when the said indenture passed between King Robert and his parliament, one extent only was mentioned in retours, viz. that of Alexander III. Nor before that period was there any occasion for a double extent here more than in England. Of this we may be convinced from what follows. In levying the casualties of superiority, such as, ward, non-entry, &c. it was not the genius of this country, to stretch such claims to the utmost, by stating the just and true rent of the land upon every occasion. Such a fluctuating estimation, severe upon vassals, would at the same time have been troublesome to superiors. The king, and in imitation of him other superiors, were satisfied with a constant fixed rent to be a general rule for ascertaining the casualties, without regarding any occasional increase or diminution of rent. The extent in the reign of Alexander III. was probably the full rent, and must have continued a pretty just valuation <441> for many years. This extent then became the universal measure of the casualties of superiority. If a barony remained entire as in the days of Alexander III. there was no occasion for witnesses to prove the rent; it was found in the rolls containing the old extent. If a barony was split into parts, the rent of the several parcels was found in the retours, being a proportion of the old extent of the whole. Hence this *quaere* in the brieve, *Quantum valent dictae terrae per annum,* came to have a fixed and determined meaning; not what these lands are worth of yearly rent at present, but what they were worth at the last general valuation; or, in other words, what they are computed to in the rolls containing the old extent.

Thus stood the extent at the date of the indenture 1326; which laid a foundation for a revaluation, not of the whole lands in Scotland, but only of what were wasted by war. Supposing now such a revolution, of which we can entertain no doubt when it was in favour of vassals, it must have been the rule, not only for levying the tax then imposed, but also for ascertaining the casualties of superiority. If so, it was necessary to take notice of this new valuation in the retours of these lands; and consequently in the brieve, which was the warrant of the retour. The clause, *Quantum valent,* contained in the brieve, could not answer this <442> purpose; because that clause regarded only the old extent, and was a question to which the old valuation of the land was the proper answer. A new clause therefore was

necessary, and the clause that was added, points out so precisely the revaluation authorised by this indenture, as to afford real evidence, that the
clause must have been contrived soon after it. The clause as altered runs
thus: *Et quantum nunc valent dictae terrae, et quantum valuerunt tempore
pacis.* It was extremely natural to characterize the old extent by the phrase
tempore pacis, not only as made in a peaceable reign, but also in opposition
to the new extent occasioned by the devastation of war. I need only further
remark, that it was necessary to engross the new clause in every brieve; because, with respect to any particular land-estate, it could not beforehand
be known whether it had been wasted by war or not.

But, beside conjecture, there are positive facts to put this matter beyond
controversy. I have not hitherto discovered a retour of land held of the king,
so ancient as the 1326; but of that period there are preserved authentic copies of many retours of lands held of bishops, monasteries, &c. who had
the privilege of a chancery. And we have no reason to doubt, but that the
great barons who had this privilege, were ambitious of copying after the
king's chancery in <443> every article. The first retour I shall mention, happens to be a very lucky authority; for it verifies a fact mentioned above upon
the faith of conjecture, that at the date of the indenture 1326, there was but
one extent mentioned in the brieve and retour. The retour I appeal to, is
that of the land of Orroc in the county of Fife, held of the abbey of Dunfermline, dated the 20th May 1328, the *Valent* clause of which runs thus:
Item dicunt quod praedictae terrae de Orroc valent per annum 12 *l.* This retour
at the same time shows, that the alteration in the *Valent* clause was not then
introduced; which is not wonderful, when the retour is but a year and ten
months after the indenture (1). The most ancient retour I have seen after
that now mentioned, bears date in the 1359, being of land held of the same

(1) Since writing what is above, I have seen a copy, not, properly speaking, of a retour,
but of a valuation of the lands of Kilravock and Easter-Gedies, *anno* 1295, in which the
Valent clause runs thus:

Quod terra de Kilravock cum omnibus pertinentiis suis, sciz. cum molendinis,
bracinis, quarellis, et bosco, valet per annum 24 lib. item dixerunt quod terra de
Easter-Gedies cum molendino et bracinis valet per annum 12 lib.

[["... that the land of Kilravock with all its pertinents, namely with mills, brew-houses,
quarries and forest, is worth £24 per annum, and they said that the land of Easter Geddes
with mill and brew-houses is worth £12 per annum."]]

abbey. Before this time, probably several years, the alteration of the *Valent* clause was made; for in this retour it runs thus: *Et dictae terrae valebant tempore bonae pacis L.* 13 : 6 : 8, *et nunc valent L.* 10 : 13 : 7. There are in that period many other retours <444> mentioning two extents, distinguishing them in the same manner. And uniformly the *valuerunt tempore pacis* is greater than the *nunc valent;* which puts it past doubt that the *nunc valent* refers to the new extent authorised by the said indenture. Some retours indeed there are of that period, where the *valuerunt tempore pacis* and the *nunc valent* are the same. But it is easy to account for that circumstance; because from the indenture it appears, that but a part of our lands were wasted by war; and the retours now mentioned must be of lands which were not so wasted.

Down to the days of our James I. the two extents mentioned in retours, were those of Alexander III. and Robert Bruce. In James's reign we observe an alteration, which cannot be explained without proceeding in the history of the public taxes. The next tax that deserves to be taken notice of, was in the reign of David II. This king was taken prisoner by the English at the battle of Durham *anno* 1346, and was released *anno* 1365; after agreeing to pay for his ransom 100,000 l. Sterling, within the space of twenty-five years. And there is good evidence that the whole was paid before the year 1383.* This immense debt, contracted for redeeming the king from captivity, came to be a burden upon his vassals, by the very con-<445>stitution of the Feudal law, abstracting from the authority of parliament. It must therefore have been levied as a public tax, which appears to be the case from the rolls of that king still extant in exchequer. And as there is no vestige of any new valuation at this time, the old extent, viz. that of Alexander III. must have been the rule; except where altered by the partial valuation in the reign of Robert I. And what puts this past doubt is, that the new extent continued to be lower than the old extent, or extent *tempore pacis,* during this king's reign, and until the reign of James I.

James I. having been many years detained in England, obtained his liberty upon giving hostages for payment of 40,000 l. Sterling, demanded under the specious title of alimony. Of this sum 10,000 l. was remitted by

---

* Rymer, vol. 6. p. 464; vol. 7. p. 417.

Henry IV. at that time King of England, upon James's marrying a daughter of the Duke of Somerset. In the parliament 1424, provision was made for redeeming the hostages by a subsidy granted of the twentieth part of lands, moveables, &c.* In order to levy this tax, a valuation was directed of lands as well as of moveables. And this new valuation of lands became proper, if not necessary, upon the following account, that the reason for making the new extent in the 1326, no longer subsisted. The lands which at <446> that time had been wasted by war, were now restored to their wonted value; and yet without a new valuation, these lands could only be taxed according to the extent 1326. And with this special reason concurred one more general, which is, that an extent, if the commerce of land be free, cannot long be a rule for levying public taxes. For by succession, purchase, and other means of acquiring property, parcels of land are united into a whole, or a whole split into parcels, which acquire new names, till by course of time it comes to be a matter of uncertainty, what lands are meant by the original name preserved on record. This reason shows the necessity of new extents from time to time; for after the connection betwixt land and the name it bears in the extent-rolls is lost, these rolls can no longer be of use for proportioning a tax upon such land.

It was appointed by the act imposing the subsidy, that this extent should be made and put in books, betwixt and the 13th July then next; and that it was made, and also that the subsidy was levied, appears from the continuator of Fordon.† He reports, that it amounted the first year to 14,000 merks, that the second year it was much less, and the people beginning to murmur, that the tax was no longer continued. But we have still a better authority than the <447> continuator of Fordon, to prove that the extent was made, viz. several retours recently after the 1424, where the new extent is uniformly greater than the old extent, or extent *tempore pacis*. These must refer to some late extent, and not to the extent 1326, which was uniformly less than the old extent. Of these retours the most ancient I have met with is dated 1431, being of the lands of Blairmukis, held of the Baron of Bothvill, in which James de Dundas is retoured heir to James de Dundas his

* Black Acts, p. 1624. c. 10. 11.
† [[Fordun, *Scotichronicon.*]] L. 16. cap. 9.

father, "Qui jurati dicunt quod dictae terrae nunc valent per annum 20 mercas, et valuerunt tempore pacis 100 solidos."*6

As there was a new extent of the whole lands of Scotland, which must have been the rule for levying the casualties of superiority as well as the tax then imposed, one is led to enquire, what was the use of continuing in the brieve of inquest the *quaere* about the two different extents? Why not return to the ancient form, specifying one extent only, viz. the present extent? In answer to this, it must be yielded, that there could lie no objection to this innovation had it been intended. But by this time the rule had prevailed of preserving inviolably the style of judicial writs; and as to questions so easy to be answered, the innovation proba-<448>bly was reckoned a matter of no such importance, as to occasion an alteration in the style of the brieve of inquest. One thing is certain, that the style remains the same without any alteration since the days of King Robert I. The brieve and retour obtained however a different meaning; so far as that the *nunc valent,* by which formerly was meant the extent 1326, came afterward to mean the extent 1424. For instance, the retour of the lands of Tullach, held of the abbey of Aberbrothock, bearing date 1438, has the *valent* clause thus: *Valent per annum L. 33 : 6 : 8, et tempore pacis valuerunt L. 10.*7 Another instance is a retour of the lands of Forglen, held of the same abbey, dated 1457, *Valent nunc per annum 20 merks, et valuerunt tempore pacis L. 10.*8 That by the *nunc valent* in these two retours must be meant the late extent of James I. is evident from the following circumstance, that instead of being less than the extent *tempore pacis,* which the extent 1326, constantly was, it is considerably greater.

As the extent 1424, was uniformly engrossed in every retour, in answer to the *quantum nunc valent* in the brieve, this practice came to be exceeding favourable to vassals in counting for the casualties due by them; because in every such account this extent was taken for the true rent of the land. By the gradual sinking of the value of money and the improvement of <449> land, the benefit which vassals had by this form of stating accounts, came

---

* This retour is in the hands of Sir John Inglis of Cramond.

6. ". . . which jurors said that the said land is now worth 20 merks annually, and in time of peace was worth 100 shillings."

7. ". . . is worth £33 6s 8d annually, and in time of peace was worth £10."

8. ". . . is now worth 20 merks annually, and in time of peace was worth £10."

to be too considerable to be overlooked. The value of the king's casualties by this means gradually diminishing, the matter was taken under consideration by the legislature, and produced the act 55. parl. 1474, ordaining, "That it be answered in the retour, of what avail the land was of old, and the very avail that it is worth and gives, the day of serving the brieve."

I once inclined to think, that it is not the meaning of this statute to require a new proof of the rent of land every time it is retoured upon a brieve of inquest. I suspected that the statute referred to some late general valuation. And I was encouraged to embrace this opinion, on finding in the records of parliament,* a tax imposed of 3000 l. for defraying the expence of an embassy to Denmark, and a general valuation appointed in order to levy that tax. Commissioners are named to take the proof, and certain persons appointed, one out of each estate, to receive the sums that should be levied. And that this must have been the case, appeared probable, upon finding that the new extent, even after this period, was no less uniform than formerly, and therefore that it could not correspond to the true rent of land, which is in a continual fluctuation. But if after all there en-<450>sued no new valuation of the land-rent of this kingdom, of which there is not the slightest vestige; the statute must be taken in its literal meaning, because it can admit of none other. I have still better authority for adhering to the literal meaning, viz. the proceedings of the sovereign court, while the statute was fresh in memory. The Earl of Bothwell, donatar to the relief and nonentry of the barony of Balinbreich, brought a reduction against the Earl of Rothes of his retour of that barony, because it was retoured to 200 merks only for the new extent, though the rent really amounted to a much greater sum. It was proved before the court, that the barony paid 500 merks of rent; and upon that medium the retour was reduced.† And the like was done with respect to the retour of the lands of Shield and Drongan, which were retoured to 42 l. of new extent, and yet were proved by witnesses to be 100 merks of yearly rent.‡

In the retours accordingly that bear date recently after the statute, we find a sudden start of the new extent, and a much greater disproportion than formerly betwixt it and the old extent. In the chartulary of the abbey

* 1467, acts 74. 79. 86.
† 22d October 1489.
‡ 13th February 1499, The King contra Crawford.

of Aberbrothock, there is a copy of a retour of certain lands, dated *anno* 1491, the particulars of <451> which are, *Terrae de Pittarow valent nunc L.* *22, tempore pacis L.* 8. *Terrae de Cardinbegy valent nunc L.* 13, *et tempore pacis* *L.* 5. *Terrae de Auchingarth valent nunc* 5 *merks, tempore pacis* 2 *merks.* In the chartulary of the abbey of Dunfermline there is a copy of a retour of the lands of Clunys, held of that abbey, bearing date *anno* 1506, *Valent nunc* 50 *merks, et tempore pacis L.* 4. I have had occasion to mention a retour of the lands of Forglen, held of the abbey of Aberbrothock, dated *anno* 1457, of which the new extent is 20 merks, and the old extent is 10 l. In the same chartulary, there is luckily another retour of the same lands, bearing date *anno* 1494, of which the *valent* clause is in the following words, *Valent nunc* *L.* 20, *et valuerunt tempore pacis* 20 *merks.* The difference in so short a time as thirty-seven years betwixt 20 merks and 20 l. of new extent, is real evidence, that the act of parliament was duly observed in making out the retour last mentioned. But from the comparison of these two retours, a more curious observation occurs, viz. that retours of lands held of subject superiors, are not much to be relied on as evidence of the old extent. In the first of these retours the old extent is stated at 10 l. in the other at 20 merks; occasioned by a blunder of the inquest, who engrossed as the old extent in the retour they were forming, the new extent contained in the for-<452>mer retour. Many such blunders would probably be discovered, had we a full record of old retours. And it need not be surprising, that in such retours little attention was given to the *valent* clause, which was reckoned a matter merely of form. For though the public taxes were levied from the king's vassals according to the old extent, yet in proportioning the relief which a baron had against his own vassals, the true rent was certainly made the rule. The new extent was of more consequence, because it was the rule for the nonentry-duties, before a declarator of nonentry was raised by a baron against the heir of his vassal.

It may be remarked here by the by, that the act 1474, is real evidence of a flourishing state of affairs after our James I. got possession of his throne. From the valuation 1424, till the said act, there passed but fifty years; and the landrent of Scotland must have increased remarkably during that period, to make the act 1474 necessary. But that monarch in his younger years was disciplined in the school of adversity. During a tedious confinement of eighteen years, he had sufficient leisure to study the arts of government, and probably he made the best use of his time. It is certain, that before his reign we had no experience and scarce any notion of a regular government, where the law bears <453> sway, and the people peaceably submit to the authority of law. But to return to our subject.

As by the statute now mentioned the superior's casualties were raised to their highest pitch, it was impracticable to support them long at that height, in opposition to the general bias of the nation in favour of vassals. The notion had been long ago broached and was now firmly established, that the vassal is proprietor, and consequently that ward, relief, and nonentry are rigorous and severe casualties. We have Spottiswoode's authority in his History of the Church of Scotland, that loud complaints were made against these casualties, early in the reign of James IV.[9] But why at this period in particular? for we do not find the same complaints afterward; at least they make no figure in the annals of more recent times. The act we have been discoursing about, affords a satisfactory answer. These casualties, by authority of the statute, were more rigorously exacted than formerly. And we shall now proceed to show, that they were very soon brought down to a moderate pitch, notwithstanding the statute. In serving a brief of inquest, the practice did not long continue, of taking a proof by witnesses of the true rent of the land.[10] If the land was once retoured as prescribed by the statute, the old and new extent engrossed in that retour were continued in the following retours. If <454> there was no retour, a proportion of the old and new extent of the whole barony was taken. And where that was not to be had, it was the method to engross a new extent bearing a certain proportion to the old extent. For the last we have Skene's authority (*voce* Extent). His words are, "The Lords of Session esteem a merk-land of old extent to four merk-land of new extent." And he cites a decision, viz. 21st March 1541, Kennedy *contra* Mackinnald, which seems to import so much; though but obscurely, because the case is not distinctly stated. The process

9. It is not obvious which passage in Spottiswoode's *History* Kames refers to here.
10. 1758, 1761 add: "The old method was revived, of making a former extent the rule."

being for the nonentry-duties of a five-merk land, it is said to have been proved, that the land paid of rent four merks for every one of the said five merks; and I must acknowledge, that the manner of expression seems to point at some general rule, rather than at a proof by witnesses. If this be the meaning of the decision, it is the first case I have observed, where this deviation from the statute was authorised by the sovereign court; and a notable deviation it was, to take such an imaginary rule for ascertaining the rent of the land, when the statute directed a proof by witnesses of the true rent. But when the act came once to be neglected, the court was more explicit in their judgments on this point. In a case observed by Balfour, (title, *Of Brieves and Retours*), 17th July 1562, Queen's Advocate and <455> Lord Drummond *contra* George Mushet, a general rule is established directly in face of the statute; which is, That when lands pay farm-victual, poultry, &c. the inquest are not bound to take inquisition of the yearly rent, nor to convert such casualties into money.[11] And the reason given is remarkable, viz. that the price of such casualties is so changeable, that no certain or fixed sum can be ascertained. This is a very bad reason upon the plan of the statute, though it serves to show the sense of the nation, which the statute had not eradicated, that the new extent ought to be fixed and uniform as well as the old. At the same time, as the landrent in Scotland was generally paid in corn, this decision was in effect a repeal of the statute; of which, we need not doubt, that proprietors whose rents were paid in money would take advantage. The act 1474, came in this manner to be universally neglected; and it was established as a matter of right, that the new extent should always be lower than the true rent: The act 6. parl. 1584, impowering the king to feu out his annexed property, has the following clause.

> Providing always that the saidis infeftments of feuferme be not made within the just avail, to the prejudice and hurt of our Sovereign Lord and his successoures: That is to say, within the dewtie to the quilkis the saidis landis are retoured, or <456> may be justly retoured, for the new extent. Quhilk new extent his hieris, with advice forsaid, declaires to be the just avail of the saidis lands, for the quhilk the samen may be set in feu-farm.

11. See Balfour, *Practicks*, p. 430.

Here it is clearly supposed, that the new extent is a favourable estimation of the rent, and lower than what is truly paid for the land.

N.B. For the materials employed in this tract, the author is indebted to Mr John Davidson clerk to the signet, whose extensive knowledge reflects honour upon the society to which he belongs. <457>

APPENDIX

NUMBER I

Form of a Letter of Slaines; referred to p. 33.

To all and sundrie whom it effeirs, to whose knowledge thir presents may come, Me   relict of the deceast   and taking burden for the children lawfully procreat betwixt me and my said deceast husband, now in their minoritie; as also we   nearest of kinne and tutores of lyne to the children procreat as said is, and all of us, with one consent and assent, and takeing burden on us for the bairnes, in respect of their minoritie and lesser age, lawfully procreat betwixt the said deceast   and me the said   Greeting in God Everlasting. Forswameikleas we, in consideratione of the repenting heart inwardly had, and manifested, declared, and showne to us, be   for the accidental slaughter of the said deceast   committed be him suddenly, without aney designe or forethought fellonie, upon the   day of   last bypast, Jaj viiC   years; and also because the said   <458> and others in his name, have made condigne satisfactione to us for the said slaughter, and hath made payment to us of certaine soumes of money, in name of kinboot and assythment: Thairfore, and for certaine other good causes and consideratione moving us, we, with one consent, and taking burden as said is, have remitted, forgiven, and discharged, and be the tenor heirof freelie remits, forgives, and discharges, the said   of all malice, rancor, grudge, hatred, envy of heart, and all occasiones of actiones, civil or criminal, which we, or aney of us, had, has, or aney wayes may have in time comeing, against the said   for the said cryme; and, be thir presents, receave him in such amitie, friendship, and heartie kyndness, as he was with us before

the committing of the said cryme, and as the samen had never been committed: And we the forenamed persones, for ourselves, and in name and behalf of the said children procreat as said is, in respect of their minoritie and lesser age, binds and obleidges us, That the said   shall never be called, persued, be way of deed or otherwayes, in or by the law, be us, or aney of us, for his committing of the said slaughter, in tyme comeing, under the paine of perjurie, defamatione, tinsell of faith, truth, and credit: And also we, for ourselves, and in name foresaid, be thir presents, will and grant, That the said   shall not suffer exyle, banishment, or aney trouble whatsomever, throw the premisses: Most humbly beseeching his Most Gracious Majestie to grant also a pardone and remissione, under the great seale, in most ample forme, to the said
for the foresaid cryme: Likeas we, or any of us, binds and obleidges us to renew, reforme, reiterat, ratifie, and approve, thir presents, alse oft and whensoever we, or aney of us, beis required thereto, in the most ample forme. In witness, &c. <459>

NUMBER II

Copy of a seisin, which proves, that the Jus Retractus was the law of Scotland in the fifteenth century; as observed p. 76.

In Dei nomine, Amen. Per hoc praesens publicum instrumentum cunctis pateat evidenter, Quod anno ab incarnatione ejusdem 1450, mensis vero Januarii die antepenultima, indictione 14ta Pontificatus Sanctissimi in Christo Patris ac Domini nostri Domini Nicholai divina providentia Papae Quinti anno quarto, In mei notarii publici et testium subscriptorum praesentia personaliter constitutus providus vir Robertus Gyms burgensis de Linlithgow exposuit qualiter per breve Domini nostri Regis de compulsione legittime obtinuit super haereditate quondam Johannis Gyms fratris sui summam octoginta quindecim librarum coram balivis dicti burgi in curia, pro qua quidem summa balivi tunc temporis existentes sibi possessionem de tenemento dicti quondam Johannis ex parte occidentali fori jacente ex avisamento consilii tradiderunt. Et quia dictus Robertus, magna necessitate compulsus, dictum tenementum alienare proposuit, ad suae vitae necessaria supportanda, eo quod nullus alius amicorum inventus fuerat qui sibi tempore necessitatis succurrere proposuit excepta solummodo Thoma de Forrest ejus consanguineo, prefatus Robertus ballivos dicti burgi cum instantia specialiter supplicavit quatenus secum usque solum dicti tenementi properare curarent, quo facto dictus Robertus totum jus et clameum quod in dicto tenemento habuit ratione dictae summae recuperatae prae-<460>fato Thomae de Forrest sursum reddidit ac sibi possessionem corporalem exinde tradidit per manus honorabilis viri Alexandri de Hathwy tunc temporis ballivi dicti burgi sibi et haeredibus suis et assignatis futuris temporibus permansuram quousque de dicta summa principali plenarie fuerit satisfactum, super quibus omnibus et singulis dictus Thomas de Forrest a me notario publico infra scripto sibi fieri petiit publicum instrumentum. Acta fuerunt haec supra solum dicti tenementi hora quasi secunda postmeridiem anno Dei mense indictione et pontificatu quibus supra, praesentibus providis viris David de Crawfurd Johanne Kemp ballivis, Thoma de Foulis Johanne Simson Thoma Henrison Henrico Cauchlyng Johanne Collano et Johanne Chalon serjandis cum multis aliis testibus ad praemissa vocatis specialiter et rogatis.

> Et ego Jacobus de Foulis clericus Sancti Andreae diocesios publica authoritate imperiali notarius praedictis omnibus et singulis dum sic ut praemittitur fierent et agerentur una cum praenominatis testibus praesens personaliter interfui, eaque sic fieri dici, vidi et audivi, indeque praesens instrumentum aliena manu ex meo mandato scriptum confeci et meis signo et subscriptione manu propria roboravi una cum appensione sigilli dicti Alexandri Hathwy ballivi propter majoris roboris et testimonium premissorum.[1] <461>

1. "In the name of God, Amen. Let it be clearly known by this present public instrument that on the antepenultimate day of the month of January in the year of incarnation 1450, the 14th indiction and the fourth year of the pontificate of our lord the most holy father in Christ, the Lord Nicholas the fifth, by divine providence Pope, in the presence of me, notary public, and the underwritten witnesses, the prudent man, Robert Gyms, an appointed burgess of Linlithgow, explained in person how he obtained the sum of ninety-five pounds out of the estate of the late John Gyms, his brother, through a brieve of enforcement (*compulsio*) from King; for which sum the bailies then existing, on the advice of the council, gave him possession of a tenement of the said late

NUMBER III

Copies of Two Rent Charges; referred to p. 110.

1. Bond Sir Simon Lockhart of Ley, to William of Lindsay Rector of the church of Ayr, for an annualrent of L. 10 Sterling out of the lands of Ley, anno 1323.

[*The principal is in the charter-chest of John Lockhart of Ley.*]

Omnibus hanc cartam visuris vel audituris Simon Locard miles dominus de Lay et Cartland infra vicecomitatem de Lanerk salutem in Domino sempiternam. Noveritis universitas vestra me pro me et haeredibus meis quibuscunque concessisse et vendidisse ac praedictas concessionem et venditionem praesenti carta confirmasse discreto viro domino Willielmo de Lindesay rectori ecclesiae de Ayr decem libras Sterlingorum annui reditus percipiendas annuatim in terris meis de Cartland et de Lay praedictis pro quadam summae pecuniae mihi prae manibus persolutae de qua teneo me

---

John which lies on the west side of the marketplace. And while the said Robert, compelled by great necessity, proposed to sell the said tenement in order to provide for the necessaries of life, and because no other friend had been found to offer succour to him in his time of need, excepting only Thomas Forrest his relative, the foresaid Robert urgently beseeched the bailies in earnest to make ready to hasten with him to the ground of the said tenement, after which the said Robert gave up all right and claim that he had to the said tenement by reason of the recuperated sum, to the foresaid Thomas Forrest, and he transferred his real possession of it through the hands of the honourable man Alexander Hathwy, at that time a bailie of the said burgh, to him and his heirs and assignees for all time to come, whereby he was fully satisfied of the said principal sum; regarding which, each and every thing, the said Thomas Forrest desired that a public record be made by me, the aforementioned public notary. These things were done on the ground of the said tenement at the second hour past noon in the year and on the day, month, indiction and pontificate as above, in the presence of the prudent men David Crawford and John Kemp, bailies, Thomas Foulis, John Simson, Thomas Henrison, Henry Cauchlyng, John Collan and John Chalon, sergeants, along with many other witnesses specially called and summoned for the foregoing.

"And I, James Foulis, clerk of the diocese of St Andrews, a notary public by imperial authority, was present in person as all and sundry the foresaid were done and acted in the presence of the forenamed witnesses, and thus I did say, see and hear them, and I therefore made the present instrument, written by another hand under my instruction, and corroborated with my own signature sign manual, along with the appended seal of the said Alexander Hathwy, bailie, as major witness and corroboration of the foregoing."

bene contentum, solvendum praedictum annuum reditum praefato domino Willielmo haeredibus suis et suis assignatis in maneriei loco de Lay supradicto per me et haeredes meos ad duos anni terminos, viz centum solidos
ad festum Pentecostes et centum solidos ad festum Sancti Martini in hieme,
primo vero termino solutionis incipiente ad festum Pentecostes anno Domini millesimo tricentesimo vicesimo tertio tenen et haben. dictum annuum
reditum decem librarum praefato domino Willielmo haeredibus suis et suis
<462> assignatis quibuscunque libere quiete bene et in pace in perpetuum,
ad quemquidem annuum reditum decem librarum fideliter et sine aliqua
contradictione solvendum loco et terminis supra dictis ut praedicitur obligo
pro me et haeredibus meis praedictam terram de Cartland et de Lay una
cum omnibus bonis et catellis in iisdem terris inventis seu inveniendis ad
districtionem praedicti domini Willielmi haeredum suorum vel suorum as-
signatorum quotiescunque defecero seu aliquis haeredum meorum defecerit in solutione dicti annui reditus decem librarum in toto vel in parte
praedictis loco et terminis, tam ad restitutionem damnorum et expensarum
si quae fuerint quam ad solutionem praedicti annui reditus nullo propo-
nendo obstante. Ego vero Simon et haeredes mei praedicto domino Willielmo haeredibus suis et suis assignatis quibuscunque praedictum annuum
reditum decem librarum, pro praedictae pecuniae summa in praedictis
manibus ut praedictum est persoluta, contra omnes gentes warrantizabimus
acquittabimus et in perpetuum defendemus. In cujus rei testimonium sigillum meum praesenti cartae apposui et ad majorem hujus rei evidentiam
et sigilli mei testimonium nobilis vir dominus Walterus Senescallus Scotiae
ad instantiam meam sigillum suum huic cartae similiter apposuit. His testibus nobili viro domino Waltero Senescallo superdicto, domino Gervaso
abbate de Newbottle, domino Davide de Lindesay, domino de Crawford,
domino Roberto de Herris, domino de Nidsdale, domino Richardo de Hay,
domino Jacobo de Cuninghame, domino Adamo More, domino Jacobo
de Lindsay, domino Waltero filio Gilberti, et domino Davide de Graham,
militibus, et Reginaldo More, et multis aliis.[2] <463>

2. "To all who will see or hear this charter, Simon Locard, knight, lord of Lay and
Cartland in the sheriffdom of Lanark, eternal greeting in the Lord. All of you, know
that I, on behalf of myself and all of my heirs have conceded and sold, and by this
present charter confirmed the foresaid concession and sale to the prudent man, Sir William Lindsay, rector of the church of Ayr, ten pounds sterling of annualrent to be gained

2. Bond by James of Douglas Lord of Balvany, from the original, found among the papers of Baillie of Walstoun.

Be it kende till all men be thir present letteris me Jamis of Duglas lorde of Balwany sekyrly to be haldyn and thrw thir present letteris lely to be oblist tyll a worschepyll man and my cusing Schir Robert of Erskyn lorde of that ilk in fourty pund of usuale moneth of Scotland now gangand for cause of pure lane thrw the forsaide Schir Robert to me lent before hand in my gret myster to be payt to the fornemmyt Schir Robert or tyll his ayre exe-cuturis or assignes at the fest of Whitsonday and Martynmas in wynter nexit eftir the makyn of thir present letteris be evynlyk porciounis in maner and forme as eftir folous, that is to say, that all the landis of the barouny of Sawlyn with the appurtiones lyand within the schiradome of Fife the quhilkis I haf in intromettyng of Alexander of Halyburton lorde of the sayd landis sall remayne with the sayde lorde with all fredomes esis & com-

---

annually from my foresaid lands of Cartland and Lay, in return for a certain sum of money paid to me in advance, of which I am well content; the foresaid annualrent to be paid to the forenamed William, his heirs and his assignees at the demesne of Lay aforesaid by me and me heirs, at two annual terms, namely one hundred shillings at the feast of Pentecost and one hundred shillings at the feast of St Martin in winter [11 November], the first payment term being at the feast of Pentecost in the year of the Lord one thousand three hundred and twenty three; the foresaid William and his heirs and assignees whomsoever, to have and to hold the foresaid annualrent of ten pounds freely, quietly, well and in perpetual peace; and so that the annualrent of ten pounds should be paid faithfully and without any gainsaying at the stated place and terms, as aforesaid, I, for myself and my heirs bind the foresaid land of Cartland and Lay along with all the goods and chattels found or to be found in those lands, to the distraint of the foresaid Sir William, his heirs and assignees whomsoever should I or any of my heirs default in the payment of the foresaid annualrent of ten pounds, in full or in part, at the foresaid place and terms, both for the recovery of damages and expenses if there be any, as well as for the payment of the foresaid annualrent, notwithstanding any reason. And I, Simon, and my heirs, warrant, acquit and in perpetuity defend against all people the said an-nualrent of ten pounds for the said Sir William and his heirs and assignees whomsoever, on account of the aforesaid sum of money paid in advance as aforesaid. In testimony of which I have appended my seal to the present charter and for the greater corroboration of this, and of the testimony of my seal, at my request the noble man, Sir Walter the Steward of Scotland has likewise appended his seal to this charter. With these witnesses: the noble man, Sir Walter, the above named Steward of Scotland; Sir Gervase, the abbot of Newbattle; Sir David Lindsay, lord Crawford; Sir Robert Herries, lord of Nithsdale; Sir Richard Hay; Sir James Cunningham; Sir Adam More; Sir James Lindsay; Sir Walter the son of Gilbert; and Sir David Graham, knights; and Reginald More, and many others."

moditeis courtis & playntis & eschetis quhill he the said lorde of Erskyn his ayris executuris and assignes be fully assitht of xl. punde as is beforsayde. And gif it hapnes as God forbede that the said Schir Robert be nocht assitht be ony manner of way of the said landis of Sawlyn I the said James oblis and byndis all my landis of the lordschip of Dunsyare to be distrenzit als wele as the landis of Sawlyn at the wyll of the said Schir Robert his ayris or assignes quhill he or thai be assitht of the forenemmyt sowme as he or thai suld strenze thair propir landis as for their awyn mail without lefe of oney juge seculer or of the kirk. In the witness of the quhilk thing to thir present letteris I haf sett my sele at Lynlithqw the aucht day of May the zere of grace MCCCC & XVIII. <464>

NUMBER IV

Old Style of Letters of Poinding the Ground, founded on the infeftment without a previous decree; referred to p. 115.

James by the Grace of God, King of Scottis, to our lovites —— —— —— —— Andrew Foreman messenger our sherriffs in that part conjunctly and severally constitute, greeting. FORASMUCHAS it is humbly meant and shown to us, by our lovite oratrix and wido Katherine Greg the relict of umquhile Alexander Forrester of Killennuch, THAT WHERE she has the lands of Wester Crow, with the pertinents, lying within the stewartry of Menteith, and sheriffdom of Perth, pertaining to the said Katherine in liferent, as her infeftment made thereupon bears: NOTTHELESS the tenants and occupiers of the saids lands rests awind to her the mealls and duties thereof, of certain terms of langtime bypast, and will make no payment thereof unless they be compelled, to her heavy damage and skaith, as is alledged. OUR WILL is therefor, and we charge you straitly and command, that, incontinent thir our letters seen, ye pass, concurr, fortify, and assist the said Katherine and her officiaris, in the poinding ad distrinzying the tenants and occupyers of the saids lands for the mealls farms and duties thereof, the two terms last bypast resting awand by them, and make the said Katherine to be paid thereof conform to her infeftment; and sycklyke

yearly and termly in time coming, and if need bees that ye poind and dis-
trinzie therefor. ACCORDING to justice as ye will answer to us thereupon.
The whilk to do we commit to you conjunct-<465>ly and severally our full
power, by thir our letters, delivering them, by you duly execute and indorst,
again to the bearer. Given under our signet at Edinburgh, the seventh day
of December and of our reign the 30 zeir. *Ex deliberatione dominorum
concilii.*

Signd J. WALLACE.

NUMBER V

Tax granted by the Parliament to Robert I. for his life, referred to p. 130.

[*The original in the Advocates Library.*]

Hoc est transcriptum indenturae concordatae et affirmatae inter Dominum
Robertum Dei gratia Regem Scottorum illustrem, et comites, barones liberetenentes, communitates burgorum ac universam communitatem totius
regni, magno sigillo regni et sigillis magnatum et communitatum praedic-
torum alternatim sigillatum in haec verba: Praesens indentura testatur,
quod, quintodecimo mensis Julii anno ab incarnatione Domini M. CCC.
vicesimo sexto, tenente plenum parliamentum suum apud Cambuskenneth serenissimo Principe Domino Roberto Dei gratia Rege Scottorum il-
lustri, convenientibus ibidem comitibus, baronibus, burgensibus et ceteris
omnibus liberetenentibus regni sui, propositum erat per eundem Dominum Regem, quod terrae et redditus, qui ad coronam suam antiquitus
pertinere solebant, per diversas donationes et translationes, occasione guerrae <466> factas, sic fuerant diminuti quod statui suo congruentem sus-
tentationem non habuerit, absque intollerabili onere et gravamine plebis
suae: Unde instanter petiit ab eisdem, quod cum tam in se, quam in suis,
pro eorum omnium libertate recuperanda et salvanda, multa sustinuisset
incommoda, placeret eis, ex sua debita gratitudine, modum et viam inveni-
re per quem juxta status sui decentiam ad populi sui minus gravamen con-
grue posset sustentari. Qui omnes et singuli comites, barones, burgenses et
liberetenentes, tam infra libertates quam extra, de Domino Rege, vel qui-

buscunque aliis dominis infra regnum mediate vel immediate tenentes, cujuscunque fuerint conditionis, considerantes et fatentes praemissa Domini
Regis motiva esse vera, ac quamplura alia, suis temporibus, eis per eum
commoda accrevisse, suamque petitionem esse rationabilem atque justam,
habito super praemissis commune ac diligenti tractatu, unanimiter gratan-
ter et benevole concesserunt et dederunt Domino suo Regi supradicto annuatim ad terminos Sancti Martini et Pentecostes, proportionaliter, pro
toto tempore vitae dicti Regis, decimum denarium omnium firmarum et
redituum suorum, tam de terris suis dominicis et wardis quam de ceteris
terris suis quibuscunque infra libertates et extra, ex tam infra burgos quam
extra, juxta *antiquam extentam* terrarum et reddituum tempore bonae me-
moriae Domini Alexandri Dei gratia Regis Scottorum illustris ultimo defuncti, pro ministeriis ejus fideliter faciend. excepta tantummodo destruc-
tione guerrae; in quo casu fiet decidentia de decimo denario praeconcesso,
secundum quantitatem firmae, quae occasione praedicta, de terris et reddi-
tibus praedictis, levari non poterint, prout per inquisitionem per vicecomitem loci fideliter faciendam poterit reperiri: Ita quod omnes hujusmodi denarii, in usum et utilitatem dicti Domini Regis, sine remis-<467>sione
quacunque cuicunque facienda, totaliter committantur: et si donationem
vel remissionem fecerit de hujusmodi denariis antequam in Cameram Regis
deferantur et plenarie persolvantur, praesens concessio nulla sit, sed omni
careat robore firmitatis. Et quia quidem magnates regni tales vendicant libertates, quod ministri Regis infra terras suas ministrare non poterint, per
quod solutio Domino Regi facienda forsan poterit retardari: Omnes et singuli hujusmodo libertates vendicantes, Domino Regi manuceperunt, por-
tiones ipsos et tenentes suos contingentes, per ministros suos, ministris Regis, statutis terminis plene facere persolvi: Quod si non fecerint, vicecomites
Regis quilibet in suo vicecomitatu, tenementa hujusmodi libertatum, regia
auctoritate, per hujusmodi solutione facienda distringant. Dominus vero
Rex, gratitudinem et benevolentiam populi sui placide ponderans et atten-
dens, eisdem gratiose concessit, quod a festo Sancti Martini proximo fu-
turo, primo viz. termino solutionis faciendae, collectas aliquas non impo-
net, prisas seu cariagia non capiet, nisi itinerando seu transeundo per
regnum, more predecessoris sui Alexandri regis supra dicti: Pro quibus prisis
et cariagiis plena fiat solutio super unguem: Et quod omnes grossae pro-
videntiae Regis cum earum cariagiis, fiant totaliter sine prisis. Et quod mi-

nistri Regis, pro omnibus rebus ad hujusmodi grossas providentias faciendas, secundum commune forum patriae, in manu solvant sine dilatione. Ceterum consensum est et concordatum inter Dominum Regem et communitatem regni sui, quod, ipso Rege mortuo, statim cesset concessio decimi denarii supradicti. Ita tamen quod de terminis praeteritis ante mortem ipsius Domini Regis plenarie satisfiat. Et quod nec per praemissa, vel aliquod praemissorum, post hujusmodi concessionem finitam, haeredibus dicti Domini Regis ant <468> communitati regni sui aliquatenus fiat praejudicium, sed quod omnia in eundem statum redeant et permaneant, in quo erant ante diem praesentis concessionis. In quorum omnium testimonium, uni parti hujus indenturae, penes dictos comites, barones, burgenses et liberetenentes residenti, appositum est commune sigillum regni: Alteri vero parti, penes Dominum Regem remanenti, sigilla comitum, baronum et aliorum majorum liberetenentium una cum communibus sigillis burgorum regni, nomine suo et totius communitatis concorditer sunt appensa. Dat. die, anno et loco supradictis. Et hoc transcriptum penes magnates et communitates praedictos et eorum successores, remansurum, sigillo regni consignatur, in testimonium et memoriam futurorum. Datum apud Edinburgum, in parliamento Domini Regis tento ibidem, secunda Dominica quadragesimae, cum continuatione dierum sequentium, anno gratiae M. CCC. vicesimo septimo.[3] <469>

3. "This is a transcript of the indenture agreed and affirmed between the lord Robert by the grace of God illustrious king of Scots and the earls, barons, freeholders, communities of the burghs and the entire community of the whole kingdom sealed by turns by the great seal of the kingdom and the seals of the aforesaid magnates and community in these words. The present indenture bears witness that on 15 July 1326, while the most serene prince the lord Robert by the grace of God illustrious king of Scots was holding his full parliament at Cambuskenneth with the earls, barons, burgesses and all the other freeholders of his kingdom assembled in the same place, it was proposed by the same lord king that the lands and rents which were accustomed of old to pertain to his crown had become so diminished by various gifts and transfers made because of the war that he did not have appropriate support for his position without intolerable charges and inconveniences to his people. Wherefore he asked of them urgently that because, both in his own person and in his property, he had sustained many adversities, in order to recover and resume the liberty of all, it should please them, out of the gratitude they owed him, to find a manner and way whereby he could be sustained in accordance with what is proper to his position, without any greater burden on his people ensuing. Which things all and singular the earls, barons, burgesses and freeholders, both within liberties and without, whether tenants of the lord king or whatsoever other lords within the king-

NUMBER VI

Lord Lile's Trial; referred to p. 180.

Parliament of King James III. holden at Edinburgh, 18th March 1481.

22 Martii quinto die parliamenti Domino Rege sedente in trono justiciae.

ASSISA

Comes ATHOLIAE   Dominus de STOBHALL
Comes de MORTON   Dominus de DRUMLANGRIG
Dominus GLAMMIS   Dominus MAXWELL
Dominus ERSKINE   WILLIELMUS BORTHWICK Miles
Dominus OLIPHANT   ALEXANDER Magister de Crawfurd
Dominus CATHKERT   SILVESTER RATRAY de Eodem
Dominus GRAY   ROBERTUS ABERCROMMY de Eodem, Miles
Dominus BORTHWICK   David MOUBRAY de Bernbougale, Miles

---

dom, with or without an intermediary, whatever their condition shall be, considering and acknowledging the aforegoing motives of the lord king to be true and, what is more, how many other benefits had accrued to them in his times through him, and his petition to be reasonable as well as just, having had common and diligent discussion upon the foregoing, unanimously, with joy and in a spirit of goodwill granted and gave to their abovesaid lord king, annually, at the terms of Martinmas [*11 November*] and Whitsun in proportion, for the entire time of the life of the said king, a tenth penny of all money from their fermes and rents, both from their lands, demesnes and wards and from whatsoever their other lands, within or outwith liberties, both within and outwith burghs, according to the old extent of lands and rents in the time of the lord Alexander [*III*] by the grace of God illustrious king of Scots of good memory who died most recently; [to be collected] faithfully by his ministers, making exceptions only for the destruction of war, in which case there shall be a decrease of the tenth penny granted before according to the size of the ferme which, by reason of the aforegoing, cannot be raised from the aforesaid lands and rents, as can be discovered by an inquest to be made faithfully by the sheriff of the place. With the proviso that all monies of this kind shall be converted entirely to the said lord king's use and utility without making any remission to anyone. And if he shall make a gift or remission of the monies of this kind before they are delivered and fully paid to the king's chamber, the present grant shall be void, and also be without strength of validity. And because certain magnates of the kingdom claim liberties of such a kind that the king's servants were not able to function within their lands, by which the payment to the lord king may perhaps be caused to be delayed, all and singular who claimed liberties of this sort gave an undertaking to the lord king that they

Accusatio super Roberto Domino Lile per rotulos ut sequitur.

Robert Lord LILE yhe ar dilatit to the King's heines that yhe have send lettres in Ingland to the tratour James of Dowglace, and to uthir Inglismen in tressonable maner; and also resavit lettres fra ye said tratour, and fra uthir Inglismen in tressonable manner and in furthering of ye Kings enemys of Ingland, and prejudice and skaith to our soverane Lord ye King, his realme and liegis. <470>

Quae assisa suprascripta in praesentia supremi domini nostri regis jurata, et de ipsius mandato super dictam accusationem cognoscere per eundum supremum dominum nostrum regem mandata, remota et reintrata deliberatum est per os Joannis Drummond de Stobhall, nomine et ex parte

---

would cause their share, and the tenants contingent on that, to be paid in full by their servants to the king's servants. That if they do not do so, the king's sheriffs, each in his sheriffdom, shall distrain the tenements of such liberties by royal authority for making payment in this way. Indeed the lord king calmly weighing up and paying close attention to the gratitude and good will of his people to him graciously granted that from the feast of Martinmas next to come, namely the first term for making payment, he will not impose any collects, not seize any prises or carriages, unless travelling around or across the kingdom in the custom of his predecessor, the abovesaid King Alexander, for which prises and carriages there shall be full payment on the nail, and that all the great supplies of the king with their carriages shall be entirely without prises, and that the king's servants shall pay in the hand without delay for all property in the collecting of such great supplies, according to the common market price of the country. But it was granted and agreed between the lord king and the community of his kingdom that the grant of the abovesaid tenth of money shall cease immediately on the death of this king, with the proviso that there shall be full payment for the terms past before the death of this lord king. And that neither on account of the aforesaid or any point of the aforesaid, after the end of a grant of this kind, shall there be a prejudice in any degree against the heirs of the said lord king or the community of his kingdom, but that all return and remain in the state they were in before the day of the present grant. In testimony of all of which the common seal of the kingdom is appended to one part of this indenture, remaining in the hands of the said earls, barons, burgesses and freeholders, while the seals of the earls, barons and other great freeholders, along with the common seals of the burghs of the kingdom, in their names and [the names of] the whole community, are appended to the other part remaining in the hands of the lord king. Given on the abovesaid day, year and place. And this transcript shall remain in the hands of the aforesaid magnates and communities and the successors, being sealed by the seal of the kingdom in evidence and for future memory. Given at Edinburgh in the lord king's parliament held in the same place on the second Sunday of Lent, with a continuation of following days, 1327." Translation taken from Record of the Parliaments of Scotland to 1707: http://www.rps.ac.uk/mss/ 1328/1.

dictae assisae et prolocutorio nomine ejusdem, dictum Robertum Dominum Lile quietum fore et immunem et innocentem accusationis et ca-
lumpniationis suprascript. Super quibus dictus Robertus dominus Lile petiit notam curiae parliamenti et testimonium sub magno sigillo ejusdem
domini nostri regis sibi dari super praemissis, quodquidem testimonium
idem dominus rex sibi concessit, darique mandavit eidem in forma suprascripta et consueta.[4]

NUMBER VII

Carta Confirmationis* Gilberti Menzeis;
referred to p. 211.

Jacobus, Dei gratia, rex Scotorum, omnibus probis hominibus totius terrae
suae, clericis et laicis, salutem: Sciatis nos, quandam literam per Robertum
de Keth militem, et Alexandrum de Ogilvy de Inverquhardy, vicecomites
nostros de Kincardin deputatos, sigillis eorum sigillatam, factam Gilberto
Menzeis burgensi burgi nostri de Aberdeen, in Curia capitali apud Bervy
tenta, anno et die infrascripta litera expressis, penes prosecutionem, dicti
Gilberti contra Joannem de Tulch de Eodem, et Walterum de Tulch filium
suum, per bre-<471>vem compulsionis capellae nostrae, per dictum Gil-
bertum impetratum de summa centum et sexaginta librarum usualis monetae regni nostri; et penes alienationem terrarum de Portarstone et de
Orcharfeldie infrascriptarum, cum pertinen. de mandato nostro, visam,
lectam, inspectam et diligenter examinatam, sanam, integram, non rasam,
non cancellatam, ac in aliqua sui suspectam, sed omni prorsus vitio et sus-

---

* Lib. 4. No. 49. 1450, July 22.

4. "The above-written assise having been sworn in the presence of our supreme lord
the king, and by his command, to examine the said accusation, [and] having by command
of our same supreme lord the king withdrawn and re-entered, it was delivered by the
mouth of John Drummond of Stobhall, in the name and on behalf of the said assise,
and forespeaker in its name, that Robert [*Lyle*], lord Lyle is acquitted and immune and
innocent of the above-written accusation and calumny. Whereupon the said Robert,
lord Lyle sought a note from the court of parliament, and the testimony of our same
lord the king's great seal, to be given to him on the aforesaid matters. This testimony
our same lord, the king, granted [and] ordered to be given to him in the above-written
and customary form."

picione carentem ad plenum intellexisse, sub hac forma:[5] Till all and sundrie thir present letteris sall heer or see, Robert master of Keth knight, and Alexander of Ogilvy of Inverquhardy sherive deputes of Kincardin, greiting, in God ay lestand, till zour universitie we mak knawin, That in ye shirriff court be us haldin at Inverbervy ye 28 day of the month of May, the zeir of our Lord 1442 zeiris, Gilbert Menzeis burges of Aberdeen followit Johne of Tulch of that Ilk, and Wat of Tulch his son, be the Kings brevis of compulsione upon a some of viii score of punds of the usuale mony of Scotlande, the quhilk some the foirsaide Johne and Wat war awande to the foirsaide Gilbert conjunctly bundyn be thair obligationes, and the quhilk some, after lauchfull processe maide, ye foirsaid Gilbert optenit and wan lauchfulli befoir us in jugement, for the payment of the ye quhilks to the said Gilbert to be maide, we, of autority of our office, and at command of our liege Kings precepts thairupone till us directit, findand no guidis of the foirsaide Johne nor Wat within our shirriffdome to mak the payment foirsaide, gert our mairs set a strop upon the landis of ye Porterstoun and of the Orchardfeldie, and gert present to the four heid courts next thairaftir halden at Kincardine erd and stane, and proferit that landis to sell for the payment of the foirsaide some; and at the last curt, quhen zire and day was passit, and the procis lauchfullie provit in the curt, the <472> foirsaide Wat of Tulch maide instance, to gar that actione be deleyit, in the plyght it then was to the next heide curt, thair to be haldin after zule; at the quhilk heide curt haldin at Kincardine the 13 day of the month of Januar, the zire of our Lord 1443, baith perties appeirit in jugement, and thair the foirsaide Gilbert

5. "James king of the Scots, by the grace of God, to all prudent men of his whole land, clerics and laymen, greeting. Let it be known to you: a certain letter by Sir Robert Keith and Alexander Ogilvy of Inverquhardy, our sheriff-deputes of Kincardine, sealed with their seals, written for Gilbert Menzies, burgess of our burgh of Aberdeen, at the head court of Inverbervy held on the year and day noted in the underwritten letter, relating to the prosecution by the said Gilbert against John Tulch of the Ilk and Walter Tulch his son under a brieve of compulsion from our chancery, that he should be obtain the sum of one hundred and sixty pounds of the usual money of our realm [*i.e.* £*160 scots*]; and relating to the alienation, by our order, of the underwritten lands of Porterstone and Orchardfield with their pertinents; [the letter] having been seen, read, inspected and diligently examined is sound, complete, not defaced or cancelled or in any other way suspect, but rather is free from any defect which would obscure full understanding of it; [is] in this form."

askit us fullfilling of law and payment to be maide him, and thairupon
present us our liege Kings precepts of commandment, to the quhilks we,
riply avisit with men of law, Gert chese upe an assise of the barony of the
Merns, the grete ath sworne, gerte tham gang out of curt to pryse to
the foirsaide Gilbert als meikle land as might content him lauchfully of the
some foirsaide; the quhilk assise well avysit income and deliverit, that the
foirsaide Gilbert sulde have, as his awn propir landis, the landis of Porterstone and the landis of Orcharfelde, with yair pertinents be tham prisit
and extendit till aucht pundis worth of land for hale payment of the aucht
score pundis foirsaide; and we, of autority of our office, deliverit to the
foirsaide Gilbert in playne curt, the landis foirsaide, to brouke and to joyse
as his awn propir landis; and for the mair sykernes we gert our mair Tome
Galmock gang with the foirsaide Gilbert to the foirsaide landis and gif him
heritable state and possessione: The quhilk possessione was gevin in presence of Hew Aberuthno of that Ilk, Johne Bissit of Kinneffe, Will. of
Strathachin, Johne of Pitcarne, Ranald Chene, and mony uthers, and this
till all that it effeiris or may effeir in tyme to cum we make knawyne be thir
present letteris, to the quhilks we have put to our sellis, the zire, day, and
place foirsaide. Quamquidem literam ac omnia et singula in eadem con-
tenta in omnibus suis punctis et articulis conditionibus et modis ac cir-
cumstantiis suis quibuscunque forma pariter et effectu in omnibus et per
omnia <473> approbamus, ratificamus, et pro nobis heredibus et successoribus nostris, ut premissum est, pro perpetuo confirmamus, salvis nobis
haeredibus et successoribus nostris, wardis, releviis, maritagiis, juribus et
servitiis de dictis terris ante presentem confirmationem nobis debitis et con-
suetis. In cujus rei testimonium presenti cartae nostrae confirmationis magnum sigillum nostrum apponi precipimus: testibus reverendis in Christo
patribus Willielmo et Johanne Glasguen. et Dunkelden. aecclesiarum epis-
copis, Willielmo domino Crichton nostro cancellario et consanguineo,
predilecto carissimo consanguineo nostro Willielmo comite de Duglas et
de Anandale, domino Galvidiae, venerabili in Christo patre Andrea abbate
de Melros nostro confessore et thesaurario, dilectis consanguiniis nostris
Patricio domino Glamis magistro hospitii nostri, Patricio domino de Graham, Georgeo de Chrichton de Carnis admiralo regni nostri, David Murray
de Tulibardyn, militibus, magistris Joanne Arons archideaconen. Glasguen.

et Georgeo de Schoriswod rectore deculture clerico nostro. Apud Striviline, vicesimo secundo die mensis Julii, anno Domini Mcccc quinquagesimo, et regni nostri decimo quarto.[6] <474>

NUMBER VIII

Act of Warding; referred to p. 217.

At   the   day of One thousand seven hundred and seventy one.

The which day   sitting in judgement, compeared and made faith; That he had searched and sought for the goods and gear of the defender   in order to have poinded and apprised the same, at the instance of the pursuer   for payment of the sums resting, decerned, and charged for; but could get none poindable to the value thereof: Therefore the Bailies ordain their officers to pass, search, seek, take, and apprehend, the person of the said   and put him in sure ward, firmance, and captivity, within the tolbooth of this city, therein to remain, upon his own proper charges and expences, ay and while he make payment of the sums resting and charged for, conform to the before-written decreet and execution, in all points. Extracted.

6. "Which letter, and all and sundry contained within it, in all its points, articles and conditions, customs and circumstances whatsoever, in all things, its form and effect, we approve, ratify and for us and our heirs and successors, as in the foregoing, we confirm in perpetuity, saving to us and our heirs and successors the wards, reliefs, marriages, rights and services of the said lands as they were due and owed to us before the present confirmation. In testimony of which we have ordered our great seal to be affixed to this present charter of confirmation. Witnesses: the reverend fathers in Christ William and John, bishops of Glasgow and Dunkeld; William, lord Crichton, our chancellor and kinsman; our wellbeloved and dear kinsman William, earl of Dougals and Annandale, Lord of Galloway; the venerable father in Christ, Andrew, abbot of Melrose, our confessor and treasurer; our beloved kinsman, Patrick, lord of Glamis, master of our hospice; Patrick lord Graham; George Crichton of Carnis, the admiral of our realm and David Murray of Tullibardine, knights; Master John Arons, archdeacon of Glasgow; and George of Schoriswood, rector of Cultre, our clerk. At Stirling, the twenty-second day of the month of July, in the year of our Lord, one thousand five hundred and fifty, and the fourteenth year of our reign."

NUMBER IX

Letters of Four Forms, issued on the debtor's consent; referred to p. 217.

James, by the grace of God, King of Scottis, to oure lovittis Robert How-ieson messenger, —— messengeris, our sherriffis in that part conjunctlie and <475> severallie speciallie constitute, greiting: FORASMEIKLEAS it is humbly meint and shawin to us, be oure lovitt Henrie Leirmonth, serviter for the tyme to umquhill mester David Borthuick of Bowhill, oure ad-vocate for the tyme: THAT QUHAIR thair is ane contract and appointment maid betwix Johnne Forrest Provest of oure burgh of Linlitgow, and He-len Cornwall his spouss as principalis, and Jerom Henderson cautioner for thaim on the ane parts, and the said Henry on the other pairt, of the dait att oure said burgh of Linlitgow the 16th day of November, in the zeir of God 1576 zeirs; be the quhilk contract the said Johnne and his said spouss salde and analeit heretablie ane annualrent of twelve punds monie of our realm zeirly, to be uplifted at Whit. and Mart. be equal portions, furth of all and haill thair four acres of land, callet the Lonedykes, lyand within the territorie and oure Sherrifdome of Linlitgow, boundet as is containit in the said contract, and to warrant the saim to the complainer frae all wardis, relieves, nonentries, and otheris inconvenientis whatever, at length specified and containit thairintill: LIKEAS they and thair cau-tioner forsaid ar bund and obliest conjunctlie and severallie for them and thair aires, to mak thankfull payment zeirly to the said Henry of the said annualrent, frae the dait of his infeftment unto the lawfull redemtion of the samen, and to fulfill divers and sundrie utheris headis, pointis, parts, and clausis, specified and containit in the said contract, to the said Henry, for thair pairt, as the samen at more length proportis; quhilk contract is actit and registrat in the Lordis buiks of our counceil and session, and decernit to halff the strenth of thair act and decreet, with letteris and executorials of horning or poinding to pass and bee direct thairupon, at the said Henries will and pleiser, as the saids Lordis decreet interponit there-<476>to, of the dait the tenth day of June 1581 zeirs, at lenth pro-portis: NOTTHELESS the said Johnne Forrest, his spouss and cautioner forsaid, will not observe keep and fulfill the forsaid contract and appointment to the said Henrie, in all and sundrie pointis and clausis thereof, as specially to mak paiment to him of the said annualrent of twelve punds monie forsaid, restand awand to the said complainer of all zeirs and terms bygane, frae the daite of the said contract, and syklike zeirly and termly in time coming, during the nonredemtion thairof, the termis of paiment being bypast conforme thairto, without they be compellit.* OURE WILL IS HEIRFOR, and we charge you strictly, and commandis, that incontinent thir oure Letters seen, ye pass, and, in our name and authority, command and charge the said Johnne Forrest, Helen Cornwall his said spouss, and the said Jerom Henderson thair cautioner forsaid, conjunctly and severally, to observe keip and fulfill the forsaid contract and appointment to the said Henry Leirmonth, in all and sundrie pointis partis and clausis thereof, and specially to mak payment to him of the said annualrent of twelve punds monie forsaid, restand awand to him, of all zeirs and termis bygane, and syklyke zeirly and termlie in tyme coming, during the nonredemtion of the samen, conform to the said contract, and the saids Lordis decreit forsaid interponit thairto as said is, within thrie days nixt after they be chargit be you thairto, under all highest paine and chairge that after may follow. THE SAIDS thrie days being bypast, and the saids persons disobeyand,† That ye chairge them zit as of before, to observe, keip, and fulfill the forsaid contract and appointment to the said Henry, in all and sundrie pointis, partis and clausis thairof, and speciallie to mak paiment to <477> him of the said annualrent of twelve punds money forsaid, restand awand, of all zeirs and termis bygane, and syklyke zeirly and termlie in tyme comeing, during the nonredemtion thairof, conform to the said contract, and decreit forsaid interponit thairto as said is, within other 3 dais next after they be chargit be you thairto, under the paine of wairding thair personis. THE QUHILKS thrie days being bypast, and the forsaids personis disobeyand,‡ That ze chairge the disobeyeris zit as of before, to observe keip and fulfill the said contract and appointment to the said Henrie, in all and sundrie pointis pairtis and clausis thairof, and speciallie to

* First Form.
† Second Form.
‡ Third Form.

mak payment to him of the said annualrent of twelve punds money foresaid, restand awand, of all zeirs and termis bygane, and syklyke zeirlie and
termlie in tyme coming during the nonredemption thairof, conform to
the said contract and decreit forsaid interponit thairto as said is, within
other thrie dais next after they and ilk ane of them be chargit be zou
thairto; or else that they within the samin thrie dais, pass and enter thair
personis in waird within oure castell of Dumbartane, thairin to remain
upon their awin expencess ay and quhill they have fulfillit the comande
of thir our letteris, and be freid be us thairfrae, under the pain of rebellion
and putting of thaim to our horn; and that they cum to oure secretar or
his deputtis, keipars of oure signet, and receive our other letteris for thair
resaite in waird within oure said castell. THE QUHILKS thrie dais being
bypast, and the saids personis or ony of thaim disobeyand,* That ze
chairge the disobeyeris zit as of before, to observe, keip, and fulfill the
said contract and appointment to the said complainer, in all and sundrie
pointis partis and clausis thairof; and speciallie to make payment to him
of the said annualrent <478> of twelve punds money forsaid, restand
awand to him, of all zeir and termis bygane; and siklike zeirly and termlie
in tyme coming, during the nonredemtion thairof, conform to the said
contract and decreit forsaid interponit thairto, as said is, within other
three dais next after they be chargit be zou thairto; or else that they, within
the samen three dais, pass and enter thair personis in waird, within our
said castell of Dumbartane, thairin to remaine upon thair awn expencess,
ay and quhill they have fulfillit the command of thir our letteris, and be
freid be us thairfre, under the said paine of rebellion and putting of them
to our horne; and that they cum to our said secretar, or his deputtis, keipars
of oure said signete, and resaive oure said other letteris for thair resaite in
waird within oure said castell. THE QUHILK last three dais of all being
bypast, and the saids personis or ony of thaim disobeyand, and not ful-
filland the command of thir oure letteris, nor zit enterand thair saids personis in wairde within oure said castell as said is,† That ze, incontinent
thairafter, denunce the disobeyeris our rebellis, and put thame to oure

* Fourth Form.
† Warrant to denounce.

horne; and escheat and inbring all thair movable guidis to oure use for thair contemption; and immediately after zour said denunciation, that ze mak intimation to the Schyrriff of oure Schyre whair our saids rebellis is, and syklyke to our thesaury and his clerkis, conform to oure act of parliament made thairanent. According to justice, as ze will answer to us thairupon; the quhilk to do, wee comitt to you conjunctly and severally our full power be thir our letters, delivering thaim be zou duely execute and indorsit againe to the bearer. Given under our signet att Edinburgh, the 17th day of *Junii,* and of our reign the 19th zeir 1586.

Ex deliberatione Dominorum concilii. <479>

The Executions written on the back thus:

* Upon the 21 day of the month of Aprile, in the zeir of God 1591 zeirs, I Robert Howison messenger, past, att command of thir our soveraign Lordis letteris within-written, to the dwelling-house of Helen Cornwall, within the burgh of Linlitgow, relict of umquhill Johnne Forrest of Magdalane personallie, and syklike, to the dwelling-house of Jerom Henderson as cautioner and sourtie for the said John Forrest and Helen Cornwall his relict, and I, conform to the tenor of the first charge containit in thir letteris within written, in our soveraign Lordis name and authoritie, commandit and chargit the forsaid Helen Cornwall and Jerom Henderson the cautioner personally, conjunctly and severally, to observe, keep and fulfill the contract and appointment aforspecifyed, to Henry Leirmonth complainer, in all pointis partis and clausis containit thairintill, and specially to mak payment to him of the annualrent of xii *libs* money forsaid, restand awand to him, of all zeirs and termis bygane, conform to the tenor of the letteris, and sylyke zeirly in time coming during the nonredemtion of the landis containit in the forsaid contract, and the Lordes decreit interponit thairto, within thrie days nixt after this my charge, under the heighest paine and chairge that after might follow; and this I did conform to the tenor of the first charge in all points, before these witnesses, &c. Sign'd by the messenger only, and sealed. <480>

---

* Execution of First Form.

* Upon the 28 day of the month of Aprile, I Robert Howison messenger, zit as of before, past att command of thir oure soveraign Lordis letteris afforspecifyed, and I personally apprehended Helen Cornwall relict of umquhill John Forrest and Jerom Henderson the cautioner, and I, conforme to the tenor of the second chairge containit thairintill, commandit and chargit thaim, and ilk ane of thaim, in all pointis, and this within other thrie dais nixt after this my chairge, under the paine of wairding of thair personnis: This I did before these witnesses, &c. And for verification of this my second chairge I have subscribit the samin, and affixit my signet thairto. Signed and sealed as before.

† Upon the 3d day of the month of May, and yeir of God aforwritten, I Robert Howison messenger, zit as of before, past to the personal presence of Helen Cornwall relict of umquhile John Forrest, and syklyke to the personal presence of Jerom Henderson, and I, conforme to the tenor of the third charge containit in the former letteris, commandit and chargit them, in our soveraign Lordis name, to observe the samin within other thrie dais, or else that thay within the said thrie dais pass and enter thair personis in waird within the castell of Dumbartane, thair to remain upon thair own expencess ay and quhile they have fulfillit the command of thir letteris, and be freed orderlie thairfrae, under the paine of rebellion and putting of thaim to the horne, and that they cum to the secretar or his deputtis, keapars of the signette, and resaive other letteris for thair resaite and waird within the said castle: And this I did conform to the tenor of the third chairge containit thairintill in all pointis. And this I did before thaise witnesses, &c. Signed by the messenger only and sealed. <481>

‡ Upon the 8th day of the month of May, and zeir of God foresaid, I Robert Howison messenger, zet as of before, past to the personal presence of Helen Cornwall relict of umquhill John Forrest, and syklyke to the personal presence of Jerom Henderson the cautioner, and I, conform to the tenor of the fourth chairge containit in the former letteris, I commandit and chargit them, in oure soveraign Lordis name and authoritie, to observe the samen within letteris thrie dais next after my chairge, or else that they

* Of Second.
† Of Third.
‡ Of Fourth.

within the said thrie days pass and enter thair personnis in waird within the castell of Dumbartane, thair to remain upon their ain expences ay and while they hae fulfillit the command of thir letteris, and freed orderlie thairfrae, under the pain of rebellion and putting of them to the horne, and that they cum to the secretar, keipar of the signet, and resaive other letteris for their resaite and ward within the said castell: And this I did conform to the tenor of the fourth chairge containit thairintill in all pointis. This I did before thir witnesses, &c. Sign'd, &c. as before.

* Upon the 21 day of the month of May, and zeir of God foresaid, I Robert Howison messenger, personally apprehended Helen Cornwall foresaid and Jerom Henderson, and I maide intimation to ilk ane of thaim, that I would denounce them oure soveraign Lordis rebellis, and put them to his heighness horn. This I did before thir witnesses, &c. Sign'd by the messenger, but not sealed.

† Upon the 22 day of the month of May and zeir of God foresaid, I Robert Howison messenger, past to the mercate-corse of the burgh of Linlitgow, and thair, be <482> open proclamation be thrie blasts of ane horne, as use is, I denounced, and put to oure soveraign Lordis heighness horne, Helen Cornwall relict of umquhill John Forrest, and Jerom Henderson the cautioner, and this conform to the tenor of thir letteris in all partis: This I did before thir witnesses, &c. And for the verification of this and my former executions I haive subscribit thir presents with my hand, and affixit my signet thairto, Sign'd, &c.

Apud Linlitgow, die sexto
mensis Junii *1591*, regrat. per

Notes of Letters of Four Forms,

‡ James, &c. Forasmeikleas (here is narrated a decreit obtain'd before the commissars of Edinburgh, att the instance of Robert White, against Sir James Crichton, decerning him to pay L. 162 Scots of principal, and L. 4 of expences; and that Robert White had thereupon raised the commissar's precept, and caused chairge the said Sir James Crichton to pay to him the

---

* Intimation.
† Denunciation.
‡ Registered 19th Sept. 1610.

saids sums, within 15 days, under the pain therein contain'd, as the said precept, shawin to the Lords, &c. testified: In and to which decreet precept and sums Robert Scott, &c. has right by assignation, &c. notwithstanding whereof the said Sir James Crichton has noways fulfillit, nor will fulfill to the said complainer as assigney forsaid, the forsaid decreet and precept raised thereupon, without he be furder compellit.) Our will is, &c. command and chairge the said Sir James Crichton to content and pay to the said complainer, the sums of money above writ-<483>ten, after the form and tenor of the said decreet and precept in all points, within 3 days next after the charge, under all highest pain, &c. which 3 days being past, to charge him within other 3 days. And so on as in common letters of 4 forms.

There is another registred 12th September, at the instance of James Wardlaw, against James Earle of Murray, proceeding upon a decreet before the Lords of councill and session, for 4000 merks, dated 2d March 1610, which decreet the said Earle will not obtemper and fulfill. Our will, &c. charge him within three days, &c. as in common letters of four forms. Given under our signette, penult day of *Maii, &c.* 1610.

Ex deliberatione Dominorum concilii.

This it seems has past upon a bill, although proceeding upon a decreet of the Lords. <484>

NUMBER X

Carta Ricardi Kine;* referred to p. 233.

Jacobus, &c. Quia direximus literas nostras Vicecomiti nostro de Selkrig, ad investigandum et perquirendum terras *quondam* Patricii Wallance, ubicunque infra bondas officii, et appretiari faciendum easdem in quantum se extendunt, pro relevio dilecti Ricardi Kine, nostri coronatoris Vicecomitatus de Selkrig, de summa viginti librarum, in qua adjudicatus erat pro dicto Patricio secundum tenorem acti adjornalis nostri, prout in eisdem literis nostris sub signeto nostro desuper decretis plenius continetur. Pro

* Lib. 16. No. 77. 1508. 29th January.

quarum executione Joannes Murray de Fallahill, Vicecomes noster deputatus de Selkrig, accedens invenit unam terram husbandiam nuncupatam Burges Walleys in burgo nostro de Selkrig, eidem *quondam* Patricio in haereditate spectantem. Et ibidem, apud capitale messuagium dictae terrae husbandiae, dictus noster Vicecomes deputatus *haeredes dicti quondam* Patricii, et ceteros omnes ad praefatam terram interesse habentes, legitime premonuit, vicesimo die mensis Septembris 1508, ad comparendos coram ipso vicecomite, vel deputatis suis, super solum dictae terrae, tertio die mensis Octobris anno praescripto, au audiendum prefatam terram husbandiam appretiari, pro relevio dicti Ricardi et terrarum suarum, quae pro dicta summa L. 20, appretiatae fuerunt. Quo tertio die Octobris dictus noster vicecomes deputatus comparuit super solum dictae terrae husbandiae, et ad capitale messuagium, ejusdem, curiam Vicecomitatus nostri de Selkrig affirmari fecit, et in eadem, *haeredi-*<485>*bus dicti Patricii* et caeteris omnibus ad prefatas terras interesse habentibus, ad audiendum eandem terram ut praemittitur appretiari, legitime vocatis, et non comparentibus, dictus noster vicecomes, per tres decem condignas personas ad hoc electas, pro predicta summa L. 20, eo quod dicta terra husbandia ad viginti solidos terrarum se extendit, legitime appretiari fecit. Qua quidem terra sic ut praemittitur appretiata, dictus vicecomes eandem *haeredibus dicti quondam Patricii,* seu cuicunque ipsam pro predicta summa emere volenti, publice vendendam obtulit. Et quia nullam personam dictam terram pro praefata pecunia emere volentem invenit, idem noster vicecomes, virtute sui officii, praedictam terram husbandiam assignavit dicto Ricardo, in plenariam contentationem et solutionem dictae summae viginti librarum, pro ipsius relevio de eadam, secundum tenorem acti nostri parliamenti. Volumus et ordinamus quod haeredes dicti quondam Patricii habeant regressum per solutionem infra septennium.[7]

7. "James, etc. Know you that we have directed our letters to our Sheriff of Selkirk, to investigate and enquire about the lands of the late Patrick Wallance [Wallace ?], wherever they lie within the boundaries of his authority, and to make an evaluation of their extent, for the relief of our beloved Richard Kine, our coroner of the Sheriffdom of Selkirk in the sum of twenty pounds of which he was cautioner for the said Patrick, according to the tenor of our act of adjournment, as is more fully contained in our letters of decreet previously given under our signet; For the execution of which John Murray

NUMBER XI

Charter of Apprising;* referred to p. 236.

Maria, &c. omnibus, &c. sciatis quia literas nostras, per dilectum clericum consiliarumque nostrum magistrum Henricum Lauder, nostrum advocatum, impetratas, dilectis nostris Willielmo Champnay nuncio vicecomiti nostro in hac parte et aliis direximus, mentionem in se proportantes, quod ipse noster advocatus de-<486>cretum coram concilii nostri dominis contra et adversus Matheum Comitem de Levinax nuper obtinuit, nostras literas super ipso decernentes ad compellendum, namandum, et destringendum ipsius terras et bona pro summa L. 10,000, monetae regni nostri, secundum formam suae obligationis in libris concilii nostri registrat. prout hujusmodi decretum latius proportat. Et quia dictus comes introitum ad terras suas et hereditates tempore promulgationis dicti decreti minime obtinuit, sed ad frustrandam executionem ejusdem ad easdem intrare noluit, idem noster

---

of Fallahill, our Sheriff-depute of Selkirk, has discovered a husbandland called Burges Wallays in our burgh of Selkirk, which pertained hereditarily to the late Patrick. And there, at the chief dwelling-house of the said husbandland, our said Sheriff-depute, on the twentieth day of September 1508, lawfully warned the heirs of the said late Patrick and all others having an interest in the foresaid land, to compear before the said sheriff or his deputy on the ground of the said land, on the third day of the month of October in the foresaid year, to hear the valuation of the foresaid husbandlands, for the relief of the said Richard and his lands, which were valued for the said sum of £20. On the third day of October our said sheriff-depute compeared on the ground of the said husbandland, and at its chief dwelling-house, making affirmation of our Sheriff court of Selkirk; and there the heirs of the said Patrick and all others having interest in the foresaid lands, to hear that land, as preceding, being valued, having been lawfully summoned, and not compearing, our aforesaid sherfiff made sure that the land was apprised lawfully by the 13 worthy persons elected for the task relating to the sum of £20, since the said land extended over 20 solidi of the lands. The lands having been valued, as aforesaid, the said sheriff publicly offered it for sale to the heirs of the said late Patrick, or to anyone willing to pay the said sum for it. And since he found no person offering to buy the said land for the foresaid sum therefore our sheriff, by virtue of his office, assigned the foresaid husbandland to the said Richard, in full satisfaction and payment of the said sum of twenty pounds, for his relief of the same, according to the tenor of our act of parliament. We determine and ordain that the heirs of the said late Patrick have regress by payment within seven years."

* Thirty-first Book of Charters, No. 294.

advocatus, per supplicationem nostri concilii dominis porrectam, alias nostras literas impetravit, virtute quarum dictum comitem precepit, quatenus ad predictas suas terras et hereditates intra viginti et unam dies intraret, ad effectum, ut hujusmodi decretum debite executioni demandaretur, eidem certificantes, quod si in id defecerit, lapsis dictis viginti et una diebus, quod praedictae suae terrae et hereditates, pro solutione dictae summae, eodem modo sicut ad easdem introitum habuisset, nobis appretiarentur, et appretiatio earundem ita legitima foret, ac si dictus comes introitum ad easdem legitime habuisset, prout prefatae aliae literae nostrae in se latius proportant. Quibus idem comes obtemperare minime voluit, prout in hujusmodi nostris literis, et in earundem executione, plenius continetur. QUAPROPTER dicti comitis terrae et hereditates pro dicta summa appretiari debebunt, veluti in eisdem infeodatus hereditarie fuisset, et terrae ejusdem quas dictus advocatus appretiari causaret, jacentes infra vicecomitatum nostrum de Renfrew, et ob magnas curas nobis pro publica concernentis sibi commissas in istis partibus tractandas, pro dictis terris appretiandis, ad vicecomitem nostrum de Renfrew antedictum accedere minime poterat, ideo alias literas nostras, dicto Willielmo et aliis suis collegis vicecomitibus nostris in hac <487> parte, direximus ad denunciandas terras et hereditates dicti Matthei comitis, pro dicta summa nobis appretiari; et ad hunc effectum curias infra praetorium nostrum de Edinburg. affigere et tenere, et ibidem supra appretiatione earundem procedere, ac si dictus comes legitimum introitum habuisset secundum tenorem aliarum nostrarum literarum prius desuper directis, et ad praemoniendum eundem, per publicam proclamationem apud cruces forales burgorum nostrorum de Renfrew et de Edinburgo respective, super 60 dierum premonitione, ad videndum et audiendum hujusmodi appretiationem legitime fieri et deduci, eo quod ipse comes nunc extra regnum nostrum extat, et penes loco desuper dispensando, et predictum pretorium nostrum de Edinburgo et crucem foralem ejusdem, ita legitima pro hujusmodi appretiationis deductione sint, quam pretorium et crux foralis burgi nostri de Renfrew ubi predictae terrae jacent, pro causis suprascriptis admittendo, prout in dictis nostris literis memorato Willielmo et suis collegis desuper directis latius continetur. Virtute quarum—and so the charter goes on to mention the denunciation of the lands to be apprised, and the apprising of the same, 13th May 1544, and the allowance of the apprising, and the giving the land to the Master of Semple, &c. dated 24th May 1547.[8]

F I N I S

8. "Mary, etc., To all . . . etc. Let it be known that we have composed these letters of ours (which have been made possible by the efforts of our beloved clerk and counsellor Master Henry Lauder our advocate) for our beloved messenger William Champnay (our sheriff in this area), and others, to give notice to them that since our said advocate has lately obtained a judgement before our Lords of Council against and in opposition to Matthew earl of Lennox, this letter conveys the judgement concerning him that his lands and goods be compelled, poinded and distrained for the sum of £10,000 Scots ['money of our realm'] according to the form of his obligation registered in the books of our council, as is more fully contained within the said judgement. And since the said earl did not obtain entry to his lands and heritage at the time of the promulgation of the said judgement, but rather determined not to enter to them in order to frustrate its execution, our said advocate, by a further supplication to our Lords of Council, secured further letters from us, in virtue of which he ordered that the said earl should make entry to the said lands and heritage within twenty-one days, for the effect as demanded by the due execution of the said decreet, certifying that if he had failed to do so within the space of twenty-one days that his foresaid lands and heritage would be apprised by us for payment of the aforesaid sum, in the same manner as if he had made entry; and the resultant appropriation would be as legal as if he had entered lawfully—as the aforesaid previous letters explained in greater detail. And the earl did not wish to comply with them in the slightest, as is fully contained in our letters and in the execution of them. On account of which the lands and heritage of the said earl ought to be apprised for the said sum, as if he had been hereditarily infeft, and even his lands which the aforementioned advocate would cause to be apprised, which lie within the Sherifdom of Renfrew, and which have been entrusted to him to administer in those areas due to a great love for me on the public's behalf; since the aforementioned lands must be apprised, he [the earl?] had not been able to come near our aforementioned sheriff of Renfrew. Therefore, we have composed another letter to William and other deputies in this area to declare that the lands and inheritance of the said earl Matthew have been apprised to us for the said sum; and in order to effect this, to set and hold courts in our tolbooth in Edinburgh, and there to proceed on their apprising, as if the said earl had made legal entry according to the rubric previously set out in the other letters above; and, for his warning thereof, by public proclamation at the market crosses of our towns of Renfrew and Edinburgh respectively, with 60 days' warning (because the earl presently lives outside our kingdom), to see and hear that this apprising has been legitimately made and deduced, at the place approved above and at our foresaid tolbooth in Edinburgh and its market cross, since they are as legitimate places for the deliberations on the apprising as the *praetorium* and forum of our town of Renfrew where the aforementioned land lies, and to deliberate over the abovewritten cases, as is contained more fully in our letters sent, as above, to the said William and his colleagues. In virtue of which . . ."

GLOSSARY
OF LEGAL TERMINOLOGY

Sources Used

Bell's Dictionary   George Watson (ed.). *Bell's Dictionary and the Digest of the Law of Scotland.* 7th ed. Edinburgh: Bell & Bradfute, 1890.

Bell's Principles   George Joseph Bell. *Principles of the Law of Scotland.* 4th ed. Edinburgh: Edinburgh Legal Education Trust, 2010.

Berger, *Encyclopedic Dictionary*   Adolf Berger. *Encyclopedic Dictionary of Roman Law.* 1953; repr. Clark, N.J.: Lawbook Exchange, 2004.

Black's   Bryan A. Garner. *Black's Law Dictionary.* 7th ed. St. Paul, Minn.: West Group, 1999.

Buckland   W. W. Buckland. *A Text-Book of Roman Law from Augustus to Justinian.* 3rd ed. Ed. Peter Stein. Cambridge: Cambridge University Press, 1963.

Dictionary and Digest   William Bell. *A Dictionary and Digest of the Law of Scotland, with Short Explanations of the Most Ordinary English Law Terms.* Edinburgh: Bell & Bradfute, 1838.

Erskine   John Erskine. *An Institute of the Law of Scotland in Four Books. In the Order of Sir George Mackenzie's Institutions of That Law.* 3rd ed. Edinburgh: Bell & Bradfute, 1793.

Glossary   *Glossary: Scottish and European Legal Terms and Latin Phrases.* Ed. Scott Styles and Niall R. Whitty. Edinburgh: LexisNexis, 2003.

Glossary of Legal Terms	Stephen R. O'Rourke. *Glossary of Legal Terms*. 4th ed. Edinburgh: W. Green, 2004.
Halkerston	Peter Halkerston. *A Translation and Explanation of the Principal Technical Terms and Phrases Used in Mr. Erskine's Institute of the Law of Scotland*. 2nd ed. Edinburgh, 1829.
Jacob	Giles Jacob. *A New Law-Dictionary*. London, 1729.
Latin Maxims	John Traynor. *Latin Maxims and Phrases Collected from the Institutional Writers on the Law of Scotland and Other Sources with Translations and Illustrations*. 4th ed. Edinburgh: William Green & Sons, 1894.
Latin-English Dictionary	John T. White. *A Concise Latin-English Dictionary*. 4th ed. London: Longmans, Green, and Co., 1880.
Law Lexicon	Joseph E. Morris (ed.). *The Pocket Law Lexicon Explaining Technical Words, Phrases and Maxims of the English, Scotch, and Roman Law*. 4th ed. London: Stevens & Sons, 1905.
OED	*Oxford English Dictionary*. (www.oed.com)
Older Scottish Tongue	William A. Craigie. *A Dictionary of the Older Scottish Tongue for from the Twelfth Century to the End of the Seventeenth*. Chicago: University of Chicago Press, n. d.
Skene	John Skene. *De verborum significatione: the exposition of the termes and difficill wordes, conteined in the foure buiks of Regiam Maiestatem, and uthers, in the acts of Parliament, infeftments, and used in practicque of this realme, and with divers rules, and common places, or principals of the lawes*. London, 1641.
Stair	James Dalrymple, Viscount Stair. *The Institutions of the Law of Scotland, Deduced from Its Originals, and Collated with the Civil, Canon and Feudal Laws, and with the Customs of Neighbouring Nations*. 2nd ed. Edinburgh, 1693.

Glossary of Terms

ab intestato	". . . from a person dying intestate. The property of any one dying without disposing of it by a valid deed, is distributed, according to certain fixed legal rules; and property so acquired is said to be derived *ab intestato*." (*Latin Maxims*, p. 6)
Act of Sederunt	". . . ordinances made by the court of session, for regulating the forms of proceeding to be observed in all actions or matters which may be brought before them . . . ; the court of session have a delegated power from the parliament, to make such statutes as they think proper for the ordering of process and the expediting of justice, 1540, c. 93." (Erskine, p. 14)
actiones in factum (actio in factum)	"An action granted by the praetor when no standard action was available." (*Black's*, p. 27)
actiones in rem scriptae	"Actions in *rem* had the characteristic that the *intention* alleged a right in the plantiff and did not mention the defendant: it was not a question of a person but of a *res*. This came to be regarded as a mark of an *action in rem* so that we get actions called '*actiones in personam in rem scriptae*'." (Buckland, p. 677)
actio metus	An action "for relieving one who had been forced by threat to go through some legal transaction . . ." (Buckland, p. 593)
actio noxalis	"An action for damage done by irrational animals." (*Law Lexicon*, p. 246)
actor sequitur forum rei	"A Roman law maxim, importing that the pursuer of an action must follow the forum of the defender; i.e. if the defender is not amenable to the courts of Scotland, the pursuer must raise his action against him in the country to the laws of which he is subject." (*Bell's Dictionary*, p. 15)

ad factum praestandum "An obligation or an order of court to perform an act other than the payment of money." (*Glossary of Legal Terms,* p. 3)

ad vindictam publicam "For vindicating the public interest." (Halkerston, p. 251)

aditio hereditatis "The entering upon, or taking up, a succession, whether in moveables or heritage." (*Latin Maxims,* p. 34)

Admiralty, High Court of [or, Admiral Court] "The Admiral's jurisdiction . . . is both civil and criminal. The first extends to all maritime causes; and so comprehends questions of charter-parties, freights, salvages, wrecks, bottomries, policies of insurance; and, in general all contracts concerning the lading or unlading of ships, or any other matter to be performed within the verge of the Admiral's jurisdiction; and all actions for the delivery of goods sent on shipboard, or for recovering their value, or where the subject of the sui consists of goods transported by sea from one port to another. . . . As to the criminal jurisdiction, the High Admiral . . . hath exclusive cognisance of the crimes of piracy, mutiny on shipboard, and others which may with propriety be called *maritime causes.*" (Erskine, pp. 51–53)

advocation ". . . an action craving a Cause to be Removed from another Judicature unto the Lords, to be discust by them, or to be remitted to another competent and unsuspected Judge." (Stair, *Institutions,* p. 652)

aliment "Maintenance, food, and clothing. By the law of Scotland, persons who, by reason of nonage, or from other causes, are unable to support themselves, are entitled, in certain circumstances, and in respect of certain relationships, judicially to enforce a claim for aliment." (*Bell's Dictionary,* p. 38)

allodial "Allodial is that, whereby the Right is without recognisance or acknowledgment of a Superior, having a

real Right in the Thing; thus are moveables enjoyed."
(Stair, p. 192)

animo remanendi "With the intention of remaining. Said of a person leaving a country without meaning to return; or, of a person resident in a foreign country with the intention of remaining there and not returning to settle in his native country." (*Latin Maxims*, p. 47)

animus possidendi "The intent to possess a thing." (*Black's*, p. 87)

antichresis "A mortgage in which the morgagee retains possession of the mortgaged property and takes the fruits (such as rents) of the property in lieu of interest on the debt." (*Black's*, p. 91)

appretiation "The valuing of poinded goods." (*Bell's Dictionary*, p. 59)

apprising "Where a debtor, who is unable or unwilling to pay his creditors refuses to dispose of his estate for their payment, he may be compelled by law to do that justice to them, which he cannot be brought to voluntarily." (Erskine, p. 403)

arles [or, earnest, arrhae] ". . . a small sum of money, or part of a larger quantity of any other commodity, given as a corroboration, symbol, or token of the completion of a bargain." (*Bell's Dictionary*, p. 349)

arrestment ". . . a Precept or Command of a Judge, ordaining the thing arrested to remain in the same case as when arrested, till such things be done as are prescribed in the Letters of Arrestment . . ." (Stair, p. 370)

assize "Sometimes signifies the sittings of a court, sometimes its ordinances, and sometimes it signifies a jury." (*Bell's Dictionary*, p. 75)

assythment ". . . insinuates the Obligation to Repair Damage sustained by Slaughter, Mutilation, or other Injuries in the Members, or Health of the Body; but it is chiefly pursued by the Wife, or Bairns, or nearest of Kin of Parties slain." (Stair, p. 75)

baillie [or, bailie] "A magistrate; also an officer appointed by a precept of sasine to give infeftment in land." (*Bell's Dictionary,* p. 84)

billa vera "A true bill." (*Latin Maxims,* p. 60)

blench [blanch] "A feudal holding where the feuduty takes a nominal form, eg one penny Scots, if asked only." (*Glossary,* p. 21)

bloodwit [or, bloodwite] "Effusio sanguinis. . . . The fine or penalty imposed for the shedding of blood." (*Black's,* p. 533)

bona fide "Made in good faith; without fraud or deceit." (*Black's,* p. 168)

bond registrable [or, registered bond] "The obligation is registered in the holder's name on the books of the debtor." (*Black's,* p. 171)

borgh of haimhald ". . . a pledge exacted from a seller of an article that it is home produce." (*OED*)

brevi manu "Without a legal warrant. The expression is used to signify the performance of an act by a person on his own authority." (*Latin Maxims,* p. 64)

brieve ". . . a writ issuing from Chancery, in the name of the king, addressed to a judge, ordering trial to be made by jury of certain points stated in the brieve. . . . These writs seem at one time to have been the foundation of almost all civil actions in Scotland." (*Bell's Dictionary,* pp. 134–35)

brieve of distress "Of old, Alienations of Lands for Money, were very rare in Scotland . . . there was then no legal Executions for Debt, against Laws or Heritable-rights, but only moveables, by a brieff of Distress or Poyndancy; by which, not only the moveables of the Debitor were poynded for his Debt." (Stair, p. 389)

brieve of right	"*Breve de recto,* the brieve of right; anciently used before the Justice-General on the decision of the ground-right and property of lands, and the reduction of infeftments; transferred to the Lords of Council and Session as early as the period of the *Regiam Majestatem.*" (*Bell's Dictionary,* p. 134)
Calata Comitia [or. *Comitia Calata]*	"One of the ancient forms of comitia convoked (*calata*) by the *pontifex maximus* for special religious purposes. There the opportunity to make a will was given to the citizens." (Berger, *Encyclopedic Dictionary,* p. 398)
calumniator publicus	public prosecutor, attorney general
capias ad satisfaciendum	"A writ to imprision the person of the defendant, after judgment has been pronounced against him, until he make satisfaction to his creditor." (*Bell's Dictionary,* p. 144)
casualty	"The casualties of superiority are certain emoluments arising to the superior, which, as they depend on certain events are termed casualties. The casualties proper to ward-holding, while it subsisted, were *Ward, Recognition,* and *Marriage.* The casualties common to all holdings are *Non-entry, Relief, Disclamation, Perpresture,* and *Liferent Escheat.*" (*Bell's Dictionary,* p. 149)
causa cognita	"The case having been inquired into; the facts being ascertained." (*Latin Maxims,* p. 71)
certans de damno evitando [*sic*]	"Striving to avoid loss." (*Latin Maxims,* p. 75)
certans de lucro captando	"Striving to make gain, or to obtain an advantage." (*Latin Maxims,* p. 76)
certiorari	"An English writ, by which a cause is removed from an inferior to a superior court, equivalent to a Scotch [*sic*] advocation or appeal." (Traymor, *Latin Maxims,* p. 76)

charge, general	"The only difference between this charge and the special charge is, that it was applicable to those heritable subjects to which the ancestor had personal rights, not completed by sasine; and the heir was charged to make up his titles to the unexecuted procuratories or precept . . . under certification that, if he failed, the creditor should have the same action against the heir and the heritage, that he would have had if he had been retoured heir in general to his ancestor." (*Bell's Dictionary*, p. 165)
charge, special	"The Special Charge, was a writ . . . issued in the Sovereign's name and passing the signet. It narrated the general charge and procedure for constituting the debt, and that the heir would not enter himself heir in special to the heritage in which his ancestor died infeft, so as to enable the creditor to adjudge that property; and it ordained the heir, within forty days, to enter himself heir in special to his ancestor, under certification that, if he failed, the creditor should have action of adjudication against him and the lands, precisely as if he had so entered." (*Bell's Dictionary*, pp. 164–65)
church regality	"All regalities, whether belonging to the church or to laymen, had originally the some right of repledging from the justices; but it was, soon after the Reformation, taken from church-regalities. The jurisdiction of church-regalities fell regularly to have been annexed to the crown, in consequence of the annexation of church-lands, by 1587, c. 29." (Erskine, p. 59)
Circuit court	"A court held by the judges of the High Court of Justiciary when sitting on circuit out of Edinburgh." (*Glossary*, p. 28)
clare constat	"It clearly appears. This is the name of a writ granted by a superior in favour of the heir of a deceased vassal, granting warrant for his infeftment and entry in the lands, deriving its name from the declaration

with which it opens, that from authentic documents laid before the superior, it *clearly appears* that the grantee is the heir." (Trayner, *Latin Maxims,* pp. 79–80)

cognitionis causa

"Where the creditor of a deceased heritable proprietor pursues the heir, with a view to constitute the debt against him, and attach the defunct's heritage, and the heir appears and renounces, the court will pronounce a decree for the amount of that debt, which is called a *cognitionis causa.*" (*Bell's Dictionary,* p. 191)

collateral

"A relative descended from the same ancestor but not in a direct line, eg a cousin." (*Glossary,* p. 30)

commissary

". . . originally an ecclesiastical judge with jurisdiction in matters of personal status, eg, legitimacy, marriage and succession." At the Reformation in 1563 a new Commissary Court was established in Edinburgh and each diocese to manage the functions of the Courts of Officials in dioceses. The commissaries virtually monopolised jurisdiction in matters of status and succession until the nineteenth century. The inferior commissaries were merged with the sheriff court in 1832 and were abolished in 1876. (*Glossary,* p. 30)

Commissary Court

See commissary.

Commissioners of Oyer and Terminer

"A royal appointment authorising a judge . . . to go on the assize circuit and hear felony and treason cases." (*Black's,* p. 265)

Commissioners of Supply

"The Commissioners of Supply are named in the acts imposing the land-tax, and are authorised to act within their respective counties." (*Bell's Dictionary,* p. 202)

composition

"In payment of money or chattels in satisfaction for an injury. . . . In Anglo-Saxon and other early societies, a composition with the injured party was recognized as a way to deter acts of revenge by the injured party." (*Black's*, p. 280)

compounding for crimes	"The offense of either agreeing not to prosecute a crime that one knows has been committed or agreeing to hamper the prosecution." (*Black's*, p. 280)
compurgator	"A person who appeared in court and made an oath in support of a civil or criminal defendant." (*Black's*, p. 282)
condictio furtive [or, *condition rei furtivae]*	"An action to recover a stolen thing." (*Black's*, p. 287)
consuetude [or, consuetudo]	"A duty or tax." (*Black's*, p. 310)
contra hereditatem jacentem	Against "an inheritance on which the *heres* has not yet entered." (Buckland, p. 174)
deathbed, law of	"By the law of deathbed, which was peculiar to Scotland, the heir in heritage was entitled to reduce all voluntary deeds granted to his prejudice by his predecessor, within sixty days preceding the predecessor's death; provided the maker of the deed, at its date, was labouring under the disease of which he died, and did not subsequently go to kirk or market unsupported." (*Bell's Dictionary*, p. 284)
debitum fundi	". . . a real debt or lien over land, which attaches to the land itself, into whose hands soever it may come." (*Bell's Dictionary*, p. 286)
decern, to	"To decern is to *decree*. Before the judgement of interlocutor of any court in Scotland can be extracted, to the effect of warranting execution, it must import a decree." (*Bell's Dictionary*, p. 287)
decerniture	"The action of decerning; a decree." (*OED*)
declarator	"A declaratory action. This is a form of action by which some right of property, or of servitude, or of

	status, or some inferior right or interest, is sought to be judicially declared." (*Bell's Dictionary*, p. 291)
declarator (on non-entry)	"A declaration by the court of a person's rights, made in an action for declaratory. The declaratory does not itself actually enforce the rights. There has to be a practical rather than a theoretical purpose to the action." (*Glossary*, p. 46)
declinator	"A written instrument declining the jurisdiction of a judge or court." (*OED*)
decreet conform	"A decree authorising the enforcement of an order or decree of some other court or body." (*Glossary*, p. 47)
decreet of cognition	"*Decreet cognitonis causa* . . . A judgement in a suit involving a plantiff suing a debtor's heir to attach the heir's lands." (*Black's*, p. 419)
de donis conditionalibus	"An English statute, enacted in 1285, that gave rise to the ability to create a fee tail." (*Black's*, p. 422)
definitive sentence (determinate sentence)	"A sentence for a fixed length of time rather than for an unspecified duration." (*Black's*, p. 367)
delict; *ex delicto*	"A civil wrong created by the deliberate or negligent breach of a legal duty, from which a liability to compensate consequential loss or injury may arise." (*Glossary*, p. 47)
diem clausit extremum	"A chancery writ, founded on the statute of Marlbury, ordering the county escheator, after the death of the chief tenant of the Crown, to summon a jury to determine the amount and value of the land owned by the chief tenant, to determine the next heir, and to reclaim the property for the Crown. It was a type of inquisition post mortem." (*Black's*, p. 465)
disseisin	"The act of wrongfully depriving someone of the freehold possession of a property." (*Black's*, p. 485)

distrain	"To force . . . by the seizure and detention of personal property, to perform an obligation." (*Black's*, p. 489)
distress	"The seizure of another's property to secure the performance of a duty." (*Black's*, p. 487)
divorce	"Judicial dissolution of marriage." (*Glossary*, p. 51)
donatio mortis causa	"A gift made in contemplation of death and effective only on the donor's death. A gift may be transferred prior to the donor's death, but if the donee predeceases the donor the gift reverts to the donor." (*Glossary*, p. 52)
donation *inter vivos*	"A gift made by one person to another whilst both parties are alive, contrasted with donation mortis causa." (*Glossary*, p. 52)
eadem persona cum defuncto	"The same person with the deceased. An heir succeeding by universal title to his ancestor, and thereby becoming possessed of all his property, with the rights and privileges attaching thereto, is held liable in payment of his ancestor's debts and fulfilment of his obligations." (*Latin Maxims*, p. 179)
effect	"That which is produced by an agent or cause; a result, outcome, or consequence." (*Black's*, p. 532)
elegit	"A writ of execution (first given by 13 Edw., ch. 18) either upon a judgement for a debt or damages or upon a forfeiture of a recognizance in the king's court." (*Black's*, p. 538)
emphyteusis	"A right of property well known in the civil law, and analogous to the feu-holding of Scotland." (*Latin Maxims*, p. 184)
entail	"A form of disposition of heritable property on a specified line of successive heirs to keep the property in the family, it often includes special provisions regarding forfeiture, alienation and borrowing." (*Glossary*, p. 55)

escheat	"... any forfeiture or confiscation whereby a man's estate, heritable or moveable, or any part thereof, falls from him." (*Bell's Dictionary*, p. 405)
escheat, liferent	"Liferent escheat is the forfeiture to the superior of the annual profits of the vassal's lands during his life, or while he remained unrelaxed, which, in like manner, formerly fell when a denounced debtor had remained a year and a day at the horn, unrelaxed." (*Bell's Dictionary*, p. 405)
escheat, single	"Single escheat is the forfeiture to the Crown of one's moveable estate, incurred not only on conviction of certain crimes, but which, until 1748, followed upon denunciation for non-payment or non-performance of a civil debt or obligation." (*Bell's Dictionary*, p. 405)
esseirs (esseyers; assayours)	"An assayer of metal or coin." (*Older Scottish Tongue,* vol. 1, p. 119)
ex delicto	"On the ground of, or arising from, delict. Delicts give rise to civil claims, as well as subjecting the person guilty of the delict to the punishment attached thereto. Thus assault gives rise to a civil claim of damages, and murder to a claim of assythment." (*Latin Maxims,* p. 197)
ex necessitate juris [or, *ex nessitate legis*]	"... from or by necessity of law." (*Black's*, p. 597)
exceptiones doli et metus	In Roman law, a defence or plea of fraud. (*Black's*, pp. 582–83)
execution, personal	*See* horning.
execution, real	*See* poind.
extent (old and new)	"... the ancient *census* or general valuation put upon all the lands in Scotland, for the purpose of regu-

lating the proportion of public subsidies or taxes exigible from them, as well as for ascertaining the amount of the casualties due to the superior . . . the new and the old extent are supposed to have been ascertained—the new extent being the valuation thus fixed, and the old extent consisting . . . of a valuation made in the reign of Alexander III., or at any rate, at some time prior to 1474." (*Bell's Dictionary*, p. 444)

extra territorium   "Beyond the territory." (*Latin Maxims*, p. 213)

fee simple   "An interest in land that, being the broadest property interest allowed by law, endures until the current holder dies without heirs." (*Black's*, p. 630)

fee tail   "An estate that is inheritable only by specified descendants of the original grantee, and endures until the current holder dies without issue." (*Black's*, p. 631)

feu [or, feuer]   "In Latin *feudum,* was used to denote the feudal-holding, where the service was purely military; but the term has been used in Scotland in contradistinction to ward-holding, the military tenure of this country, to signify that holding where the vassal, in place of military service, makes a return in grain or money. . . ." (*Bell's Dictionary*, p. 456)

feu-duty   "The *reddendo* or annual return from the vassal to the superior in feu-holding." (*Bell's Dictionary*, p. 457)

fideicommissum   "Trusts; that is, trusts for carrying out the last wishes of a deceased person." (*Latin Maxims*, p. 225)

fieri facias   A writ that enables a defendant's goods and chattels to be levied as payment of debt or damages. EL.

fisk   ". . . the Crown's revenue. This term is usually applied by Scotch law-writers to the moveable estate of a person denounced rebel, which was, by our older practice, forfeited to the Crown." (*Bell's Dictionary*, p. 462)

forisfamiliation	"... the separation of a child from the family of his father. The son is said to be *foris familiat* by the father, when, with his own consent and good will, he received from his father any lands, and is put in possession thereof before his father's decease, and is content and satisfied therewith; so that he nor his heirs may not claim or crave any more of his father's heritage." (*Bell's Dictionary*, p. 470)
formulae actionum	"... formula for regulating juridical proceedings." (*Latin-English Dictionary*, p. 384)
forum	"A court of tribunal appropriate for the exercise of jurisdiction for a particular purpose." (*Glossary*, p. 68)
forum delicti	The place where the offence was committed.
fredum	"... a Composition made by a Criminal, to be freed from Prosecution, of which the third Part was paid into the Exchequer." (Jacob)
frith	"A firth or estuary." (*Older Scottish Tongue*, vol. 2, p. 572)
furtum manifestum	"The case where the thief was caught in the act, or in the place where the theft was committed, or before he reached the spot to which he intended to convey the stolen property." (*Latin Maxims*, p. 234)
furtum nec manifestum	"Where none of the circumstances of *furtum manifestum* had place." (Traymor, *Latin Maxims*, p. 234)
haeres factus	"An heir in trust; a trustee. This name is given to the person or persons appointed by the testator's settlement to succeed to his estate, in order that they may fulfil the purposes of the testator's will." (*Latin Maxims*, pp. 242–43)
haeres natus	"An heir who succeeds in respect of birth or relationship" (under *haeres factus*). (*Latin Maxims*, p. 240)
heir of conquest	"Those heritable rights to which the deceased has succeeded as heir to his ancestor, are sometimes

termed *heritage* in a strict sense, in contradistinction to *conquest*, which term is applied to such heritable rights as the deceased has acquired by singular titles, *e.g.,* by purchase, donation, or even excambion." (*Bell's Dictionary,* p. 229)

heir of entail "A person entitled to succeed to entailed land. The title 'heir of entail' is retained after succession." (*Glossary,* p. 73)

heir of line "Until 1964 a person entitled to succeed to a deceased's heritable property under the rules of primogeniture, eg the eldest lawful son." (*Glossary,* p. 73)

heir of provision "A person who succeeds by express provisions in eg a settlement." (*Glossary,* p. 73)

heir-male "The nearest male relative who is related to the deceased only through a male." (*Glossary,* p. 73)

heredes cum beneficio inventarii ". . . we have now borrowed from Roman law. R.22 s.2, 3, 4. *C. jure delib.* as an expedient, by which an heir, who is doubtful whether his ancestor's estate be sufficient for satisfying his debts, may enter upon inventory, *cum beneficio inventarii,* without the risk of subjecting himself to the debts farther than the value of the estate amounts to." (Erskine, pp. 621–22)

hereditas jacens (haereditas jacens) "(An inheritance that is not taken up.) An estate in Scotland is so called when, after the ancestor's death, no title to it has been made by his heir." (*Law Lexicon*)

horning "After a debt is constituted, either by a formal decree, or by registration of the bond, or other ground of debt, the creditor may obtain letters of horning, issuing from the signet, and directed a messenger, who is required to charge the debtor to pay the debt, or perform the obligation within a limited time, under pain of rebellion." (Erskine, p. 250)

house-mail	"House-rent." (*Older Scottish Tongue*, vol. 3, p. 167)
hypothec	". . . a security established by law in favour of a creditor over a subject belonging to his debtor, while the subject continues in the debtor's possession. The Roman law recognised many hypothecs over moveables; but the law of Scotland, having regard to the inexpediency of such liens in a commercial and trading country, admits of but few hypothecs." (*Bell's Dictionary*, p. 513)
impune	"Without punishment, with safety." (Berger, p. 493)
in capite	"A type of tenure in which a person held land directly of the Crown." (*Black's*, p. 764)
in civilibus	In civil matters.
in familia	In the family.
in favorem fisci	In favour of the property of the monarch or treasury.
in foro contentioso	"In the forum of contention or litigation." (*Black's*, p. 783)
in gremio	"In the body of, eg any clause or words contained in a deed or document." (*Glossary*, p. 78)
in hereditate jacente	"In the estate of a deceased person, which has not been entered upon or taken up by the heir." (*Latin Maxims*, p. 262)
in integrum	"Entirely; to the fullest extent." (*Latin Maxims*, p. 263)
in medio	"The property or money held by the pursuer in an action of multiplepoinding is called the fund *in medio*, because it is, or may be, subject to the claims of all the claimants, and yet belongs to none of them. It is thus common to them all, and forms the centre or substance of the litigation." (*Latin Maxims*, p. 267)
in rem singularem	Against an individual thing.

in solatium	"Compensation; esp. damages allowed for hurt feelings or grief, as distinguished from damages for personal injury." (*Black's*, p. 1397)
in terrorem	"As a warning or deterrent." (*Glossary*, p. 78)
in universum jus defuncti	In the universal right of the deceased.
in valorem	"For the value; or, according to the value." (*Latin Maxims*, p. 278)
Infeft, infeftment	"Investment of title to heritage in a new owner, formerly by symbolically giving him sasine or possession by delivery of earth and stone, now by recording the deed in the General Register of Sasines or registering the title in the Land Register of Scotland." (*Glossary*, p. 80)
infeftment of annualrent	"The sasine is an annualrent payable out of the lands, and in the lands themselves in security, when duly recorded in the Register of Sasines, vests a feudal estate; but it is still of the nature of a mere burden, which payment of a debt, or confusion, or mere renunciation of the security, must extinguish." (*Bell's Principles*, p. 350)
inquest, brieve of	"The Shiereffe is Iudex the breive of inquest, quhair be ane desiris to be served and retoured narrest and lauchfull aire to his predecessor." (Skene, p. 132)
inter vivos	"Between living persons." (*Latin Maxims*, p. 25)
interlocutory sentence (interlocutory judgement)	". . . any judicial order or interlocutor pronounced in the preparation or disposal of a cause either in the Court of Session or in an inferior court, which is not decisive or the whole merits of the suit." (*Bell's Dictionary*, p. 578)
inventory	". . . a regular list of articles, or of an estate, describing each article fully and precisely by itself, and seriatim, so as to point out every article of which the estate consists." (*Bell's Dictionary*, p. 581)

irritant clause	"... clause by which certain prohibited acts specified in a deed, if committed by the person holding under the deed, are declared to be void and null." (*Bell's Dictionary*, p. 586)
ius retractus	"The right of certain relatives of one who has sold immovable property to repurchase it." (*Black's*, p. 868)
jure gentium	"By the law of nations." (*Black's*, p. 854)
jurisdictionis fundandae gratia	For the sake of establishing jurisdiction.
justiciars	"... law officers instituted by William the Conqueror to assist the sovereign in administering the law." (*Law Lexicon*, p. 197)
Laburrows [or, Lawburrows]	"... letters passing under the signet, running in the Sovereign's name, and obtained at the instance of one who had, or thought he had, reason to apprehend danger to his person or property from the acts of another." (*Bell's Dictionary*, p. 642)
lease for life	*See* liferent.
leil [or, lele]	"... legally valid, legal, lawful, just, rightful." (*Older Scottish Tongue*, vol. 3, p. 666)
letters of apprising	*See* apprising.
Letters of Four Forms	"The Decreets of the *Lords of Session* for attaining their effects, have *Letters* in the *Kings* Name, Commanding the Parties Decerned to pay and perform as is Descerned. These of Old, were, by *Letters of four Forms*, as they were called: The *first* was a Charge to pay or perform, without any Certification; The *second* was a Charge to the same effect, but with Certification that Horning would be direct; The *third* was Horning; the *fourth* was Caption. But these being Tedious and Expensive, every Form being returned to Edinburgh, before the next were granted;

The *first* two were laid aside, and only Horning and
Caption remained." (Stair, p. 722)

letters of general
charge; special charge

See charge, general; charge, general special.

Letter under the
Signet

"Signet Letters are writs for enforcing the decrees of
courts, or for attaching the property of debtors, or
for citing defenders or other parties in actions before
the Court of Session. These run in the name of the
Sovereign, and are authenticated by the signet."
(*Bell's Dictionary,* p. 659)

levari facias

"In English law, a writ of execution directed to this
sheriff for levying a sum of money upon a man's
lands and tenements, goods and chattels, who has
forfeited his recognisance." (*Bell's Dictionary,* p. 660)

lex talionis

"The law of retaliation, by which a person was made
suffer as a punishment for his offence, the same
injury as that which he had inflicted, or attempted to
inflict." (Trayner, *Latin Maxims,* p. 328)

libel

"This term, in the law of Scotland, is used in different significations; it is applied to the form of the
complaint, or the ground of the charge on which
either a civil or criminal prosecution takes place. It is
also applied to scandal reduced into writing." (*Bell's
Dictionary,* pp. 660–61)

lien

"In English law, an obligation, tie, or claim annexed
to, or attaching upon, any property, without satisfying which, such property cannot be demanded by
its owner. Before the introduction of the term *lien*
into Scotch legal phraseology, the right to retain the
property of a debtor was recognised under the right
of *retention;* but . . . it has become general to employ
the terms lien and retention indifferently to signify
the same right." (*Bell's Dictionary,* p. 662)

liferent

"A liferent right entitles the liferenter to use and
enjoy the subject of the liferent during life, without

destroying or wasting its substance. . . . The legal liferents in the Scotch law are the terce and the courtesy." (*Bell's Dictionary*, p. 663)

litiscontestation ". . . a term applied, in the Roman law, to the case where both parties to a suit had stated their pleas judicially. It was held as a species of contract between them, that they should abide by the decision of the judge on the facts as proved." (*Bell's Dictionary*, p. 667)

locus originis The place of origin.

locus poenitentiae "Place or opportunity for repentance, or change of intention." (*Latin Maxims*, p. 338); ". . . a power of resiling from a bargain, before any act has been done to confirm it in law." (*Bell's Dictionary*, p. 670)

lyning [or, lining] "The measuring out of holdings in order to the settlement of boundaries, chiefly or only with burghs." (*Older Scottish Tongue*, vol. 3, p. 795)

Lyon Court "The court of the Lord Lyon King-of-Arms . . . the Lord Lyon King-at-Arms [is] an officer . . . who has wide jurisdiction in the Court of the Lord Lyon in all heraldic matters and who is responsible for the ordering of state ceremonies. His functions correspond to those discharged in England by the Earl Marshal and the Garter King of Arms." (*Glossary*, p. 99)

mala fide; mala fides "In bad faith; lacking good faith; *mala fides* (nominative) bad faith." (*Glossary*, p. 100)

mora "Delay. This word signifies technically undue or culpable delay, and subjects the person against whom it can be charged to the consequences which arise from it." (*Latin Maxims*, p. 360)

mortis causa "Deeds made in contemplation of death are so called, because the prospect of death is the cause which induces their execution." (*Latin Maxims*, p. 362)

nemo potest mori pro parte testatus et pro parte intestatus	"No one can die partly testate and partly intestate." (*Latin Maxims*, p. 379)
nexus or lien of property	"Bond, tie, fetter or connection." (*Glossary*, p. 109)
nobile officium	"... generally speaking ... the equitable power vested in the [Court of Session], whereby it interposes to modify or abate the rigour of the law, and, to a certain extent, to give aid where no remedy could be had in a court confined to strict law." (*Bell's Dictionary*, p. 741)
non-entry	"... the casualty ... which fell to the superior where the heir of a deceased vassal neglected to obtain himself entered with the superior; or, as it is otherwise expressed, failed to renew the investiture." (*Bell's Dictionary*, p. 742)
oath of purgation	"Purgatory oath ... An oath taken to clear oneself of a charge or suspicion." (*Black's*, p. 1100)
ob denegatam justitiam	On account of denied justice.
ob non solutum canonem	"On account of unpaid canon or feu-duty." (*Latin Maxims*, p. 412)
obligations *ad facta praestanda*	"An obligation *ad factum praestandum,* is an obligation to perform an act." (*Dictionary and Digest*, p. 419)
obligor	"... the debtor in an obligation." (*Bell's Dictionary*, p. 751)
obtorto collo	"By the throat." (*Latin Maxims*, p. 414)
pacta liberatoria	"... bargains whereby a real right is either passed from or restricted. Such agreements form an exception to the general rule, that writing must intervene in all that related to land, in order to bar the *locus poenitentiae* or power of resiling." (*Bell's Dictionary*, p. 758)

pannel	"The accused person in a criminal action." (*Bell's Dictionary*, p. 760)
pars soli	"*Partes soli*—Parts of the soil. Trees are said to be *partes soli*, and as such go to the heir, and not to the executors." (Halkerston, p. 75)
patria potestas	"This was the name given to that power under which, under the civil law, a paterfamilias had over all the members of his family; the family including his wife, children, and grandchildren, as well as those who became members of the family by marriage or adoption." (*Latin Maxims*, p. 442)
peine fort et dure	"The punishment of an alleged felon who refused to plead, consisting of pressing or crushing the person's body under a heavy weight until the accused either pleaded or died." (*Black's*, p. 1153)
pendere poenas	To pay a penalty.
perambulation	"Actions upon brieves of perambulation were authorised by the act 1579, c. 79, and were intended to settle the line of march between conterminous properties." (*Bell's Dictionary*, p. 798)
personam [sic] *standi in judicio*	"A person or character entitling one to appear in a lawsuit to vindicate his right, and that whether in the character of pursuer or defender. This right is common to all, except those who have been deprived of it by the operation of the law, or those who have never yet attained it." (*Latin Maxims*, p. 456)
pignus praetorium	"A legal pledge; a pledge given by the law, or the magistrate who administers it." (*Latin Maxims*, p. 458)
poind, poynd	"Poinding . . . A judgement creditor's seizing of a debtor's property to satisfy the debt." (*Black's*, p. 1177)
praetium affectionis, pretium affectionis	"The price of regard; sentimental value; the value of a thing due to the owner's regard for it, irrespective

	of intrinsic value, as with heirlooms." (*Glossary,* p. 127)
precept	"A warrant or order." (*Glossary,* p. 126)
primer seisin	"The right of the Crown to receive, from the heir of the tenant who died in possession of the knight's fee, one year's profits of the inherited estate." (*Black's,* p. 1363)
primogeniture	". . . the rule of law, whereby the eldest son is preferred to the younger ones in the succession of heritage." (*Bell's Dictionary,* p. 850)
pro interesse (pro interesse suo)	"According to his interest; to the extent of his interest." (*Black's,* p. 1228)
pro parte testatus et pro parte intestatus	"Partly testate and partly intestate." (*Latin Maxims,* p. 379)
procurator	". . . a general term for a person who acts for or instead of another, and under his authority. Thus, the person whom the vassal directs to make resignation in the hands of the superior is termed his procurator." (*Bell's Dictionary,* p. 858)
procurator fiscal	". . . the officer at whose instance criminal proceedings are carried on." (*Bell's Dictionary,* p. 859)
procuratory	"An authority, mandate or commission to a person to act for another." (*Glossary,* p. 130)
prohibitory clause(s)	"Prohibitions against altering the order of succession, against alienating the land, and against contracting debts, whereby the lands may be burdened or affected by diligence." (*Dictionary and Digest,* p. 969)
pupillar substitution	"The nomination of a person to take as heir in place of, or to succeed, a descendant who is under the age of puberty and in the potestas of the testator, if the descendant has failed to take the inheritance or has died before reaching puberty." (*Black's,* p. 1444)
purpresture	". . . a feudal delinquency, [now obsolete,] inferring a total forfeiture of the fee. It was incurred by the

vassal encroaching on the streets, highways, or commonties belonging to the superior." (*Bell's Dictionary*, p. 876)

quantum valent dicta terrae per annum

What these lands are worth per year.

querela inofficiosi testamenti

"The complaint against an inofficious testament. A testament was considered *inofficiosum* under the civil law when, although validly and formally executed, it violated by its terms those duties which affection and natural obligation made incumbent upon the granter." (*Latin Maxims*, p. 508)

quia emptores terrarum

"The English statute, West. 3, 18 Ed. I. st. 1, is so called from the introductory words. Its intention was to put a stop to subinfeudations, by declaring that a vassal might sell his lands, provided he sold them to be held of his superior by the tenure and services due. The statute was at one time thought to have been introduced into Scotland by Robert I. stat. 2, c. 24, § 2; and there have been speculations as to the causes of it not having produced the same effect in Scotland as in England, where feudal forms were, by the statute, rendered no longer necessary." (*Bell's Dictionary*, p. 879)

quia spoliatum ante omnia restituendus

"A maxim importing that spuilzied goods must be returned before any discussion takes place as to the rightful owner of them." (*Latin Maxims*, pp. 583–84)

quod actor sequitur forum rei

"The plantiff ought to follow the court of the defendant. A maxim adapted from Roman law importing that the plantiff in an action must bring his action against the defendant in that country to the laws of which the defendant is amenable." (*Law Lexicon*, p. 11)

quod diem clausit supremum

See *diem clausit supremum*.

quod mortuus sasit vivum

"A maxim of English law which signifies that the moment a man dies his real estate vests in his heir-at-law, without any service of other legal proceeding being taken by the heir to establish his right." (*Latin Maxims*, p. 367)

quod non est factum	"Non est factum, a plea denying that the deed on which the plantiff sued was the defendant's deed." (*Law Lexicon*, p. 242)
quod pater est quem nuptiae demonstrant (pater est quem nuptiae demonstrant et quem nuptiae)	"He is the father whom the marriage indicates to be so." (*Latin Maxims*, p. 440)
quod potior est conditio possidentis (potior est conditio possidentis)	"The condition of a possessor . . . is stronger." (*Latin Maxims*, p. 466)
ratione domicilii	"On account of domicile." (*Latin Maxims*, p. 541)
record of court	Recorded in the books of the court.
reddendo	"That clause in a charter which sets forth the payment to be made or service to be rendered by the vassal to the superior, in return for the lands held by the former of the latter." (*Latin Maxims*, p. 545)
reduction	"To set aside or annul . . . a deed, contract, decree or award." (*Glossary*, p. 139)
regality, lords of regality	". . . originally a territorial jurisdiction conferred by the King. The lands were said to be given in liberam regalitatem; and the persons receiving the right were termed Lords of Regality. The civil jurisdiction of a lord of regality was equal to that of a sheriff; but his criminal jurisdiction was much more extensive, as he was competent to judge in the four pleas of the Crown, and possessed the same criminal jurisdiction with the Justiciary, excepting in the case of treason." (*Bell's Dictionary*, p. 897)
relief	"A payment made by an heir of a feudal tenant to the feudal lord for the privilege of succeeding to the ancestor's tenancy." (*Black's*, p. 1293)

rei vindicatio	"An action under the civil law by which the owner of a subject claimed the subject itself; a real action, as opposed to condictio, which was a personal action under which the delivery of the thing itself could not be enforced, but its value might be recovered. The *vindicatio* was only competent to the true owner against the possessor for the time being." (*Latin Maxims*, p. 547)
remainder	"A future interest arising in a third person—that is, someone other than the creator of the estate or the creator's heirs—who is intended to take after the natural termination of the preceding estate." (*Black's*, p. 1294)
remeid	"Remedy." (*Older Scottish Tongue*, vol. 7, p. 269)
renovatio feudi	A renewal of the feu.
rent charge	"The right to receive an annual sum from the income of land, usually in perpetuity, and to retake possession if the payments are in arrears." (*Black's*, p. 1299)
rent seck	"A rent reserved by deed but without any clause of distress." (*Black's*, p. 1299)
repledge (repledging)	". . . a power formerly competent to certain private jurisdictions to demand judicially the person of an offender accused before another tribunal, on the ground that the offence had been committed within the repledger's jurisdiction." (*Bell's Dictionary*, p. 912)
res judicata	"A case, or matter decided; a final judgement." (*Latin Maxims*, p. 553)
res singularis	The property of an individual. (*Latin Maxims*, p. 556)
resolutive clause	". . . in order to make the prohibition [of an irritant clause] effectual . . . a resolutive clause, is required, whereby the right of the contravener is resolved and put an end to on his committing the acts against which the irritancies are directed. It is by the joint aid

	of these two clauses that the object of the maker of the deed is obtained." (*Bell's Dictionary,* p. 586)
retour	"The points aforesaid being cleared, and instructed to the Inquest, the Service is the Sentence or Decreet: which ought to be sealed with their Seals, and with the Seal of the Judge, to whom a Brieve is directed, and is returned to the Chancery, whence it is called a Retour, being registrat there, and extracted; till which it is not compleat: neither doth the Service ordinarily instruct the active Title but only the Retour." (Stair, p. 473)
reversion	"(1) in relation to heritage, a right of redemption which may be legal, as in adjudication for debt, or convential, as usually set forth in the terms of a heritable security; (2) the right of the fiar to heritage at the end of a liferent." (*Glossary,* p. 146)
sasine	"The act formerly symbolising the legal acquisition of heritable property." (*Glossary,* p. 149)
secundum vires hereditatis	"According to the extent of the succession; that is, the value of the estate succeeded to." (*Latin Maxims,* p. 567)
secundum vires inventarii	"According to the extent of the inventory." (*Latin Maxims,* p. 568)
seisin	"Possession of a freehold estate in land; ownership." (*Black's,* p. 1362); "A formal Season [*sic*], is the Instrument of a Nottar-Publick, bearing the delivery of a Symbolical Possession, by the Superiour or his Bailie to the Vassal or his Actuary." (Stair, p. 200)
separatio bonorum	"The separation of the heir's property from the estate he inherited." (Berger, p. 701)
short hand, pledge or poynd	Without the intervention of a judge.
slains, letters of	"Letters subscribed by the relations of a person who had been slain, declaring that they had received an assythment, and concurring in an application to the

Crown for a pardon to the offender." (*Bell's Dictionary*, p. 1018)

solvere | "To pay (a debt)." (*Black's*, p. 1400)

spuilzie | "... the taking away of Moveables without consent of the Owner, or Order of Law, obliging to Restitution of the things taken away, with all possible profits, or Reparation thereof according to the estimation of the Injured, made by his *juramentum in litem*." (Stair, p. 84)

Statute of merchants | "One of two 13th-century statutes establishing procedures to better secure and recover debts by, among other things, providing a commercial bond that if not timely paid, resulted in swift execution on the lands, goods, and bonds of the debtor. 13 Edw., ch. 6 (1283); 15 Edw., ch. 6 (1285)." (*Black's*, p. 1421)

stellionate | "Any fraudulent or deceitful act (obsolete)." (*Glossary*, p. 161)

stipulatio | "Stipulation; the mode by which, under the civil law, a verbal obligation was constituted." (*Latin Maxims*, p. 586)

stirpes | "*Per stirpes*—according to the stems or stocks (*stirpes*) of the family instead of *per capita* among individual members of the family. In succession, where the estate is to be divided *per stirpes*, it is not just the survivors who benefit; the share of the predeceasing beneficiary is divided among his children or remoter issue. Called succession by right of representation." (*Glossary*, p. 120)

sui et necessarii heredes | "These are those in the *potestas* of the deceased who become *sui juris* at his death, and *posthumi* who would have been in that position if born soon enough." (Buckland, p. 305)

superior | "In feudal tenure the person holding heritable property immediately from the Crown (the paramount superior) who grants land to a vassal in return for the payment of feuduty." (*Glossary*, p. 163) suspension

"The means by which injury of rights, occasioned or threatened by court decrees, sentences or orders and diligence, is prevented." (*Glossary*, p. 164)

tack

"(1) A lease or tenancy, especially of a farm or mill (obsolescent); (2) the land held in tack; (3) a payment levied by a feudal superior (obsolete)." (*Glossary*, p. 165)

tam infra burgos et regalitates quam extra

Both within and without the burgh and regality.

terce

"Liferent of one-third of the heritage of a deceased husband conferred on a widow who had not accepted provision under his will (obsolete since 1964)." (*Glossary*, p. 166)

titulo universali

"By a universal title. An heir who succeeds to the estate of his ancestor is said to acquire or hold such succession by universal title." (*Latin Maxims*, p. 600)

ultimus haeres

"Last heir." (*Latin Maxims*, p. 608)

ultra vires

"Beyond the power; in excess of the authority." (*Latin Maxims*, p. 610)

usque ad sententiam

"Until the pronouncing of judgment." (*Latin Maxims*, p. 612)

usufruct

". . . the Power of disposal of the Use and Fruits . . . without making profite, or disponing to others." (Stair, p. 273)

valent

"Value or worth." (*OED*)

vassal

"In feudal tenure the owner of the *dominium utile* of land, his right of ownership being conditional on fulfilling certain obligations imposed by his superior." (*Glossary*, p. 176)

vergelt

"In ancient Teutonic and Old English law, the price set upon a man according to his rank, paid by way of compensation or fine in cases of homicide and

	certain other crimes to free the offender from further obligation or punishment." (*OED*)
virtute officii	"By virtue of his . . . office; by the authority invested in one as the incumbent of a particular office." (*Black's*, p. 1565)
vitious intromission	In Scots law, *intromission* is the assuming of the possession and management of property belonging to another; *vicious intromission* is an heir's unwarrantable intromission with the moveable estate of the ancestor. (*Bell's Dictionary*, pp. 580–81)
wadset	". . . The giving of a Wedd or Pledge in Security." (Stair, p. 327)
ward, casualty of	"By this casualty the superior was entitled to the full rent of the ward-lands after the vassal's death during the heir's minority, because the heir, in that period, was incapable of performing military service. . . . Ward expired when the heir, if male, reached majority. In females, it lasted only till fourteen, at which age women became marriageable by the old law. This casualty was abolished in 1747." (*Bell's Dictionary*, p. 1114)
warrandice	"An express or implied personal obligation . . . of a granter (eg a seller or lessor), especially of heritable property, to indemnify the granter in case of eviction on some grounds existing before the grant or sale." (*Glossary*, p. 178)
writ	"A written command, precept, or formal order issued by a court in the name of the sovereign, state, or other competent legal authority, directing or enjoining the person or persons to whom it is addressed to do or refrain from doing some act specified therein." (*OED*)

BIBLIOGRAPHY

The aim of this bibliography is to allow the reader to identify all works quoted from or otherwise cited by Kames in *Historical Law-Tracts*. Where it can be identified, it is the particular edition of a work which Kames cites that is listed here. In some cases, a suggestion is made as to the edition that Kames might have used, given the holdings of the Advocates Library in Edinburgh or the National Library of Scotland. Where the edition used by Kames cannot be identified, a standard modern edition is sometimes listed here instead.

The Acts of the Parliament of Scotland, A.D. MCXXIV–MDCCVII. Ed. Cosmo Innes and Thomas Thomson. 12 vols. London, 1814–52.

The Ancient Laws and Customs of the Burghs of Scotland. Ed. Cosmo Innes and R. Renwick. 2 vols. Edinburgh: Scottish Burgh Records Society, 1868–1920.

Anderson, James. *An Historical Essay, Shewing That the Crown and Kingdom of Scotland, Is Imperial and Independent.* Edinburgh, 1705.

————. *Selectus Diplomatum et Numismatum Scotia Thesaurus.* Edinburgh, 1739.

Aristotle. *Nicomachean Ethics.*

————. *Politics.*

Bacon, Francis. *Essays or Councils, Civil and Moral.* Ed. Brian Vickers. London: The Folio Society, 2002.

————. *Of the Advancement and Proficience of Learning or the Partitions of the Sciences.* Trans. Gilbert Watts. Oxford, 1640.

Bacon, Matthew. *A New Abridgment of the Law.* 5 vols. London, 1736–66.

Balfour of Pittendreich, Sir James. *Practicks, or a System of the More Ancient Law of Scotland.* Edinburgh, 1754.

"Black Acts": *The Actis and Constitutiounis of the Realme of Scotland.* Edinburgh, 1566.

Boece, Hector. *The Chronicles of Scotland . . . translated into Scots by John Bellenden.* Ed. Edith C. Batho and H. Winifred Husbands. 2 vols. Edinburgh: William Blackwood, 1938–41.

Bolingbroke, Henry St. John, Lord Viscount. *Works.* 5 vols. London, 1754.

Bosman, Willem. *A New and Accurate Description of the Coast of Guinea.* Trans. anon. London, 1705.

Bracton, Henry. *De Legibus et Consuetudinibus Angliae Libri Quinque.* London, 1569.

Caesar, Julius. *De Bello Gallico.* Trans. H. J. Edwards. Loeb Classical Library. William Heinemann: London, 1917.

Carpzov, Benedict. *Jurisprudentia Forensis Romano-Saxonica.* Frankfurt am Main, 1638.

"Chartulary of Aberbrothock": *Liber S. Thome. de Aberbrothoc.* 2 vols. Edinburgh: Bannatyne Club, 1848–56.

"Chartulary of Paisley": *Registrum Monasterii de Passelet.* Edinburgh: Maitland Club, 1832.

"Chartulary of the abbey of Dunfermline": *Registrum de Dunfermlyn.* Edinburgh: Bannatyne Club, 1842.

Cicero, Marcus Tullius. *De Oratore.* Trans. E. W. Sutton. Loeb Classical Library. London: William Heinemann, 1942.

The Code of Justinian [Codex]. Vols. 12–15 of *The Civil Law.* Trans. S. P. Scott. 17 vols. Cincinnati: Central Trust Co., 1932. [Available online at http://www.constitution.org/sps/sps.htm]

Codex Legum Antiquarum. Frankfurt, 1613.

Coke, Sir Edward. *The Second Part of the Institutes of the Lawes of England.* London, 1642.

"Constit. Crim.": *Constitutio Criminalis Carolina: Commentatio in Constitutionem Criminalem Carolinam Medica.* Ed. Michael Alberti. Halle, 1739.

Cowell, John. *A Law Dictionary: or, The Interpreter of Words and Terms, Used Either in the Common or Statute Laws of England.* London, 1708.

Craig, Sir Thomas. *Jus Feudale Tribus Libris Comprehensum.* Edinburgh, 1655.

Cujacius, Jacobus [Jacques Cujas]. *De Feudis Libri V.* Leiden, 1566.

"Curia quatuor burg": "Curia Quator Burgorum Edinburgh Stirling Berwick et Roxburgh": in *Acts of the Parliament of Scotland,* ed. Thomson and Innes, vol. i, pp. 703–4.

Curtius Rufus, Quintus. *De Rebus Gestis Alexandri Magni.*

Davies, Sir John. *A Discoverie of the State of Ireland.* London, 1613.

The Digest of Justinian. Ed. Theodor Mommsen and Paul Krueger. Trans. Alan Watson. 4 vols. Philadelphia: University of Pennsylvania Press, 1985.

Dirleton, Sir John Nisbet of. *Some Doubts and Questions, in the Law; especially of Scotland.* Edinburgh, 1698.

Drury, Robert. *Madagascar: or, Robert Drury's Journal, during Fifteen Years Captivity on That Island.* London, 1729.

Duck, Arthur. *De Usu et Authoritate Juris Civilis Romanorum, Per Dominia Principium Christianorum.* London, 1678.

Fitz-Herbert, Anthony. *The New Natura Brevium . . . Corrected and Revised.* London, 1704.

"Fleta": *Fleta seu Commentarius Juris Anglicani.* London, 1647.

Fordun, John of [Johannis de Fordun]. *Scotichronicon, cum supplementis et continuatione Walter Boweri.* 2 vols. Edinburgh, 1752.

Gellius, Aulus. *The Attic Nights.* Trans. John C. Rolfe. Loeb Classical Library. 3 vols. London: William Heinemann, 1927–28.

"Glanvil": *The Treatise on the Laws and Customs of England Commonly Called Glanvill.* Ed. and trans. G. D. G. Hall. Oxford: Clarendon Press, 1993.

Heineccius, Johann Gottlieb. *Antiquitates Romanae Jurisprudentiam Illustrantes.* Strasbourg, 1734.

———. *Elementa Juriis Civilis Secundum Ordinem Pandectarum.* Amsterdam, 1731.

Herodotus. *The History.* Trans. Isaac Littlebury. 2 vols. London, 1709.

Home, Henry, Lord Kames. *The Decisions of the Court of Session, From Its First Institution to the Present Time, Abridged and Digested under Proper Heads, in Form of a Dictionary.* 2 vols. Edinburgh, 1741.

———. *Essays on the Principles of Morality and Natural Religion.* Edinburgh, 1751. Ed. Mary Catherine Moran. Indianapolis: Liberty Fund, 2005.

———. *The Statute Law of Scotland, Abridged with Historical Notes.* Edinburgh, 1757. 2nd ed. Edinburgh, 1769.

Homer. *Iliad.* Trans. Alexander Pope. 6 vols. London, 1715–20.

———. *Odyssey.* Trans. Alexander Pope. 5 vols. London, 1725–26.

Hope, Sir Thomas. *Minor Practicks, or, A Treatise of the Scottish Law.* Edinburgh, 1726.

Horace. *Odes and Epodes.* Trans. Niall Rudd. Loeb Classical Library. Cambridge, Mass.: Harvard University Press, 2004.

Jacob, Giles. *A New Law-Dictionary.* London, 1729.

Justinian's Institutes. Ed. Paul Krueger. Trans. Peter Birks and Grant McCleod. London: Duckworth, 1987.

Justinus, Marcus Junianus. *Historiarum Philippicarum T. Pompeii Trogi Libri XLIV in Epitomen Redacti.*

Kempfer, Engelbert. *The History of Japan, Giving an Account of the Ancient and Present State and Government of That Empire.* Trans. J. G. Scheuchzer. 2 vols. London, 1727.

Kolben, Peter. *The Present State of the Cape of Good-Hope: or, A Particular Account of the Several Nations of the Hottentots [etc.].* Trans. Medley. 2 vols. London, 1731.

Lambard, William. *Archaionomia, sive, De Priscis Anglorum Legibus Libri.* London, 1568.

The Laws and Acts of Parliament Made by King James the First, and His Royal Successors, Kings and Queens of Scotland. Collected . . . by Sir Thomas Murray of Glendook. 2 vols. Edinburgh, 1682.

"Leg. Burg.": *Leges Quatuor Burgorum:* in *Acts of the Parliament of Scotland,* ed. Thomson and Innes, vol. i, pp. 329–56.

Lobo, Jerome. *A Voyage to Abyssinia. . . . With a Continuation of the History of Abyssinia . . . by Mr. Legrand.* Trans. Samuel Johnson. London, 1735.

Lucan. *The Civil War: Books I–X.* Trans. J. D. Duff. The Loeb Classical Library. London: William Heinemann, 1928.

Mackenzie, George. *The Institutions of the Law of Scotland.* Edinburgh, 1684.

———. *The Laws and Customes of Scotland, in Matters Criminal.* Edinburgh, 1678.

Meursius, Johannes [Meurs, Johannes van]. *Themis Attica: sive De Legibus Atticis Libri II.* Utrecht, 1685.

Mevius, David. *Commentarii in ius Lubecense libri quinque: ad explicationem eiusdem solidam, pro docenda vera statutorum ratione, exponendis eorum recessibus & informando fori usu.* Frankfurt, 1700.

"Mod. Ten. Cur.": "Modus Tenendi Curias Baronum": see "Forme and Manner of Baron Courts," in *Regiam Majestatem,* ed. Skene, pp. 100–118.

"New abridgement of the law": i.e., Bacon, *New Abridgment.*

The new actis and constituvtiones of parliament maid be the rycht excellent prince Iames the Fift Kyng of Scottis 1540. Edinburgh, 1541.

"Quon. Attach.": *Quoniam Attachiamenta:* see *Regiam Majestatem,* ed. Cooper, pp. 305–84.

Racine, Jean. *Andromache*. Trans. Douglas Dunn. London: Faber and Faber, 1990.

"Reg. Maj.": *Regiam Majestatem. The Auld Lawes and Constitutions of Scotland.* Ed. and trans. John Skene. Edinburgh, 1609.

Regiam Majestatem Scotiae, Veteres Leges et Constitutiones. Compiled by Sir John Skene. Edinburgh, 1609. Ed. and trans. T. M. Cooper. Edinburgh: The Stair Society, 1947.

Ruddiman, Thomas. *An Introduction to Mr. James Anderson's Diplomata Scotiae.* Edinburgh, 1773.

Rymer, Thomas. *Foedera, Conventiones, Literae, et cujuscunque Generis Acta Publica, inter Reges Angliae, et Alios.* 20 vols. London, 1704–35.

Selden, John. *Janus Anglorum; or, The English Janus.* Trans. Redman Westcot. London, 1682.

Shaftesbury, Anthony Ashley Cooper, third earl of. *Characteristicks of Men, Manners, Opinions, Times.* 3 vols. [London,] 1711. Ed. Douglas Den Uyl, Indianapolis: Liberty Fund, 2001.

Shakespeare, William. *Works.* Ed. Alexander Pope and William Warburton. 8 vols. London, 1747.

Siculus, Diodorus. *The Historical Library.* Trans. G. Booth. London, 1700.

Skene, John. *De Verborum Significatione. The Exposition of the Termes and Difficill Wordes conteined in the Foure Buikes of the Regiam Majestatem.* Edinburgh, 1641.

Sophocles. *Tragedies.* Trans. Thomas Francklin. 2 vols. London, 1758–59.

Spelman, Henry. *Archaeologus in Modum Glossarii ad Rem Antiquam Posteriorem.* London, 1626.

———. *English Works . . . Publish'd in his Life-Time; together with His Posthumous Works, Relating to the Laws and Antiquities of England.* 2 vols. London, 1723.

Spottiswood, John. *The History of the Church of Scotland.* London, 1655.

Stair, James Dalrymple, Viscount of. *The Institutions of the Law of Scotland . . . in IV Books.* 2nd edition. Edinburgh, 1693.

The Statutes at Large, from Magna Charta, to the Thirtieth Year of George the Second, Inclusive. Ed. John Cay. 6 vols. London, 1758.

Tacitus, Cornelius. *Dialogues, Agricola, Germania.* Trans. William Peterson. Loeb Classical Library. London: William Heinemann, 1914.

Texeira, Pedro. *The History of Persia.* Trans. John Stevens. London, 1715.

The Twelve Tables. In vol. iii of *Remains of Old Latin,* ed. and trans. E. H. Warmington. The Loeb Classical Library. Cambridge, Mass.: Harvard University Press, 1938.

Vinnius, Arnoldus. *In Quatuor Libros Institutionium Imperialium Commentarius Academicus et Forensis.* 2nd ed. Amsterdam, 1655.

Virgil. *Aeneid.* Trans. H. Rushton Fairclough, rev. G. P. Goold. Loeb Classical Library. 2 vols. Cambridge, Mass.: Harvard University Press, 1999–2000.

Voet, Johannis. *Commentarius ad Pandectas.* 2 vols. Leiden, 1698.

Walker, Obadiah. *The Greek and Roman History, Illustrated by Coins and Medals.* London, 1692.

Wilkins, David. *Leges Anglo-Saxonicae Ecclesiasticae et Civiles.* London, 1721.

Wood, Thomas. *An Institute of the Laws of England; or, The Laws of England in Their Natural Order, According to Common Use.* 2nd ed. London, 1722.

INDEX

This book is set in Adobe Garamond, a modern adaptation by Robert Slimbach of the typeface originally cut around 1540 by the French typographer and printer Claude Garamond. The Garamond face, with its small lowercase height and restrained contrast between thick and thin strokes, is a classic "old-style" face and has long been one of the most influential and widely used typefaces.

Printed on paper that is acid-free and meets the requirements of the American National Standard for Permanence of Paper for Printed Library Materials, z39.48-1992. ∞

Book design by Louise OFarrell, Gainesville, Florida
Typography by Grapevine Publishing Services, Madison, Wisconsin
Index by Kate Mertes, Alexandria, Virginia
Printed and bound by Sheridan Books, Inc., Chelsea, Michigan